A Tale of Two Churches

St Eugrad's and St Gallgo's in the Parish of Llaneugrad cum Llanallgo, Anglesey

A Story Over 1500 Years in The Making...

By: Gillian Kellett Hodkinson

Contributors:
Beth Hampson and Graham D. Loveluck

St Eugrad's

Painting by Emyr O. Parry, 2011

St Gallgo's

Painting by Pat Singleton

First Edition: August 2022
ISBN: 9798846875272

Author Contact Information
Email: ukgills@comcast.net
829 Bluebonnet Ct., Marco Island, FL 34145 USA

Dedications

This book is dedicated to:
King Maelgwyn Gwynedd who donated the land for these (and many other) churches.
Brothers Eugrad and Gallgo for their devotion in founding these enduring places of worship and their sister Peithian whose place of worship was somewhere in between.
The Clergymen, Churchwardens, Lay Readers, Organists, and Congregations.
Those who were christened, married, and buried in the churches and churchyards.
Those who financially and otherwise ensured that the church buildings endured.

The book title is a nod to Charles Dickens and his book, *A Tale of Two Cities,* which was published in the same year as the *Royal Charter* Wreck. Dickens visited Moelfre and Llanallgo and eloquently wrote about the wreck and the incredible work of the Reverend Stephen Roose Hughes.

Acknowledgements

I am indebted to Beth (Elizabeth) Hampson of Moelfre and Graham Loveluck of Marianglas for their substantial contributions to this book. One very wet and cold winter, Beth decided to identify as many rectors of St Gallgo's as she was able. In addition to names and dates, she found but also a variety of information from parish registers, newspapers, census records and even the Crime and Punishment database in the National Library of Wales (NLW!) She documented all this information and very kindly provided it to me long before this book was ever conceived of. When I began my research, I quickly realized that the extent and quality of her work would save me literally hundreds of hours, and for that I am extremely grateful. Graham has long taken an interest in the history of the churches and is one of the most knowledgeable people that I have come across on the local history of the area. During his time as curate and then rector of our churches, he published a number of articles in the parish magazine and shared much of his research with me, as well as articles and books that also saved me scores of hours. He also made an enormous contribution serving as Editor of the chapter on the clergymen, the lion's share of the book, which was no mean feat, and I am exceptionally thankful for his help and guidance and input.

The saying "it takes a village" is literally true in this case, and I am extremely grateful to all of the following for their various contributions – providing information, family knowledge, fact-checking, photographs, obtaining documents from local archives when Covid restrictions prohibited my travel and help with various translation to name a few. In no particular order, they include Philip Hughes, Dawn Hughes, Gwen Meredith Williams, Emyr Roberts, Ffion Kellett, Lynne Kellett, Iwan Kellett, Jaci Huws, Peter Day, Eileen Clarke, Sioned Harper, Tom Roberts, Bryn Jones, David Hughes (son of rector Hugh Hughes,) Elena Johnson, Vicki Louise Smith, Chris Hughes, Sue Watkinson, Delyth Roberts Pwll Bachgen, Patrick Hussey (nephew of Arthur Gordon Ware,) Eleanor Jones (granddaughter of Cedric and Margaret Wild,) Alma Salt (relative of rector Robert Williams,) Sioned Boardman, Pixy Tom, Arwyn Owen, Heather DeFer, Valmai Jones (mother of Dafydd Elgan Jones,) Colin Haywood, Pat Singleton, Emyr O. Parry and Philippa Parry. My sincere apologies if I omitted to mention you by name, thank you all!

The resources and staff in our various Welsh Archives - the National Library of Wales, Anglesey Archives and Bangor Archives are simply fantastic. Even with Covid disruptions in service the staff were absolutely brilliant, with very fast responses to my inquiries and even when working from home, they always got the documents to me very quickly once they returned to work in the archive. Without this incredible support it would have taken me so much longer to complete this project. Thank you!

Lastly, a great big thank you to my family – my husband Mel and kids Tom and Emrys, who have supported me in my quest/obsession to unearth the history of these churches.

Table of Contents

Introduction 1

Chapter One: A Tale of Two Brothers 3

Chapter Two: The Church Buildings 5
  St Eugrad's 7
    Structure and Renovations 7
    St Eugrad's in Pictures 13
  St Gallgo's 23
    Structure and Renovations 23
    St Gallgo's in Pictures, 2022 36

Chapter Three: Memorials in the Churches 42
  St Eugrad's 42
    John Williams, Bodgynda 42
    The Parke Family 42
    John Croome 44
    William and Marian Williams 45
    Colonel Lawrence Williams, OBE, DL, JP, Kathleen, and Elinor Henrietta 46
    Francis Idris Williams of Bodelwyddan 48
    Margaret and Lionel Frederick Southwell Sotheby 49
    Margaret Anne Edwards 51
    Arthur Gordon Ware, BA 53
    William Rees Hughes, BA 54
    Cedric Harry Wild, F.I.MA 54
    Sir Lawrence Hugh and Sara Margaret Helen Williams 56
  St Gallgo's 58
    Anne Gruffydd, 1635 58
    John Hughes, 1755 and Mary Griffith, 1763 of Glanrafon 58
    Robert and Elizabeth Hughes, Glanrafon 60
    Mary Hughes and John Ellis, Taicroesion 60
    Grace Jones, Glanrafon 61
    Edward Williams, Ty'n Y Llan 62
    The Reverend Lewis Owen 63
    Elizabeth, Wife of William Lewis 63
    Henry Molyneux Blevin 64
    Isaac Lewis, Ty Hir 64
    The Reverend John Lewis Davies 65
    Richard Williams, Croesallgo 65
    The Reverend Robert Williams 66
    David William Irons 67
    Dafydd Elgan Jones, Gwynfryn 68
    Unidentified Royal Charter Victims 69

Chapter Four: The Clergymen 70

Introduction	70
Peter de Morteyn, 1328 – Unknown	71
Interim to 1379	73
Hywel ab Adda Grwn (Arthur Grwn), 1379 - 1385	75
Iorwerth ap Ievan (or Blethyn ap Iorwerth ap Ievan), 1391 - 1399	76
Iorwerth ap Dafydd, 1399 - 1436	76
Dafydd ap Iorwerth Vychan, 1436 - Unknown	77
Syr Dafydd Trevor, 1504 or before– 1527/8	77
Gruffydd ap Tetur, 1504 or before – Unknown, Curate	77
William Nant, B.Can.L., 1527/8 - 1550	79
Richard ap Ieuan Taylor and Sir William Griffith, 1550 – 1587	81
David ap Robert, 1554	84
Owen Byner, 1574 - 1580	84
William Evans, 1580 – 1595	85
Richard Puleston, MA, 1592 - 1596	86
David Rowlands, 1596 - 1610	87
Hugh Griffith, LL.D., 1610 - 1617	89
Robert Griffith, MA, 1617 - 1631	90
Michael Roberts, MA, 1631 - Unknown	92
John Payne, 1631 – 1658	94
Hugh Humphreys, MA, 1658 - 1668	95
Owen Wood, 1668 - 1668	97
Edward Wynne, MA, 1669 – 1670	97
Richard Hughes, 1670 - 1687	100
Maurice Jones, B.D., 1687 - 1697	101
Francis Prichard, MA, 1697 - 1704	105
Rowland Griffith, MA, 1704 - 1712	108
Evan Foulkes, BA, 1710 – 1712	109
William Wynne, BA, 1712 - 1717	109
Hugh Jones, MA, 1717 - 1735	111
Robert Jones, BA, 1735 - 1739	112
Lewis Owen, 1739 - 1771	113
John Williams, 1771 - 1792	118
John Richards, 1784 – 1797	119
Pierce Owen Mealy, MA, 1792 - 1801	121
Richard Lloyd, 1801 - 1830	125
Hugh Hughes Wynne, BA, 1826 - 1830	129
Robert Davies, MA, 1830 - 1834	130
John Griffith, MA, 1834 - 1852	132
Stephen Roose Hughes, MA, 1852 - 1862	140
Alban Griffith, 1862 - 1863	154
James Morris, 1863 - 1874	156
John Evans, 1874 - 1883	164

John Williams aka Glanmor, 1883 - 1891 167
Griffith Bees Jones, 1891 - 1899 174
John Lewis Davies, 1899 - 1929 181
John Henry Parry, 1929 – 1937 189
Robert Williams, 1937 - 1940 192
Arthur Gordon Ware, B.A, 1940 – 1943 195
Glyn Evans, BA, 1943 – 1954 199
Thomas "Tom" Woodings, BA, 1955 – 1958 201
William Rees Hughes, BA, 1958 – 1973 206
Hugh Hughes, BA, 1974 – 1982 210
Philip Hughes, 1983 – 1995 213
Graham D. Loveluck, BSc., Ph.D., F.R.S.C., 1987 – 2004 215
Honourable Mention: Peter and Pat Day 218

Chapter Five: Charity 221
Wills and Bonds 221
Charities Commission Inquiries of 1833 and 1895 224

Chapter Six: Ghosts and a Goblin 239

References and Sources 249
Photographs, Illustrations & Newspaper Articles 249
Journal Articles 252
Books, Essays, Articles 253
Crown, Legal, Church and Misc. Other Documents 254
Wills 255
Websites 255
Subscription and Free Online Databases -Various Records 256
Personal Contribution/Memoirs 256

Introduction

St Eugrad's as a place of worship was over 1500 years old when the last Sunday service was held at 2pm on December 6th, 2020. My brother, Justin Kellett, and his son Iwan were there for that historic event, but sadly due to the Covid restrictions, I was unable to travel to Wales to attend myself. However, I was there in spirit and later watched the service on a video recording that was made for me.

Growing up in the village of Marian-glas, I attended St Eugrad's and in 1981 I was married there. In 1989 I moved to the USA where my two children were born, and I brought both of them "home" to be christened in St Eugrad's. My parents are buried in the tranquil churchyard as are my grandparents, great grandparents, and many other relatives. The church is near and dear to my heart, and when I learned that it was being closed, I felt compelled to research and document its history in an enduring way. My first thought was to produce a booklet, but as I delved into the over 1500 years of its existence, I found much more information than I had imagined, and it became clear that it was a much bigger project – hence this book.

The St Gallo's church in the neighbouring parish of Llanallgo for centuries has been part of the same benefice as St Eugrad's, with a single parson or rector and/or curate. Also, the church founders, Eugrad and Gallgo were brothers, and they founded their churches at the same time. The story of one could therefore not be told without the story of the other.

The topics are varied and include what is known about the founding of the churches, the church buildings and restoration efforts over the years, the stories of the people named on the memorial tablets inside the churches, charitable contributions and financial legacies left in Wills and the stories of the clergymen who served our churches. The latter is by far the largest chapter and is presented as a journey through time. I decided to include significant events that happened during their tenure which would have directly affected them and/or their parishioners. It is therefore much more interesting than just a few dates and names and offers a glimpse into what life was like for a rural clergyman and his parishioners. Finally, no book of mine would be complete without a chapter on the legendary local ghosts and, in this case, a goblin!

The following are comments on naming conventions. The churches and their churchyards are referred to as St Eugrad's and St Gallgo's and unless otherwise specified, all burials are in the churchyards. Llaneugrad and Llanallgo refer to the parishes. Marian-glas and Moelfre are the villages within the parishes. I have used the modern, or most recent, spelling of house names and locations throughout, regardless of how they appear in the various documents, with a couple of exceptions – I chose to use the Welsh names for Penrhosllugwy and Llannerch-y-medd. The title *Lord of Llaneugrad* refers to the owner of all/most of the

Llaneugrad lands and is not an official title that was ever used, but a nod to the Lord of the manor in the old feudal system. It is also the title of a book I wrote with my nephew, Iwan Kellett, on the ownership of the Llaneugrad lands over time.

The book involved a substantial amount of original research from historical documents and, where information is taken from the work of others, I have endeavoured to go back to the original source document to verify the facts. Wherever it makes sense, references to sources are weaved into the narrative, and a complete list of sources is included as an appendix.

I have strived to make the book as accurate as possible, however, this quote applies:

> *To have no errors is a privilege above the condition of humanity.*
> *Happiest are they who have fewest of them.*
> Hor. lib. I. Sat. iii (and adapted by Gill)

If you notice any errors, I would be very grateful if you would report them to me – thank you.

Chapter One: A Tale of Two Brothers

In researching the origins of the churches, I came across some discrepancies in various publications for when the churches founded. Samuel Lewis in his 1833 *A Topographical Dictionary of Wales* states that the churches were founded in about 605AD. Angharad Llwyd gives the same date in her essay *A History of the Island of Mona,* the Prize Essay in the Royal Eisteddfod in Beaumaris in 1832, and it is also quoted on the Wikipedia page for both St Eugrad's and St Gallgo's. Several other scholarly texts state that they were founded in the preceding century, and there appears to be supporting evidence for this earlier founding.

All of the texts agree that the churches were founded by the brothers Eugrad and Gallgo, sons of Caw, the King of Strathclyde "Caw Twrcelyn" who came to Anglesey with his family. Caw had a large number of children, and one of his sons was the famous Gildas, known as "Gildas the Wise", a monk who wrote the scathing religious attack *De Excidio et Conquestu Britanniae*, which recounts the history of the Britons before and during the coming of the Saxons. He is one of the best-documented figures of the Christian church in the British Isles during the sub-Roman period and was renowned for his Biblical knowledge and literary style. In his later life, he emigrated to Brittany where he founded a monastery known as St Gildas de Rhuys. He was born around 500 AD and died in about 570 AD, and if Eugrad and Gallgo were his brothers, then they lived in the sixth and not seventh century. Everyone also agrees that the land upon which their oratories were built was granted to them by King Maelgwyn of Gwynedd, who, it is said, died of the Justinian plague in about 547AD and is supposedly buried on Puffin Island. Incidentally, Maelgwyn was also blasted by Gildas in his work *De Excidio et Conquestu Britanniae.* He says that Maelgwn overthrew his paternal uncle to gain the throne; that he had taken up life as a monk but then returned to the secular world; that he had been married and divorced, then remarried to the widow of his nephew after being responsible for his nephew's death; and that he was tall! The churches (or cells as they are known) were therefore actually founded in the early 6th Century, making them over 1500 years old or thereabouts.

Eugrad was also known as Egreas and Gallgo as Alleccus, and the Monk of Rhuys told their story in a text entitled *Life of Gildas,* and the following is an excerpt from that work: "*Egreas, with his brother Alleccus and their sister Peteova* [Peithian]*, a virgin consecrated to God, having also themselves given up their patrimony and renounced worldly pomp, retired to the remotest part of that country* [Anglesey]*, and at no long distance from each other, built, each one for himself, an oratory, placing their sister in the middle one. Both of them alternately, each on his own day, used to celebrate with her the daily hours and the mass; and taking food with her after the vespers, and returning thanks to God, they returned before sunset, each to his own oratory; for each of them used to celebrate the vigils separately in* *his own oratory. Now those blessed and holy men Alleccus and Egreas, with their saintly sister, after contemning, as was said before, all the wealth and luxuries of the world, strove with the whole bent of their soul to reach the celestial country, and devoted their lives to fasting and prayers. At last, they were called by God, and received the reward of their labours. They were buried in the oratories which they had built, and are preserved there, famous, and illustrious for their constant miracles, and destined to rise again in glory."*

I found another interesting claim that Eugrad appears in one of the tales in the Welsh medieval masterpiece, the *Mabinogion* – he is Ergyryad in the story of Culhwch, which would make him a contemporary of the legendary King Arthur.

He is also thought to be the Ergat found in Brittany. According to the book, *The Lives of the British Saints*, he is patron saint of Tréouergat near Ploudalmezeau where a part of his skull is supposed to be preserved. His Holy Well is also there, and there is a statue of him in Eucharistic vestments holding a book. He was invoked, and his well waters resorted to, for the treatment of rheumatic diseases. He was a disciple of Saint Illtyd who founded nearby Lanildut and, when there was a famine in Brittany at one time, Saint Illtyd went there with corn ships from Wales, so perhaps that was how Eugrad ended up in France. The Holy Well is about a twenty-minute walk south of the church and, according to that same book, the local landowner was Seigneur of Penguer at one time and he was so fed up with pilgrims crossing his land to get to the well that he filled it in. Shortly afterwards he was troubled with

1. The Holy Well at Tréouergat

2. Close up of the Statue

3. Likeness of Eugrad from *"The Lives of the British Saints"*

sickness and became so alarmed that he constructed the Holy Well of cut stones which bear the arms of Penguer.

Chapter Two: The Church Buildings

We can only guess what the buildings looked like for the first few hundred years, but we do have an idea of what St Eugrad's looked like from the 12th century and St Gallgo's from the late 15th century, as those structures still form part of the buildings today. It is assumed that the churches are still in their original location as there is no evidence to suggest that they moved. In *The Life of Gildas,* sister Peithian's cell is described as "in the middle" of the brother's cells. It has been suggested in various texts that the old, ruined chapel building at Llugwy might be on the site of her cell, however, it is not "in the middle" between St Eugrad's and St Gallgo's. The unnamed author of *The Life of Gildas* was either Gildas himself, or someone who obtained the information directly from him, so why would he claim this if it were not the case?

4. Llugwy Chapel in 2022

According to *Medieval Anglesey* by A.D. Carr, medieval churches were built within easy access of nucleated settlements, and there are various remains of ancient settlements around the Llanallgo and Llaneugrad area and I created a map to show the locations of the churches

The Church Buildings

in relation to these settlements. The Cadw website records that they date from prehistoric times to the fourth and fifth centuries and later. Prof. Carr also says that settlements were typically built on well-drained soils close to the coast and continued to develop in the same locations, so this map is likely what the area looked like as Eugrad and Gallgo founded the churches. There were later settlements, but as the buildings were made of less durable materials than the limestone hut circles, nothing is left of those in their original form. Looking at the map, St Gallgo's is right in the middle between St Eugrad's and Llugwy chapel and this led me to wonder if Llugwy chapel was the original site of Gallgo's cell, and if the current site of St Gallgo's church was where the brothers placed Peithian. It would fit much better with the *Life of Gildas* account, however, there are other considerations. The ruined chapel is described in various texts as a "chapel of ease" and the 1960 publication by the Royal Commission on Ancient and Historical Monuments states that it is a chapel of ease to St Michael's, Penrhosllugwy. This makes sense because Penrhosllugwy was a maerdref – with land that was cultivated by bondsmen and belonging to the local King. It had a greater population than other townships, so it would be much more likely to need a chapel of ease.

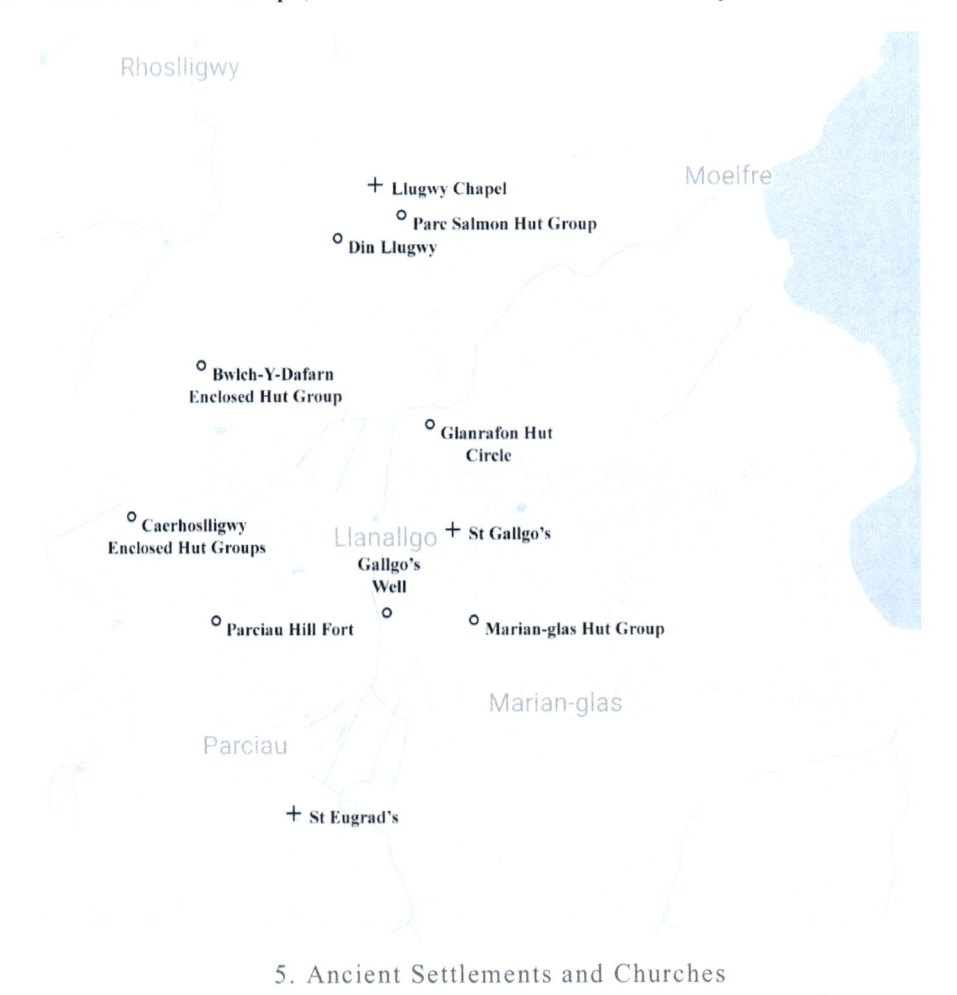

5. Ancient Settlements and Churches

As an aside, after Edward I conquered Gwynedd, and Wales came under English rule, the maerdrefi then all belonged to the King of England or Prince of Wales.

Where then was Peithian's cell? Assuming she really was in the "middle" of the churches, when a line is drawn between them, it passes right by Ffynnon Gallgo or Gallgo's well, and given its importance with its healing waters, this is the most logical location. If "middle" is meant to mean halfway, then this would be at the location of the old Amlwch Lodge, but there isn't an obvious reason for the choice of this location for her other than the proximity to the nucleus of the township of Nantmawr next to the hill fort of Bryn Ddiol. I have been unable to find any information as to how Peithian fell by the wayside in terms of a permanent place of worship, but she did, and I would guess that it was because there was not a demand for three different permanent places of worship in such close proximity.

St Eugrad's
Structure and Renovations

The diagram is roughly to scale and was drawn by the author from information contained

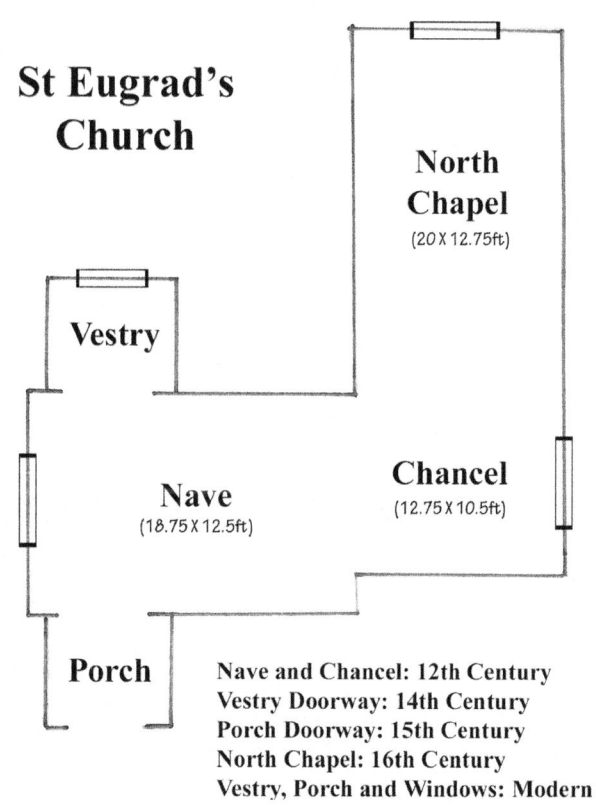

St Eugrad's Church

North Chapel (20 X 12.75ft)

Vestry

Nave (18.75 X 12.5ft)

Chancel (12.75 X 10.5ft)

Porch

Nave and Chancel: 12th Century
Vestry Doorway: 14th Century
Porch Doorway: 15th Century
North Chapel: 16th Century
Vestry, Porch and Windows: Modern

6. St Eugrad's – Plan from 1960 Publication

in *A Survey and Inventory by the Royal Commission on Ancient and Historical Monuments in Wales and Monmouthshire* dated 1960. St Eugrad's is described as being typical of a lesser parish church built during the period of native rule (1100 – 1282.) It was a small plain building with little ornament consisting of a nave separated from a narrower square chancel by a round arch. The diagram shows the structural modifications and their timing through the ages. There is a blocked-up window (barely visible today but can be seen in the 1859 illustration) in the south nave wall that dates back to the 12th century, and the existing windows are from modern times. The window in the south wall of the chancel seen in the 1859 sketch if also now blocked up. The door on the north wall dates from the 14th century, but the door on the south wall dates from the 15th century, but it is not known whether it was new then or replaced an earlier doorway.

Inside the church, the font is said to probably date from the 12th century and is a plain tapered bowl 15 inches high with a projecting band at the base. It is wonderful that it has survived through the centuries, and I wonder just how many children have been christened from it over all of those years.

Another treasure of historical interest is a crucifixion on the north wall of the nave, thought to be from 13th century. It is a crudely carved figure on a wheel-cross with pierced spandrels and it can be seen in its original

7. The 12th Centruy Font

place outside the church in an 1859 illustration which appears later in this chapter.

Anyone who has been inside the church will agree that the nave and chancel are very small. Today, there are four pews on each

8. The 13th Century Crucifix

side of the nave, and each can fit roughly three people for a total of only about 24. There is some standing room at the back of the church, but the overall size of the ancient structure I suppose reflects the small parish population at the time it was built. The church was in the medieval township of Nantmawr, and although some believe that the nucleus was at the current farm of Nant Uchaf, others have written that there were signs of a medieval town at Parciau Home Farm next to Bryn Ddiol, the hill fort. I tend to believe that latter position and this is based on a range of information from archaeological publications and descriptions of old structures, legal conveyance, and loan documents to the work of the bard, Watcyn Clywedog.

It wasn't until the late 13th century that an "owner" (granted the township by Crown for the duration of their life) of Llaneugrad/Nantmawr lands is first documented. He was Tudur Fychan who was descended from the Tribe of Iarddur of Penhesgin Isaf, Llansadwrn, and although he started out as a supporter of Llewelyn the Last, he turned against him, aligned with the King, Edward I, and was handsomely rewarded. According to the *Calendar of Patent Rolls*, On 21st August 1284, he was granted the Kings Township of Nantmawr "*to hold without question of the King's bailiffs, provided that he behave himself faithfully to the King hereafter.*" Indeed, he remained loyal to Edward and on 18th May 1290 he was awarded £20 for his expenses for performing the services. I wonder if it was Tudur who had the crucifixion made for the church.

The north wall of the chancel was demolished, and the north chapel added in the 16th century. This was the century that Robert ap Owen ap Meurig/Meyrick of the House of Bodeon was the *Lord of Llaneugrad* and he lived in Caerfryn, a house that was next to Bryn Ddiol. It must have been either Robert, or his son Owen (grandfather of Sir John Bodvel who lived in Caerfryn from 1555,) who helped to get the expansion to the church.

The earliest sign of a refurbishment that can be specifically dated, is a carved wooden panel on the south wall of the chancel next to the altar. It bears the initials IB AB and the date 1644. The lettering is gilded, but whoever did this missed the "I" and therefore it is reported incorrectly in all sorts of places as "BAB". The initials are those of Colonel John (written Iohn back in those days) Bodvel and his wife Ann. In the early 1640s, John, a Royalist, had returned to Anglesey to prepare to defend his home against Cromwell's army and also to get it ready for his English wife to live in. He refurbished Caerfryn for her, and evidently refurbished the church at the same time. The panel was originally part of the pulpit and was still on it in 1844 according to the 1859 *Archaeologica Cambrensis* article described below. Colonel John Bodvel led quite a tragic later life, and for those interested in more details, I recommend the following reading: *The Lords of Llaneugrad* by Gillian Kellett

9. John & Ann Bodvel Panel from 1644

Hodkinson and Iwan T Kellett, 2020 available on Amazon; *The Tragedy of Colonel John Bodvel* by the late Prof. A.H. Dodd in Transactions of the Anglesey Antiquarian Society, 1945 or *Y Cyrnol John Bodvel* in the journal *Cymru* Vol 45, available on the National Library of Wales Journals website.

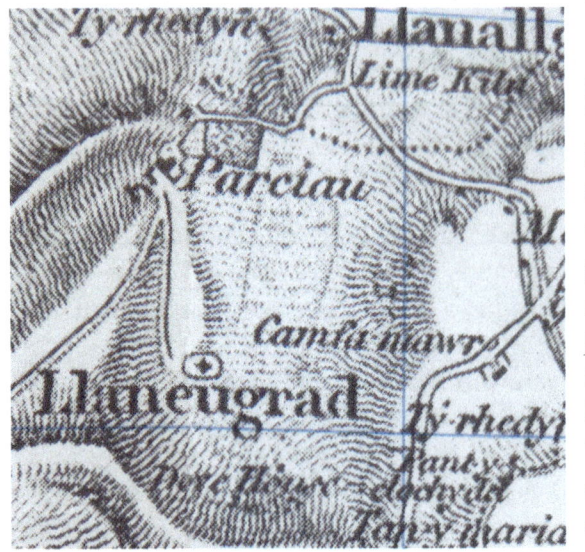

An account of medieval buildings in the parishes Llanallgo and Llaneugrad is in the "Mona Mediaeva" section of the April 1859 issue of *Archaeologica Cambrensis*. It states that "*at the time when this account was written (1844), the church was in a state of great neglect, but it is deserving, from its architectural peculiarities, of being carefully preserved.*" It is also noted that the only other medieval buildings were outbuildings belonging to the manor house, which "*formerly stood to the southeast of the church*". It goes on to say "*Not far from the church, on the southern side, are the remains of a park wall; the mansion standing within has most probably been replaced by a modern farmhouse. A doorway, which once led perhaps into the garden, or 'plesaunce,' still exists, highly picturesque, covered with ivy, and bearing the date 1575.*" I think the author may have made a mistake - there was no modern farmhouse to the south or south-east of the

10. 1841 Ordnance Survey Map

11. Sketch of St Eugrad's from the April 1859 Edition of *Archaeologica Cambrensis*. Colour added by Gillian Kellett Hodkinson

church in 1844. The only farmhouse that could be described as not far from the church was Parciau farm, where Michael Richards lived, and that is to the north of the church, not the south. An undated sketch of the exterior of St Eugrad's is included in the article which appears to show the church in good repair. Perhaps it is an artist's impression, or perhaps the neglect was to the inside the church. This neglect may have contributed to the missing register entries in the time of the Reverend John Griffith (1834 – 1852) which are described later in this book.

The next recorded refurbishment was a few years later. The Reverend Alban Griffith became rector of the churches in August 1862 and in September he launched a fundraising effort to renovate St Eugrad's and it was reported in the *North Wales Chronicle* newspaper

LLANEUGRAD.

A circumstance of considerable interest was witnessed last Sunday, in this secluded parish. It may not be generally known that the ancient church of this parish has been for many years in such a delapitated state, that no service has been performed in it. Neglect and desolation are written within its sacred precincts. Its solitude has been only occasionally disturbed when the mortal remains of some of the inhabitants were laid in the grave, where their forefathers had for years found a quiet resting place. The Incumbency of the parish, with the sister church of Llanallgo (now so celebrated as the place where the Royal Charter was wrecked) has passed into the hands of the Rev. Alban Griffith, formerly a missionary in the Diocese of Llandaff, and since Curate of Portmadoc. His public services have been hitherto confined to the labours of the latter church. During the past week, steps were taken to bring together the people of the surrounding district to the old church of which we write. At the hour named, from every quarter were seen people of various ages, wending their steps along the steeps which surround the ancient edifice, and soon there were congregated between two and three hundred persons. The services were conducted in the open air, by the Rev. Mr. Griffith, Rector of the parish. He commenced by reading the Litany, at the close of which he delivered a sermon to a very attentive audience. The proceedings were confined to the Welsh language. The responses and hymns were joined in and sung by the congregation, and the many voices of praise awakened echoes which were new among the craggy heights, which had such a romantic aspect to the scenery around. The preacher chose for his subject the history of the Jews, at that interesting period, when with joy and gladness they returned from their captivity, and entered upon their work of restoring their favourite city, and especially the temple where they were wont to worship their own and their father's God. He afterwards spoke of the piety which in days gone by, led to the erection in this country, of temples for the Worship of the Most High, and had provided for the maintenance of religious means among the people. He pointed to the Church of the land as the geatest ornament to the country, and around which the affections of the nation still clung. He spoke of the circumstances under which they had met, and of the happiness which he felt in learning that the attachment which had long slept in the bosoms of those around him, had now been awakened, and their zeal for their Church, which their fathers venerated, was about to lead them to use measures to repair the desolation which was painful to witness, and once more to open the gates of their Zion to the exercise of praise and prayer. We understand that the Rector of the parish is about to make a public appeal to the sympathy and support of the friends of the Church of England, to aid him and his parishioners in the extensive work of restoration, which the venerable fabric requires. Noble examples have been set by one of the land-owners of the parish and other gentlemen. We may mention the name of Mr. Hughes, of Kinmel, who has generously subscribed £50 towards the undertaking. We heartily wish the new Rector every success in his labours in rebuilding the shattered walls of his church, and especially in guiding the steps of his parishioners in the good old paths, which under God's blessing cannot fail to lead to the virtue and happiness of his flock. We have much pleasure in directing the attention of our readers to an advertisement which appears in another column. It is known to many of them that in the churchyard of Llaneugrad, are many of those who perished in the wreck of the Royal Charter.

12. *North Wales Chronicle* 13th September 1862

as follows:

By 2nd October an added £3 had been raised in minor donations and on 18th October, the North Wales Chronicle reported on two more donations, £5 from Richard Lloyd Edwards Esq of Nanhoron, Llangian and £3 from Miss Catherine Wynne Edwards of Hirdrefaig,

Llanffinan. Alban would not live to finish the fundraising nor see the church restored, as he died on 5th February 1863, and the task of finishing the fund-raising and overseeing the renovation fell to his successor. He was the Reverend James Morris, and the work was completed in time for the 3rd of October 1868 Harvest Thanksgiving service. It was reported in the newspaper that the church had been "*lately restored*" and that a large number of parishioners assembled for the service. After James read the prayers, an excellent sermon, to suit the occasion, was preached by Reverend John Richards of Amlwch.

In 1868, William Williams and his nephew, Robert, bought over 2000 acres of the Llaneugrad lands. William and his wife Marian were leasing Plasgwyn at the time and, when they had to give up the lease, they decided that Parciau would be their new home. William began building a mansion in Autumn 1872 on grounds next to the church, and they moved in on 3rd August 1875, their fourth wedding anniversary. When he bought it, the estate was in a wild and uncultivated state, and he employed many men to clear it of stones and rocks as well as hedges and walls from the myriad of small enclosures on the land. William also built roads for better access to his home, and one of them was the current driveway next to Bangor Lodge, enabling much easier access to St Eugrad's.

The church building also benefited from the Williams family making Parciau their home. William's sister, Margaret, was extremely wealthy having married Sir Henry Peyto-Verney, the 16th Baron Willoughby de Broke. After her husband died, she had the "Marble Church" at St Asaph built in his memory at a cost of £60,000. She generously donated £100 towards the renovation of Bangor Cathedral in 1879, and earlier, she had spent £400 on restoring St Eugrad's from a ruin at the same time that the mansion was being built. This is when the castellated porch was added and the crucifix was moved from above the south door to the

LLANEUGRAD.—On the 19th inst. the annual thanksgiving service for the late bounteous harvest was held at the venerable church of Llaneugrad, which has lately undergone a complete restoration, through the munificence of Mr William Williams, Parciau, and Mrs Williams, who take a lively interest in all that concerns the church in this and the adjoining parishes. Owing to the unpropitious state of the weather, the sacred edifice was not so well filled as it is on Sundays. The English morning prayers were said by the rector, the Rev. John Evans, in his own impressive manner, and a powerful and effective discourse was delivered by the Rev. Hugh Thomas, M.A., rector of Llaneilian, from Exodus xxiii. 16. The singing was greatly admired. Mason's beautiful anthem, "Lord of all power and might," being well rendered. The hymns were 223 and 360 A. and M. Tallis's responses were used, with accompaniments on the harmonium kindly presented to this church by Mrs Williams. After the service a liberal collection was made. We must not omit to render praise to Miss Pickett, of Parciau, and Mr W. Roberts, Tynyborth, for their valuable aid on all occasions to the choir of this church.

13. *North Wales Chronicle* 30th October 1875

LLANEUGRAD.

ATTRACTIONS TO VISITORS.—No English visitor attracted to the picturesque north coast of Anglesey should leave without visiting the above church, especially since there are always English services. This little unique, secluded oratory will be found in the woods of Parciau, surrounded by a mossy churchyard, which still retains the remarkable oval figure of a once Druidical "high-place" consecrated to devotion perhaps some thousand years before the Christian era. And here some of those who perished in the ill-fated "Royal Charter" sleep with the dead of many ages, under a carpet of beautiful hyacinths and wild flowers of summer. This was once the cell of St. Eugrad, who built and endowed it in A.D. 604. The late munificent Lady Willoughby d'Broke, restored it from a ruin at an expense of some £400, and it is religiously kept in trim by Mrs Williams of Parciau and family. A neat new stone was lately supplied, and the reading-desk, pulpit, and altar have been carpeted and upholstered with rich crimson-velvet cushions and hassocks. Externally, it is luxuriously over-grown with ivy, and seems to want nothing to finish the picture but a miniature spire.

14. *North Wales Chronicle* 9th June 1888

north wall of the nave, just to the right of the vestry. The church bell was also replaced at this time with one from the same maker as that in the clock tower at the mansion. The *North Wales Chronicle* ran a story on the renovation on 30th October 1875, and a few years later on 9th June 1888, it ran an advertisement for St Eugrad's as an *"attraction to visitors"*, which included details of the refurbishment completed in the 1870s. Living next door, Mrs Williams, and her daughters and some of the servants always ensured that the church was kept in immaculate condition and was appropriately decorated for special services.

It was a few more years before I found records of various other work performed. An order dated 1925 transferred the burial ground from the commissioners of Church Temporalities in Wales, under Welsh Church Acts, to the Rev. John Lewis Davies and the Parish Council, who are still to this day responsible for the churchyard. Further renovations to the exterior of the church building were carried out in the 1930s based on the plan dated 11th November 1936 and it seems that these were chiefly drainage upgrades. In 1978, a certificate authorising a minor alteration was granted by the Archdeacon, and a new electric organ installed.

A very interesting discovery was made in 1987 during the tenure of Phillip Hughes. The church was re-roofed, and more work was done to correct subsidence in the floor of the Chancel. As the floor was excavated, a number of bones of very tall adult men were unearthed. Work had to be halted and the police brought in to investigate. Forensic examination found them to very old and, according to the North Wales Police, "*if foul play was involved, then the perpetrators have been judged by a higher authority than ours!*" The whole area was then excavated, and the remains then reinterred in a large grave under the Chancel aisle, and the work recommenced. According to Phillip, "*who they were we have no idea, it is claimed that Cromwell's troops stabled their horses in the church during the Civil War, but the bones are likely to be later than that. We stopped at the Chancel Arch, who knows what may be under the floor of the 'Far End' as it was called*". The only record I have come across for a burial inside the church is that of John Williams of Bodgynda who died in 1721 and for whom there is a memorial tablet in the church. The church records survive from the late 1600s, but they give us no clue as to who these men were, so their identity will remain, if not to God, then to us, a mystery forever.

St Eugrad's in Pictures

Join me on a photographic "tour" of St Eugrad's with interior pictures showing how it was in the year it closed. Pictures of the driveway down to the church in spring are also included, it is a beautiful and peaceful walk at any time of the year. The photographs were taken by Dawn Hughes, Gwen Meredith Williams, Peter Day and the author.

The Church Buildings

15. The Road Down to the Church Lined With Wild Garlic and Bluebells

16. The Dovecote

The Church Buildings

17. The Hill to the Church Gate in May With the Wild Garlic

18. The Door, Come on in!

19. The Crucifix & Bowl

The Church Buildings

20. Fonts and Bell Rope

21. Vestry

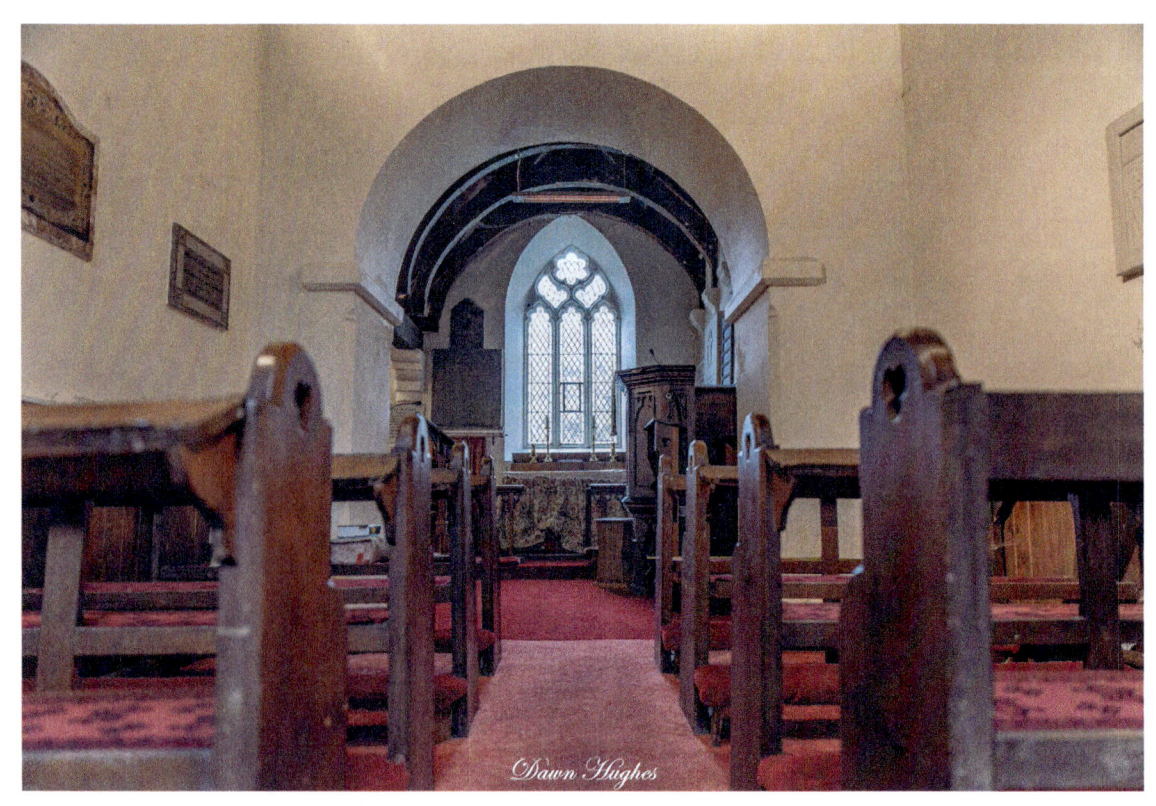

22. View to the Chancel from the Back of the Nave

The Church Buildings

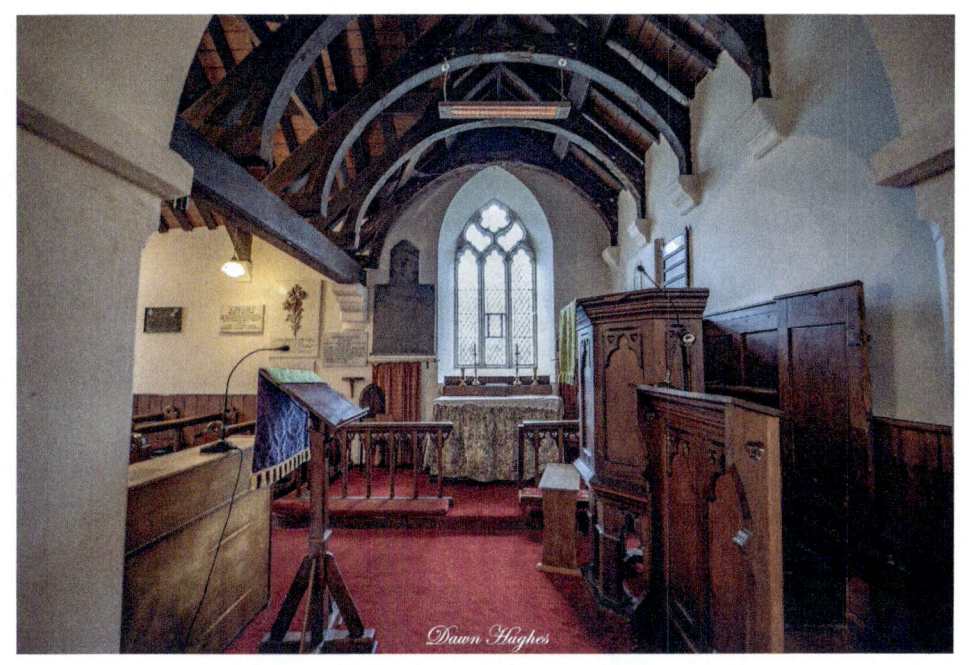

23. Organ, Altar and Pulpit from the Chances Arch

24. Candles on the Altar

17

The Church Buildings

25. The Altar and Bodvel Panel

26. North Chapel

The Church Buildings

27. View to Pulpit from the End of the North Chapel

28. View Towards Nave from Sir Lawrence Hugh Williams' Pew

The Church Buildings

29. View of the Nave from the Altar

30. Front View. Grave of the Reverend John Phillips with the Railings

The Church Buildings

31. West Side View of Nave and Castellated Vestry and Entry Porch

32. View of the Rear

The Church Buildings

33. East Side, Chancel Window and North Chapel

St Gallgo's
Structure and Renovations

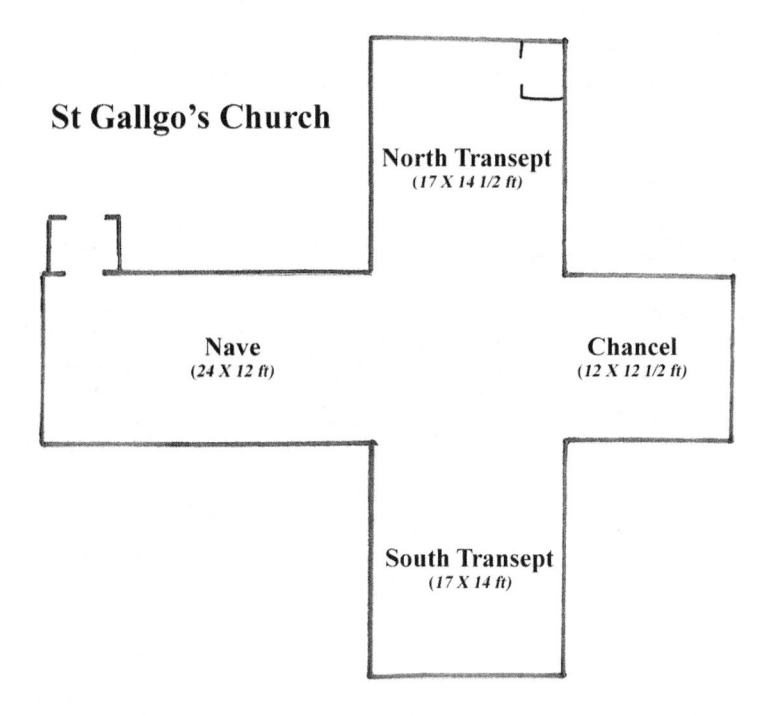

St Gallgo's Church

- North Transept (17 X 14 1/2 ft)
- Nave (24 X 12 ft)
- Chancel (12 X 12 1/2 ft)
- South Transept (17 X 14 ft)

34. Plan from 1960 Publication

The diagram is roughly to scale and was drawn by the author from information contained in *A Survey and Inventory by the Royal Commission on Ancient and Historical Monuments in Wales and Monmouthshire* updated 1960. The Chancel and Transepts date from the 15th century, so it was built much later than St Eugrad's church. According to *The Diocese of Bangor in the Sixteenth Century* by Arthur Ivor Pryce, MA, there was quite a revival in church building in the late 15th century, as the Owain Glyndwr uprising and Wars of the Roses had a negative impact on the church, and many needed repairs. The structures were made larger than before, and many were replaced with finer and more nobler buildings. The new St Gallgo's church was close to the township of Dafarn, which likely had its nucleus somewhere in the vicinity of Glanrafon Uchaf.

The bell pre-dates the church building and is from the late thirteenth century. It has the letters "AVE MARIA GRACIA PLENA" inscribed on it, together with the imprint of the reverse of an Edward I penny from Durham mint. The bell is unique, and its origins have not been proved. The coin is no later than 1285, and probably struck about 1281 and it is apparently exceptional to find an impression of such an early coin, and unusual that the coin can be dated given that it is the reverse of the coin that is imprinted. The bell is 16 5/8 inches in diameter and weighs 56.1kg. In 2000 the bell lost its clapper, and so the bell was removed for repair and renovation. The bell had been previously repaired at some point during its history with a false crown staple of lead which was removed to accommodate the new crown staple and clapper assembly. The cost of £3000 was met almost entirely by grants from the Isle of Anglesey Charitable Trust, the Council for the Care of Ancient Churches, and the Diocesan Trust (W.G. Roberts Trust). The renovation, repair and rehanging were carried out by Eayre and Smith of Derby, while the initial removal of the bell was carried out by Thomas Brothers of Moelfre. Graham Loveluck took the photographs of the bell through the process, and I include four of them here.

35. Before. The headstock was removed prior to the bell being lowered to the ground. The stock was made of pine. Removal was easily achieved as the gudgeons were virtually corroded through.

The Church Buildings

36. In good company at the works of Eayre and Smith, Derby

37. The bell on site prior to replacing in the turret. The new oak headstock, the stainless steel straps, the stainless steel gudgeon plates and the sealed cast iron bearing housings and the new clapper

8. The Bell in Place

The Royal Commission on Ancient and Historical Monuments report also describes a Communion Table, or Altar, in the vestry with turned legs and a modern top, dated 1726. This is the date that the table was gifted, and several experts have told me that based on the style, it is their opinion that the table was made much earlier than that, likely the mid to late 1600s. The inscription reads "The Gift of x E x M   A x D x 1726" and above the "E" are the lowercase letters "m" and "s," which I am told is possibly the abbreviation for mistress. I would think that it very likely that the donor had a strong connection to the church, and I set about trying to find out possible candidates.

The Church Buildings

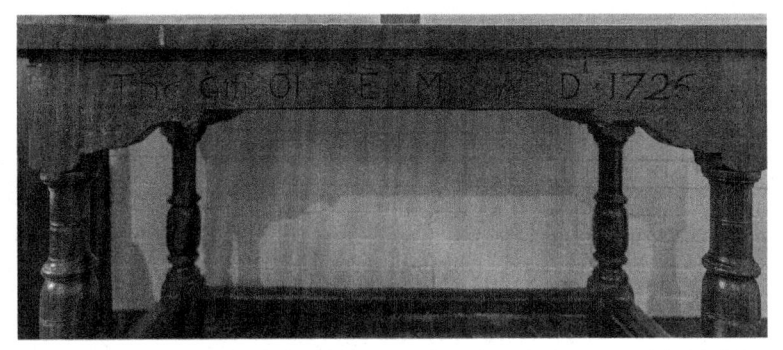

39. Close-up of the Communion Table Donated by EM

The records are sparse for that timeframe, and I was not able to find a definitive answer, however, there is a strong possibility that I came across in a review of the Wills of Llanallgo residents and parish records of that era. Owen Morris, a yeoman, was buried inside the church on 15th February 1725 but I cannot find him in the JEG Pedigrees for the Glanrafon, Ty'n Llan or Pentre Erianell families, but must have been an important member of the community to be buried inside the church. His wife was Elin Hughes, and following patronymic naming convention, she did not adopt her husband's last name after marriage, so she probably wasn't the donor. Also, Elin re-married only six weeks after her husband's death, in St Gallgo's to a Rowland Williams. Owen left small legacies to brothers Robert and John and sisters Jane and Elin Morris, and I think it is quite possible that it was Elin who donated the table, perhaps in memory of her brother. Glebe terriers recorded lands and property in a parish owned by the Church of England and held by the clergyman as part of the endowment of his benefice, and which supplied the means by which the incumbent (rector, vicar, or perpetual curate) could support himself and his church. A terrier dated 14th December 1899 lists a silver Alms Bason 12 ½ inches in diameter in St Gallgo's that bears the inscription "Llanallgo E.M. 1721". I would guess that this is almost certainly the same person who donated the Communion Table. Sadly, the bason is no longer in the church and nothing is known of its fate. In the book *The Church Plate of the Diocese of Bangor* by Edward Alfred Jones published in 1906, there is the following description of the same item: "*ALMS DISH. A large, circular pewter Dish, which has been plated, inscribed on the back 'LLANALLGO E x M 1721.' Marks illegible. Diameter, 12 1/2 in. These initials probably refer to Elizabeth Mealy, third daughter of the Rev. Richard Parry, M.A., of Perfeddgoed, Bangor, Rector of Llanddeiniolen. Her husband was John Mealy, of S. George's, Middlesex, gent. Her brother, Owen Parry, married Margaret, daughter of the Rev. Hugh Jones, M.A., of Brynhyrddin, Pentraeth, Rector of Llanallgo 1717-35.* I do not believe that it was Elizabeth who donated the Alms dish as she was born after the date on the dish in 1726. She and John Mealy were the parents of one of our rectors, the Reverend Pierce Owen Mealy who was born in 1757 and served in our churches from 1792 to 1801.

A new rectory was built in the late 1700s by the Reverend Pierce Owen Mealy who was from wealthy family and born and raised in London. There is no record of what the rectory building was like when he came to our parishes in 1792, but it must not have been large enough for him. Pierce took out a 25-year mortgage, borrowing £200 from the Reverend Peter Williams of The Friars, Bangor who was headmaster of the grammar school from 1794 to1803. He built the very large three-storey house that is today known as The Cloister and it was quite impressive, especially for a small rural parish. Pierce only got to enjoy it for a very short time as he died on 2nd April 1801 aged only about 44.

In December 1802, the Reverend John Skinner took a 10-day tour through the Isle of Anglesey, and his notes and some of his sketches were published in *Archaeologica Cambrensis* in 1908. He was accompanied for part of his journey by the Reverend John Richards of Llannerch-y-medd, who was curate of our churches from 1784 to 1797, and somewhat of an expert on local history and ancient monuments. The church must have been in good repair as it is not noted otherwise, but Skinner did write that there was a "*mutilated memorial*" on the north wall near the altar, of a knight in armour kneeling before an altar, said to be that of Sir John Bodvel who had a residence in the parish. The Reverend John Richards also told him that when the foundation for the new rectory was dug, "*the workmen discovered a square vault formed of a solid composition resembling thick tile supposed to be an ancient burying place.*" I wonder if the remains of St Gallgo were in the vault. [

40. Skinner's Sketch of St Gallgo's and the Rectory

The next documented tour, a few years later, was by the Welshman Richard Fenton, who was born at St David's in Pembrokeshire, and was a barrister, topographer, antiquary, poet, and scholar. His *Tours in Wales (1804 – 1813)* was published in 1917 by the Cambrian Archaeological Association and edited by John Fisher, BD. As part of his Anglesey tour, he visited St Gallgo's on his way to Amlwch on Thursday 16th August 1810, and notes: "*Pass the Church of Llanallgo, which is most slovenly kept, the windows being broken, so as to admit Pigeons and other birds, which produced abominable litter, and which the rural Dean should prohibit. On the Northside of the Chancel, on an old mural tablet, ornamented with Urns and other Emblems of mortality and the shortness of life, is the Effigy of a Warrior, kneeling on a hassock, opposite to a desk with a book on it, with his helmet on the ground. It is said to be meant for a Sir John Bodvill. The Monument may be about the time of Queen Elizabeth or James first*".

Putting together the two accounts of the memorial, Sir John Bodvel became *Lord of Llaneugrad* in 1604 when he reached twenty-one years old. He married Bess, the daughter of the formidable Sir John Wynne of Gwydir, and it was Sir John Wynne who helped to get the young Bodvel's career off the ground. He also decided to get him knighted. The King was charging huge amounts of money for a knighthood and turning down offers of £300 - £400 and so he tasked his son, Richard, to somehow make it happen. Richard managed to arrange for Bodvel to be knighted in Ireland by the Lord Deputy for the more reasonable sum of £100 - £120. This was a very big deal, and if the memorial was indeed for Sir John Bodvel, and it was erected to commemorate this event, then it would date to around 1615, in the time of King James I.

It is interesting that Fenton mentions that the church is dilapidated with broken windows in 1810, only eight years after the last tour. The rector at this time was the Reverend Richard Lloyd who served from 1801 to 1830, so he had quite a long tenure and, living next door, I would have thought that he and his wife would make sure the church was kept clean and free of birds. Fenton's comment that the rural Dean should stop the bird's from producing their "abominable litter" inside the church is also curious, why would he not invoke Richard's name or title? Fenton's tour was in the months following an incident in the rectory, the full account of which is told in the chapter Ghosts and a Goblin, when Richard's daughter, Grace, hit a maid with a poker on the head and the maid later died in May of 1810. Grace was accused of murder by the dead maid's stepfather, and her trial was to be held in September 1810, so perhaps Richard was too preoccupied with that to worry about the state of the church. Despite its *"slovenly"* appearance and *"abominable litter"*, christenings and marriages were still being conducted in the church, with two marriages conducted about a week before Fenton's visit. John Parry and Mary Hughes (Pant Y Gaseg) were married on 8th August, and William Williams and Elizabeth Robert (Boldon) were married on the 10th. As an aside, these couples became related by marriage in 1843 when John and Mary's son, John, married William and Elizabeth's daughter, Ruth, in St Gallgo's.

The Mona Mediaeva section of the April 1859 issue of *Archaeologica Cambrensis*, described St Gallgo's building as *"one of the better kind in Anglesey"*, and it goes on to say *"It is probable that all the walls were lowered perhaps a century after their erection, for the east window of the chancel is at present placed unusually high under its gable, and in a manner that could never have been meant by its original designer. The timbering of the chancel roof in fact comes athwart, and cuts off, the apex of the rear-arch of the east window."* There are now no traces of two features mentioned. One is a chapel at the west end of the nave which was thought to be perhaps of an earlier date than the church building. It was lighted by a loop in the gable and was entered through a slightly pointed doorway in the south side. It was connected to the nave by an almost circular archway and was known as Capel y Ffynnon. It was here that visitors to Ffynnon Gallgo came to give thanks for and to pray for healing at the well which lies in between the two churches. The area is called Bryn Myfyr to this day and was the old name for Glanrafon Uchaf. The second is the remains of a rood screen, a common feature in late medieval church architecture. It was between the chancel and nave and might originally have been surmounted by a rood loft carrying the Great Rood, but by 1844 there was no sign of a rood loft.

The chancel had remains of stalls with poupée heads. The font is described as a circular basin on three steps and probably of the same date as the actual building. It is curious that the memorial tablet to Sir John Bodvel is not mentioned at all. The piece concludes with *"The workmanship of this church is more careful than usual and shows that it was erected by some person of munificent disposition."* The church served the old medieval township of Y Dafarn which was an episcopal township, owned by the Bishop of Bangor and not the King, as was the neighbouring township of Moelfre. Perhaps it was the Bishop of Bangor who was the person of munificent disposition.

Llanallgo Church, Anglesey.

41. Drawing from April 1859 Edition of *Archaeologica Cambrensis*

After the *Royal Charter* was wrecked in October 1859, the Reverend Stephen Roose Hughes turned the church into a sort of mortuary where the victims were laid out in the hope that they could be recognized using information from relatives, or by the relatives themselves, some of whom journeyed to the little church. The seating was removed, and the services were held in the National School just down the road. Many of the victims were not able to be identified and they were placed in a large grave next to the West wall of the nave which was later extended over this grave.

An account of the funerals was included in the *Illustrated Times* 19th November 1859 edition, together with a sketch depicting several burials. Graham and Llio Loveluck have an original similar sketch by H.N. Ball that Llio inherited from her grandfather, William Daniel Williams of Ty'nygongl. In a note with the sketch, William records information given to him by Owen Owen of Croesallgo (1848 – 1926): The Reverend Roose Hughes in the white robe; Standing in the grave, Edward Williams of Ty'n Llan (1808 – 1894) and old lady Mary Rowlands, an imbecile, who attended every funeral in the district. Both sketches depict sombre gatherings, and it is interesting to note that the female mourners are dressed in the traditional Welsh attire (I am loathe to describe it as a costume) with the distinctive hats.

42. Sketch of Burials from the *Illustrated Times* 19th November 1859

43. Sketch of Royal Charter Burials by H.N. Ball

LLANALLGO.

THE CHURCH.—Last Sunday Divine Service was held at the National Schoolroom. Owing to a meeting held lately at the above schoolroom, at which a resolution was passed "that our Church is not worthy to be called the House of God." The building is much behind both in design and repair, so the services for the future will be held in this parish at the schoolroom, until the Church be restored and repaired. The new rector (Rev. G. B. Jones) intends to make an earnest appeal to all who love the Church to help him in this movement. A wealthy body like the Church of England will, no doubt, come forward at once and relieve the rector. Many relations of them that perished in the wreck of the "Royal Charter" will be glad to contribute towards making the church a memorial church of that sad accident. The late rector (Glanmor) intended, like David, King of Israel, to improve and decorate the House of God. He received sums of money for this purpose, and placed them under the care of Mr J. Rice Roberts, Tanygraig, Pentraeth, and also left behind a list of sure promises. He started the work, and thought to bring the church in his days into a good repair, but he left the work to his successor to finish.—*Correspondent.*

44. *North Wales Chronicle*
1st August 1891

LLANALLGO.

REOPENING OF PARISH CHURCH.—The Bishops of Bangor, acting for the Bishop of Llandaff, the patron of the parish living, reopened the parish church of Llanallgo, the other day, after restoration, at an outlay of over £500. The rector of the parish, the Rev G. B. Jones, who succeeded the late Rev John Williams (Glanmor), has been most strenuous in his efforts to collect funds for the work. It will be remembered that those who perished in the illfated steamer "Royal Charter," some 34 years, off the coast of Anglesey were buried in the quaint churchyard of this church. A beautiful monument has been erected in the church in memory of the sad event. The Rev G. B. Jones was curate of Carnarvon during the vicarship of the late Dean Edwards.

45. *Caernarvon & Denbigh Herald*
14th July 1893

When the Reverend Griffith Bees Jones took over in 1891, St Gallgo's was once more in quite a dilapidated state and his predecessor, the Reverend John Williams, known by his bardic name, Glanmor, had been raising funds with a view to refurbishing it. The *North Wales Chronicle* reported on efforts in the 1st August 1891 edition.

Before the restoration work began, draper and antiquarian, D Griffith Davies, BA, local secretary in Caernarfonshire for the Cambrian Archaeological Association, was invited by Mr Lloyd Griffith of Holyhead (a local secretary for Anglesey) to visit St Gallgo's to see if there was anything of archaeological interest worthy of preservation. By this time the screen and stalls had disappeared, and the chapel at the west end of the nave was also gone. D Griffith was also surprised that the mural table for John Bodvel was not mentioned. The tablet was made of plaster and by now was crumbling away and in order to preserve it, someone had "*literally plastered over with lime-wash, so that the detail of the ornament, which, from the faint indications now visible, must have been fairly good, have, in a great measure, disappeared.*" Neither Alban, nor anyone who had lived there in the past, could tell them who the tablet was for, and so they concluded that it must have been for Sir John Bodvel. Certainly, the timing and circumstances would support that. He states that the aim of the restoration was to extend the nave over the graves of the unclaimed bodies of the Royal Charter victims, making the nave a sort of memorial chapel. He also noted that there was an intention to move the obelisk, which was on the grave, into the church, and comments "*will be a most unsightly object in a church of this size, so it is to be hoped that this intention may be abandoned.*" It was not abandoned.

The Church Buildings

It took almost two years to finish the fund raising and complete the restoration work and the Caernarvon and Denbigh Herald reported on the completed work on 14th July 1893. The photograph, numbered 45a, includes a young boy standing next to the obelisk. I wonder who he was?

A memorial stone was set in the exterior wall of the church at the commencement of the work in 1892 by Mrs John Rice Roberts of Pentraeth.

45a. The Obelisk in the Church

45b. Memorial Stone

The Reverend John Lewis Davies served in our churches from 1899 to 1929, and in 1909 it was the 50th anniversary of the wrecking of the Royal Charter. Expecting many visitors, he wanted the churchyard to look at its best. He conducted a fundraising effort, placing an advertisement in the *North Wales Weekly News* on 6th August appealing for funds. A copy of this postcard is in the Anglesey Archives, the original had been loaned by the widow of the Reverend Arthur Gordon Ware, and pre-dates the 1934 refurbishment. The church looks very nicely done up, so perhaps the card was made to commemorate the 1909 refurbishments, as this was such a significant anniversary.

> The Rector of Llanallgo, in Anglesea, is appealing for funds for the repair of his church yard, in connection with the forthcoming fiftieth anniversary of the wreck of the Royal Charter, which took place on the coast near by. One hundred and forty of the wrecked people lie in the churchyard. The wreck is graphically described by Dickens in his "Uncommercial Traveller."

46. *North Wales Weekly News* 6th August 1909

LETTER FROM DICKENS.

The appeal is addressed to all lovers of Charles Dickens, as well as to the friends of the church. To those who send contributions a facsimile of a personal letter from Dickens to the Rev S. R. Hughes will be sent in acknowledgement.

For months after the disaster bodies were recovered over a wide area, many off the Irish Coast and many off the coast of the Isle of Man. Nearly 230 were removed to the Parish of Llanallgo, in which the parish church is situated, and were interred there.

The Rev S. R. Hughes and his brother, the Rev. H. R. Hughes Rector of the adjoining Parish of Penrhos, together with the Misses Moulsdale and Mrs Hughes, devoted themselves heroically to this gigantic task.

48. 4th November 1933 Newspaper Appeal

In 1926, an order by the commissioners of Church Temporalities in Wales under the Welsh Church Acts, transferred the burial ground, to the Reverend John Lewis Davies and the Council of the Parish of Llanallgo.

The Reverend John Henry Parry (1929 – 1937) placed an advertisement in several newspapers on the 4th of November 1933, appealing for funds to *"restore and beautify"* the church with the aim of raising about £600. A committee was formed, of which John was a member, and it included the churchwardens, Lord Boston, Col. Lawrence Williams, and the great nephew of Reverend Stephen Roose Hughes, Reverend S.R.P. Moulsdale who was the Principal of St Chad's College, University of Durham. They came up with a very clever way to attract donors: all those who contributed to the fund would receive a copy of the famous Charles Dickens letter to Reverend Stephen Roose Hughes. No wonder there are quite a few copies of this letter existing today as the fundraising

47. Pre-1934 Postcard of Interior of St Gallgo's.
Reproduced with Kind Permission of Anglesey Archives

was quite successful. In 1934, John received permission for the modifications in the form of a Faculty (permission): *"To the Rev. John Parry, Rector of Llaneugrad cum Llanallgo to carry out improvements and alterations in the chancel of the Parish Church of Llanallgo including re-arrangement of the fittings and the seating."* Amongst other improvements, the chancel was panelled in memory of the Reverend Stephen Roose Hughes.

An upgrade in 1938 was made with the kind generosity of Mrs Margaret Williams of Croesallgo who paid for electric lighting to be installed in memory of her husband.

A conveyance document dated 1951 transferred the burial ground adjoining the church of St. Allgo by the council of the parish of Llanallgo to the Representative Body of the Church in Wales.

> AFTER the wreck of the Royal Charter on the coast of Anglesey in 1859 a memorial to those who lost their lives in the disaster was set up in the parish church of Llanallgo nearby. The interior of the church has lately been restored; the work was completed last September. As a result the memorial has now been removed from the church and placed in the churchyard.

49. *Western Mail* 27th May 1952

The next update to the interior of the church occurred in 1952, during the tenure of the Reverend Glyn Evans (1943 – 1954) when the seating was revised, and the pews were replaced with new chairs. Although it is believed that the pews that were removed were taken to St Michael's in Penrhosllugwy, the ends of the pews in St Michael's today look different from those of St Gallgo's per the pre-1934 photograph. In this same update, the Royal Charter Memorial obelisk was moved from inside the church to the graveyard.

An electric organ was installed in 1978, and the church was re-roofed during the tenure of the Reverend Phillip Hughes (1987 to 1993,) and the new section of the churchyard was consecrated and opened.

Perhaps even in death, the Reverend Stephen Roose Hughes continues to watch over the Royal Charter victims and their final resting place, because it was surely some sort of a "divine intervention" that saved St Gallgo's from burning down on the chilly morning of Wednesday 1st September 2004. Pat Parry, who lives in Henefail, discovered the fire, and tells me *"It started with my sister-in-law, Jean, buying me some flowers for my birthday. They still had lots of life in them when we were going away on holiday, so I was going to give them to my daughter, but she forgot to take them, so I decided to take them to church on our way to the airport if we had time. It was a pretty big 'if,' as I am always last minute when leaving the house, and I thought the chances of getting David [her husband] to take a detour past the church were slim. Anyway, on the day we were indeed in plenty of time. I nearly changed my mind because I was wearing light coloured trousers and didn't want to spill water on them. Then it occurred to me that I could fill the vase when I got to church from the tap outside. So off we went. When we got to the church there was smoke coming through the roof slates, I cautiously opened the door but closed it again quickly as the church was full of black smoke. I shouted to David to call the fire brigade which he did. We couldn't hang around to see what was going on, so we called round to Dr Loveluck's house to tell* him. *I had to persuade him that it really was a fire and not just smoke from the incense he had been burning to deter bats. He came with us back to the church. Not long after the fire brigade arrived, and we left them to it. That's about it really. Turns out that mice had been gnawing at the wires near the pulpit. The thing is, if we had been a little earlier, I would also probably have thought that the burning smell was incense. According to the fire brigade if we had been 10 minutes later the fire would have been well established.*" The photograph shows the seat of the fire, and the damage caused to the vestry. Smoke damage was considerable but seven weeks to the day it happened, the church was re-opened by Anthony, Bishop of Bangor.

St Gallgo's in Pictures, 2022

The following photographs were all taken by Dawn Hughes in 2022.

50. Entrance

The Church Buildings

51. Looking Back Down the Path to the Gate. Ty'n Llan in the Background

52. View to the Chancel from the Back of the Nave at the Entrance

The Church Buildings

53. Vestry and West Transept

54. East Transept

The Church Buildings

55. The Chancel

56. Window Above the Altar

The Church Buildings

57. View to the Nave from the Chancel

58. The Nave and Bell

The Church Buildings

59. Rear of the Church. The Old Rectory (Now The Cloister) in the Background

60. Rear View of the Church

Chapter Three: Memorials in the Churches

St Eugrad's
John Williams, Bodgynda

"*Underneath lyeth ye Body of John Williams who lived att Bodgynda 33 yrs dyed January ye 17th 1721 Aged 73. He left 50 pounds to be layd out att interest for ye benefit of ye poor of Llanigrad Llanfair mathafarnitha & Llanddona where he was born*"

John was born in Llanddona in about 1648 and was a tenant of Bodgynda, Llaneugrad, where he lived for 33 years. He died on 17th January 1721 and was buried inside the church underneath his memorial tablet. He left an enduring charity, the full story of which is told in the chapter on Charity. The executors of his Will were his wife, Hester Parry, and his nephew, Rowland Jones, who also has a memorial tablet in the church.

61. John Williams, Bodgynda

The Parke Family

Upper Tablet: *Underneath is interred the remains of Rowland Jones and wife Mary Thomas. He died December 20th, 1757, She Died April 12th 1763 He Aged? years She Aged? Years* Lower Tabet: *In Memory of OWEN THOMAS of Park who died December 23, 1785, aged 62. ALSO, of Margaret his Wife, who died December 19, 1794, aged 69/ And also of Owen their son, who died September 24, 1763, aged 4 yr. Likewise of Elizabeth their Daughter, who died May 25, 1796, aged 44. AND LIKEWISE of Anne Daughter of William Edward of Llanfaes, who died December 17, 1790, aged 18.*

The upper tablet is in memory of Rowland Jones and his wife, Mary Thomas who were tenants of Bodgynda and later, roughly 500-acres of the Parke, later known as Parciau. Rowland was a Gentleman, and nephew of the above John Williams of Bodgynda. Rowland and Mary became tenants of Bodgynda sometime after John's death and their daughter, Margaret, was born there and christened in St Eugrad's on 7th December 1725. Rowland took up the tenancy of Parke sometime after 1749 and he died there and was buried in St Eugrad's on Christmas eve 1757. The inventory with his Last Will and Testament included many livestock which, together with his goods etc, were worth £213, which was no small fortune at that time, and this estate was equally divided between his wife and daughter. The tenancy of Parke then passed to their son-in-law Owen. Mary died intestate on 12th April 1763, and administration was granted to Owen in the right of his wife, and so the two halves of Rowland's estate came back together.

62. The Parke Family

The lower tablet is in memory of Margaret and Owen and two of their children, Owen who died aged four in 1763 and Elizabeth who died aged 44 in 1796. Margaret grew up in Bodgynda and was living there when she married Owen, who was from Llanfihangel Tre'r Beirdd, in St Eugrad's on 11th February 1746/7. They began married life in Bodgynda where their first child, Mary, was born and she was christened in St Eugrad's on 21st June 1747. Perhaps it was when Rowland and Mary moved to Parke, that Owen and Margaret became tenants of, Brynhyrddin, Pentraeth, before moving to Parke after Rowland died. Owen and Margaret had three further children christened in St Eugrad's: Owen in 1759, Jane in 1762 and Margaret in 1765. Owen did very well farming Parke and, when he died on 23rd December 1783, the inventory of his goods was valued at £396 4s 3d. Margaret took over the tenancy after her husband died until her own death on 19th December 1794.

Curiously, there is another person memorialized on this tablet, Anne, the daughter of William Edward of Llanfaes (Tyddyn Llanfaes,) died aged 18 in 1790. I do not know if or how she was related to this family or why she would be named on their memorial tablet.

John Croome
An Officer and a Gentleman, Hero of the Royal Charter

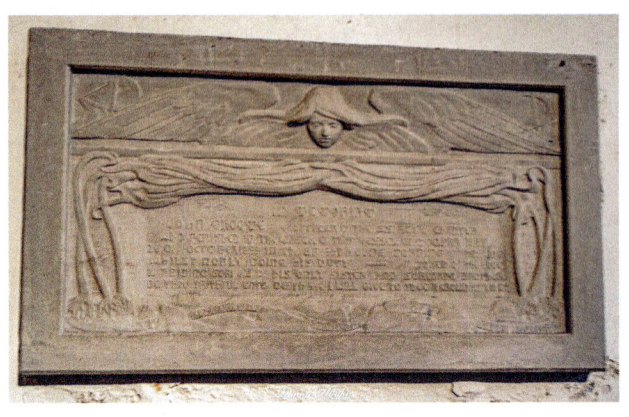

"IN MEMORIAM. JOHN CROOME 4TH OFFICER ON THE SS ROYAL CHARTER WHO PERISHED IN THE WRECK OF THAT VESSEL IN MOELFRE BAY 26TH OF OCTOBER 1859 IN THE BRIGHT YOUNG MORNING OF HIS LIFE WHILST NOBLY DOING HIS DUTY – A TOKEN OF THE LOVE AND ABIDING SORROW OF HIS ONLY SISTER AND SURVIVING BROTHER. BE THOU FAITHFUL UNTO DEATH... I WILL GIVE TO THEE A CROWN OF LIFE."

63. John Croome

John was born in Bristol in 1840 to civil engineer John and his wife Rachel née Shill. The following is from the *Sheffield Daily Telegraph* 21st November 1859: "*He was a cadet on the Royal Charter from her first voyage and was appointed 4th Officer on the journey before her last. At the time of his appointment, he had not served out his time, but he was a very clever and gentlemanly young man, a good scholar, and a clever draughtsman, which talent he inherited from his father who was a mechanical draughtsman with the firm of Penn & Son, the celebrated marine engine-boilermakers of London. Although he was a mere youth in years, he was a man possessed of sterling nautical qualities.*"

His obituary in the Cardiff Times reads: "*On the 26th of October, to the indescribable grief of his family and friends, in the 20th year of his age, John Croome, second surviving son of Mr John Croome, late of the Bristol Ironworks, St Phillip's. He was a junior officer of the ill-fated Royal Charter, and a letter from Messrs. Gibbs, bright and Co. to his father states 'he was last seen, we understand, quite self-possessed, and cheerfully endeavouring to cheer up a number of passengers, and, we believe, was washed away with a number of them when the ship parted in two'.*"

His body was washed up in Llaneugrad parish (so likely on either Traeth Bychan or Dinas beach), in the first week of December, together with the body of Samuel Bleaver, second steward. The Reverend Stephen Roose Hughes did not record the exact burial date in the parish register, but John was buried

64. John Croome's Grave

sometime in December 1859. His headstone reads: "*Sacred to the memory of John Croome Esquire, C.E. of Bristol and London. In his 20th year. He was the Junior Officer of the ill-fated steamship Royal Charter and was lost in the fearful wreck of that vessel in the adjacent bay of Moelfre on the morning of Wednesday the 26th day of October 1859. He was the last Officer on board and the only one whose remains were recovered and interred, as his were beneath this tablet. Extract from Official Report: "Even at that frightful moment, we have in evidence, that the 4th officer Mr Croome and the crew spent some 20 minutes in trying to save the female in the fore-part of the ship". For God shall bring every work into judgement, with every secret thing, whether it be good or whether it be evil. Ecclesiastes XII C14.5."* R.I.P. Brave Young Man.

William and Marian Williams

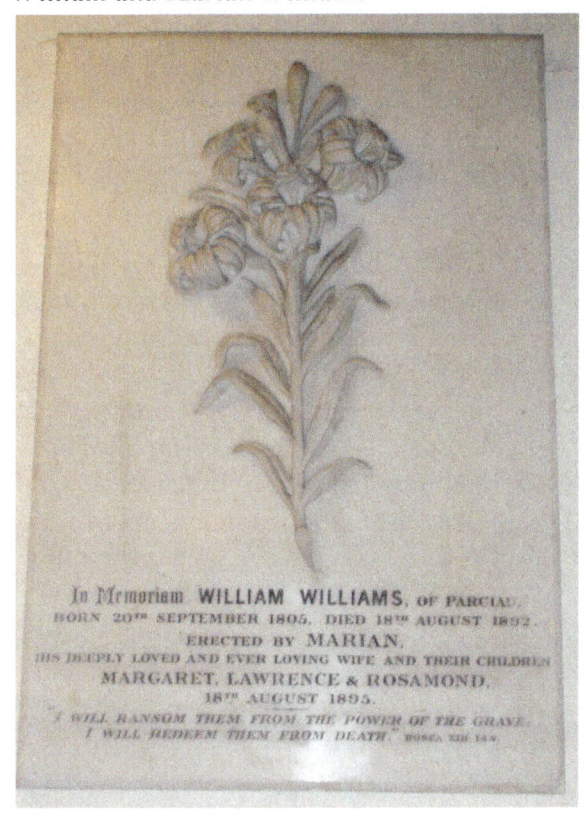

65. William Williams of Parciau

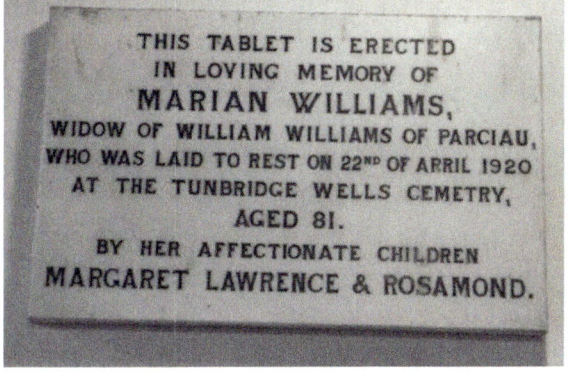

66. Marian Williams of Parciau

"In Memoriam WILLIAM WILLIAMS, OF PARCIAU. BORN 20TH SEPTEMBER 1805, DIED 18TH AUGUST 1892. ERECTED BY MARIAN, HIS DEEPL LOVED AND EVER LOVING WIFE AND THEIR CHILDREN MARGARET, LAWRENCE & ROSAMOND, 18TH AUGUST 1895. "I WILL RANSOM THEM FROM THE POWER OF THE GRAVE; I WILL REDEEM THEM FROM DEATH." HOSEA XIII.14.V."

"THIS TABLET IS ERECTED IN LOVING MEMORY OF MARIAN WILLIAMS, WIDOW OF WILLIAM WILLIAMS OF PARCIAU, WHO WAS LAID TO REST ON 22ND OF APRIL 1920 AT THE TUNBRIDGE WELLS CEMETY, AGED 81. BY HER AFFECTIONATE CHILDREN MARGARET LAWRENCE & ROSAMOND."

William was the son of Sir John Williams (1761 - 1830), the first Baronet of Bodelwyddan, and Margaret née Hughes, the heiress of Ty Fry, Pentraeth. Sir John became

Baronet in 1798 and the family lived in Bodelwyddan Hall in St Asaph. William was the youngest of their nine children and he was born on 20th September 1805. William first married Arabella Pretyman in June 1855 in the church of St George Hannover Square in London. She was the daughter of the Reverend George Thomas Pretyman (Chancellor of Lincoln Cathedral) and Amelia née Tower. William was a much-loved figure on Anglesey, and the wedding was a cause for big celebration with a very large event held in his home village of Pentraeth. They were married for 12 years but did not have any children. Arabella died in June 1867 and is buried in St Margaret's church, Bodelwyddan. In 1871, William married 32-year-old Marian Scott, the eldest child of Major-General Sir William Henry Scott of Thorpe House, Thorpe and Harriet Alethea née Stanley who was the daughter of the 1st Baron Stanley, Sir John Thomas Stanley. He and Marian were well-beloved figures in the parish and were extremely generous, holding tea parties for the children of Llaneugrad and Llanallgo as well as annual clothing drives for the poor of the parish. One of the highlights for the workers on the estate was the annual harvest Thanksgiving dinner they put on. In 1883, 40 workers attended and enjoyed a splendid spread of roast beef and plum pudding. Earlier that same year, in January, Marian gave clothes to the needy, as well as a liberal bonus of four shillings and six pence. They must have been absolutely delighted! There are many regular reports in the local newspapers of these types and other events that were cherished and enjoyed immensely by the workers and parishioners.

William was 86 when he died on 18th August 1892 in his home, and he is buried in St Eugrad's in the family crypt, the entrance to which had been decorated with "*great care and taste.*" There were several magnificent stems of the lilium auratum, each bearing over a dozen blossoms, all of which had been grown in the open air in the flower garden adjoining the mansion. A newspaper commented that this was "*a thing to be rarely seen in this bleak northerly clime of ours.*" As William set up his Parciau estate, he employed primarily local people from Anglesey and there was an influx of workers into the parish. When he bought the Llaneugrad lands, there was no village of Marian-glas, just empty common land. In his 20 or so years, the Llaneugrad population increased from 215 to 285 (33%,) and the number of houses grew from 48 to 66, an increase of 38%, quite an impact on this little community. Marian is buried in Tunbridge Wells, where she died on 18th April 1920.

Colonel Lawrence Williams, OBE, DL, JP, Kathleen, and Elinor Henrietta

LAWRENCE WILLIAMS OF PARCIAU BORN 25TH APRIL 1876 DIED 6TH JUNE 1958 AND HIS WIFE ELINOR HENRIETTA WILLIAMS BORN 7TH JUNE 1886 DIED 3RD MAY 1980 THIS TABLET IS ERECTED TO THEIR MEMORY BY FRANCIS WILLIAMS, VIOLET PEARSON, PENELOPE CORRIGAN, AND LAWRENCE WILLIAMS.

"IN LOVING MEMORY OF KATHLEEN WILLIAMS. DIED FEB 1ST 1905. ERECTED OCT 1905. BY HER DEVOTED HUSBAND & LOVING MOTHER 'SIMPLY TRUSTING'"

Memorials In the Churches

IN LOVING MEMORY OF
KATHLEEN WILLIAMS.
DIED FEB 1ST 1905.
ERECTED OCT 1905.
BY HER DEVOTED HUSBAND
& LOVING MOTHER,
"SIMPLY TRUSTING."

67. Kathleen Williams Wife of William

LAWRENCE WILLIAMS
OF PARCIAU
BORN 25TH APRIL 1876 DIED 6TH JUNE 1958
AND HIS WIFE
ELINOR HENRIETTA WILLIAMS
BORN 7TH JUNE 1886 DIED 3RD MAY 1980
THIS TABLET IS ERECTED TO THEIR MEMORY BY
FRANCIS WILLIAMS, VIOLET PEARSON,
PENELOPE CORRIGAN AND
LAWRENCE WILLIAMS.

68. Lawrence and Henrietta Williams

Lawrence was born in Parciau in April 1876. He was educated at Harrow school and admitted to Trinity College, Cambridge on 25th June 1894. He took up a career in the army with the Duke of Cornwall's Light Infantry (DCLI) and was 2nd Lieutenant in 1896, promoted to Captain in 1899, Major in 1902, Lieutenant Colonel in 1911 and Colonel in 1919. He served in the South African war from 1898 until 1901, then both of the world wars. In Llaneugrad (and elsewhere locally), he was affectionately known to almost everyone as "the Colonel"; I shall call him that.

He first married Catherine Elizabeth Anne Griffith Phibbs (Kathleen), the daughter of the late Colonel George Phibbs of Knoch Brach, County Sligo, Ireland, and his wife Frances Charlotte Griffith Bramston-Smith. His cousin, Reverend Watkin Williams, Dean of St Asaph officiated at the wedding, which was on 1st December 1897 in All Souls Church in Marylebone, London. They lived in Plas Llanddyfnan and had four children: Mona Rosamund Alice born on 24th December 1898; Sir Reginald Lawrence (7th Baronet Bodelwyddan) born on 3rd May 1900; Violet Kathleen Mary born on 4th May 1902 and Sir Francis John Watkin (8th Baronet Bodelwyddan) on 24th January 1905. Kathleen was only 28 when she died in Plas Llanddyfnan a week after Francis was born and is buried in St Eugrad's. The Colonel found love again in the Bodelwyddan side of the family, and on 12th September 1909 he married his cousin Elinor Henrietta Williams in St Margaret's church, Bodelwyddan. She was the daughter of Sir William Grenville Williams, 4th Baronet of Bodelwyddan and his wife, Elinor Harriet Hurt Sitwell. They had two children: Penelope Lawrence born on 25th June 1925 and Lawrence Hugh born on 25th August 1929.

The Colonel had a very illustrious career in the army and in civilian life. He was Deputy Lieutenant of Anglesey and on the Anglesey County Council for 56 years, and a magistrate from the age of 23 until he was 75 years old. In the January 1938 King George VI's New Year's Honours, he was admitted to the Order of the British Empire. He made a significant contribution with his service to the RNLI and the Moelfre lifeboat. He was Honorary Secretary for over 50 years from 1905, and in 1948 he was appointed a life Governor of the RNLI, which is the highest award given to an honorary worker. The Colonel was the last *Lord of Llaneugrad*, as by now much of the Llaneugrad parish lands were owned by several individuals which was a familiar story over much of Britain. He passed away in his mansion home on 6th June 1958, Henrietta died on 3rd May 1980, and they are buried together in the family crypt.

69. Lawrence and Henrietta Wedding

Francis Idris Williams of Bodelwyddan

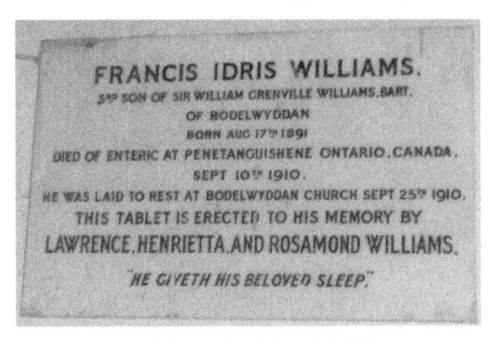

70. Francis Idris Williams

"FRANCIS IDRIS WILLIAMS. 3RD SON OF SIR WILLIAM GRENVILLE WILLIAMS, BART. OF BODELWYDDAN BORN AUG 17TH 1891 DIED OF ENTERIC AT PENETANGUISHENE ONTARIO, CANADA. SEPT 10TH 1910. HE WAS LAID TO REST AT BODELWYDDAN CHURCH SEPT 25TH 1910. THIS TABLET IS ERECTED TO HIS MEMORY BY LAWRENCE, HENRIETTA, AND ROSAMOND WILLIAMS. HE GIVETH HIS BELOVED SLEEP."

Francis was the youngest surviving brother of Elinor Henrietta, the Colonel's wife, and he was born on 17th August 1891 in Bodelwyddan. He attended Dunchurch boarding school in Dunchurch, Warwickshire and decided to pursue a career in the church. He was due to start at the University of Oxford in 1910, but before that, he and his aunty Mary Charlotte Lucy Williams, his father's sister, decided to holiday in Canada. They set sail from Liverpool on the *Empress of Ireland* on 29th July 1910, travelling in first class and arrived in Quebec on 4th August at 4 o'clock in the afternoon. Before allowing passengers off the ship, the ship's surgeon certified that he had examined the passengers and that none of them were, amongst other things, *"afflicted with a contagious, infectious or loathsome disease"*.

Their destination was Toronto and no doubt they intended to explore the surrounding area. Around 21st August, Francis started feeling unwell, but they decided to travel to Penetanguishene, a coastal town about 100 miles north of Toronto, perhaps it was part of their itinerary or perhaps it was to get him some fresh seaside air to help him recover from his ailment. However, his symptoms worsened, and Dr Philip Howard Spohn was called to attend to him on August 29th and diagnosed typhoid fever. Francis then suffered a perforated intestine, which was always fatal back in those days, and died eight hours later on Saturday 10th September. He was only 19 years old. Poor Mary must have been devastated to lose her young nephew, and she now had the sad task of telegraphing the news to their family back home and arranging for him to be taken back to Liverpool.

His body arrived in Liverpool on Friday 23rd September and was driven by motor car to Bodelwyddan church on Saturday morning for a private funeral at noon with only immediate family and residents of Bodelwyddan in attendance. The Reverend Trevor Owen officiated, and the coffin was covered with "*an immense number of wreaths*" that had been sent from all over the country. He was said to be of "*a most admirable disposition*" and was survived by two brothers, Sir William Willoughby then 5th Baronet of Bodelwyddan and Hugh Grenville who would become the 6th Baronet and his big sister Elinor Henrietta of Parciau who no doubt had the memorial put up in St Eugrad's.

Margaret and Lionel Frederick Southwell Sotheby

71. Margaret and Lionel Sotheby

"*TO THE GLORY OF GOD AND IN LOVING MEMORY OF MARGARET WIFE OF WILLIAM EDWARD SOUTHWELL SOTHEBY SHE WAS THE ELDEST DAUGHTER OF WILLIAM WILLIAMS OF PARCIAU SHE FELL ASLEEP 21T APRIL 1922 AGED 47 AND IS LAID TO REST IN THIS CHURCHYARD ALSO IN REMEMBRANCE OF THEIR SON LIONEL FREDERICK SOUTHWELLL WHO LAID DOWN HIS LIFE FOR KING AND COUNTRY AT AUBERS RIDGE IN FRANCE SEPTEMBER 25TH 1915 AGED 20 YEARS*".

Margaret was the eldest child of William and Marian Williams born on 4th July 1874 in Parciau and married William Edward Southwell Sotheby on 24th October 1894, in the church of St George Hanover Square, London. Her sister Rosamond was her bridesmaid, brother Lawrence (the Colonel) walked her down the aisle and cousin, the Reverend Watkin Williams, Dean of St Asaph, officiated. Margaret and William had two sons, Lionel Frederick Southwell born on 16th August 1895 and Nigel Walter Adeane born in 1896. The family initially lived at Cippenham House in Burnham, Buckinghamshire, moved to Sussex Lodge, Slough and were living in Menaifron Farm on the Menai Straits in Anglesey at the start of World War I. Margaret passed away on 21st April 1922 in the Cottage Hospital Caernarfon and is buried in the family vault in St Eugrad's.

Lionel educated at Langley and then followed in his father's footsteps to Eton College where, like most boys, he joined the officers' training course, which was an army class. He left Eton in Christmas 1913 to seek civil employment in business, and in preparation for this, he went to Berlin and spent seven months studying German at the Institute of Tilly. He arrived back in England in mid-July 1914, just a few weeks ahead of the start of the war. He was 18 when he enlisted in the army on 15th August 1914 with the 4th Battalion of the Argyll and Sutherland Highlanders. He chose this regiment because it was the Regiment of his uncle, Capt. Herbert George Sotheby, a career Army officer who was Captain of the 2nd Battalion. He was 2nd Lieutenant 4th Argyll & Sutherland Highlanders and also 1st & 2nd Black Watch.

I got to know this brave young man quite well through his diary and letters that were quite by chance selected for a book written by Donald C. Richter, a Professor of History at Ohio University in the United States of America. It is called *Lionel Sotheby's Great War, Diaries and letters from the Western Front* and I highly recommend it to those who wish to learn more about Lionel and the Great War from a young Officer's perspective. Even though the officers largely came from well-to-do or educated backgrounds, had access to better provisions at the front and lived in tents versus the accommodations for other ranks, their war experiences were the same as their men they commanded. They wore similar uniforms, endured the same cold, rain, trenches, mud, gas and shelling, machine gun fire and lived the same consequences of tactical errors. When it came down to risk of injury or being killed on the front line, your rank didn't matter at all. Lionel approached the war with a somewhat (for me anyway) unexpected optimism and cheerfulness and complete acceptance of any hardship. From the beginning he was quite sure of his fate in the war and seems to have determined to make the most of his earthly days. From his writings I don't think I am exaggerating when I say that he enjoyed his time in the Army. The following is a quote from his diary not long before he was killed: "*Once you leave the firing line with some illness, it is like being wounded, you return to England and take your turn in coming out. I have no intention of leaving the line, it amuses me intensely, as one becomes totally callous of the dead and death that are around you. Horrible to say but this is the truth.*" He goes on to say "*I don't know what I shall be like after this war, I feel I am passing through a peculiar stage, just as a caterpillar becomes a chrysalis and then a butterfly. I cannot explain. It comes unseen and makes you oblivious of almost everything at times, save one intense desire to kill, kill, kill the Germans in front.*"

In April 1915 he went on his first leave home and returned just in time for the battle of Aubers Ridge on 9th May. He wrote letters to his brother and mother detailing the carnage and his lucky escape – 15 of the 16 Officers were either killed (11) or wounded (four) and Lionel was the only one unscathed. On that day 500 men were killed and wounded and so instead of a company of 200 men, he was left to command only 25. For some time, he felt guilty about surviving, but wrote to his mother on 24th May noting that he had completely recovered his spirits again. On 25th September 1915, his battalion was involved in an offensive of the battle of Loos. Casualties were huge, numbering 363 including 92 killed or missing presumed killed and 271 wounded. Five Officers were killed that day and, among the bodies never recovered, was that of 21-year-old 2nd Lieut. Lionel Sotheby. Major Wauchope, the Battalion commander, wrote to his father that *"he was wounded and continued leading his men until a grenade struck him and killed him"* and this must have brought closure for his parents, because if he was classed as missing, they would have to wait until eventually he was "presumed dead" which would often be after a year.

Lionel left a letter with the family solicitor to be opened *"in the eventuality of my going out on the ebb tide and not returning"*. It was essentially a Last Will and Testament and had a list of mostly his army articles to be given to various people as "*souvenirs*". Uncle Bootie and Aunt Hennie (The Colonel and his wife) were to receive his prismatic compass. He left his money to brother Nigel as well as any other effects that Nigel may want. Although he said his mother and father could choose what they wanted from his belongings not bequeathed, he preferred that they remember his *"one-time existence"* without the need for visual objects. He left another letter to his parents, school, friends and brother and the envelope bore the words *"on my attaining still greater happiness"*. It said that he feels no remorse and talks about how he has been spared often but that his time will assuredly come and that it is a great honour to die for his country and asks them to be thankful that such an opportunity was given to him. It must have been as hard to read the letter as it was to lose him. He was awarded the 1915 star, the Victory, and British medals.

Margaret Anne Edwards
School Teacher Extraordinaire, The Angel in the Churchyard

"TO THE GLORY OF GOD AND IN LASTING REMEMBRANCE OF MY LOVING AND DEARLY LOVED WIFE MARGARET ANNE EDWARDS HEAD TEACHER OF THE SCHOOL IN THIS PARISH 1902 – 21 WHO DIED 5 JUNE 1921 IN HER 47TH YEAR. "A good life hath but a few days but a good name endureth for ever. Rejoicing in Hope."

Margaret was born in Lodge, near Brimbo Denbighshire in about 1875 to coal miner Ellis Jones and his wife Margaret. She must have shown early promise and desire to become a teacher,

72. Margaret Anne Edwards

because in the 1891 census, she was a 16-year-old pupil teacher. These student teachers attended a centre that provided professional training by the best teachers in the elementary school system, and most students who took part in centre programmes spent half of their training on theory at the centralized school and half of their training with hands-on teaching in schools. In the 1901 census she was living at home with her parents in Lodge, Brynteg and was an assistant school mistress. She was about to leave one Brynteg and take up a post in another one some 80 or so miles away on Anglesey. The post of headmistress for the Llaneugrad Council School was advertised in the 14th of August 1903 edition of the *North Wales Chronicle*. There were 30 pupils, the salary was £80 a year and a house and applications were to be made to the Reverend John Lewis Davies of Llanallgo Rectory. Margaret applied and was given the job, an excellent decision for both her and the school, as it turned out.

72a. Margaret's Grave

Margaret was a remarkable teacher, turning the school into one that was regarded by the school inspectors as a "*model school in every way*" according to a report dated 20th June 1913. This report is a glowing one, and the inspector praises Miss Jones and the children: "*the tone and work of the school is difficult to speak about without using what may seem to be extravagant praise*"; "*She deserves the greatest credit for her ceaseless efforts to study the best methods of teaching and for the sympathetic, stimulating and intelligent manner in which she trains the children under her care*"; "*The children are happy, alert and intelligent and take a pride in their school.*"; "*The school is abundantly and beautifully decorated with flowers which are brought in daily by the children*"; "*In the singing lessons the children's voices are exceedingly rich and resonant*"; "*they sing with perfect timefulness and a brightness of tone.*" They had a wide variety of lessons all using the latest teaching techniques of the day, including illustrations and models mostly created by the children. They were taught in English and Welsh (unusual for that time), and they even kept a small garden in the school playground. Margaret must have been much loved by her 56 pupils, as she seemed to make the school a fun and homely place. Suffice it to say that our children of the village, including my grandmother Katie Owen née Jones and her sister Maggie who attended, received an excellent education from this talented teacher.

In his memoirs of Marian-glas, Hugh Griffith the actor talks about his old Llanallgo school teacher, "Old Scŵl", as he called him, and he seemed like he was quite a character indeed. He was Margaret's husband. His name was William Robert Edwards, born in Towyn, Merionethshire around 1870 to David Edwards, a Letterpress Printer, and his wife Margaret. In 1901 and 1911 he was lodging in Glanrafon Uchaf, Llanallgo and was first a schoolmaster in Llanallgo council school and then Head Teacher in the new Llanallgo School. They were married in Rhosddu church in Denbighshire on 8th January 1916 and, after their marriage, they lived in the Llaneugrad schoolhouse.

They had a wonderful five and a half years of married life and then suddenly on 5th June 1921, Margaret passed away peacefully at home after suffering a haemorrhage from a gastric ulcer and cardiac collapse. She was only 46 and William was with her when she died. She was buried in St Eugrad's on 10th June, and I can only image how distraught the children were to lose their beloved teacher. In his memoirs, Hugh mentions the beautiful memorial Old Scŵl had raised for her. I am a frequent visitor to St Eugrad's when I visit Anglesey, and I am familiar with the stories of many who rest there and often have a walk around to pay my respects to them. I have stopped at one of the more unusual memorials many times and wondered who rests there. It turns out to be Margaret's grave and is indeed very beautiful. Hugh says that Old Scŵl was quite lost for a time without her; it is obvious form the memorials that William thought the world of his wife, and that she was highly regarded and well loved. William continued to live in the Llaneugrad schoolhouse through 1922 but by 1925 had moved out of the parish. He served as headmaster of the Llanallgo school for 35 years and passed away on 10th May 1955 at Eugrad Villa, Maes Y Coed Ave, Old Colwyn and is buried in the Old Colwyn Cemetery.

Arthur Gordon Ware, BA

"ARTHUR GORDON WARE. BA. RECTOR OF LLANEUGRAD LLANALLGO 1940 – 43"

Arthur was rector of our churches from 1940 to 1943. His memorial tablet was put up in 1945. See the Clergymen chapter for his story.

73. Arthur Gordon Ware

William Rees Hughes, BA

74. William Rees Hughes

"WILLIAM REES HUGHES B.A. RECTOR OF LLANEUGRAD AND LLANALLGO 1958 – 73. PEACE PERFECT PEACE."

Rees was rector of our churches from 1958 to 1973. See the Clergymen chapter for his story.

Cedric Harry Wild, F.I.MA
Churchwarden of Llaneugrad

75. Cedric Wild

"In Memory C.H. Wild Churchwarden 1970 – 82"

The memorial for Cedric is on the Hymn Board in the church. Cedric was born in Smethwick, Staffordshire on 13th May 1902 to schoolteacher Walter and his wife Lily née Noris, both of whom were born in Birmingham. Cedric was an exceptional student and an extremely intelligent boy; he was already taking university level courses and passing the exams when he was 16 and attending George Dixon secondary school. He went to University of Birmingham and graduated with a bachelor's degree in chemistry in June 1921 when he had just turned 19. He went on to do a master's degree in science, graduating in June 1922 after turning 20. His first teaching job was at The King's grammar school in Grantham where he taught until 1926. One of its most famous pupils was Isaac Newton, who attended from 1655 to 1660, some 260 odd years before Cedric taught there.

He married Margaret Griffiths in Liverpool in 1933. Margaret was born on 25th November 1906 in Bodifir, Moelfre and was the daughter of Captain Ebenezer and Ann Griffiths who had built Olive Branch in 1938 for their retirement home. Cedric and Margaret had two

76. Cedric and Margaret Wild

children, Judith, and Martin. Judith married Gwilym Thomas, and she still lives in Bronallt in Marian-glas, and Martin sadly passed away on 29th January 2021. After they were married, Cedric and Margaret lived in Rhiwlas, Llangefni for a time, and in the 1939 register he was a schoolmaster, presumably at the Llangefni County school.

The following is an excerpt from the book, *The People of Llaneugrad Volume I*, and records the memories of Jenny McRonald who told me: "*My parents were lifelong friends of Cedric and Margaret. Margaret was a pupil of Cedric's that is how they met. They lived near us in Shrewsbury Road, Oxton, Birkenhead from 1950s and later in a flat in Oxton until they built Swn y Coed. Cedric was a brilliant mathematician, and I was relieved when he met Richard (my husband) and they were able to discuss Maths for hours which took the pressure off me. He was a lecturer latterly in Kirby Liverpool at Teacher training college. Previously he had taught at The Holt and Collegiate schools in Liverpool where I think he taught one of the Beatles. Judith (his daughter) and I often reminisce that he would have been in his element now with computers. I can see him now at the large room at the top of the stairs at Swn y Coed surrounded by his books and with the view of Traeth Bychan all around him. A lovely man.*" I can well imagine this because Cedric became a Fellow of the *Institute of Mathematics and its Applications*. It was a very prestigious institute, and a Fellow was of the highest standing possible, and quite an accomplishment.

Cedric was a churchwarden of our church from 1972 until 1982, and I do remember that Margaret played the organ in the church (after Daisy Rees Hughes), so they were quite a team. Cedric died on 28th May 1982 in Swn Y Coed and Margaret died on 31st January 1993 and they are buried in St Michael's, Penrhosllugwy.

Sir Lawrence Hugh and Sara Margaret Helen Williams

"In loving memory of Lawrence Hugh Williams of Parciau 1929 – 2018 and his wife Sara Margaret Helen 1927 – 2016 Love is Immortal"

77. Lawrence and Sara Williams

Sir Lawrence was born on 25th August 1929 in Llanddyfnan, the youngest son of The Colonel and Elinor Henrietta, and he grew up on the Parciau estate. According to Burke's Peerage 107th Edition, he was educated at Royal Naval College, Dartmouth, Devon and was in the Royal Marine Corps, becoming a Captain. He was in the Korean War in 1951 and the Cyprus Campaign in 1955 and was Lieutenant-Commander between 1965 and 1987 in the Royal Navy Auxiliary Service. He married Sara Margaret Helen Platt in Beaumaris church on 23rd September 1952. Margaret was born in December 1927 in Manchester to Sir Harry Platt, the extremely famous and highly accomplished orthopaedic surgeon, and his wife Gertrude Sarah née Turney. The couple lived in Old Parciau and had two daughters, Emma, and Antonia.

In the 1950s, a new business plan was needed to preserve the ownership of the remaining Parciau estate after many farms had been sold off. Someone once told me, perhaps my father, that it was Major Corrigan's (husband of Penelope, Lawrence's sister) idea and plan to set up a caravan park on the estate. Tourism was a great source of revenue for the island and Llaneugrad benefited in so many ways from this. The local shops thrived from the added business from the "visitors" as they were known, and I believe that without the caravan park, Marian-glas would not have developed into the size of village that it became. Hilda and William Darlington form Leigh, Lancashire built a house on the top of the hill next to the caravan park sometime between 1945 and 1950, which they aptly named Haul a Gwynt (sun and the wind). Hilda died in 1963, and not long after that, Lawrence and Penelope bought the house and turned it into the only pub in the parish, The Parciau Arms, which was a centre of social life for many for many years.

When Sir Frances John Watkin Williams, 8th Baronet of Bodelwyddan died on 3rd January 1995, the title passed to brother, Lawrence, and he became the 9th, and last, Baronet. Sir Lawrence also served as one of the last High Sheriffs of Anglesey in 1970. Margaret died on 14th November 2016, and Lawrence passed away peacefully in his home on 19th April 2018. They are buried together in St Eugrad's, and I think that it is very fitting that the stone that commemorates them comes from my brother, Justin Kellett's, local quarry in Moelfre. It was engraved by stone carver, letter cutter and designer Teucer Wilson of Norfolk.

Memorials In the Churches

78. Lawrence and Sara's Gravestone

Sir Lawrence's funeral was held on Saturday 19th May at 2.30pm and the Reverend Dr Kevin Ellis, the Reverend Pauline Jones, and the Reverend Canon Dr Graham Loveluck officiated. A funeral tea was held on the field next to the church after the service. In the service, his daughter Emma gave the following reading from the work of the Armenian American novelist, playwright, and short story writer, William Saroyan (1908 – 1981): *"I am not going to try to comfort you. I know I cannot. But try to remember that a good man can never die. You will see him in the streets, you will see him in the houses, in all the places of the town. In the vineyards and orchards, In the rivers and the clouds, in all things here that make this world for us to live in. You will feel him in all things that are here out of love and for love, all things that are abundant and the things that grow. The person of a man may leave or be taken away, but the best part of a good man stays. It stays forever. Love is immortal and things are made immortal by love."*

St Gallgo's
Anne Gruffydd, 1635

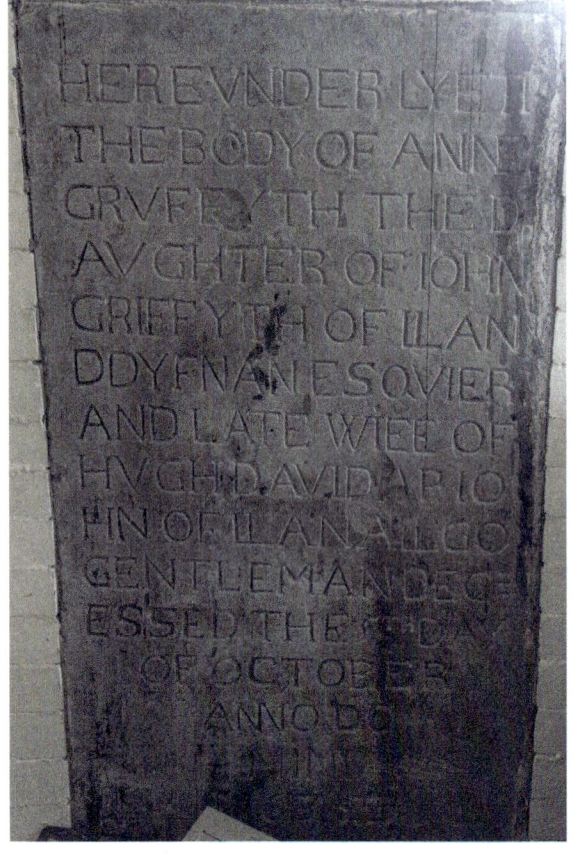

"Hereunder lyeth the body of Anne Gruffyth the daughter of John Griffyth of Llanddyfnan Esquire and late wife of Hugh David ap John of Llanallgo Gentleman deceased the 5th day of October Anno Domini 1635"

Anne was the daughter of John Griffith III of Llanddyfnan and his wife, Elin Bulkeley, daughter of Robert Bulkeley of Gronant (great granddaughter of the original William Bulkeley who moved to Beaumaris and founded the Bulkeley dynasty). Anne first married Hugh ap David ap John ap Madog of the Tre'rdafarn family of Llanallgo, and I suspect that she lived at Glanrafon Isaf. After Hugh died, she married John ap Llewelyn, MA, who was made rector of Llaneilian on 13th May 1603. John had died by 20th August 1612 when his successor took over, according to the church succession records.

79. Anne Gruffydd

John Hughes, 1755 and Mary Griffith, 1763 of Glanrafon

"Underneath are interred the Remains of John Hughes of Glanrafon Gent. And of Mary his Wife who was a true friend and a Loving Mother. He died 27th February 1755 Age 61 years and she died 19th September 1763 Age 62"

John was of the Tre'rdafarn family and was the great, great, great grandson of the above Anne Gruffyth. His wife, Mary Griffith, was his mother's first cousin and the daughter of Robert Griffith, second son of John Griffith VII of Llanddyfnan and his wife Grace. Grace, who was the daughter of William Mostyn, Archdeacon of Bangor, had first married Morris Lewis of the Trysglwyn family, so Robert was her second husband. In 1707, Robert took up a 21-year lease on Llaneugrad Parke and was rent collector for the Anglesey estate of then *Lord of Llaneugrad*, Simon Folkes, so Mary very likely grew up in Caerfryn. The couple had seven children, and three of them also have memorials in the church.

Both left Wills with monetary legacies to the children alive at the time. John left specific pieces of furniture, including cabinets, cupboards, and tables to his eldest son John that he would inherit after Mary died, and he specified that they must remain in Glanrafon and be passed down with the house to his son's heirs. Mary inherited the balance of the estate's worth and if she re-married then it would be shared amongst the surviving children at the time of that marriage. He left his lands in Llanfair ME to Mary to sell for *"best advantage"* to help pay his debts and the legacies. Out of curiosity I looked to see if I could work out what the lands were. There is only one John Hughes responsible for Land Tax in Llanfair ME in the years from 1752 leading up to his death, so this might well be him, and his property was variously called House Willow, House Wilim and Yr House and eventually was simply called R'House. Some relatives of mine lived there, and I have often wondered about the origin of the name, and now I know. Mary does not appear to have re-married, and at the time of her death, she owned a herring boat that she left to son Robert and daughter Mary along with some silver spoons. She also left a small legacy to niece Ann Lewis, the daughter of her nephew Ambrose Lewis and her grandson Thomas Ellis.

80. John Hughes and Mary Griffith

Their eldest son John attended Oxford University, matriculating on 19th March 1738 aged 17 and graduating with a BA on 12th March 1742. He became rector of Llandegfan cum Beaumaris when his predecessor, also John Hughes, died in 1754 and he married Grace Bulkeley on 16th July that year. They both died in 1762 when he was only 41 and she was 39, so it was likely to have been from some sort of infectious disease. They were both buried in Beaumaris church, Grace on 17th March and he on 19th June. Even though the *JEG Pedigrees* list children for them, I do not believe that this is correct, as I cannot find any children christened in his churches or in Bangor Cathedral, and there are no children listed in his Will. In fact, he left all his properties to brother Robert for life and then to Robert's heirs, sons first and then daughters. If Robert had no children, the properties were to go to sister Grace and her heirs, then sister Mary and her heirs if Grace had no heirs, and finally sister Jane and her heirs if Mary had no heirs. He had quite a few properties in addition to Glanrafon – he owned Pen Y Bryn in Llanallgo and several properties in Llaneilian, which I believe he must have all inherited from his father, although I have not specifically traced the ownership of the Llaneilian properties. As it turned out neither Robert nor Grace had any children, and so Glanrafon and the other properties passed to Mary and her heirs. One other point of interest is that the inventory in John's Will is by far the longest inventory I have seen in these local Wills, and it is much more detailed than I have seen before. The inventory is taken by room or area and there is a list of contents of the brewing house, and in the cellar, there were 6 barrels, four half barrels and four dozen glass bottles so Glanrafon was definitely an alehouse in 1762.

Robert and Elizabeth Hughes, Glanrafon

"Underneath is Interred Robert Hughes of Glanrafon Gent Died 24th April 1777 Aged 50 Likewise Underneath is Interred the Remains of Elizabeth Hughes the Wife of the above Robert Hughes and Daughter of Griffith Landon in the Parish of Llaneilian, who departed this life on the 10th day of April 1777"

Robert and Elizabeth (who used her patronymic name, Griffith), were married in St Gallgo's on 30th January 1764 by the Reverend Lewis Owen and they did not have any children. They died within a couple of weeks of each other, and considering his young age, I would imagine that they died of some sort of infectious disease. He wrote his Will on 21st April 1777, and it was the

81. Robert and Elizabeth Hughes

shortest Will I have come across for someone of means. He left three pair of sheets and two blankets to his aunt Jane Hughes, two guineas to infant John Brereton, and all the rest of his goods etc to his sisters Mary and Jane, who were to take care of all his debts and keep the rest. I was not able to definitively prove who John Brereton was, but given the quite unusual name for the area, a strong possibility is the infant christened on 27th April 1777 in Penmynydd, who was the son of Roger and wife Jane.

Mary Hughes and John Ellis, Taicroesion

"Beneath are deposited the Remains of MARY, Daughter of the late John Hughes of Glanyrafon Gent. and Wife of John Ellis of Taicroesion, Gent. She died June 1, 1795, aged 61. Likewise Underneath is interred the Remains of John Ellis, the Husband of the above Mary Ellis, and the Son of the late Thomas Ellis of Taicroesion, Gent. who departed this life on the 13th day of January 1810, Aged 75."

82. Mary and John Ellis

Glanrafon Gent. And Wife of John Ellis of Taicroesion, Gent. She died June 1, 1793, aged 61. Likewise Underneath is interred the Remains of John Ellis, the Husband of the above Mary Ellis, and the Son of the late Thomas Ellis of Taicroesion, Gent. Who departed this life on the 13th day of January 1810, Aged 75"

Mary and John were married in St Gallgo's on 1st April 1760 and, as the Reverend Lewis Owen was away at the time, John Bulkeley who was curate of Bodedern officiated. He and John Ellis were first cousins from the Dronwy branch of the Bulkeley family, as was Robert Bulkeley, curate of Llandrygarn who was one of the witnesses. As an aside, John Bulkeley's son was Sir John Bulkeley, Knight and he married Ann Owen, his maid servant. After he died in 1819, married the celebrated Calvinistic minster, John Elias. Mary and John had five children, four boys and a girl. It was their eldest son, Thomas Ellis, who would inherit the Glanrafon family estate after his mother's sister, Grace Jones, died and he also inherited Taicroesion.

Grace Jones, Glanrafon

83. Grace Jones

"Underneath is Interred the Remains of Grace Jones the Wife of Leonard Jones Excise Officer late of Holyhead and the daughter of John Hughes of Glanrafon Gent who departed this life on the 29th day of December 1809 Aged 89"

Grace and Leonard were married in St Gallgo's on 2nd November 1757. He died about 12 years after they were married and was buried on 29th June 1769 in Holyhead, so Grace was a widow for 40 years. Leonard left a Last Will and Testament when he was in a *"middling state of health"* and *"not to live long"*. Curiously, he said that he was leaving the Will *"to avoid any"* [piece of document missing] *that may happen amongst my relations"*. He left £30 to his natural (illegitimate) daughter Elinor Jones, so I am sure that this explains what the relations might have been unhappy about. He left the rest and residue of his estate (goods, chattels, ready money, mortgages, bonds, notes, securities, and personal estate) to sole Executrix Grace. Grace also left a Will and updated it later, adding a Codicil. The main beneficiaries were nephew Thomas Ellis and his children. His son John Hughes Ellis received the £300 mortgage she had on Pen y Bryn and a further £600 in the codicil. His son Richard was left £130, his daughter Grace was left £50 and all her plate and linen (worth £6 5s according to her inventory) and his daughter Mary received £21. Thomas received the rest and residue of her goods etc. and the inventory reveals that she had given a £200 mortgage on Glanrafon, but it does not say who was the purchaser. She had a large amount of cash, £368 8s 10 1/2d and was due £94 in rents and about £7 rent from a house in Caernarvon. The total value of her inventory was about £698 after £60 was paid in debts and funeral expenses. Grace was of Holyhead according to her Will, so she did not live in Glanrafon, presumably

Edward Williams, Ty'n Y Llan

"In Memory of EDWARD WILLIAMS of Ty'n y Llan, who died Feb 2, 1770, aged 63"

Edward was a mariner and fisherman of Llaneugrad at the time he married Ann Lewis of Llanallgo in St Gallgo's on 9th January 1743. He was likely the son of William Jones Owen, and christened on 3rd March 1706 in St Eugrad's. Ann was the daughter of carpenter Lewis Thomas, and his wife, Sarah Williams. Ann was born in Ty'n Llan in 1721 and grew up there. After they married, Edward and Ann lived in Nant Bychan township where they had seven of their nine children. Ann's father died intestate in 1759 and her mother in 1761 after which Edward and Ann then moved to Ty'n Llan.

Edward died intestate and Ann took out a Bond together with Richard Davies of Gell, Llanallgo parish, to administer his goods. According to his inventory, he owned a half-share in a boat with six nets and five anchors and an old sloop. He was buried on 4th February in the churchyard, and not inside

84. Edward Williams Ty'n Llan

the church. The intent must have been to have Ann memorialized on the same tablet as him as there is a lot of room underneath his inscription. Ann died in March 1813 aged 94 and is also buried in St Gallgo's. She left an extensive Will with legacies to all her surviving children as well as to her many grandchildren. Curiously, she had put a legal document in place with Owen Anthony Poole, solicitor of Caernarfon with a covenant that limited the use of Ty'n Llan and Ty'n y Rhedyn. The properties were divided in half and then one half went to daughter Jane Williams for her natural life. The other half went to her eldest son John and his heirs, who would also inherit his sister's half after her death. I believe that John may have been Ann's illegitimate son from before the marriage, and perhaps that is why the covenant was needed to ensure that he inherit.

Memorials In the Churches

The Reverend Lewis Owen

"Erected to the Memory of Lewis Owen Clerk Rector of Llaneugrad and this Parish which he faithfully Served for 32 years he died May the 28th 1771 Aged 71. Henry Prichard Grandchild of the Said LO was here interred who died July 2nd 1771 Aged 1 year & 9 Months"

His full story is told in the chapter on Parsons, Rectors, and Curates.

Elizabeth, Wife of William Lewis

"Also Elizabeth the Wife of William Lewis, who died 2 Feb 1788 aged 31"

85. The Reverend Lewis Owen

There was space left above her name on the memorial, which I assume was for her husband, but for whatever reason his name was never added. Elizabeth was born in Frigan, Llaneugrad to Land Steward William Thomas and his wife Jane, and she was christened in St Eugrad's on 1st July 1757. She and William were married in St Eugrad's on 13th November 1785, and he was living in Amlwch parish at the time. I suspect that he was related to the Trysglwyn Lewis family but cannot find a definitive link. The couple had their only child, Lewis Williams, in 1785 and he was christened in St Gallgo's on 13th November. I suspect that Lewis was brought up by relatives and William then moved

86. Elizabeth, Wife of William Lewis

away from Llanallgo and is buried elsewhere as I could not find a burial for him there. Lewis remained in Moelfre, becoming a shopkeeper, and he died in 1852 and is buried with his wife, Jane, in St Gallgo's.

Henry Molyneux Blevin

"In affectionate Remembrance of HENRY MOLYNEUX BLEVIN, who was lost in the Royal Charter, off the coast of Anglesey, October 26 1859, AGED 22 YEARS AND 11 MONTHS"

87. Henry Molyneux Blevin

Henry was born in Liverpool and christened on 15th January 1837 in St Nicholas church, Liverpool. He was the son of Master Printer, James Blevin and his wife, Hannah née Rimmer. At the time of the 1851 census, aged 14, his occupation was watchmaker, so he must have had a change of career, because he was a Steward on the Royal Charter and in his 23rd year when he lost his life. There is a grave for him in St Eugrad's, but no record of his burial in the parish register. The fact that there is a grave means that his remains were washed up in that parish on either Traeth Bychan or Dinas beach and subsequently buried. The memorial for him in St Gallgo's is mounted on the door and is a funeral memorial card. The headstone on his grave reads: *In affectionate remembrance of HENRY MOLYNEAUX BLEVIN who was lost in the 'Royal Charter' October 26, 1859, age 22 years.*

Isaac Lewis, Ty Hir

"In memoriam ISAAC LEWIS of Ty Hir Moelfre who as a crew member lost his life during the sinking of 'The Royal Charter' on October 26th 1859 aged 21 years and is buried beneath this church. From his family descendants Sunday October 25th 2009"

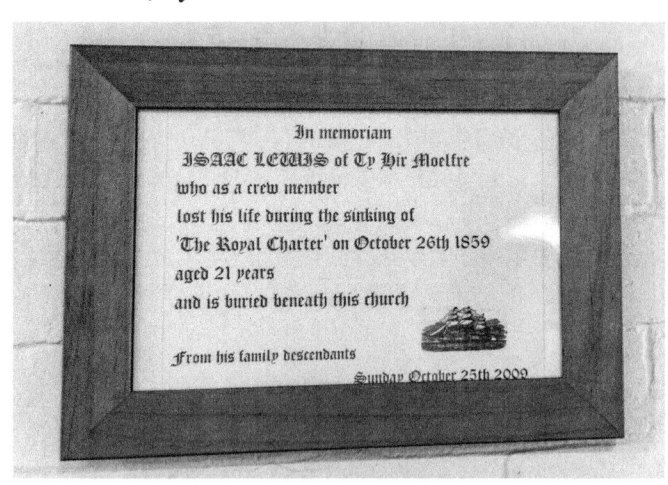

88. Isaac Lewis

Isaac was born on 24th September 1838 in Ty Hir to Captain John Lewis (abt. 1799 - 1883) and Jane née Williams (abt. 1798 - 1845) from Penrhosllugwy, one of four sons who would all pursue careers on the sea. Isaac was a member of the crew on the Royal Charter and was apparently drowned in sight of his father off the rocks. *The*

> An affecting account was related of one of the seamen belonging to the Royal Charter. His name was Lewis, a native of Moelfra, and it was said that his father resided within a stone's throw of the spot where the dreadful catastrophe occurred. The father recognised his son on the wreck, and they hailed each other in agonising terms. "Oh," cried the young man, "I have come home to die!" He then made an effort to reach the shore by means of the hawser, but was struck by a terrific sea and drowned in the presence of his father. It was stated on Saturday evening that the body had been recovered and removed to his father's cottage.

89. *Liverpool Mercury* 31st October 1859

Liverpool Mercury reported his story on 31st October 1859. Whilst the report about the father and son exchange may have been true, the statement that his father recovered his body that night and brought him home is definitely "fake news". According to the *North Wales Chronicle* on 17th December, Isaacs' body was picked up at Moelfre on Tuesday 13th December and identified by his marked stockings and tattoo "IL" on his arm. He was buried on 15th December in St Gallgo's. He was only 21 years old. His father was one of the 29 local heroes who risked life and limb to rescue the ships' hero, Joseph Rogers, and who were instrumental in saving the lives of several of the crew and passengers. Capt. and Mrs Lewis, along with many other families, also took in and cared for survivors including a Mr. Russell whose wife and two daughters were left on what remained of the ship to drown as he was, to his horror, washed overboard. He was rescued on the rocks and taken to Ty Hir to recover.

The Reverend John Lewis Davies

"TO THE GLORY OF GOD AND IN LOVING MEMORY OF JOHN LEWIS DAVIES RECTOR OF LLANEUGRAD-CUM-LLANALGO 1899 – 1929 WHO DIES ON JAN 27TH (SEPTUAGESIMA SUNDAY) 1929 AGED 69 YEARS. THIS TABLET IS ERECTED BY HIS WIFE & CHILDREN R.I.P."

John's story is told in the Clergymen chapter.

90. The Reverend John Lewis Davies

Richard Williams, Croesallgo

"TO THE GLORY OF GOD AND IN MEMORY OF RICHARD WILLIAMS, CROESALLGO, LLANALLGO THIS CHURCH WAS RE-ILLUMINATED BY HIS WIFE, MARGARET WILLIAMS AUGUST 1938."

Memorials In the Churches

91. Richard Williams, Croesallgo

Richard was born in Llanfair ME on 4th November 1868 to Captain David Williams and Ellen née Thomas and the family were then living in Figin Bach, Llaneugrad. He was a mining geologist and went with some of his brothers to the gold rush in the Klondike where they made their fortunes. The family built several notable properties in the area including Fron Heulog, Olgra and Cae Marl. Margaret was the great, great granddaughter of the Reverend Richard Lloyd who served in our churches, and her maternal family had Croesallgo for a couple of generations starting with her great grandmother, Margaret Lloyd. Margaret was born in Croesallgo on 16th September 1888 to Ellen née Owen and Owen Williams from Newborough. She married Richard sometime before 1923 and the couple had four children. Richard was about 20 years older than his wife, and he died on 25th August 1937 and is buried in St Gallgo's. It was the following year that Margaret, who was a Lay Reader in the church, had the electric lighting installed. She later married medical practitioner, Owen Vaughan-Jones, who had a medical practice in Bangor for many years, and she died in Croesallgo on 5th November 1967.

The Reverend Robert Williams

"TO THE GLORY OF GOD AND IN LOVING MEMORY OF ROBERT WILLIAMS RECTOR OF THIS PARISH 1937-40 WHO DIED ON SEPTEMBER 22nd 1940 AGED 38 YEARS. THIS TABLET IS ERECTED BY HIS DAUGHTER AND FAMILY R.I.P"

His full story is in the Clergymen chapter.

92. The Reverend Robert Williams

David William Irons
Lay Reader

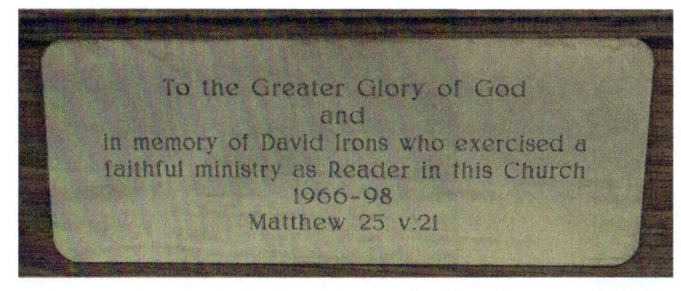

"To the Greater Glory of God and in memory of David who exercised a faithful ministry as Reader in this church 1966 – 98 Matthew 25 v.21"

93. David Irons

David was born during WWI on 21st May 1916 in Hampshire to George David Irons and Mabel Louise née Mudge. He married Patricia "Pat" Irons in 1943. She was born on 14th May 1920 in Southampton. Both David and Pat were very active in the church and David was also a founder member of Radio Ysbyty Gwynedd. The couple lived in Bryn Hyfryd, Llansadwrn for many years. The 3rd January 1992 edition of the Caernarfon and Denbigh Herald carried this delightful piece about Pat. David passed away on 14th May 1998 and Pat died the following year.

Pat's ready to have a go

By Liz Carter

KEEP going or you will end up in a wheelchair is advice that children's author and lay preacher Patricia Irons knows only too well.

For Mrs Irons, of Bryn Hyfryd, Llansadwrn, was born with a congenital spine condition.

When her husband David proposed, she had just had a renewed attack of back trouble and was in a hospital, in a plaster cast.

"The nurses were delighted and kept popping round to see if he had kissed me yet," she said. "I always jokingly say that I only said yes because of the wartime sweet rations he gave me."

Mrs Irons has actually had 42 operations, both major and minor, and has spent more time under anaesthetic for the various treatments she has had, than she can remember.

Until six years ago, when she started coming to Plas Menai, Caernarfon to have lessons, she could not swim.

Since then, she has won numerous cups, trophies and awards, starring as best swimmer in her age group (she is 71!) She has also swum for charity as well as playing table tennis for Anglesey.

She does all the digging in their lovely rambling garden, taking special pride in their shrubs which include mimosa.

"I'll have a go at anything," seems her obvious motto which she proved yet again when husband David had a sore throat.

"He was due to go and preach in Llanfairfechan," said Mrs Irons,"The people who had asked him were terribly disappointed that he could not go, when I rang to tell them.

"Rashly and really joking, I said I would go instead, if they liked. They rang me back and took me up on my offer."

Now Mrs Irons is well known as a lay preacher though, as she hastily asserts, she has no qualifications whatsoever.

A favourite venue is the Presbyterian Church on Castle Square, Caernarfon, twice a year or so where she has given the special Children's Address before the Sunday school.

And, when addressing children, she tells parables that she has made up herself.

Mrs Irons has just had her second book of children's parables, entitled *Which Way? This Way* published by the charitable Headquarters Publishing Company in Ealing, London, copies available from her at £1.50p.

It is delightfully illustrated in pen and ink by her good friend Keith Williamson who lives with wife Christine and children Nicholas and Christopher at Bryn Eglwys, Llansadwrn, and works at Ysgol David Hughes.

Pictures of such characters in her little book as The Stubborn Donkey, Fred the Industrious Spider and Dusty Doll add greatly to its charm.

Her first book of the same title, published in 1989 is for children aged four to 10 while this one is for older ones. Now she is working on a third.

"So many children's books today are full of blood and thunder," said Mrs Irons " Mine are little peaceful stories which the adults, reading them to children going to bed, seem to enjoy as well."

Mrs Irons worked as a nurse during the war at a Southampton Hospital and remembers having to move hospital beds out into the corridors during the Blitz. She told the frightened children stories to calm their fears.

Years later, a good friend, former IPC magazines editor Mrs Carys Morgan of Tan-y-Ffynon, Bethel, collected together the stories Mrs Irons had written for church newsletters and magazines and found a publisher for them in a book as a surprise.

Mrs Irons has more time on her hands now her family are grown-up. Son Keith is a chartered surveyor with a family of his own in Carlisle and daughter, Vivienne, also married with children, has a shop in Cromer, Norfolk.

Mrs Irons' husband David is a founder member of Radio Ysbyty Gwynedd and still conducts his Memories programe for the hospital radio.

Mrs Patricia Irons with her dogs

94. *Caernarvonshire and Denbigh Herald*, 3rd January 1992

Dafydd Elgan Jones, Gwynfryn

95. Dafydd Elgan Jones

96. Dafydd Elgan Jones

"*Dafydd Elgan Jones Gwynfryn – Moelfre 15:09:1987 – 14:05:2013 Atgyweiriwyd y ffenest hon Er Cof cariadus amdano ga neu deulu Rhagfyr 2014 December.*" Transalation: This window was repaired in loving memory of him by his family.

Dafydd was brought up in Moelfre with his parents, elder brother, and younger sister. He first went to sea at 3 months old, along with his brother Gerallt. They travelled worldwide on bulk carriers until both brothers had to attend school in Moelfre and later Amlwch. Dafydd was a talented artist and a film fanatic, he studied art and design in college but decided against going to university. Although he had colour blindness, dyslexia, and epilepsy, he enjoyed life with his wide circle of friends. After years of working at various hotels and cafes locally, he discovered his love for cooking and pursued it, working onboard a ferry as a chef for Stena Line. After suffering a seizure on the vessel, he had to be seizure free for a year before he could go back onboard to work. During this time, he was offered kitchen work at the Coastal Cafe in Moelfre, a job he really enjoyed. Sadly, Dafydd lost his life to epilepsy in 2013 at 25 years old. His family decided to repair a window at Llanallgo Church in his memory, a much-loved son and brother who will never be forgotten.

Unidentified Royal Charter Victims

When the nave was extended in 1892/3, it then covered a grave holding the remains of 67 unidentified victims of the Royal Charter wreck. There was nothing inside the church to indicate that the grave was there, or to memorialize them. In 2022 Graham Loveluck had this memorial tablet made and mounted on the wall to mark their final resting place.

96a. Memorial Tablet in St Gallgo's

Chapter Four: The Clergymen

Introduction

I have been able to find 54 men who were parsons/rectors/curates from 1328 AD through to the very last rector, the Reverend Canon Dr Graham Loveluck who retired in 2004. The names were obtained from several sources, including *Calendar of Patent Rolls* (various kings), *Calendar of Papal Registers*, *Mona Antiqua Restaurata*, *Anglesey Antiquarian Transactions*, *theclergydatabase.org.uk*, a handwritten list of rectors from 1739 to 1983 in the Llaneugrad christening register, surviving parish registers and a variety of newspaper reports.

The earliest information on the churches I have been able to find comes from the Norwich Taxation of 1254, but it does not name any clergymen. The church in Wales by this time had a territorial framework of diocese, archdeaconry, and rural Deanery, but the parishes as we know them had probably not yet been set up. There were two Deaneries called Cantref and Dindaethwy & Twrcelyn. Cantref included three commotes - Menai, Malltraeth and Llifon. Dindaethwy & Twrcelyn included the commote of Talybolion. In the valuation recorded in 1254, the two churches were valued individually, and historians appear to have assumed that they were part of the same benefice at that time, although a source for that information is not provided in any of the texts. I therefore believe that it is possible that they were not combined into a single benefice at the time and may have each had their own parson. Of the 72 Anglesey churches listed, 29 had a Llan prefix and others were named after the townships that they were situated in or nearby. St Eugrad's was called Nant as it was in Nantmawr and St Gallgo's was called Dafarn as it was in the township of Y Dafarn. The income (tithes, oblations, and income from the glebe) of the parson of St Eugrad's was seventeen shillings nine pence and that of the parson of St Gallgo's was eight shillings ten pence. By way of comparison, the income of parson of the neighbouring maerdref of Penrhosllugwy was valued at one pound, fifteen shillings and sixpence. All the clergymen of England and Wales had to pay a tenth of their valuation to fund the King's crusade. The amount of that tenth for most churches is listed in the original document but there are a few churches for which that information is missing, including our churches. The calculation, though, is straightforward, and a tenth of their value would be one shilling and nine pence for the parson of St Eugrad's and ten pence for the parson of St Gallgo's. A cursory review of the valuations for the Archdeaconry of Northumberland which appears next on the roll, reveals that the Welsh churches were exceptionally poor compared to their English counterparts and so the tenth for our men was a very lot of money to "give up" and especially for something that was half a world away and had no impact on their daily lives.

By way of background, Henry III was King of England from 1216 until 1272 and the Crusades to the Holy Land were popular during his rule. They were also very expensive, and to fund a crusade for Henry, Pope Innocent IV granted Henry the tenths of all ecclesiastical incomes of England and Wales for three years, a commitment that was extended by his successor after Innocent's death the following year. Both the annual income and personal property of the clergymen were included in the valuation, and as we might imagine, it was not a popular tax, and the property valuation could be quite controversial. The task of valuing and collecting the monies fell to three men, the bishops of Norwich and Chichester and the abbot of Westminster. The bishop of Norwich, Walter Suffield, was in charge, and hence the tax became known as the "Norwich Tax". The task was divided between them, and the valuation for the Bangor diocese came under Norwich's responsibility.

In the 14th century the Welsh had not yet given up on their independence and North Wales in particular was a rebel stronghold. The rebels would be caught periodically and, by the early 1300s would be imprisoned in the newly built Beaumaris Castle. Three prisoners being held in the castle in 1320 were Jevan Cutta (Ieuan Cwta), David ap Kenewreck (Dafydd ap Cynwrig) and Mereduc Thloskorn (Meredydd Llys Coron?) and they managed to escape. Although their crime is not specified in the rolls, it is likely that they were rebels as one of them would be run to earth in St Gallgo's church and killed according to page 48 of *Medieval Anglesey* by AD Carr. This man was Ieuan Cwta, and he was of the gwely (family) Wyrion Sandde of Bodafon. He had 18 virgates (llathen in Welsh) or yards of land for which he had paid 10 pence annually towards the collective rent of the gwely. He must not have had a legal heir as his lands escheated to the King and a tenant had still not been found by the time of the 1352 Extent. I believe that Dafydd ap Cynwrig was possibly Dafydd Lloyd ap Cynwrig of Trefeilir, who was at one time one of the soldiers in Edward I's army. According to *Welsh Soldiers in the Later Middle Ages* by Adam Chapman, a surviving plea roll records that Dafydd was accused of stealing a horse and he said that he had bought the animal at Carlisle, "*at the time the Welshmen came to Scotland*". I was not able to find out who the third man was nor what happened to these two. The constable of Beaumaris Castle at the time was John de Sapy. He had been constable of Newport Castle until 14th March 1318, and Sheriff of Caernarfon from 8th August 1316. On 9th March 1320, the King pardoned him for their escape, so perhaps Dafydd and Meredydd were caught or met the same bloody end as Iuean and thus John de Sapy had redeemed himself, at least for a time. John was himself later branded a rebel and on 30th March 1324 was ordered to appear before the King to answer the charges, and a couple of months later, on 22nd May, it was documented that he and others owed the most reviled medieval courtier and reputed King's lover, Hugh Despenser the younger, the enormous sum of £200. I imagine that the money was paid, as by 1325, John had received a knighthood and was back in favour as the keeper of Rockingham Castle in Northamptonshire.

Peter de Morteyn, 1328 – Unknown

I include Peter here as *potentially* the first documented parson of St Eugrad's. The *Calendar of Patent Rolls* states that he was presented to the church of "Lannerghaern" in the diocese of Bangor on 27th February 1328 by the King (Edward III,) as the Bishopric of

Bangor was vacant. "Lannerghaern" has been interpreted to be Llaneugrad, but as it is such an unusual spelling, I should include that there is also a parish in the diocese called Llanengan or Llaneigan (various spellings are used) which could be another possibility. The rolls appear to be written using anglicized phonetic spelling of placenames, and many of them are difficult to decipher, probably also due to the accents of the time. Unlike the later entries for appointments to our churches, the record of Peter's appointment makes no mention of Llanallgo, which could either corroborate that it is Llanengan, or showing that our churches were separate benefices in 1328, as suspected in the 1254 Norwich Taxation.

On 2nd March 1328, Peter was granted the "portion" that Caducan Thloit (Cadwgan Lloyd) lately had in the church of Kellennokvaur. This was Clynnog Fawr in Caernarfonshire, one of a handful of very wealthy Collegiate churches in the diocese. As of 21st January 1328, he also held the benefice of the church of Brantfield in the diocese of Lincoln, in the King's gift, owing to the voidance of the abbey of St Albans. Peter was a king's cleric, and this plurality of benefices/posts was how king's clerics (and others) were rewarded to give them a more substantial income. They would live and work in one of their churches and hire more junior clerics or curates to take care of their other parishes. The Bishop of Ely Peter also granted Peter another benefice – that of Outwell in Norfolk - in 1328. It was here that Peter lived, at least for a time, as the King (Edward III) tried to get him a house and some land. Back in the reign of Edward I, it was noted in the *Norwich Domesday* book that the rector of Outwell at that time had neither house nor land. In 1333, Edward III sought to remedy that and allowed two tenants to let 3 acres of land to Peter as well as a messuage (house) for him to live in. Ten years later, on 18th April 1343, it was noted in the *Calendar of Patent Rolls* that the licence never took effect, and all three parties had "*gone the way of all flesh*" so Peter died sometime between 1333 and 1343. He had resigned from Outwell in 1334, but I could not find any other information on his St Eugrad's post.

Entry 1030 in the *Calendar of Inquisitions Postmortem* records that on 26th January 1328/9 (just before Peter's appointment,) the King ordered the justice of Wales, Roger de Mortuo Mari, to conduct an "Inquisition" of the township of Nantmawr. It was held on Saturday 8th September 1329, the feast of St Gregory the Pope. It was found that there were "*no demesne lands, homages or villeins in the town of Nantmaur, but there are 45 tenants who pay the King yearly 4l. 10s. [£4 10 shillings], besides going to the King's army for a day at their own expense and doing suit of court every three weeks; the pleas of the town are of the yearly value of 10s.*" Demesne lands were those held in direct possession by the King, homages were titled tenants who had paid homage to the Lord of the manor and villeins were tenants legally tied to the Lord. The courts were local hearings held to keep law and order in the township and tried all but the most serious of crimes.

In the same entry it is noted that the King has granted Nantmawr to Res ap Tuder (Rhys ap Tudur) "*for life without any yearly rent or other services except going in the King's army at his own expense.*" In 1284 Tudur Fychan (10th great uncle of Sir John Bodvel) had been granted the township for life, and according to the *JEG Pedigrees*, Rhys was his son. It is interesting that Edward II granted the township to Rhys's son David for life in 1322/3.

Rhys was *Lord of Llaneugrad* for only a short time as in 1331/2 a new Lord was named and Nantmawr was back in English hands. On 3rd February William de Shaldeford was granted Nantmawr town for life at an annual rent of 100 shillings.

There was also a new magistrate the same year when on 21st March the King committed *"during good behaviour"* of the *"bailiwick of the rhaglawry, rhingildship and woodwardship of Nantmaur"* to William de Pillarton, king's pantler at the same rent that others had paid. As pantler, he was in charge of the king's pantry and in 1329 he was constable of Northampton Castle.

Interim to 1379

The plague arrived from Europe in the Autumn of 1349, and although records of its early impact have not survived, the later records paint a bleak and devastating picture. The mortality was so great that it triggered a change in the ownership and tenancy of lands. The Bond tenants (who were bound or tied to the land) and the Free tenants (who were not bound to the land) all paid rent on their lands to the Lord. In Nantmawr this was the *Lord of Llaneugrad* and in Y Dafarn, it was the Bishop of Bangor. The tenancy of lands was passed down from generation to generation to the heirs of the head of the gwely, and the land was subdivided between heirs. This inheritance was known as "braint" or privilege. As the population increased and there were more surviving heirs, this model was not one that could last indefinitely and still have large enough pieces of land to be inherited for the heirs to make a living. This dilemma went away with the Black Death because it wiped out an estimated third to a quarter of the Anglesey population leaving large amounts of land with no tenants. In some cases, the only option left to the rhingyll (magistrate in charge), was to let the land for grazing at a substantially lower price than if it were rented. The old feudal system no longer worked financially or from a tenant point of view and it began to crumble. Many men of the church also perished in the plague, a sign that they were fulfilling their pastoral duties of visiting the sick to hear their confessions and conduct last rites for them.

One of the consequences was that it became increasingly possible for tenants to move around, and there were more "immigrants" who came in to take up vacant tenancies. When they did so, they had to pay a "fine" (usually fourpence) to the prince for their protection. In the Commote of Twrcelyn, there were nine immigrants in 1350-1 and 33 in 1354-5. These immigrants were men of various standing and the difference between Free and Bondsmen continued to fade as the old tenurial model continued to break down, and more men became landed proprietors.

In 1352, a survey of most of Anglesey was conducted, by a man called John de Delves, to assess the state of land and tenants at that time from a financial point of view. John travelled around the island, making a record for each of the Commotes of the king's lands. The church owned substantial lands on Anglesey with rents paid to the Bishop of Bangor. Y Dafarn was a church-owned township and is not included, but Nantmawr belonged to the

Crown and was included. The Lords of Llaneugrad at this time were Edmund de Wauncy, knight, who held two parts of the township for the term of his life by the grant of the lord prince and Thomas de Bodenham and his wife Alice held the third part as her dower. Heirs of the gwely in the township ae named and are our earliest known parishioners:

A Free gwely called Gwely Hywel ap Llywelyn. The heirs were Iorwerth ap Hywel ap Llywelyn, Dafydd Goch ap Hywel ap Llywelyn and others. Their annual rent was a total of 23 shillings which was paid in four installments of five shillings and nine pence. They would pay 10 shillings gobrestyn, relief and amobr to Edmund, Thomas, and Alice. Interestingly this family also owned, by right of braint (heritage) a share in a free Mill in the commote of Dindaethwy.

Four and a half gwelyau of the nature of tref welyog or hereditary township and these were bond tenants. They were:

Gwely Dafydd ap Ewrydd. The heirs were Einion ap Adda and Iorwerth ap Bleddyn. Annual rent was 54 shillings.
Gwely Pyll ap Isaac. The heirs were Cadwgan ap Iorwerth, Dafydd ap Ednyfed and others. Annual rent was 42 shillings and six pence.
Gwely Cynwrig ap Elidyr. The heirs were Iorwerth ap Madog, Madog ap Cynddelw and others. Annual rent 51 shillings and two pence.
Gwely Madog ap Nynnio. The heirs were Madog ap Philip, Ednyfed ap Dafydd and others. Annual rent was 53 shillings.
Half of Gwely Cathaearn ap Cynwrig. The heirs were Iorwerth Ddu, Trahaearn ap Madog and others. Annual rent 21 shillings and eight pence.

These four and a half gwelyau owed suit (payment) to the prince's mill of Melin Bryn Gwydded, each a twenty-ninth measure. They also paid 10 shillings for relief, gobrestyn and amobr to Edmund, Thomas, and Alice. In addition to all of this they also owed a sum of £12 five shillings and four pence to the Sheriff for the two tourns.

Relief (ebediw in Welsh) was a fee to be paid to the Lord by an heir to enable him to take up his inheritance. Gobrestyn was a fee paid in addition to relief to take up an inheritance when the heir was not a direct descendent of the deceased. Amobr was a fine for the loss of a woman's virginity and payable to the Lord when she married, or on other relevant occasions. The Tourn, set up in 1284, was the sheriff's criminal court held twice a year where five representatives of the township would be questioned under oath and would have to confess to all the offences and breaches of law that had occurred in the township in the previous six months. These were minor breaches of public order that did not affect the crown, and apparently, the unfree, or bond communities could pay a fine to avoid them having to report them at the tourn.

From their names, the heirs of the free gwely appear to be the sons of Hywel, but the heirs of the four and a half bond gwelyau do not appear to be sons and perhaps this was because of the plague, and these are the closest surviving family members who thus became the heirs.

According to the Angharad Llwyd prize-winning essay, Einion ap Adda, heir of Dafydd ap Ewrydd, spent some time in prison in Pontefract (for what I do not know) but when there, he apparently received an old copy of the Laws of Hywel Dda from the constable or governor and which is now in the Hengwrt collection at the National Library of Wales.

Hywel ab Adda Grwn (Arthur Grwn), 1379 - 1385

By 1379, the two churches were part of the same benefice and I wonder if this was because of the Black Death, which would have significantly reduced the value of the parishes, making financial sense to combine our two parishes. Llanallgo has always been described as annexed to Llaneugrad and this was presumably because it was worth about a half of the Llaneugrad income.

Hywel was an upper-class Anglesey cleric, and his father was one of the Welsh burgesses of Beaumaris in 1327. The very expensive 100 years' war was continuing to rage and in 1377 Parliament had granted a tax to be paid to the King to finance the war. Every beneficed person had to pay an additional 12 pence, known as the clerical subsidy. The tax was revised in 1379 to be fairer and is known as the Poll Tax of 1379. The task of collecting the Clerical Poll Tax in the Archdeaconry of Anglesey fell to Hywel, who was also rector of Llanallgo and Llaneugrad.

Hywel was later presented by the King on 7th February 1385 to the church of St "Donwenne" (Dwynwen) on an exchange with the king's clerk Nicholas Slake. Dwynwen's reputation as the patron of lovers was widespread and pilgrims came to visit the church from near and far. As a result, this was one of the wealthiest churches in Anglesey thanks to these pilgrims, and so it was quite a promotion for Hywel. Nicholas Slake was a very ambitious cleric, and I believe that the exchange meant that Nicholas was granted the benefice of Llaneugrad and Llanallgo which was worth considerably less. However, by 16th October the same year, he had also been granted the Archdeaconry of Chester in the king's gift and so he too got a promotion out of the move. Hywel was one of the bailiffs in Newborough in the years 1385-6 and from 1386 to 1390 he was also one of the farmers of the borough.

Hywel's appointment does not seem to have been without controversy. There were some who were not happy with him being placed in Llanddwyn, and this was brought to the attention of the King, who issued the following on 14th November 1387: *"Mandate to the justices and chamberlains of North Wales and those supplying their place, and to the sheriff of Anglesey in Wales to arrest and bring before the King and council all impugners of the king's title to present Howell ab Adda Grwn, late parson of Nantmawr with the chapel of Llanallgo, in the diocese of Bangor, to the church of St Donwenne [Dwynwen] in the same diocese, on an exchange with Nicholas Slake, and any persons who by process in Court Christian seek to disturb the possession of the said Howell in prejudice to the Crown."* Whether anyone was brought before the King I have not been able to discover, and perhaps just the threat itself was enough to silence the impugners.

Iorwerth ap Ievan (or Blethyn ap Iorwerth ap Ievan), 1391 - 1399

According to the *Calendar of Patent Rolls*, Jor' ap Jevan (Iorwerth ap Ievan) was presented to Llaneugrad as rector on 7th February 1391, in the gift of King Richard II as the Bishopric of Bangor was vacant.) There is a variance in his name in the roll, because when the King ratified him as parson on 15th February 1392, the name in that record was Blethyn ap Iorwerth ap Ievan. I believe this must have been the same person because the 1392 record was of a ratification and not a new appointment, and it raises the question of whether he was Blethyn or Iorwerth. He must have done a good job because on 18th April 1399 Richard II gave him the "portion" of the cure in the parish church of Aberdaron that had previously been held by Llewelyn Ysgolaic. His appointment was ratified on 18th October the same year by Henry IV who was then on the throne.

During his tenure, the township of Nantmawr in Llaneugrad was owned by the son-in-law of Goronwy Fychan ap Sir Tudur Fychan of Penmynydd. Goronwy Fychan had inherited Penmynydd from his father in 1382. He had two children, Tudur and Morfydd. After Tudur died, Morfydd became the heiress and she had married Gwilym ap Gruffudd ap Gwilym (I shall call him Gwil), heir to the very substantial estate of Penrhyn. It was Gwilym who was the *Lord of Llaneugrad*. Goronwy Fychan had been one of Richard II's Squires of the Body and was also a first cousin of the famous Owain Glyndŵr, which must have put him in quite a dilemma during the Glyndŵr uprising.

Iorwerth ap Dafydd, 1399 - 1436

On 12th February 1399, Richard II presented Jor' ap David to the church of Llaneugrad. He was ratified on 18th October 1399 by Henry IV, and it was noted in the rolls that the chapel of Llanallgo was annexed.

The rector took care of the souls and wellbeing of his parishioners, and he also played an important role in passing on the news of the day. News would come from a variety of sources, such as the church hierarchy, local landlords and officials and elsewhere. Through his sermons in the church and visits with parishioners, he would also exert his influence probably with varying degrees of success. From his name I assume that he was a local Welshman and as such he would be familiar with local sentiments about Welsh independence. Iorwerth had only been in his role for just over a year when the Owain Glyndŵr uprising began.

The uprising created quite some turmoil in the Penmynydd family as Sir Tudur Fychan's remaining sons had ties and loyalty to the King and Crown, yet Owain was close family. Two of them, Rhys and Gwilym, believed fiercely in Owen's cause which they gladly joined. Morfydd's husband and Penrhyn heir and *Lord of Llaneugrad*, Gwil, was pulled in different directions, especially when he saw that Owain's supporters were having their lands confiscated. Initially he valued his lands more than he valued Owain's cause, but there was mounting pressure from within the family for him to join the cause. Rector Iorwerth would have been keeping exceptionally close tabs on this situation and he would have had to be quite careful in how he passed on the news to his parishioners. Gwil eventually gave in to the family pressure, aligned with Owain in 1402 and had his lands confiscated. Llaneugrad had a temporary new Lord, an Englishman called Hugh Mortimer, although it is doubtful that he ever stepped foot in the parish. Gwil was more of an astute businessman than a rebel, and he saw an opportunity to profit from the situation. In 1405 he aligned with the King and obtained the land of 27 known rebels, including his own lands that had been taken. Gwil was back as *Lord of Llaneugrad*. To complete the story of the uprising, by about 1412 Owain Glyndŵr had disappeared, and life settled back to the ordinary and everyday challenges and trials. Iorwerth stayed on until 1436 when he resigned from the position.

The earliest surviving Register of a Bishop of Bangor is that of Bishop Benedict Nicolls, 1409 – 1417, and it was the last register completed for a great number of years. The Bishopric had suffered greatly during the Owain Glyndŵr uprising with the cathedral being partly destroyed and it suffered further during the Wars of the Roses and was not restored until the end of the 15th century. To give an idea of what life was like in these turbulent times, at the 1446 General Chapter of the Augustinian Canons, the Visitors for the diocese of Lichfield said that they had not visited the Augustinian houses in North Wales partly because they could not speak the Welsh language and partly because travelling was not safe in Wales. According to *The Diocese of Bangor in the Sixteenth Century,* there is a surviving record of a complaint from 1464 by the clergy and people of St Asaph, Bangor, and the border dioceses that *"the number of murderers and ravishers of virgins and of other women, of thieves and robbers had so increased as to make life hardly safe."*

Dafydd ap Iorwerth Vychan, 1436 - Unknown

According to the *Calendar of Patent Rolls,* David was presented to the church of Llaneugrad in the gift of Henry IV on 28th October 1436 upon the resignation of Iorwerth ap David. This is all the information I have on him and there is then a gap in the records until 1504.

Syr Dafydd Trevor, 1504 or before– 1527/8

Gruffydd ap Tetur, 1504 or before – Unknown, Curate

Much of the information about Syr Dafydd Trevor comes from an article published in the *Transactions of the Anglesey Antiquarian Society,* 1934 by Irene George MA who drew what little information there is about him directly from a variety of manuscripts and documents. There are those who have published that he was rector of our churches during the Owain Glyndŵr uprising, but that happened 100 years before his time.

Although he went by the name of Dafydd Trevor, he was born David ap Hoell ap Ieuan ap Iorwerth, and his place of birth is as uncertain as his pedigree. In *Cwrtmawr* manuscript 561, his place of birth is given as Llanddeiniolen and in his poem "*Cywydd i ofyn Geifr*" he says that Morgan ap Hywel, Llanddeiniolen, is his "ewythr" (uncle) although Irene points out that bards also loosely used that term for a friend or patron.

He appears on the list of Clergy of the Bangor Diocese in the Warham return of 1504 as rector of Llaneugrad and was a "Magister", so he possessed a university degree and as such used the title "Syr" (Sir). Dafydd was the rector, but he also employed a curate, Gruffydd ap Tetur (which I believe was some sort of phonetic spelling or Tudur based on other men of the same name in the register). I do not have any other information of Gruffydd. The fact that he employed a curate may be a sign that he did not spend all of his time in our parishes, and perhaps spent more time in Bangor as he was also listed in the return as a Canon of Bangor Cathedral church. There are a couple of gaps in the register of clergy between 1525 and 1534 other than a couple of entries for 1530, so it is not known exactly how long he was rector of our churches. However, there are clues in some documents. In 1513 he was involved in a lawsuit and the legal document described him as "late of Llanallgo", and in a conveyance document dated 1524, when he sold Tyddyn Hwfa near Llangeinwen church to Owen Holland, he is described as the current rector of Llanallgo.

As a young man Dafydd saw the first Welsh man crowned King of England (and Wales) when Henry VII defeated Richard III at the battle of Bosworth Field on 22nd August 1485, and he wrote an elegy for Henry after his death. When Henry VIII succeeded his father in 1509, little did the men of the church suspect that their world was about to be turned on its head. Although Dafydd witnessed Henry VIII fighting with the Pope to secure a divorce from his first wife, he died before the earth-shattering separation from Rome and the dissolution of the monasteries a few years later.

In his time as rector of our churches, the *Lord of Llaneugrad* was Robert Owen ap Meurig of the House of Bodeon (great-grandfather of Sir John Bodvel), and he lived in the house called *Caerfryn* which was near to the church and Bryn Ddiol hill fort. I imagine that he and Dafydd were good friends, as they were both cultured men and would share a common interest in country and world events. Robert was very well connected through his wife's family, which I am sure came in useful to both Dafydd and Gruffydd for obtaining up to date information on latest developments at the country level. The great-grandfather of Robert's wife, Sian, was John ap Meredydd of Rhiwaedog, one of the most influential men of his time in North Wales and one of the two leaders who put together a large army from North Wales to support Henry VII at Bosworth Field. Robert also had his own family connections. His father, Owen, had fought on the battlefield with Henry VII and, upon his return home, his father had the beautiful east window in Llangadwaladr church dedicated to him and his wife Elin who was the daughter of William Bulkeley, founder of the Beaumaris Bulkeley dynasty.

In the book *Gwaith Syr Dafydd Trefor*, edited by Rhiannon Ifans, she says that "*many of his poems are requests for gifts, namely a bow, a mare, a rosary, and a harp. He also composed songs of praise and elegies, and religious songs (albeit not as many as one might expect), among them a delightful song of praise to St Dwynwen, patron saint of Welsh lovers. Although Sir Dafydd Trefor greatly enjoyed the company and prosperous lifestyle of the gentry, he sang of the brevity of life and the transitoriness of its finery. His songs are an interesting reflection of the life of a cultured priest on Anglesey during the period immediately preceding the Protestant Reformation.*"

The *Cambrian Register Vol III* dated 1818 has this delightful entry. It is in a section written by Richard Llwyd of Beaumaris who was known as Bardd Y Wyddfa or The Bard of Snowdon:

"The intelligent rector of Llanallgo, in 1480, Sir Dafydd Trevor addressing the statue of this Prince over the grand entrance into the castle of Caernarfon, thus expressed himself:

> *Where! ye now astonished cry-*
> *Where does mighty Edward lie;*
> *He that gave these ramparts birth,*
> *When prostrate Cambria lean'd on earth?*
> *Here still his image, rais'd on high,*
> *Attracts the thoughtful, curious eye;*
> *But he, long humbled from a throne,*
> *Lies far beneath a massy stone."*

The Poetical Works of Richard Llwyd includes the original Welsh verse by Sir Dafydd:

> *P'le mae Edwart, plwm ydych!*
> *Gwr a wnai y Gaer yn wych;*
> *Mae ei ddelw, pe meddylien',*
> *Wych yn y porth, uwch y pen;*
> *Ynteu yn fud hwnt yn ei fedd;*
> *Dan garreg dew yn gorwedd.*

An elegy for Dafydd by Ieuan ap Madoc suggests that he died in 1527 or early 1528 as it talks about two other bards who died before him, Tudur Aled, who is known to have died in 1526, and Lewis Môn who is known to have died in 1527. According to Edward Lhuyd FRS (the Welsh naturalist, botanist, linguist, geographer, and antiquary), Dafydd Trevor was buried in Llanallgo. At the time he wrote this, he said that some of the parishioners could then point out the site of his grave. If he is buried in Llanallgo, he was likely the rector there at the time of his death. There is no record of the resignation or death of Gruffydd ap Tetur which must have happened in the period of the missing records.

William Nant, B.Can.L., 1527/8 - 1550

With the gaps in the register of clergy, it is not possible to pinpoint the year of his appointment with any certainty, but it is very likely that was appointed on the death of Dafydd Trevor. He died as rector of St Eugrad's and St Gallgo's in 1550, but I was not able to find the year that he was appointed

William appears on page 302 in the *J.E. Griffiths Pedigrees* (Erw Gwyddel & Chwibren, Llansannan) as a descendant of the Hedd Molwynog tribe and the son of David Lloyd and Mallt, the daughter and heiress of Griffith ap Madog ap Llewelyn Vychan of Llwyndurys.

The family surname was Lloyd, and his brother was a Lloyd, so how he came to use "Nant", I have not been able to prove it, but I believe it to be a shortened form of Nantmawr, the township. William attended University of Oxford and studied Canon Law, graduating with a bachelor's degree on 12th July 1525.

Although priests were forbidden to marry in the Catholic Church, apparently in Wales this was long ignored, and it was quite common for "obstinate" Welsh clergymen to marry. In fact, in the 1504 Warham Return for Bangor Diocese there were no fewer than 43 clergy who were charged with keeping "concubines", so-called as the marriages were not recognized as such by the Western Church. If the information is correct, then William probably married as according to Page 267 of the *J.E. Griffiths Pedigrees*, William had a daughter called Agnes who married John, son of Ifan Vaughan of the Bach Y Saint family (who were descended from Owen Gwynedd) and his wife Nes who was from Denbighshire.

William served our parishes during a very turbulent time for the church, and I imagine that it must have been incredibly stressful and personally challenging. Not only did he have to deal with the changes himself, but he also had to guide his parishioners through these revolutionary times. There were likely many discussions with his colleagues in the neighbouring parishes as the consequences from the drama in the palace were felt, one by one. It began in the late 1520s with the lack of support from Rome for Henry VIII to divorce his first wife, Catherine, to "trade her in", so to speak, for a more fertile wife who could bear him a son – Anne Boleyn. After lots of back and forth, it was clear that he was not going to get what he wanted under the Catholic Church, so he took matters into his own hands, and, ignoring the Pope's authority, secretly married Anne in January 1533. He then had his first marriage declared null and void in a special court at Dunstable Priory, and his second marriage later declared legal. He did not stop there. The Act in Restraint of Appeals in 1532 had abolished the right of appeal to Rome and the 1534 Acts of Supremacy now recognised Henry's status as head of the church in England – he had essentially "fired" the Pope. In response, Pope Clement excommunicated Henry, although this wasn't made official for a while. William and his parishioners must have been following these shocking developments not only with trepidation, but probably like a modern-day soap opera, with a morbid fascination and eagerness to see what was going to happen next.

Another major event for the Welsh people followed soon after. The 1535 (and later, 1542) Laws in Wales Acts officially annexed Wales into the Kingdom of England, a move that was apparently not unpopular with Welsh gentry as it gave them equality with their English counterparts. One of the local effects was that English was now to be used in the courts instead of Welsh and I am sure that none of the parishioners spoke English at that time. The courts in those days were quite busy with all sorts of business from minor misdemeanours and transgressions to managing aspects of daily life such as confirming property inheritances, approving marriages, and collecting the proper charges for those events either in livestock, goods, or money. Although the court documents would be recorded in English, I would imagine that the conversations on court days would still have been conducted in Welsh.

An Act in 1536 heralded a more earth-shattering change - the dissolution of the monasteries, priories, convents and friaries, a move that sent shockwaves through the Church of England and its clergy. The Catholic Church was exceptionally wealthy, and Henry was a very extravagant spender. The monies he collected from the dissolution of the monasteries etc as well as those that were formerly paid to Rome, came in handy to fund his exorbitant lifestyle, although he always seemed to be on the verge of financial ruin. Waltham Abbey was the last of the country's abbeys to close on 23rd March 1540, marking the end of an era. Closer to home, the monastery on Ynys Seiriol (Puffin Island) was dissolved in 1536, Penmon Priory in 1537, Llanfaes Friary in 1538 and Holyhead monastery sometime soon after that. The Saints Seiriol and Cybi must have been turning in their graves as the saying goes.

The Llaneugrad and Llanallgo parishioners must have heaved a collective sigh of relief when after six marriages, two divorces, two beheadings and some of the most sweeping changes the country had experienced in a very long time, England's most-married monarch passed away on 28th January 1547. His nine-year-old son Edward VI succeeded him and since he was underage, a regency council was formed to manage the country's affairs. It was not the end of the changes, though, because the new church had yet to be set up. Henry had mostly taken things away and put himself in charge, but under Edward, the religious reformation began in earnest, and the Church of England was transformed into a recognisably Protestant body. It was these changes that had the biggest impact on the daily lives of the clergy and their parishioners. The 1548 Clergy Marriage Act abolished the prohibition on marriage of priests and those in the Welsh clergy who were married must have been somewhat relieved to have the pressure lifted. On 15th January 1549, the Act of Uniformity imposed a Book of Common Prayer, which was a sort of new protestant church "handbook".

These were two very big changes for everyone to get to grips with, but William would not really have enough time to make these different practices feel like the "new normal". Perhaps it was because of all the stress and trials and tribulations of the recent years, or perhaps he had contracted one of the prevalent incurable diseases of the time from his parishioners or maybe it was from some other cause, but William died a relatively young man, somewhere close to 2nd August 1550. As he had graduated from university in 1525, he must have been only around 50 years old.

An article in *Archaeologica Cambrensis* in 1900 records that William was an official of William Glyn, the Archdeacon of Anglesey from 1524 to 1537, and that he had his own seal. It measured 48 X 32mm and was of black or very dark red wax. Under a gothic-type canopy with tabernacle work at the sides, a capped figure is seated and holding a key in his left hand and in his right hand a sword, there is also an indecipherable motto.

Richard ap Ieuan Taylor and Sir William Griffith, 1550 – 1587

This is a "Tale of Two rectors" as I could not find out the exact dates of their individual tenures from the existing records and their story is quite an unusual one. Both rectors were married men, and when the country was returned to Catholicism by Queen Mary I, they were forced to choose between their marriages and their careers...

King Edward VI was only 15 when he died on 6th July 1553 from some sort of lung disease. He had reigned for six years, during which time, long-lasting changes were made to the Church of England. Edward knew that he was terminally ill, and he really wanted his changes to the church to endure. His successor was his catholic half-sister Mary, but knowing that she would undo his reforms, he (possibly influenced by others) decided to change the succession. He drew up a document in June 1553 and named his cousin, Lady Jane Grey, great granddaughter of Henry VII, and her male heirs as successors to the Crown. Jane was a committed Protestant, and he knew that his reforms would be safe under her rule. Jane was proclaimed Queen on 10th July 1553, but as Mary's popularity grew, Jane's supporters abandoned her. Nine days later she was deposed, and Mary was declared Queen on July 19th. Jane was sent to the Tower and she and her husband were executed on 12th February 1554. The entire church would have very closely followed these developments, and most definitely by our next rector, Richard ap Ieuan Taylor, who succeeded William Nant in 1550. I have not been able to find out any information on his origins or family or exactly when he was married, but I do know that he was a married man in 1554.

Meanwhile, on the other side of the island in the parish of Llanfaethlu/Llanfwrog, Sir William Griffith who had been rector there since 30th May 1544, would also have been following events closely as he too was a married man. He was from the Carreglwyd family of Llanfaethlu and was the son of Edmund Griffith of Porth Yr Aur, Caernarfonshire and Talybont, Llangeinwen and his wife Jonet, who was the daughter of Meredydd ap Ifan ap Robert of Gwydir. William married Elizabeth, the daughter of Griffith ap Robert of Carne, Llanfair-yn-neubwll and they had seven children, four boys and three girls but the *JEG Pedigrees* does not give the years of birth, nor the year that William and Elizabeth were married, but I do know that it was before 1554.

Once on the throne, Mary I set about undoing as many of the church reforms as she was able. Reinstating the monasteries etc was not going to be possible as their lands had been largely given away to nobles, and she was not going to strip them of these lands and risk having them turn them against her. She began replacing the Protestant bishops with Catholic ones, and her first Parliament in October 1553 abolished Edward's religious laws and, amongst other things, reinstated clerical celibacy. Married priests were called up on to abandon their wives and families and have their marriages dissolved or face fines and loss of their benefices. The Welsh clergy were going to be held to these new standards like they had not been in the earlier Catholic Church.

Whether they expected it or not, when it happened, this must have come as a shock to Richard and William, and it put them in quite a quandary – a choice between their wives and family or their jobs. When push came to shove, they both loved their wives and families more than they wanted to keep their jobs, and in July 1554 they were both deprived of their benefices due to their married status and they were not the only ones on Anglesey. Of the 23 other rectors, three who were in the same quandary made the same choice. They were Hugh ap Robert of Newborough, Gregory ap Llewelyn of Llanidan and Rowland Meyrick of Llangadwaladr (later Bishop of Bangor in 1559) and they were all deprived of their benefices in June of 1554. The new incumbents of these three parishes served there until their deaths in 1596, 1579 and 1572 respectively, and the three ousted clerics do not appear to have been granted another benefice on Anglesey during Mary's reign. However, something less common happened with Richard and William and I have not been able to find out who was responsible, although I know that Williams's patron was Edmund Bulkeley and Richard's patrons were Robert Griffith and others. By their patronage they appear to have endorsed a swap of benefices at a time when the Bishopric of Bangor was vacant for the whole of 1554. Bishop Arthur Bulkeley (grandson of William, the founder of the Beaumaris Bulkeley dynasty) had died in the spring of 1552/3 and was not replaced until September 1555 when another Anglesey man, William Glynn, who was born at in Heneglwys and who had been rector there from 1551 was appointed largely because of his catholic sympathies. Both the Llaneugrad/Llanallgo and Llanfaethlu/Llanfwrog benefices were in the bishop's gift, and in prior vacancies, it had fallen to the monarch to appoint new rectors. That did not appear to happen this time, but I do not know why.

On 13th and 19th July 1554 respectively, William and Richard were appointed to each other's benefice. Both appointments showed that the new rector replaced one who had been deprived of the benefice since they were a married man. The Llanfaethlu/Llanfwrog parish was worth about £20 and Llaneugrad/Llanallgo worth about £14, so William would have been taking a step down and it would have been a promotion for Richard, but the records seem to hint at some sort of a sharing arrangement. This is what makes it difficult to decipher the dates of tenure for them in the different parishes. William was about 49 years old when all this happened, and he and his wife had seven children, but as their dates of birth are not given in the *JEG Pedigrees* it is not possible to know if they were all born before these events.

Thankfully for the married priests, the return to Catholicism was only to last a handful of years, as the 42-year-old Queen Mary I died in November 1558 during a flu epidemic. She was succeeded by her Protestant sister Elizabeth I, and with a 44-year reign, Good Queen Bess would return the country to Protestantism, and bring some much-needed stability to both the church and our two rectors as it was once more acceptable to be a married clergyman. I have not been able to find out if or when Richard and William were restored to their respective benefices and in 1558, they were both listed as rector of Llanfaethlu/Llanfwrog. This supports that there was a sharing arrangement, rather than a straight swap and in 1561 Richard is listed as rector of Llaneugrad/Llanallgo per the *The Survey of Bangor Cathedral* by Browne Willis.

After the death of Robert Owen ap Meyrig, his son Owen became the *Lord of Llaneugrad*, and he and his wife Elin lived in Caerfryn from about 1555. Their son and heir, Richard, died at the beginning of the Summer of 1573 when he was young and still single and his father commissioned a eulogy for him by a bard (name unknown) which describes the family lineage and praises the young boy and his talents, as well as describing the grief of his four sisters and parents. In one part it alludes to him being glad to have the "bear from his head" which might mean that he died from something like meningitis or perhaps a brain tumour or injury. It also talks about him returning to Bueno, which at first, I thought might mean that he was buried in St Beuno's in Trefdraeth, his mother's family church. However, the Trefdraeth parish records from that time survive in very good condition and there is no entry for his burial. I therefore imagine that he was buried in St Eugrad's with Richard officiating.

The Reverend Richard died the following year in 1574, and William Griffith succeeded him as rector on 9th August, and he also kept the Llanfaethlu/Llanfwrog benefice until his death, aged 71, on 17th November 1587.

Whatever happened and how it happened, it appears that all's well that ended well. During his solo tenure, William gave his personal attention to Llanfaethlu/Llanfwrog, and was aided in Llaneugrad and Llanallgo parishes by two curates, Owen Byner and William Evans. Before I go ahead to tell their stories, there is a record of another potential rector around the parish swapping time, David ap Robert.

David ap Robert, 1554

On page 54 of the *JEG Pedigrees* (Plas Gwyn and Llwynogwen family), David ap Robert is noted as being rector of our parishes in 1554. I have not been able to find any other reference to him or his tenure, and he is not listed in the Bangor Diocese clergy. He was the son of Robert ap Rhys, heir of Meylltern and Elin, daughter of Robert Griffith of Plas Newydd. In 1596 his nephew, David Rowlands, would become rector of our parishes. If he did serve in our churches then it was probably only for a brief time, and perhaps as a stopgap until the permanent arrangement was made for Richard and William.

Owen Byner, 1574 - 1580

From 1575, the archbishop of Canterbury was Edmund Grindal. In 1576 he visited the Bangor Diocese and several Anglesey churches and those present in these churches during his visits were recorded in a register that was aptly named Grindal's Register. Per this register, on 16th July 1576, Syr William Griffith was the rector and Owen was curate. I assumed that he was appointed after the death of Richard ap Evan in 1574, although technically he could have been appointed any time between then and the visit of the archbishop.

From his family name, I do not believe that he was from an Anglesey family but was likely from one of the Byner (or Bynner) families of Montgomeryshire. By 1580 William Evans had replaced him, but I do not know exactly when he left. In 1595 he (together with others) was served a Writ of Commission to preside over depositions taken for a Star Chamber case of a dispute over the lease of the rectory of Llanfair Caereinion.

William Evans, 1580 – 1595

William was the next curate and was appointed after he had been ordained as a priest in Bangor Cathedral on 25th December 1580 by Bishop Nicholas Robinson. Interestingly, William's lay sponsor was the *Lord of Llaneugrad*, Owen of Caerfryn, which suggests that William was either local to the parish and attended Llaneugrad church, or that he had some sort of family connection to Owen. In the early 1580's, Owen and Elin's daughter, Catherine, married Thomas Bodvel, who was heir to the Caernarfonshire Bodvel estate. Given that it was traditional for brides to marry in their home parishes, the wedding perhaps took place in Llaneugrad church. If so, then either curate William Evans or the Reverend William Griffith would have been the officiating minister.

Owen of Caerfryn was a very shrewd businessman, and in addition to those he inherited from his father, he obtained much more land all over Anglesey during his lifetime. Thomas Bodvel's father, Hugh Gwyn of Bodvel, and Owen made an agreement to have their estates inherited by the son of Thomas and Catherine. He was the famous Sir John Bodvel and was born in 1583 in Bodvel Hall. Sadly, Catherine died in or shortly after childbirth, and the bard who was commissioned to write a eulogy for her mother in 1595 referred to the depth of sadness at Bodvel but made no mention of Llaneugrad. I do not know if she was brought home to be buried or if she was buried in the Bodvel family church in Llanor.

The Bodvel family were staunch Catholics and did not give up their faith after Mary I died. Hugh Gwynn Bodvel, along with other gentry, were accused of recusancy (refusal to attend the protestant church) by Elizabeth I's favourite, the Earl of Leicester, who went to any lengths in his attempt to obtain lands in North Wales. They had got on the wrong side of Leicester in 1578 over a very silly attempt by Leicester at land grabbing, and eight of them, including Hugh Gwynn Bodvel, had been imprisoned for a time at Ludlow. He cut some sort of a deal with Leicester, and by 1581 the recusancy accusations had all but stopped. That year an Act of Parliament was passed that called for heavy fines for practising Catholicism and must have been cause for anxiety in both the Bodvel household and that of Catherine's parents in Llaneugrad. Hugh Gwynn Bodvel began to toe the line so to speak and was finally able to climb the career ladder as was expected of someone of his status and heritage. I am not sure whether he ever made peace with the Earl of Leicester, but it wasn't until after Leicester's death in September 1588 that Hugh Gwynn was appointed High Sheriff of Caernarfonshire.

Other notable events that took place during William's time in our parishes include the beheading of Mary Queen of Scots in 1587, the same year that our rector William Griffith died. In 1588 the Spanish Armada was defeated off the coast of Flanders but, of much greater interest to our men of the church, was the publishing of the first Welsh translation of the whole bible by William Morgan. He was Bishop of Llandaff and St Asaph, but it was whilst he was vicar of Llanrhaeadr-ym-Mochnant in 1578 that he began his translation of the Old Testament. I would imagine that this was warmly welcomed not only by curate William Evans, but also by the Welsh speaking parishioners of Llaneugrad and Llanallgo. It would be the first time they would hear bible passages read in their own language.

During a visit to the parish by a church elder in 1587, William was still listed as curate, and the next record in the *Clergy of the Church of England Database* lists him as a curate in Amlwch church in 1595 during a similar visit.

Richard Puleston, MA, 1592 - 1596

Richard was born in 1548 in Allington, Denbighshire, the fourth son of Sir Roger Puleston of Emral, Flintshire and his wife Anne, daughter of Richard Grovesnor of Eyton. The Puleston family originally came from Normandy and settled near Newport in Shropshire. One branch of the family moved in 1283 to Emral which became their family seat for many generations. Richard attended University of Oxford obtaining his BA on 16th December 1573 and MA on 30th March 1577 and was appointed rector of Astbury in Cheshire that same year. On 16th December 1592 he was appointed rector of our churches and the entry for him in *Dictionary of Welsh Biography* by A.H. Dodd describes it as a "sinecure" rectory meaning that he had the financial benefit but did not do the work, so he would have a local curate – possibly still William Evans - but I have not been able to confirm this. Richard held the post for almost four years, and on 28th July 1596 he resigned when he was appointed rector of Kingsworthy in Hampshire.

Richard married Alice Lewis, the daughter of David Lewis of Burcot in Oxfordshire with whom he apparently had 11 children. His eldest son John became a notable Welsh barrister and judge, and eventually inherited the Emral estate in 1634 upon the death of his uncle/first cousin, Sir George Puleston (the texts vary as to what the relationship was) Richard's second son was also called Richard and he followed in his father's footsteps in the church, obtaining his Doctor of Divinity in 1627. He also held the rectories of Hope in 1616 and Kingsworthy in 1618 which seems to have led to some confusion in the records as to the tenure of his father in those rectories.

The first wife of Owen of Caefryn, Elin, died in 1595 and was buried on Palm Sunday the 13th of April in the parish church of Trefdraeth, the location of the seat of the Trefeilir family and her home parish. Owen loved her very much, and he had quite a bit of money, as he commissioned at least six eulogies for her by various bards.

Elin was not even cold in her grave when Owen married again on 27th April, two weeks to the day after his first wife was buried. He married in the parish church of Trefdraeth and to another Elin (Elin II) who was the widow of John ap Owen, heir of Trefeilir and the nephew of the first Elin and so Owen married his nephew's widow. Elin II was the daughter of Morris Gruffudd, heir to the Plas Newydd Estate, and his wife Jane, who was the daughter of John Wynn ap Hugh of Bodvel. Therefore, Owen and Elin II were also related by marriage to the Bodvel family; Elin II and Owen's son-in-law Thomas Bodvel were first cousins. Owen and Elin II continued to live in Caerfryn, and probably worshipped in St Eugrad's and I would imagine that he gave money to the church and either he or his father probably paid for the 16th century addition of the North Chapel.

David Rowlands, 1596 - 1610

David was born around 1567 so was about 29 or 30 when he was appointed rector on 1st September 1596. His half-brother was Bishop of Bangor, Henry Rowlands. They had the same father - Rowland ap Robert of the Plas Gwyn and Llwynogan, Llanedwen family and David's mother was his second wife. David attended New Hall, University of Oxford matriculating on 24th November 1581 aged 14 but there is no record of a graduation in the alumni database. There were quite a few monumental events during David's tenure, many of which had quite an impact on local life.

Early in his tenure, Elin II (wife of Owen of Caerfryn) died in August 1597. She was buried in St Gallgo's on 28th August 1597 having not yet reached her 40th birthday and I would imagine many parishioners attended her burial and I am sure that David officiated. Owen commissioned the bard Hugh Machno to write a eulogy for her, and although the bards were paid to say very nice things, this eulogy is exceptionally complimentary and paints a vivid picture of a very kind, compassionate and noble lady. It appears the parishes must have undergone some sort of adverse happening - perhaps a bad harvest or a maybe one of the plagues of disease that were prevalent in those times, because he says that there were many in the parish in need of charity, and that Elin was giving to those in need, was open to any request and did not turn anyone down. He further says that the parish was going to suffer greatly after her death. Later in the eulogy, there is a piece about her being good in her day, good to the end and good after her death and that there was a "rhagorfraint" or large inheritance/legacy to Caerfryn, so she perhaps left provisions for the parish in a Last Will and Testament, although I have not yet been able to find one. There are also several references to her death being a shock, so it sounds like it was sudden and unexpected, and I am thinking that she might have died in childbirth, or perhaps from one of the lethal diseases of the time.

The next few years were relatively quiet on a local and country level, but the death of Elizabeth I on 24th March 1603 must have caused a new round of anxiety for David and his parishioners. She had reigned for over 44 years, and many considered them to be the "golden years". With the country stable, people had come to know what to expect. The new King was the son of Mary Queen of Scots, and he became James VI of Scotland and I of England. This was a big change as the two sovereign states of England and Scotland were united under a single monarch, and it must have generated some anxiety while the people waited to see what this might mean for them.

In January 1604, a meeting was held at Hampton Court Palace between the King, Puritan leaders and nine Anglican bishops which resulted in the King James Bible, a version in English vernacular which came to be known as the authorized version, as it was the only one to be used and read in churches. I wondered what then happened in our Welsh churches with the parishioners only speaking Welsh, but I note with relief from the National Library of Wales website that the Welsh bible continued to be used in Welsh churches.

James was not as harsh as his predecessor in his treatment of Catholics, but something happened on 4/5th November 1605 that undermined his trust in them and led to two Acts of Parliament. The story of Guy Fawkes and what became known as the Gunpowder Plot is quite famous, so I won't go into detail. Essentially, a group of catholic dissidents were going to blow up the King and Houses of Parliament on the eve of the opening of the second session of James' first English parliament. One of them, Guy Fawkes, was caught guarding a pile of wood and 36 barrels of gunpowder. Fawkes and his associates were arrested, and he was executed on 31st January 1605.

Both Acts that were passed in 1606 affected both the church and parishioners. The Popish Recusants Act of 1605 came quickly after the gunpowder plot and barred Roman Catholics from the legal and medical professions, prevented them from being a guardian or trustee and allowed magistrates to search their houses for arms. It also required a new oath of allegiance, and the recusant was to be fined £60, or to lose two-thirds of his land, if he did not receive the sacrament of the Lord's Supper at least once a year in his Church of England parish church. The second Act was a new one to me - having grown up with "bonfire night" – a community or family affair with a huge bonfire, fireworks, hotpot, and my mother's best-in-the-world treacle toffee, I had no idea that it originated from an Act of Parliament!

There was a sense of national thankfulness and relief that James and his family had survived, and the "Observance of 5th November" Act (which became commonly known as the "Thanksgiving Act") was proposed and passed, as James' saving was thought to be through divine intervention. It was required that all "*Ministers in every Cathedral and Parish Church, or other usual Place for Common Prayer ... shall always upon the fifth Day of November say Morning Prayer and give unto Almighty God Thanks for this most happy Deliverance*". During the service the minister had to "*publicly, distinctly and plainly*" read out the text of the act and it required all persons to "*diligently and faithfully resort to the Parish Church or Chapel accustomed*" on 5th November and "*to abide orderly and soberly during the Time of said Prayers, Preaching or other Services of God.*" Apparently, A new form of service was even added to the Church of England's Book of Common Prayer, for use on that date. David, along with every other minister, had to give warning to his parishioners publicly in the church at morning prayer on the Sunday beforehand. There were no prescribed penalties for not adhering to the Act, and so I do not know what happened in our parishes, I would imagine that it was especially difficult to hold the service when 5th November fell on a workday. There are a few instances of celebrations with fires and gunpowder in some of England's towns that have been documented from as early as 1607, but it is not known how long it took for these to take hold across the whole country, and I can't imagine Anglesey being at the leading edge, but who knows. Interestingly, the Act was not repealed until much later in 1859.

On 12th April 1606, a new flag for the union between England and Scotland was specified in a royal decree. The flags of England and Scotland were joined together forming the flag of England and Scotland which was to be flown on ships.

Owen of Caerfryn married for a third time, but I don't believe that this would have been in one of our churches as his third wife, Jane, was from Bangor. She was the daughter of Sir

William Williams, Baronet, of Vaynol, and his wife Ellen, the daughter of William Williams of Cochwillan. They had a daughter, Elin, perhaps born in Caerfryn and christened in St Eugrad's. By the time Owen wrote his Last Will and Testament on 27th November 1607, the family had moved out of Caerfryn and were living in Treithon in Aberffraw. Owen died in 1608 but his grandson, John Bodvel, had already inherited lands and the Caerfryn house from his grandfather when turned 21 in about 1604. John Bodvel first married Mary, the daughter of Sir Harry Bagnall of Plas Newydd, but she died on 27th January 1605. He became a suitor for Elizabeth, the formidable daughter of the equally formidable Sir John Wynn of Gwydir, Llanrwst. Sir John's servant, Humphrey Lloyd, arranged a visit with her via John's future father-in-law. Sir John Wynn was a very important and influential man of his time, and his daughter, whom he called Bess, was a very demanding woman who complained about anything and everything, even the most trivial things (according to her father). Despite this, he doted on Bess, and she was his favourite. John Bodvel must have been on his best behaviour because she found him to be an acceptable husband and they were married in the late Summer of 1608 at Gwydir. David's half-brother Henry Rowlands, Bishop of Bangor was at Gwydir for the occasion and so I would imagine that he was the one who conducted the marriage ceremony. Given his position, I wonder if our Reverend David was also there.

David died in 1610 aged only about 40 years old and I was not able to find where he is buried.

Hugh Griffith, LL.D., 1610 - 1617

Hugh was appointed after the death of David Rowlands and, according to J.E. Griffiths, he was the son of Thomas ap Hugh ap Llewelyn of Ty Marian Heilin, Llanddyfnan and his wife Anne daughter of Owen ap Gruffydd ap Howel ap Tudur of the Marian Deilog family of Llanddyfnan. He is noted in the *JEG Pedigrees* as Sir Hugh Griffith, so had a degree. I was unable to find how he came to use the surname Griffith; perhaps it was after his grandfather on his mother's side of the family. There is no record of a Hugh Griffith at either of the two universities of the day, but there is a record of a Hugh Thomas from Anglesey who attended St Edmund Hall of University of Oxford and obtained a degree in 1603 and a master's degree in 1606, which is in the right timeframe, and it could be that he was using his patronymic surname at the time of his degree, adopting Griffith later in life.

Hugh became rector of Llansadwrn from 19th August 1609 until 28th May 1611, and again from 5th November 1617 until 6th January 1635. He was appointed rector of our churches on 4th December 1610 and by this time, John Bodvel and wife Bess were living in Caerfryn. John had built the Dovecote in the field near the church and, perhaps also by then, had started building a new house next to it. When Hugh arrived in the parish, John's father-in-law, Sir John Wynn of Gwydir was trying to get John on the career ladder and the appointment of Sheriff of Anglesey. In those days you needed to be well-connected, and Sir John Wynn had friends and family in high places. One of his cousins, Robert Lewys of Penmachno, and a lawyer at Gray's Inn, handled his personal and administrative legal affairs. Another cousin, John Panton from Henllan, was Secretary to the Lord Chancellor of England. Sir John had them work together to get John Bodvel appointed Sheriff of Anglesey. On 8th November 1610, Robert Lewys wrote to Sir John to let him know that the Lord Chancellor was told by a man called Thomas Edwards not to appoint Bodvel as Sheriff as he was *"a young man and no housekeeper"*. John Panton intervened, pointing out that Bodvel was indeed a householder, and based on this, together with an assurance that Panton had Sir John's letters confirming the fact, he was elected Sheriff of Anglesey for 1611.

That same year, the King James Bible was finally published, and John and Bess became parents, their daughter Mary was born after a difficult pregnancy. I do not know if she was christened in St Eugrad's or in Llanor, the church local to Bodvel Hall. Sir John Wynn continued to work on his son-in-law's career, and he turned his attention to getting him knighted. The King charged a lot of money for knighthoods and evidently was turning down offers as high as £400 which Sir John did not want to pay. He tasked his son Richard with finding a cheaper way to get John knighted, which he did, and John was knighted in 1614 by the Lord Deputy for somewhere between £100 and £120.

The long heatwave in the Summer of 1613 destroyed both grass and crops and was disastrous for tenants who found themselves then unable to pay their full rent, and for the landowners who depended on that rent. Crops had to be bought from other counties to avoid starvation, and both Caernarfonshire and Anglesey were badly affected. John Bodvel was affected and perhaps this is the reason that his new house next to the Dovecote was never completed. The harsh Summer was followed by a very wet Winter with flooding in much of Caernarfonshire, and John and a pregnant Bess could not return to Caerfryn until after the flooding subsided. Their daughter was born in Caerfryn on 26th August 1614 with Bess's mother in attendance, and they named her Catherine after John's mother, and I would imagine that she was christened in St Eugrad's. After his father died, John and Bess made Bodvel Hall their home and for the first time in a while, Llaneugrad did not have a resident landlord.

Reverend Hugh was collated canon secundus and Chancellor of the Diocese of Bangor on 10th March 1616 and he left our churches the following year, exchanging benefices with Robert Griffith, rector of Llansadwrn on 5th November 1617. He was appointed rector of Llanddyfnan on 8th April 1822, a position he held through 1636 until he resigned. In 1625 he was Chancellor of the Diocese, acting alone for four years and after that jointly with William Griffith, LL.D.

Robert Griffith, MA, 1617 - 1631

There are no references to his origins in the sources listing his tenure. He had a master's degree obtained from one of the two English universities at the time, Cambridge, or Oxford. A search of the alumni databases of both universities yielded two possibilities for Oxford, one from Caernarfonshire who attended Brasenose College and obtained his masters on 17th

June 1605 and the other of unknown origins who attended Christ Church and obtained his masters on 14th June 1611. He shall therefore remain a man of mystery.

His first post on Anglesey was rector of Llansadwrn which he took up on 28th May 1611 and stayed there until 5th November 1617, when he swapped benefices with Sir Hugh Griffith and became rector of our churches. There is no record of when he left or whether he died in post, and it is possible that he was rector until Michael Roberts took over in 1631.

The first major event of Robert's tenure happened at the beginning of 1617/8 with the birth of a son to Sir John and Bess Bodvel. He was named John after his father, and he was destined to become the next *Lord of Llaneugrad* and to make Caerfryn his home. The colonization of America had begun to accelerate, and in 1619 the first African slaves were brought to an English colony in Virginia. On 16th September 1620 the Mayflower ship left Plymouth with 102 passengers, known as the Pilgrims, and it would arrive several weeks later at what would become known as Plymouth in Massachusetts. The Winter of 1620/1 in Britain was a particularly severe one, the Thames froze over and there was 13 days of continuous snowfall in Scotland where only 35 out of 20,000 sheep survived on Eskdale Moor. Although I could not find documentation, Anglesey must also have been affected, and I wonder if any of our parishioner's animals also perished. The people would perhaps fare better than animals as the area was then densely wooded, so there would be plenty of fuel for fires, assuming Sir John Bodvel and other landowners in Llanallgo allowed them to cut down trees which were very valuable assets back then.

In 1623 there was a great famine and a new sickness with a high mortality rate and Wales especially was affected. By 23rd June, a third of London was down with the plague. It was only a matter of time before it would spread north, and it was desperate times survival-wise and financially, making it more challenging for the Reverend Robert and the church to take care of the poor and sick. *The Calendar of Wynn Papers* (Wynn's of Gwydir) are a rich source of information for that period. Two of Sir John Wynn's sons complained to each other that their father was *"not inclined to afford them the same means as other gentlemen of quality"* but they acknowledged that trade was decreased, money was scarce, rents had fallen, the price of land was half of what it was, and their father could not receive the third part of his rents. Even the great Sir John Wynn was feeling the pinch and had to borrow money. The situation was the same for all landowners and so no doubt Sir John Bodvel and Bess were also affected, although they would not starve to death like many parishioners. In a letter to Sir John Wynn dated 23rd August 1623, John Pigott promised that he would send venison to Bodvel when thoroughly cooled, a side of venison and hoop of wheat to Sir John Wynn at his Gloddaeth home, and a buck to the Bishop of Bangor (Lewes Bayly). He says that he *"cannot come by the lemons mentioned in the note, because they are under lock and key in my lady's closet"* and adds that *"the beer shall be brewed next week."* How the other half lived...

The King died on 27th March 1625 and his son Charles, the Prince of Wales, became King Charles I. After a reasonably stable period, chaos, trouble, and a great deal of strife were about to be unleashed by a King who was a bit too big for his breeches, and who would end up plunging the country into Civil Wars. He got off on the wrong foot by marrying the Roman Catholic French princess Henrietta Maria, which worried many members of the Commons who feared that Charles would lift restrictions on Catholic recusants and undermine the official establishment of the reformed Church of England. Although Charles told Parliament that he would not relax restrictions, he had secretly signed a treaty with his brother-in-law, Louis XIII of France, promising to do exactly that! The clergymen of the country must have been holding their collective breaths wondering what might happen next. Charles believed in the divine right of kings and was not about to be overruled by Parliament. He began to quarrel with them over all sorts of things including money, wars, and religion.

Meanwhile in Wales, even though he was still a relatively young man of 48, Sir John Bodvel's health was failing him, and he drew up his Last Will and Testament on 18th September 1631 and died a few months later. His son John was only 14 and would not be able to inherit his father's estate until he turned 21, so in the meantime he became a ward of the King. Sir John left monies for the repair of various churches: 10 shillings each to Bangor Cathedral and Llanor church (the Bodvel local church) and 20 shillings each to St Eugrad's and St Gallgo's. It was also in this timeframe that the Reverend Robert either died or left our parishes and thus he would not be the one to spend the legacies from Sir John.

Michael Roberts, MA, 1631 - Unknown

An article in the *Journal of the Welsh Bibliographical Society* supplies much of Michael's story. The Welsh Bible for the people did not become available until 1630 and the corrector for the press was none other than our next rector, Michael Roberts. The copy of the Bible he was given at the time was stolen and he had to call upon the Bishop of Bangor to help retrieve it. In a letter dated 10th December 1672 that he wrote to Bishop Robert Morgan, he says *"My Welsh Bible given me in 1630, when I was corrector for that impression, was stole out of my house in Llwydiarth Esgob. I strongly conceive the crime of sacrilege belongs to the cognizance and censure of the Ecclesiastical Court. Your Lordship will do me a special kindness if I may recover my Bible. Richard Jones the one-eyed of Pentraeth, commonly called 'Dick y gof' did discover my said Bible with Humphrey Lewis, at his house in Tregarnedd. He is dead, yet I hope my Bible is not buried with him. His widow is married to William Owen Humphrey, within the rectory of Heneglwys-Eglwys, in Anglesey. I have civilly sent sundry messages for my book. Her last answer, by John Edmund, was very stout and daring. She bade me take my course. Good my Lord, I entreat your help and good favour for the recovery of my Bible."* I was not able to find out if he was successful in retrieving his Bible.

Little is known of his origins or early life, but from his Last Will and Testament dated 4th April 1678 we know that his father was born in Llandrygarn, Michael was born and christened in Llanedwen, and he left monies to the poor of both those parishes. According to the *JEG Pedigrees* his father was Evan ap Robert and his sister Elin married three times, her second husband being Richard Bolton of Beaumaris. Richard and Elin had two daughters,

Joannet and Mary and Michael left his lands at Llwydiarth Esgob and his half-share in lands at Pen Yr Orsedd in Anglesey to Mary who was the youngest daughter. From the parish burial records for Beaumaris, it is possible that she was the Mary Bolton who died shortly after Michael and was buried in July 1678, but I was unable to confirm that this is her. There is no record of what happened to the bequeathed lands between this time and the time of the Reverend Francis Prichard who later owned Llwydiarth Esgob.

Michael attended Trinity College Dublin, obtaining his BA in 1620 and MA in 1623. He left the following year for the University of Cambridge, where he became a student at Caius College, before moving to the University of Oxford on 13th July 1624. He became a Fellow of Jesus College in 1625 and gained his Bachelor of Divinity on 8th July 1630. He was ordained a priest in Oxford on 19th September 1629. The Bishop of Bangor, Lewis Bayly died on 26th October 1631 and with his successor was not yet named, it was the King who presented him to the benefice of Llaneugrad and Llanallgo on 24th November 1631, to add to the benefice of Llanbadrig that he had been appointed to in 1628. The benefices provided him with income, and he continued to live in Oxford, engaging a local curate to carry out the pastoral duties. He did not take his DD Statutes within the timeframe prescribed by the College, so in 1637 he was removed from his Fellowship. In 1639 the King also presented him to the benefice of Llangynwyd in Glamorganshire as vicar. In a letter, he did say that he had lived on Anglesey with his mother for a period in later life until 1648, and I wonder if he ever came to the churches to conduct services.

When Civil War broke out in 1642, both Michael and the *Lord of Llaneugrad*, Colonel John Bodvel, were on the side of the Royalists. John was serving in parliament at the time, and the King gave him arms to defend his Anglesey home consisting of 20 headpieces, 20 belts, 20 swords 50 match, with saddles, coats, carbines, and other accoutrements. He left London to take up residence in Caerfryn and it is therefore likely that both Michael and John were on Anglesey at the same time. Either at the hands of John, or more likely his forefathers, over 1400 acres of the estate in Llaneugrad then known as Llaneugrad Parke was surrounded by a 5 feet high stone wall. The entrance to the Parke was just down Lôn Las from Bangor Lodge on the right-hand side as you head towards Brynteg (obviously these are modern day directions.) There was a Gatehouse called Greglas, and the access to the church and Caerfryn would have been across the fields and past the Dovecote that had been built by Sir John Bodvel at the beginning of the 1600s. Colonel John's wife, Ann, had grown up in wealthy circumstances in an English city and was used to city luxury, and so he needed to renovate his ancestral home to make it appropriately comfortable for her and their daughters as he intended to bring them to Caerfryn to keep them safe during the war. Ann was devoutly religious and was used to worshipping in grand city churches, and he also renovated St Eugrad's for her. A carved wooden panel, which once adorned the pulpit, survives today to commemorate this renovation, and is described in the chapter covering the plaques inside the churches.

In 1648 Michael was sent for to become Principal of Jesus College, Oxford. The second Civil War had broken out that same year, and the following year, Charles I was tried for treason and sentenced to death. On a very chilly 30th January 1649, he donned two shirts so that he wouldn't shiver with cold and have that mistaken for fear, and at 2 pm he placed his head on the block and a single, clean stroke of the axe removed his head. His son, Charles Prince of Wales, was declared King in Scotland (where he would rule only until 1651), but he would not take over the throne of England, Scotland, and Ireland until the restoration in 1660.

Michael's time in Oxford was by all accounts a difficult one, initially he was neither trusted by the Royalists nor the Puritans, and then he was accused of fraternizing with the enemy and other offences, including delinquency, but was later acquitted. The accounts of his tenure as Principal are not to his favour, and his story would fill a book all on its own but is beyond the scope of this one. He was "ejected from his position" as Principal of Jesus College in 1657 by Cromwell (as he told the Bishop of Chester in 1671 on his way back from a visit to Anglesey) and was not able after that to earn himself a position despite his considerable efforts.

Along with losing the money from his Fellowship, his long absences from Anglesey had also led to a loss of other income. The properties that he inherited from his father had relatives as tenants, and although initially they had paid him rent, in 1678 he wrote that for the last ten years, they had simply stopped paying him. He said that he was going to try and get the monies out of them without having to resort to legal measures which he says they know he abhors and was going to pay a visit to Beaumaris to try to obtain the rent. I was unable to find out if he succeeded.

The rest of his career is full of controversy and poverty and destitution (his own words.) In May 1679 he breathed his last and was around 79 or more when he died and was buried on the 3rd of May at St Peter's Oxford. If you are interested in his full story, it is in *Journal of the Welsh Bibliographical Society* dated 1st August 1923 written by Miss M Foljambe Hall who concludes her article with the following paragraph: "*Welsh literature owes a great debt to Dr Michael Roberts; and, even if the cloud which has overshadowed his reputation for upwards of two hundred years has not completely lifted, it has, perhaps, been shown that he scarcely deserves to be known to posterity as a place-man who was 'rich yet obscure'.*"

John Payne, 1631 – 1658

John Payne is listed as cleric from 1631 in the 1930 *Anglesey Antiquarian Society Transactions* article. He also paid the Land Taxes on the tithes in 1650. His tenure began when Michael Roberts became rector, so John was the local curate who took care of our parishes and was paid by Michael. Michael also might have hired someone to collect the tithes for him, which would make sense as this could be a very difficult task. The reason I suspect this is that the Last Will and Testament of David ap John Thomas of Llaneugrad who died in 1636 has something I have not seen before. After the usual legacies, the rest of the Will consists of a long list of tenants of both Llaneugrad and Llanallgo and the monies owed by them to him, which I suspect could be tithes, as they were far too low to be Land Taxes.

John's successor took over from him upon his death in 1658, and I could not find where John is buried.

Hugh Humphreys, MA, 1658 - 1668

I was not able to find out any information on his origins, neither the *JEG Pedigrees* nor the university alumni databases shed any light, so he shall remain a man of mystery from that point of view. His first wife was Margaret Williams, the daughter and sole heiress of John ap Thomas Wynn of Amlwch and they had six children, two sons and four daughters. Their younger son, Robert, became a physics professor and was rector of Llansadwrn from 1682 to 1684 and rector of Llanfechell from 1691 to 1710.

By the time Hugh became rector, Col. John Bodvel's marriage had broken down completely and husband and wife were living apart. Col. John had ceased to live on Anglesey, so Caerfryn was now empty and there was no local landlord. Col. John's story is a tragic one that is too long to include here and is told in the book *The Lords of Llaneugrad*.

Hugh had barely arrived in his new job when Oliver Cromwell died in September 1658, and Oliver's son Richard, who was much weaker than his father, took over. Because of his weakness, a coup was mounted, and Parliament ended up returning Charles II from exile to England, and the monarchy was restored. Money was in short supply for the new King, and when Parliament calculated that the Royal Household would need the princely sum of £1,200,000 a year, they realized that there was a shortage of about £300,000. It was decided to make up this shortfall by introducing what is known as the hearth tax, or chimney money as it was called then. Every dwelling had to pay one shilling at Michaelmas (29th September) and Lady Day (25th March) for each fireplace or stove and understandably, the king's subjects did not warmly greet this. For the very poor, it was simply not affordable and so there were some loosely written rules that allowed for exemptions. There must have been great anxiety in our parishes because they were very poor overall, and Hugh would have been their first port of call with their complaints. He was also responsible for ensuring that those who were exempt were recorded accordingly and it must have been a thankless task.

From the surviving hearth tax returns for Llaneugrad in 1662, nine dwellings were exempt from payment and two of the occupants, Jane Owen, and Morris ap Ellys, were paupers receiving relief from the parish. There were 12 dwellings that had only one hearth and two wealthier dwellings with multiple hearths. One of those was Bodgynda, occupied by John Lloyd, Gentleman and it had three hearths. The other was Caerfryn, the former home of Col. John Bodvel, who had used it as collateral with the 1244-acre Llaneugrad Parke parcel to raise money in 1654 using a special sort of leasing arrangement. The lessor was Joseph Hearne, a London lawyer, and although Joseph received the monies from the profits of the lands, I doubt that he ever set foot on Anglesey or ever lived in Caerfryn. I would imagine that a housekeeper or skeleton staff were retained to keep the house in good order, and this may be why, in 1662, it was recorded as having only one hearth, perhaps the only one that was in use. This did not last because, in 1664, the Crown hired professional tax collectors to an effort to improve the tax collection process, Caerfryn was then recorded as having six hearths - more in keeping with the description of the restored Caerfryn in the cywydd written in around 1645 by Watcyn Clywedog for John Bodvel and his wife (ref the book *The Lords of Llaneugrad*).

Col. John died in London on 28th March 1663, when he was only 46 years old. Bodvel owned land in both parishes, and although the Llaneugrad Parke lands were leased out, the Bodvel family had kept the freehold and they eventually passed to his grandson Charles Bodvel Roberts, daughter Sarah's son. In the meantime, though, these lands continued in the "daily" hands of the absentee London lawyer who, to all intents and purposes, was the *Lord of Llaneugrad*. In fact, Col. John was to be the last Lord to live in the parish for around another 200 years or so until William Williams came to live here in around 1870.

In May 1668 Hugh left our parishes and became rector of Trefdraeth, where he spent the rest of his life. His wife Margaret died shortly afterwards and was buried in Trefdraeth on 3rd November 1670. Hugh's second wife was Jane Hughes of the Porthllongdy, Llanbedrgoch family, and they had two daughters, Martha, and Mary. Martha married Ambrose Lewis, rector of Llanrhyddlad and she was to be a very lucky beneficiary of her rich uncle's Last Will and Testament! Jane was the daughter of Thomas and Jane Hughes, and her eldest brother was none other than Owen Hughes, better known as "Yr Arian Mawr" or "Big Money". I will now digress a little and tell Yr Arian's story (there is a good reason for inserting this here, I promise). Owen had a fire in his belly and ambitions way beyond his humble beginnings, and he began to build wealth starting with a lease of land from the Bulkeleys in Beaumaris. In a strategic move, he gained a monopoly over the most important of the Menai Strait's ferries at the time, later securing a lease for 30 years from the Crown that would not be contested until he had made quite a fortune for himself. He then became a "rich attorney of Beaumaris" and was gradually buying up estates in Caernarfonshire and Anglesey, including the Madryn estate and the Llysdulas estate on Anglesey. In 1661 he married Margaret, the daughter of Ifan Wynn of Penllech, but they did not have any children, and Margaret died before him.

He divided his land and properties into two parts. The Anglesey lands in Talybolion, Twrcelyn and Llifon were left to William Lewis, the eldest son of niece Martha and her husband Ambrose, and William took up residence at Llysdulas. The rest of the Anglesey estates in Tindaethwy, Menai and Malltraeth, together with the Beaumaris properties and the Caernarfonshire estates, were left to Peter Bodvel, the eldest son of his niece Ann by her husband Lloyd Bodvel. His joint Executrixes were his nieces Ann Bodvel and Martha Lewis who also received all his personal estate, goods, chattels etc to share between them.

In his Last Will and Testament Yr Arian described his estate as *"not very great but far beyond my deserts"* Talk about the understatement of the year! In fact, his accumulated wealth and estates jump-started a new dynasty whose property ownership and influence were to rival, if not exceed, that of the other great Anglesey landowners. They were the copper barons of Parys Mountain, and founder, Reverend Edward Hughes, would come to own just about all of the Llaneugrad lands in 1805 thanks to him marrying the niece and heiress of

William Lewis - Mary - who was the great granddaughter of Hugh Humphreys! I wonder what Hugh would have thought about that.

Hugh wrote his Last Will and Testament in April 1680 and died later that year or at the beginning of the next year, as it was proved in Bangor on 19th January 1680/1. His wife had already passed away and his two daughters Mary and Martha were not yet of age but were made joint Executrixes under the direction of a Hugh Davies. Hugh left the following legacies: To his daughters Elin 40 shillings; Ann £4; Jane £3 and Dorothy £5. To son John five shillings and son Robert all his books. Martha and Mary were to get the rest of his goods and estate after paying his debts and funeral costs.

Owen Wood, 1668 - 1668

He was the eldest son and heir of Arnold Wood, Gentleman, of Isallt, Holyhead, and he took up the position of Rector on 8th June 1668. According to JE Griffiths, Owen is related to the Wood family of Rhosmor, and his 1930 *Anglesey Antiquarian Transactions* article refers to page 132 of the *Pedigrees*, but neither he nor his father appear on that page. There is a Hugh Wood of Isallt, so this is presumably his brother who is mentioned in Owen's Last Will and Testament. Owen married Dorothy Deane, the daughter of Sydney Jones and Richard Deane, a merchant of Beaumaris. Sydney's father, Humphrey Jones, was from the Castellmarch family and a mayor of Beaumaris, and his wife Catherine was the daughter of John Wynn of Bodewryd. The couple did not have any children, as he died not long after they were married.

He must have known that he was terminally ill because he drew up his Last Will and Testament on 31st December 1668 and Dorothy was the sole Executrix. In it he says that he is the eldest son and that his father had bestowed upon him a considerable estate in lands in the parish of Holyhead and elsewhere on Anglesey. His mother was still alive at this time and was entitled to her jointure from the estate. Owen left his mansion house of Isallt with all its appurtenances and lands (excluding his mother's jointure) to his wife Dorothy for the duration of her life. After Dorothy's death they were to go to his brother Hugh. His sister Dorothy was given 50 shillings and brother Hugh and each of his sisters received 12 pence. He also left 12 pence to the Cathedral church of Bangor and two shillings to the reparation of Llanallgo church, where he wished to be buried. This seemed curious to me given that he was only rector there for such a short time, and I wonder if he had any other association with the parish, or whether it was customary at the time for rectors to be buried in the churches that they were serving when they died.

After Owen died, Dorothy married the Reverend Richard Hughes of the Cymunod family of Bodedern (Page 36 *JEG Pedigrees*) who would become rector of our parishes in 1670.

Edward Wynne, MA, 1669 – 1670

According to *Dictionary of Welsh Biography,* Edward was born on 17th February 1644/5, the son of John Wynne of Bodewryd Esq. and his wife Elin who was daughter, and co-heiress of John Lewis of Chwaen Wen, which she inherited on her father's death. He was a cousin of Owen Wood's wife, Dorothy Deane; his grandfather Edward and her grandmother Catherine were siblings. Edward was educated at the University of Cambridge and graduated MA on 22nd March 1670/1. He was ordained deacon on 23rd September 1666, and he held the living of Meylltern from 22nd June 1668 for a few months before coming to our churches on 17th February 1668/9, his 24th birthday.

As previously mentioned, one of the duties of the rector was to supply certification of the persons exempted from paying the hearth tax. For the 1670 returns, a new pre-printed form was supplied especially for that purpose and both the rector and churchwardens had to certify, and two Justices of the Peace had to verify the certificate. Both certificates for this year for Llaneugrad and Llanallgo survive, with 19 names / dwellings for Llaneugrad and 15 names / dwellings for Llanallgo that were exempted from payment.

Edward was rector of our churches for only a brief time and moved to Llantrisant on 7th October 1670. Earlier that year on 1st June, Charles II and Louis XIV of France signed the secret Treaty of Dover. In return for £200,000 or so annually (and more), Charles promised to go to war with the Dutch, and in secret he further promised to relax the laws against Catholics, to gradually re-Catholicize England, and that he would himself convert to Catholicism. This didn't remain a secret for too long as Charles began to act in 1672, once again plunging the church into another period

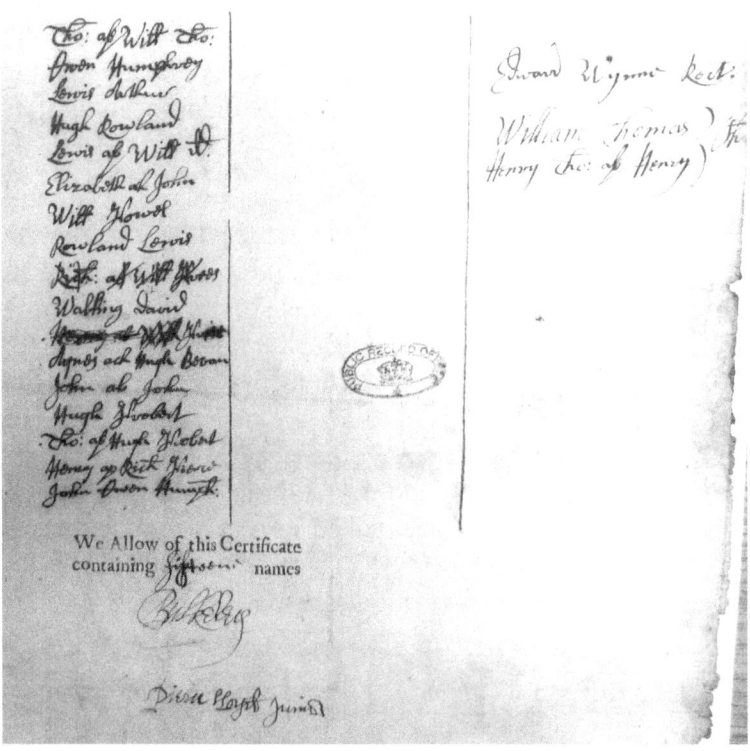

97. Llanallgo Hearth Tax Certification 1670

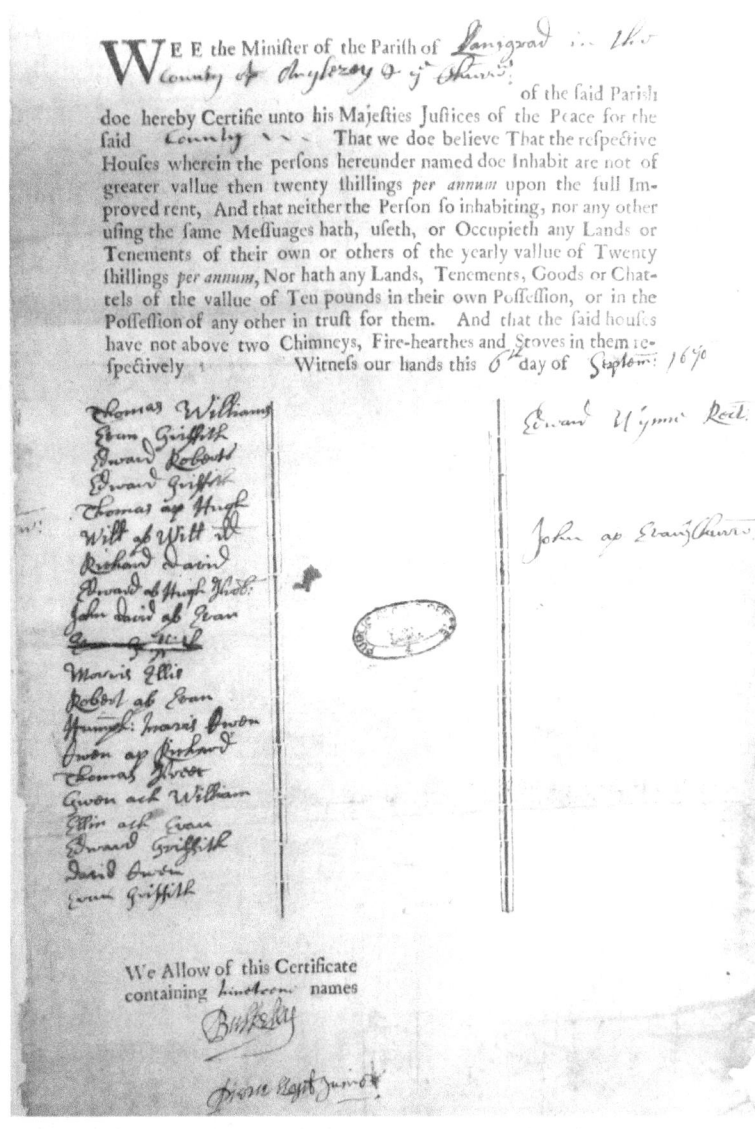

98. Llaneugrad Hearth Tax Certification 1670

of uncertainty.

Meanwhile in Llantrisant, Edward married Margaret, the eldest daughter of Robert Morgan, DD Bishop of Bangor on 3rd January 1671/2. On 4th November 1672 he was appointed to the benefice of Llanddyfnan which had been held in trust, unoccupied, by his father-in-law who also licenced him to Llantrisant. The couple already had three children, John, Ann, and Elin and were expecting their last child when Edward must have learned that he was terminally ill causing him to make his Last Will and Testament on 27th February 1680/1. His father John had died on 30th January 1669/70 and his eldest son and heir, also named John, died not long afterwards on 16th March 1670/71 so Edward had inherited the family estate and was a wealthy man. He appointed three good friends and kinsmen as Trustees: John Humphreys, Dean of Bangor, Thomas Mostyn of Bodewryd and Hugh Williams of Chwaen Issa, Gentleman. They were made overseers of the Will to ensure that the legacies were appropriately handled. He also asked John Humphreys to help his wife in the education of his eldest son and heir (John) and asked that he be brought up in the protestant religion. Provisions were made for a university education for him also with £20 a year until he was 16 and then £50 a year after that. Edward died a very young man aged only 38 on 21st March 1681.

I found one provision in his Will quite interesting, that for their unborn child. If it was to be a girl, then she would have equal shares in the profits of his estate with the other siblings per an earlier clause. If it was to be a boy then he would have only so much as the Trustees should think is enough to maintain him in school until he was fit to be a clerk bound to an

Attorney, then enough to keep him bound to an Attorney or any other convenient position as they shall see fit, and for him to have £30 once he had completed his time with the Attorney, or his apprenticeship in his calling. The baby achieved so much more than this, and perhaps credit is due to the Trustees.

The child turned out to be a boy, who was named Edward after his father, but life often doesn't work out the way that you plan it or want it to be. Edward's eldest son and heir, John, enrolled in Christ Church Oxford on 31st March 1691 aged 15 and then became a student of the Inner Temple in 1693. He married Blanche, the daughter of Pierce Lloyd of Lligwy and their only son Edward died as an infant in 1701. John himself died in 1707 and his inheritance passed to his brother Edward. Edward must have been an exceptionally bright and ambitious boy and the Trustees saw fit to enable him to have much more accomplished career than that envisioned by his father. He was enrolled in Jesus College Oxford on 18th December 1698 aged 17, obtained his BA in 1702 and MA in 1705. He was fortunate that his mother lived at Bodewryd and took care of the estate, freeing him up to further pursue his studies. He received his bachelor's and Doctorate in Canon Law on 15th March 1710/11 and in 1707 became Chancellor of Hereford, a post previously held by his uncle Bishop Humphrey Humphreys. Edward was also a very progressive farmer and was the first farmer to grow turnips on the island of Anglesey. He is also traditionally credited with being a patron of the poet Goronwy Owen in his youth and he was one of the chief men of Anglesey in the first half of the 18th century. Upon his death, the family estate passed to sister Ann who had married Robert Owen of the Penrhos Isa family of Holyhead.

Richard Hughes, 1670 - 1687

According to the *JEG Pedigrees*, Richard was from the Cymunod family of Bodedern and was the son of Richard ap Owen ap David Lloyd ap Hugh of Plas Coch, and his father and grandfather were both clergymen. His mother Ann was the daughter of William Bulkeley of Brynddu whose daily diaries survive today and can be found online at the University of Bangor Archive. Richard married Dorothy Deane, the widow of rector Owen Wood, and became rector on 5th November 1670, so Dorothy found herself once more living in Llanallgo. They had five children: two daughters, Gloria, and Sidney, and three sons who all became clergymen. Owen was Chancellor of Bangor and rector of Aberffraw and Trefdraeth and Prebendary of Penmynydd, Holland was vicar of Hemingford Grey in Huntingdonshire and Bulkeley was vicar of Bangor and of Llanddeusant with Llanbabo and Llanfairynghornwy from 1762 until his death in 1768.

The country was in quite a bit of turmoil during the 17 years that Richard spent as our rector, and a couple of the more interesting events are covered here. A scandal happened in London on 9th May 1671 – a man called Thomas Blood disguised himself as a clergyman and tried to steal the Crown Jewels from the Tower of London. He was apparently caught at once because he was too drunk to run off with his haul and was later condemned to death. However, after secret talks with the King, and to the amazement of many, he was pardoned.

Rumour has it that Charles also gave him a very handsome pension in return for him spying on the nonconformists.

On 15th March 1672 Charles began to act on his secret part of the Treaty of Dover. He issued the Royal Declaration of Indulgence, which suspended execution of Penal Laws against both Protestant nonconformists and Roman Catholics. This created all sorts of consternation in Parliament and on 8th March the following year, he was compelled by them to withdraw it, as it was too generous to Catholics. Quite what Richard and his fellow clerics thought of all of this I have no way of knowing, but I have to imagine that the events of the reign of Mary I would still be remembered, and the prospect of another enforced celibacy of the clergy must have served to worry Richard and Dorothy considerably.

On a local level, a shipwreck off Anglesey in 1675 must have created quite a stir. His Majesty's Yacht Mary was the first Royal Yacht of the Royal Navy. She was built in 1660 by the Dutch East India Company and bought by the City of Amsterdam to give to Charles II on the restoration of the monarchy, as part of the Dutch Gift. She struck The Skerries in thick fog on 25th March while en route from Dublin to Chester, and quickly broke up and sank with the loss of 35 lives; 39 managed to scramble their way to safety. There are still parts of the wreck there today, and the Mary was featured in 2018 on a TeliMôn episode of The Shipwrecks of Anglesey. Maritime archaeologist, Lowri Roberts from Moelfre, presented this episode. Her grandfather, Gwilym Hawes, was headmaster of Llanallgo school for many years, and author of the very interesting booklet titled *Journey's End* about St Gallgo's and The Royal Charter Shipwreck. The TeliMôn short program is very interesting and can be found on their Facebook page or on the following website: www.telimon.com/shipwrecks-of-anglesey-hmy-mary-llongddrylliadau-ynys-mon-hmy-mary/

On 5th February 1685, a dying King Charles II was received into the Catholic Church in a private ceremony which was arranged by his Catholic brother James, and he died the following day at noon. James acceded to the throne, and the clergymen of the country must have collectively held their breath in anticipation of what might happen next.

Richard was appointed to Llanddeusant with Llanbabo and Llanfairynghornwy on 21st October 1687, a benefice that had previously been held by his father. This benefice was worth more than twice that of Llaneugrad and Llanallgo, so it was a promotion for him. Richard and Dorothy lived in Llanfairynghornwy, and he stayed rector until his death in late 1693. Dorothy survived him and was the beneficiary of all his goods, chattels, cattle, debts, and credits and was the sole Executrix of his Last Will and Testament which was proved in Bangor on 18th January 1693/4. He was succeeded on 10th January that year by his older brother William. Interestingly, almost 150 years after his death, his great, great, great grandson would become rector of our churches.

Maurice Jones, B.D., 1687 - 1697

Maurice was rector from 21st October 1687, and he came from a wealthy Denbighshire family. He was born about 1663 to John ap Richard ap John William and Mary Lloyd of Llanychan parish. He had two brothers, Richard, and Robert, and three sisters, Elizabeth, Dorothy, and Sidney. Elizabeth was the only sibling who married, and she wed Pierce Foulkes Esq of Meriadog. Maurice attended the University of Oxford, matriculating on 18th June 1680 aged 17, he obtained his BA in 1684, MA on 5th February 1686/7 and a BD in 1694.

Maurice came to our churches at a time when much of the Bodvel estate, which included the Llaneugrad lands and some in Llanallgo, had just come under the ownership of an English Barbados sugar plantation owner, Samuel "Sam" Hanson. I was quite surprised to find that the *Lord of Llaneugrad* was a slave owner. Sam's story is quite an extraordinary one and is told in full in the book *The Lords of Llaneugrad*. The research into this man "necessitated" me taking a field trip to Barbados to meet with the family who owns the plantation today. It was a very rewarding trip, as one of the owners is also local amateur and brilliant historian named John Knox, and he shared his wealth of knowledge of the history of the era, including of the large number of Quakers from Wales (and England) who escaped persecution and made Barbados their home.

John told me that Sam was a Quaker. He was also a bit of a pirate and had a trading business that was more illegal than not as far as the records go. As his businesses was flourishing, he fell afoul of a Governor of Barbados and ended up with his plantation being ruined and his trading ventures seriously curbed in those waters. The Bodvel estate was up for sale at this time as the owner, Charles Bodvel (grandson of Col. John,) needed the money, and he had no interest in his Welsh heritage. He had become Earl of Radnor after his paternal grandfather died and he inherited estates in Cornwall. I wondered why an English Barbados plantation owner be interested in buying lands in North Wales. After further research I believe that Sam bought the Bodvel estate to gain access to Bardsey Island, a pirate's haven that had been in the Bodvel family for a few generations, and the out-of-the-way quiet bays of Traeth Bychan and Moelfre where ships could dock in the dead of night to unload their merchandise, unseen by the import tax collectors stationed in the official ports. Sam could continue his business using well-established trade routes along the North Wales coast and he likely stepped right into the shoes of the Bodvels. He could not have found himself in a more fortunate position as his sugar plantation was struggling to recover from the Governor's tyranny, and the waning sugar trade was crippling many plantations in those years. Goodness knows what Maurice and the locals thought of all of this, although I would imagine that some of them were "in on the action" so to speak. I also think that the legend of the Parciau Goblin began at this time and its story is included in the Ghosts and Goblin chapter.

More changes were afoot on the religious front in Maurice's early tenure, as on 4th April 1687 James II issued the Declaration of Indulgence which suspended all penal laws against dissenters and Catholics. He did this hoping to have a Parliament elected that could repeal the laws, and on 4th May 1688 he required that this Declaration be read in every Anglican pulpit. Whether Maurice read this or not I do not know, but apparently very few Anglican clergymen did so. I think that our rural churches were so off the beaten track that Maurice must have felt quite safe doing what he wanted and ignoring James' remote dictate to read an English document to his Welsh parishioners. This stressful time for our clergy thankfully did not last long and on 23rd December 1688 in The Glorious Revolution, James was deposed, and he fled to France in exile. This marked the end of a century of turmoil, confirmed the primacy of Parliament over the Crown, and James II was to be the last Catholic monarch.

In 1687 Sam died in Barbados and his Last Will and Testament was proved on 13th August that year. His 22-year-old son, Samuel, who had come to England in 1680 to study in Gray's Inn and become a lawyer, inherited his estates and was the new *Lord of Llaneugrad*. In 1690, he married Jane Griffiths, spinster of Hammersmith parish in Middlesex who was the daughter of William Griffith of Cefnamlwch and great granddaughter of Jane, the daughter of Owen of Caerfryn, Parciau and the sister of Catherine, mother of Sir John Bodvel. So, the now "Lady" of Llaneugrad was the great, great granddaughter of Owen of Caerfryn. Samuel might have stayed in Bodvel Hall in 1690, as he served as Sheriff of Caernarfonshire that year and he had clearly become well enough known and respected amongst the gentry of the area to be elected to this office. The following year he served as Sheriff of Anglesey and in both posts, he was granted permission by the King to live outside those counties whilst still holding office.

James' successor was his Anglican daughter Mary and, together with her Protestant husband William III of Orange, they jointly ruled the country from February 1689, and I am sure at this point, the clergymen of the Church of England heaved another collective sigh of relief. On 24th May that year, the Act of Toleration received Royal assent and was quite a landmark as it allowed freedom of worship to nonconformists such as Baptist, Congregationalists, and Presbyterians, allowing them to have their own places of worship as well as schoolteachers, as long as they accepted certain oaths of allegiance. Although it specifically excluded Roman Catholics, it was a step forward towards freedom of worship and as such it led to a reduction in attendance at Church of England churches as people now had choice as to where they wanted to worship without fear of recrimination. The very next day, a big weight was lifted from Maurice's shoulders (and every other rector's I should imagine), as the dreaded Hearth Tax was collected for the very last time and then abolished.

In late 1692, Samuel Hanson fell ill and wrote his Last Will and Testament, he died in 1693 aged only 28 and without producing an heir. He left his household stuff and personal estate to his wife Jane, but per his father Sam's Last Will and Testament, the properties and lands went to his sister Elizabeth, together with the financial mess that he unfortunately left behind him. Samuel was a lawyer, not a businessman, and the trading business suffered in his hands. Elizabeth had married into a very old, and well-established English family from Norfolk, the Folkes of Rushbrooke, Suffolk, and her husband, Simon was unable to deal with the financial situation that he inherited – these were the days when the husband became the owner of anything his wife inherited unless expressly stated otherwise in the Last Will and Testament.

On 28th December 1694 Queen Mary II died of smallpox aged only 32 leaving poor

William to rule alone, and without leaving an heir. Her younger sister Ann (whom they had had a major row with and thrown out of Court) was now called back to Court as William's official heiress. The year 1695 was a very wet one with an exceptionally cold Winter and apparently it was so cold that the wine in the glasses froze at the Palace of Versailles. Closer to home the Thames froze over and the snow that lasted until April and arctic sea ice had extended around the entire coast of Iceland. In the midst of this Winter freeze, on the last day of that year, another property-based tax was introduced – the window tax that levied a fixed two shillings on every house and an added flat rate per window above 10 windows in a dwelling. Later records (1760) would suggest that only a small number of properties in our parishes would qualify to pay this tax, as the poor were exempted.

In addition to our benefice, Maurice held the benefice of Llanychan in 1690 and Cerrigydrudion was added in 1697 after he left our churches. In 1702 he became cursal canon of St Asaph, and he was the first of the siblings to die, passing away on 17th September 1725. Richard, his eldest brother, had inherited the family wealth from his father, but Maurice had a lot of money of his own, and left several legacies. He left £20 to buy a silver flagon for the communion table in Cerrigydrudion church to be bought by his Executor, brother Richard. He left a charity which was to be administered by the rector and churchwardens and it is quite an interesting tale. First, he left £20 with the interest to be used for relief of the poor of Llanychan or, if there were none to be found, then it was to be applied to apprenticing or schooling of poor children. There was a further £100 to be invested and the interest was to be used for either apprenticing of poor children or for the relief of poor clergyman's widows with preference given to the parish of Llanychan. Richard was also responsible for investing the £120 to generate interest for the charity.

Richard died in 1730 and in his Last Will and Testament, he directed his Trustees to lease or mortgage his dwelling house and property in Maes Maen Cymro and property called Erin Fadog and adjoining lands to raise £120 to either purchase lands, or to invest it to yield £6 annually, for the charity that Maurice had defined. Gilbert's Returns were reports from parishes on both poor law expenditure and charitable payments to the poor during the three years prior to 1786 and came about because of the Relief of the Poor Act of 1782. In 1786 the trustees chose to invest in Ponthilin farm in Llanynys that was vested in a Mr Yorke. The £6 was now a rent-charge on that property, which was owned by the Yorke family, and they paid it annually to the churchwardens.

Mr Yorke was Phillip Yorke Esq. of Erddig, famous as the author of *Royal Tribes of Wales*, and he married Diana Wynn (great granddaughter of Maurice's sister Elizabeth) who had inherited the property and was the sole heiress of Dyffryn Aled. Phillip and Diana faithfully paid the £6 annually. He died in 1804 and Diana died the following year and their eldest son, Pierce Wynne Yorke, inherited the considerable Dyffryn Aled estate, including Ponthilin. When Pierce died in 1837, his personal estate was worth almost £3,000, and so he was not short of a bob or two as the saying goes. However, for some unknown reason, according to the *1838 Commissioners Report* on Charities to the House of Commons, he decided to simply stop paying the rent-charge and the charity ended with him and when

Ponthilin was sold to Colonel Joseph Peers, the rent-charge appears to have been removed from the Title Deed. The loss must have been a great blow to the churchwardens and the poor of the parish who had come to depend on Maurice's legacy, but it was a common story with these sorts of perpetual charities. The only other charity that survived was one of 20 shillings a year left by Maurice's sister Sidney. I wonder if his mother and Maurice were turning in their graves at this act of meanness, but perhaps even in death they were able to exact their revenge. Pierce happens to be one of the famous ghosts of Dyffryn Aled that appeared in the house, and the grimmest of them all: he manifests as a corpse in a coffin. According to the book *Haunted Wales: A Guide to Welsh Ghostlore*, the ghost of a corpse is quite unusual and possibly unique. I like to think that it was Diana and Maurice simply refusing to let him rest in peace…

The church at Llanychan has a lovely marble plaque on the wall above his grave inside the church commemorating Maurice (Robert, Sidney, Dorothy, and Richard are also buried inside the church), and it details his charity that is no more. The plaque says of him: *"He was strictly regular in performing all the duties of his calling; unblemished in his life; conscientiously just in all his actions"*. Sorry to say that sI do not think that the last statement can be said of Pierce Wynne Yorke.

Francis Prichard, MA, 1697 - 1704

According to the Oxford Alumni records, Francis was born about 1667 and was the son of Richard Owen of Harlech, although I believe that he had more ties to Anglesey than Harlech. He matriculated at Jesus College Oxford on 13th March 1683/4, obtained his BA in 1687 and MA in 1690. He was a master at Beaumaris school for a while and was appointed rector of our churches on 20th May 1697.

King William III died on 8th March 1702, two weeks after he fell off his horse when it tripped over a molehill in Richmond Park and apparently, his Jacobite opponents started drinking toasts to the mole, *"the little gentleman in the velvet coat"*! Anne Stuart, the second daughter of James II, became Queen, and both her and her husband were in very poor health and thankfully, it was a stable time for Francis and the church for the next couple of years. At the local level Simon Foulkes continued to struggle with finances, sinking deeper into debt with the legacies from his father-in-law's Will that he had to pay to his sister-in-law on her marriage and birth of her children. It did not help that he was an extravagant spender, and by 1702 he had racked up £12,000 in debt and had to go in exile to Holland to avoid his debtors. Samuel Hanson junior's wife re-married and left Bodvel Hall and Simon and Elizabeth moved there with their daughter Elizabeth, and in 1703/4, Simon was appointed Sheriff of Caernarfonshire. I do not know whether they ever visited the Anglesey estates or whether he met Francis or corresponded with him.

Francis served as rector of our churches until his appointment to Llanrhuddlad on 30th June 1704, but he was only there for a few short months as he died at the end of that year aged only about 36. He knew he was terminally ill because he drew up his Last Will and

Testament on 16th November and declared *"...considering the certainty of death and the uncertainty of the hour thereof..."*. His wife Ellen was his sole Executrix, and the Will was proved on 9th January 1704/5 with an inventory of goods to the value of £99. He wished to be buried in private in Llanrhuddlad church, and he gave a shilling to Bangor Cathedral and five shillings to buy bread to be distributed to the Llanrhuddlad parish poor about a week or a fortnight after his burial.

He left a small number of legacies including 12 books to his dear brother Owen Prichard as a *"poor token of the great love and affection"* they had shown for each other. He left the rest of his books to his *"well beloved"* brother William Price, BA wishing his *"serious perusal of them and all good books to God's glory and his own advantage"*. If I have the right man, William Price, BA also attended University of Oxford, his father was William Price of Anglesey, and the younger William was rector of Llanddeusant in 1707. Given that he uses the term "brother" for both men with different surnames and fathers, I assume that Frances' mother was married twice.

Frances' legacy to widow Ellen set me off on another challenge that unearthed some interesting history. He left her and her heirs forever his property (house and lands etc) in Llandyfrydog and Coedana called Llwydiarth Esgob. Her surname was "Prichard" in the Will, but I cannot tell whether he used her married name or whether she was born a Prichard as it was common back then for women to keep their maiden name rather than adopt their husband's name. That he owned Llwydiarth Esgob leads me to believe that he must have been in the line of inheritance from rector Michael Roberts (1631 – Unknown). After many hours of searching through the *JEG Pedigrees,* many Wills, and parish records, I have not been able to draw the line of inheritance. One thing I point out here is that the *JEG Pedigrees* might lead one to assume that the Hughes family (of which Hugh Hughes, the famous Bardd Côch, was an heir) owned Llwydiarth Esgob. However, a review of the family Wills and the Land Tax records shows that they were tenants and owned other properties on the island.

By 1722 Llwydiarth Esgob was owned by a Lewis Evans and his wife Ellen, and I suspect that this Ellen was Francis' widow. However, I have not been able to find a marriage in the few surviving parish records for that time, and it is therefore impossible to say one way or another.

I wondered if there was a connection between the Reverend Francis and the Prichard family that owned Llwydiarth Esgob over 100 years after he died and decided to research the ownership and inheritance further. The next owner of record was William Thomas, Gentleman of Bodafon Uchaf, Llanfihangel TB, who paid the Land Tax on Llwydiarth Esgob from 1760 until his death in 1772. I do not know how he came to own the property. His daughter Elizabeth married Edward Morris of Llangwyfan, and they inherited Llwydiarth Esgob when William died in 1772, becoming the first owners in many years to live there. The inheritance of the property was defined expressly in William's Last Will and Testament, and after Edward and Elizabeth died, it passed to their daughter Jane and her heirs. In 1788 Jane married a Gentleman who happened to own what was the best Inn on the road from London to Holyhead, Gwyndy in Llandrygarn. He was James Knowles, the son of Charles

Knowles, Gentleman and Innkeeper and his wife Lydia and James was christened in Llangefni church on 10th May 1763. As Jane's husband, James then became the owner of Llwydiarth Esgob for the duration of his life, and he redeemed the land tax on it in 1798 after Jane's parents had both died, and so there are no further records of tenancy or ownership after that year in the land tax records. He and Jane never lived there but rented it out to a tenant and, in 1798, that tenant was a Robert Prichard and he lived there with his wife Ann and family and his mother, Elinor Jones, and their descendants lived there for many generations.

I now digress for a few paragraphs covering the story of James and Jane and Gwyndy for those who may be interested. They started out married life in Gwyndy which James had eventually inherited after his father died in 1773 when James was only 10 years old. According to the book *Secret Anglesey,* the Inn at that time had stabling for 21 horses, 15 beds and three parlours, a kitchen, bar and cellar with brewery and dairy. It was also used as a post-house with its own post-mark and, occasionally, as a courthouse. It was a very busy place that was popular with the increasing number of travellers of the day and seems to have received good reviews from those who documented their travels in print. James was a highly respected member of the community and was a Trustee of the estate of William Griffith of Hafod Y Bryn, Holyhead. Over time, he took up leases on a few properties on the island. On 1st October 1799 he leased the farms of Gwyndy and Bodychen for a period of 21 years at a rent of £150. Other properties he appears to have leased include Henblas in Llandrygarn and Rhydyspardyn in Heneglwys. He must have been quite an ambitious man, and doing well at the Inn, but at some point, he seems to have bitten off more than he could chew. However, it came about, James found himself borrowing money and was soon in debt that he was unable to clear. On 11th November 1806 one Owen Davies wrote to William Jenkins, both Methodists, that their brother William Jones (who was superintendent of the Beaumaris circuit) had bought a horse that didn't suit him, and he sold it to James for 14 guineas. James did not have the money to pay him and asked him to return for the money, but by that time he was bankrupt and poor William was said to be "*exceedingly distressed*". Whether he ever got his money or his horse back I do not know.

On 28th March 1807, The Cambrian newspaper announced an auction that would take place on 27th April 1807 of "*a Capital Inn and Other Premises*" by order of the Assigns of James Knowles, bankrupt. The properties were: Gwyndy Inn plus the farm of "*upwards of 200 acres in a high state of cultivation, for the remainder of a lease for two lives, the youngest only ten years old, and for a term of 18 years certain, at a very moderate rent. The Inn has been lately enlarged and improved at a very great expense, is capable of accommodating the late great increase in travellers, and there are but few better houses upon the public road between Holyhead and London.*" Also, all the Life hold estate and interest of James in several farms in Coedana, Llandyfrydog, Llandrygarn and Heneglwys called Coedana Farm, Llwydiarth Esgob, Henblas and Rhydyspardyn. It adds that the new and elegant household furniture of Gwyndy together with the farming stock, horses, carriages etc will be sold early in May. It must have been at this auction that Robert Prichard, then tenant of Llwydiarth Esgob, bought the property for the family. I have proved that they did not acquire it through inheritance, and so are perhaps not related to our rector Francis Prichard.

I feel compelled to finish James' story. He went on to run the Hibernian Arms in Holyhead and in 1809, the minister of Holyhead church and the churchwardens had to certify as to his good character, and Robert Prichard of Llwydiarth Esgob and Innkeeper James Fisher, Gent of Llannerch-y-medd put up a Bond of £10 each to warrant that James would keep good order at the common Inn for which he had a licence until 10th October 1810.

On 11th April 1812 a warrant was issued for his arrest for a debt of £100. He was arrested and put in Beaumaris gaol and from there, on 5th June, he gave a full account of his effects which was published in the newspapers. It wasn't until 22nd September 1812 that under the "Act of Insolvent Debtors" that he and another prisoner were released from the gaol. So, poor James spent more than five months in Beaumaris gaol. For anyone who has ever visited it, you can imagine that this had to be the most miserable time of James the Gentleman's life. It appears that they then left Holyhead and moved to Coedana. In 1811 he was owed money from spinster Mary Morris of Bangor and by 20th December 1815 it was James' wife who obtained Power of Attorney to receive these monies from Mary and so perhaps James was in jail again or had died by this time. This is where I lose track of the Knowles and the story finally ends.

With the building of the A5 by Telford in 1822, Gwyndy was no longer on the main route to Holyhead, and it sadly went to rack and ruin. However, it apparently is still a hive of activity now "inhabited" by those who lived or died there over the years. Gwyndy was the subject of an episode of TeliMôn "Yr Ochr Arall" (the Other Side) which can be found on their Facebook page or at the following website should you be interested: telimon.com/yr-ochr-arall-the-other-side-02-gwyndy/

Rowland Griffith, MA, 1704 - 1712

According to the *JEG Pedigrees*, Rowland was the son of Owen Griffith of Trefdraeth and the daughter of Thomas Wynn of Rhyd Y Groes. He was christened in Trefdraeth church on 6th December 1658, and his mother was named as Mary in the parish register. He was named after his paternal grandfather, Rowland Griffith of Plas Llangadwaladr, who was married to Ellen Meyrick, the daughter of Richard Meyrick of Bodorgan. He attended Jesus College Oxford, matriculating on 19th February 1674/5 aged 16, obtained his BA on 24th March 1678/9 and MA in 1682. He was appointed to our churches on 30th June 1704.

In the same year that Rowland came to our churches, Queen Anne implemented the Queens Bounty, a scheme to increase the income of the poorer clergy of the Church of England. It came about because the Toleration Act of 1689 caused a drop in attendance in the Church of England churches and, together with an increasing number of challenges in collecting the tithes, it led to a reduction in the income of incumbents. The intent was to buy land to attach to a living so that the incumbent would benefit from the land and the resulting increased remuneration. A lottery system was used, and to start with, those benefices with an income less than £10 a year were entered. As far as our benefice was concerned, we can see from the values given in *Mona Antiqua Restaurata*, that in the time of Elizabeth I there were seven benefices out of the 24 on Anglesey that would have qualified for the lottery, and Llaneugrad/Llanallgo had an income of £9 11 shillings. As time went on, the poorest benefices were supplemented and incomes boosted, and the minimum qualifying amount was increased, and was under £50 by 1810. I do not know the exact year when our benefice "won the lottery" so to speak, but I strongly suspect that this was when the quillets of land on the farms of Glanrafon Isaf and Tynllan in Llanallgo were acquired (see the chapter on Charity).

The Acts of Union were passed on 12th May 1707, combining England and Scotland, and creating the United Kingdom of Great Britain with a single Parliament, but there would be no local impact on our parishes as Wales had long been a part of England. At the local level, Elizabeth Folkes, (wife of the *Lord of Llaneugrad*) died in June 1708 and on 22nd January 1710, he married Jane Webb in London. Jane was oblivious to the true extent of his financial woes until after the marriage was done and dusted, and it came as a great shock to her. She then took charge and moved them to live in Bodvel Hall for several years, although their daughter Elizabeth did not go with them but was raised by her mother's sister, Silence Hanson, who had married Simon's brother Thomas. Away from the London city life, Simon had little opportunity to fritter away more money and Jane later said that *"with close and frugal living over a number of years"*, they were able to put together £6,000 to pay off some of his creditors. The Llaneugrad (and their other) lands must have been quite profitable to amass such an amount, so the weather must have been kind with some very good harvests during that time.

Rowland served in our churches for a little over eight years and was 54 when he died in late 1712. There is no burial record for him in the church of his home parish of Trefdraeth, so I think he is buried in either St Eugrad's or St Gallgo's, but the parish records and Bishop's Transcripts are missing for that year for both churches. If he made a Last Will and Testament, it has not survived.

Evan Foulkes, BA, 1710 – 1712

Evan was born around 1690, the son of Foulk of Eglwys-fach, Caernarfonshire (Oxford Alumni database) and he attended St Mary Hall, University of Oxford. He matriculated on 19th May 1702 aged 18 and obtained his BA on 19th February 1705/6 from Christ's College. His name appears as the minister in the Bishop's Transcripts for births, marriages, and deaths for the years 1710 and 1711 and so perhaps Rowland was ill, and Evan was a curate helping with the pastoral duties. I assume that he stayed at our churches until Rowland's successor took over as Evan was assigned to Trefriw, Caernarfonshire in 1713.

William Wynne, BA, 1712 - 1717

William was the son of Hugh Wynn of Clegyrog Plas, Llanbadrig and his wife Barbara.

William acquired Clegyrog from his elder brother who had originally inherited but later mortgaged his lands to him. William attended the University of Cambridge, matriculating in 1681 and graduating with a BA in 1684/5. He was appointed rector of Llanbadrig on 5th July 1691 where he remained until he was appointed to our churches on 8th November 1712.

William married Florence Wynn, daughter of Captain William Wynn of the Pengwern, Llanwnda family and Florence Griffith, daughter of Rowland Griffith of Llangadwaladr, a relative of William's predecessor. It was a second marriage for Florence who had first married Howel Lewis of Gwredog, Amlwch on 5th November 1693 but by 9th January 1699/1700 he had died, leaving her a young widow with six small children. Howel owned two properties in Llandyfrydog, Ty Mawr (next to Llwydiarth Esgob) and Tyddyn Traian, and they were placed in Trust, with the monies generated from them to be used by his mother and then Florence after his mother's death. The exact arrangement is difficult to decipher as the document is very old and illegible in places, but he did make some provision for Florence and his children.

William and Florence lived at Clegyrog, and it was there that William was taken ill in 1709, and likely believing that he would shortly die, he drew up his Last Will and Testament on 18th November. It was a simple Will, and unusually for a clergyman, he did not leave anything to a church or parish poor. Florence was executrix, and everything was left to her, her heirs, and assigns. She was to sell Clegyrog, pay off his debts and lay out the rest of the money at interest for the benefit of herself during her lifetime and then for the survivors of his children. His loving friend, Ambrose Lewis (rector of Llanrhyddlad and son-in-law of rector Hugh Humphreys who served in our churches from 1658 to 1668), was overseer, and was to give good advice to Florence. Whatever the illness was, he made a recovery and lived for another eight or so years.

Queen Anne died on 1st August 1717 and dissenters and nonconformists offered prayers of thanks for her death as they believed that they had narrowly escaped what could have been a new era of persecution. The Schism Act was about to be implemented and it required anyone who wished to manage or own a public or private school, or act as tutor, be granted a licence from a bishop, to conform to the liturgy, and to have taken the rites of the Church of England in the past year; luckily for them it was never implemented.

The big news at the local level was that Elizabeth Folkes, daughter and heiress of Simon and Elizabeth Foulkes had met and fallen in love with Sir Thomas Berney, 5th Baronet of Park Hall, Reedham in Norfolk. Elizabeth was in Bath with her ailing aunt Silence (who had gone there to restore her health,) when she met him, and Simon's brother Thomas negotiated the marriage settlement. As Simon had been unable to pay the legacies due under Sam Hanson's Will, Thomas and Silence had come into possession of two thirds of his Welsh lands, including those in Llaneugrad and Llanallgo. Thomas made sure that Sir Thomas Berney was aware of his prospective wife's financial situation, but (unusual for the time) this was actually a love match, and the marriage went ahead. Thomas managed the estates on their behalf and collected the rents from a local manager who had been installed by Simon in 1709. Sir Thomas and Elizabeth were married on 27th September 1716 in Bath church and after a honeymoon period in London at her parents rented house, they went to live in his Norfolk home, and I do not believe that they ever set foot on Anglesey.

On 17th March 1715/6, a new Bishop of Bangor was appointed who was to make the name Bangor quite famous. Benjamin Hoadly was born in Kent and was the first Englishman to serve as bishop since the Restoration, and he was the first of twelve bishops over the next 85 years who had no knowledge of Welsh and were largely non-resident (ref *Portraits of an Island.*) He was chaplain to King George I and he started the most bitterly fought ideological battle of the 18th century, which became known as the "Bangorian Controversy". It began in earnest after he preached a sermon to George I on 31st March 1717 titled "The Nature of the Kingdom of Christ" and his text was John 18:36, "My Kingdom is not of this world". This offended the sticklers for ecclesiastical authority and started a battle of pamphlets – both for and against his extreme views. We do not know what William's personal view on the matter was, but I must imagine that the whole affair stimulated much lively discussion amongst him and his Anglesey peers as each pamphlet was published. Benjamin rarely visited any of his dioceses and lived in London where he was very active in politics, and I wonder how many of any of the Anglesey clerics actually met the man.

William served our churches until he died in October 1717 and was buried in St Gallgo's on 21st October 1717. Florence must have died before him as his Will was proved on 4th February 1717/8 by William Wynne and Richard Hughes on behalf of his children: Hugh, William, R(illegible), Anne and Jane Wynne.

Hugh Jones, MA, 1717 - 1735

Hugh was born in about 1689, the only son and heir of Hugh Jones of Brynhyrddin, Pentraeth, and his wife Margaret who was the daughter of Thomas Bulkeley of Pyllaubudron. Hugh matriculated at Jesus College, University of Oxford on 11th March 1706/7 aged 17, obtained his BA on 22nd February 1710/11 and his MA in 1715. He was appointed to our churches on 17th March 1717/8. He was married twice. His first wife was Grace, the daughter of Robert Davies of Caerhun, Caernarvonshire and they had five children (Hugh, Robert, Margaret, Elizabeth, and Catherine). Grace's brother Hugh had inherited the Caerhun estate, but he died childless in 1721 and Grace inherited the estate and as was the case back then, Hugh became the owner. Hugh also inherited the Brynhyrddin estate from his father, and so ended up quite a wealthy man.

It was only about six months after Hugh's appointment, on 28th August 1718, that the *Lord of Llaneugrad*, Simon Folkes, died in his London home. His daughter, Dame Elizabeth Berney, and her husband Sir Thomas Berney inherited his estates and extensive debts and, to discharge some of the debts, they conveyed all the Anglesey and Caernarfonshire lands to Silence and Thomas Folkes on 9th and 10th December 1720 and Thomas became the new *Lord of Llaneugrad* for the next 11 years. He died in December 1731 leaving all his estates to Silence.

Hugh was appointed vicar of Caerhun and rector of Llanbedr-y-Cennin in the Autumn of

1735. Grace died in September 1743 and was buried in the church at Caerhun on the 9th. Hugh married for a second time to another Grace, the daughter of Griffith Lloyd of Cymryd and they had two children, Martha, and Rowland. Hugh died in Caerhun on 23rd January 1754 and was buried in the church on 26th January. He did not forget his ancestral parish, though, as in his Last Will and Testament he left 40 shillings to the poorest and most sickly people of the parish of Pentraeth to be distributed amongst them by the minister and warden directly after his decease. His eldest son Hugh inherited both estates and adopted the surname Davies, the Caerhun family name. He died unmarried in January 1771 and left everything to his sister Catherine. As a complete aside, but by way of making connections, Hugh's daughter Margaret married Reverend Owen Parry of Perfeddgoed, Bangor and Owen's sister was the mother of a future rector of our churches, Pierce Owen Mealy.

Robert Jones, BA, 1735 - 1739

Robert was born in about 1686, the son of John of Llanfeirian, Anglesey (this is my best guess as to the parish - it is spelled in the Oxford Alumni record as Llanvehenen). He matriculated at the University of Oxford on 29th March 1704 aged 18 and obtained his BA in 1707. According to the *JEG Pedigrees* page 103, he married Jane Lloyd, the daughter of Montague Lloyd of Hafod Y Gors and his wife Elizabeth née Michael of the Glan Y Gors family of Llanfihangel Ysceifiog. He was rector of Bodedern in 1723 and was appointed rector of our churches on 1st October 1735.

Not long after Robert took up his post, the poor widows of Llaneugrad had a windfall. Silence Folkes (wife of the previous *Lord of Llaneugrad*,) died in January 1735/6, and she left the very large sum of £100 to them and their counterparts in Llanor. It was to be paid out at £5 a year in each parish for 10 years and Love Parry and Thomas Edwards were to decide the recipients as *"the greatest objects of charity"* as well as make the payment. Love Parry was a Caernarfonshire man of the Cefn Llanfair, Llanbedrog family and would be familiar with the Llanor parish so it is possible that Thomas Edwards was an Anglesey man who would have knowledge of Llaneugrad, however, I have not been able to find out who he was. I am sure, though, that the Reverend Robert would have been crucial in the decision-making process as part of his overall responsibility for the poor of the parish.

The next *Lord of Llaneugrad* was Sir Thomas Hanmer 4th Baronet, of Betisfield, Hanmer in Flintshire. He acquired the estate upon his marriage in 1723 to Elizabeth Folkes, daughter of Thomas and Silence. It was an arranged marriage, and he was chosen for financial and status reasons. There was a large age difference, Elizabeth was 18 and Sir Thomas was a 47-year-old widower, and it later turned out the marriage was doomed from the wedding night. Elizabeth eventually took a lover - Tom Hervey (he became known as "mad" Tom Hervey) a son of the Earl of Bristol. Tom was Sir Thomas' godson, and his father and Sir Thomas were the best of friends. Shortly before her death, Silence had a heart to heart with Elizabeth and Sir Thomas and, realizing that the marriage was now a sham, she broke the entail (predefined inheritance) on the estate, enabling Elizabeth to make her own choice as to who would inherit. After Silence died, Elizabeth left her husband and went to live with Tom, and they had a son who they called Thomas.

On the religion front, the Methodist movement was, in Robert's time, in its very early stages and John Wesley had his great religious experience at a Moravian church in Aldersgate, London in 1738 shortly after arriving back from America. Three years before that on Whitsunday 1735, Howel Harris had undergone a similar experience in Talgarth Church in Breconshire and Howel would later pay yearly visits to Anglesey. In these early days, though, the churches on Anglesey were not affected.

I found an interesting snippet about Robert on page 313 in the book of Richard Fenton's *Tours in Wales*. He was apparently a South Walian (even though his father was from Anglesey) and he *"said in the hearing of old Williams of Llandegai, when he had his living given him, he was obliged to borrow a horse for the journey, as he had none of his own, to take possession of it; and riding over Penmaen, the horse lost his step and fell with him over the precipice. The horse was dashed to pieces, but he providentially escaped with little hurt. He had a horrid custom of swearing in relating this story; swore a great oath that he was obliged to pay for the horse, though he had hazarded his own neck"*. Quite which living this referred to, I cannot say. Although the *JEG Pedigrees* claim that he was rector of Bodedern in 1723, he is not in the *Mona Antiqua Restaurata* list of Anglesey clergymen.

On 24th July 1739 he became rector of Llaneilian where he stayed until August 1762 when he resigned aged about 76. I was unable to find a burial record for him.

Lewis Owen, 1739 - 1771

Lewis was born in 1700 in Merionethshire and became rector on 24th July 1739. He served our churches for 32 years making him the longest serving rector for quite some time. Previously he was a curate in Aberffraw for Owen Hughes (son of our Reverend Richard Hughes, 1670 – 1687) who was chancellor of Bangor, prebendary of Penmynydd and rector of Trefdraeth. Whist in Aberffraw he received a great compliment from William Bulkeley of Brynddu (b. 1691, d. 1760) whose daily diaries for 1734 – 1743 and 1747 – 1760 survive and are online at the University of Bangor Archives. The diaries make for a fascinating read, recording daily weather and the activities of a minor Anglesey landowner of the time. Bulkeley also wrote about the sermons preached in church and he was not impressed most of the time. However, the sermon given on 29th August 1737 struck a chord and his entry for that day reads: *"The Wind W. S. W. raining very hard long before day & a dirty mizling rain almost all day long. Went to Church about ii* [2 o'clock] *where I heard a very good Sermon preached by Lewis Owen the Curate of Aberffraw (a Meirionnydd-Shire man) on Levit. Chap.19th. vers. 12th."* To be judged "very good" by William was praise indeed so Lewis must have delivered an impressive sermon.

As he arrived in our parishes, a drama was about to unfold with the *Lord of Llaneugrad* which started with the parish (and other) lands receiving a dramatic "haircut" and resulted in an embarrassing scandal that would play out in a very public forum. Dame Elizabeth

Hanmer (née Folkes) was taken ill with some sort of progressive disease, and in her Last Will and Testament dated December 1739 she left her English estates to lover Tom Hervey and the Welsh estates were left to the use of her husband for the rest of his life, and after he died, they would pass to Tom. Elizabeth died on 24th March 1741 aged only 34.

Timber was expensive in those days and there were extensive woods and forests on the Welsh lands which made them very valuable. The first thing Sir Thomas Hanmer did after Elizabeth died was to have all the trees cut down on all the Welsh lands in Anglesey and Caernarfonshire that would be inherited by Tom, and he sold the wood. With his own vast estate, he cannot possibly have needed the money, and I can't help wondering whether it was an act of revenge against Tom for stealing his wife, as it would greatly devalue the lands that Tom would inherit. He was not called mad Tom Hervey for nothing, and Tom was not going to take this lying down. He wrote a letter to Sir Thomas and was cheeky enough to point out that he should be grateful that his wife had eloped with the son of his greatest friend! He also said that he wished Sir Thomas would have offered him right of first refusal to buy the wood and asked to buy it for the sake of the inheritance. He also claimed that he had been denied a request to pay a visit to Sir Thomas and asked for an answer to his letter. The answer came quickly in a letter dated 12th December 1741. Sir Thomas was incredulous that Tom should want to meet with him or even correspond with him. He also said that he had the right to dispose of what he owns however he pleases and was upset that Tom suggested it should be otherwise. He goes on to say that he would much rather sell his wood to others than to Tom. Tom replied but Sir Thomas returned the letter unopened precipitating an outrageous reaction from Tom. What he did next was a most despicable thing. He published a pamphlet for anyone to buy for a shilling containing these letters and another one to Sir Thomas. It is a very long letter with a lot of ranting and raving and an account of Elizabeth's words in her final hours but, unforgivably, it gave an account of Sir Thomas' and Dame Elizabeth's wedding night and the fact that the marriage was never consummated. Quite what Lewis and our parishioners made of the scandal I do not know, but the removal of the trees must have had local impact on agriculture, and it would have taken a very long time for the woods to regrow.

The Bishop of Bangor between 1747 and 1756 was and Englishman, Zachary Pearce, and in 1749 he sent out elaborate visitation questionnaires to his clergy in which they were asked about the number of Methodists, non-conformists, and Papists in their parishes. In response, some clergy gave specific numbers, a few gave names, others gave very vague responses, and some were careful to add that the Dissenters continued to attend church. Lewis's response was as follows: *"There are none that call themselves Methodists in Llanallgo, and there are but two reported cases in Llaneugrad parish who most commonly frequent the Methodist conventicles and very seldom attend the divine service of their parish church, though often admonished to do the same."* It seems that virtually all parishioners were at that time loyal to the church. By 1763 this had changed in Penrhosllugwy according to William Morris who then said that the Methodists and the Non-conformists have come together, and it is impossible to know which are which and the congregation of Penrhosllugwy church had declined almost to nothing. The two disciples were Owen Wenog (Owen Thomas Rowland who is said to have preached the first Welsh sermon in Liverpool) and the son of Twm Rolant the smith and they preached on Bodafon Mountain. It was a similar story across much of Anglesey.

Lewis played a vital role in the education of his parishioners. In 1731 a man called Griffith Jones, who was rector of Llanddowror in Carmarthenshire, and an enthusiastic member of the Society for the Promotion of Christian Knowledge (SPCK), started what became known as the Circulating Schools which aimed to teach people to read. They were so named because they would circulate around the rural parishes, mainly in the Winter months when farm work was relatively slack, and they would stay in one place for approximately three months and then move on to another location. The curriculum was in Welsh and consisted only in the study of the Bible and the catechism of the Church of England and thus they helped to create a country with a literate population who had a deeper knowledge of the Christian scriptures. They started in Carmarthenshire and soon spread throughout the rest of the country with dozens of men, women and children flocking to them.

At Lewis' invitation, Circulating Schools were held at Llaneugrad in 1751/52 with 40 scholars and in Llanallgo in 1751/52 and 1752/53 with 70 scholars. Lewis created quite an atmosphere of expectation by mentioning the supply of Bibles which were on their way from the SPCK in London. The supply to Anglesey was slow and William Morris (one of the famous Morris brothers or Morrisiaid Môn) wrote a letter to his brother Richard to speed up their delivery. When they finally arrived in January 1755, Lewis received the largest share of the 50 Bibles and 56 New Testaments.

Griffith wrote several accounts of the state of these Circulating Schools, and he included some of the testimonials relating to the master and scholars that he had received from the parish rectors and curates. The publication covering the period Michaelmas 1751 to Michaelmas 1752 included a testimonial written by Lewis for Llanallgo school dated 20th June. The school had 46 attendees. It reads: *"This is to certify that O.O.,* [only the initials were given] *Master of the Welsh charity school in the parish of Llanallgo, did behave himself soberly, and perform his duty faithfully and honestly, during the last quarter, as well as before, by following the rules prescribed; and upon examination I found his scholars very much improved, having made a considerable proficiency in reading the Welsh language, in singing psalms; and diligently instructed in the Welsh church catechism, and other short questions in the principles of religion. I heartily join with my parishioners in sending our grateful acknowledgement, and sincere thanks to the pious and generous benefactors of this most laudable charity, bestowed upon our poor ignorant fellow-creatures; praying for their success in this world, and their abundant reward in that which is to come."* Lewis also wrote another certificate which he concluded with: *"The children's parents are highly pleased and satisfied with the conduct of the said schoolmaster, and join with me in sincere and hearty thanks to, and prayers for the good benefactors, and pious promoters of this most necessary and laudable charity."*

Lewis was a great friend of the Morris brothers and he no doubt also knew the great poets, Goronwy Owen and Hugh Hughes (Bardd Côch of Llwydiarth Esgob in Llandyfrydog). In

1763 a book was published by The Honourable Society of Cymmrodorion which was an anthology of contemporary poetry by Goronwy, Hugh and Lewis Morris (eldest of the Morris brothers) and others. Titled *Diddanwch Teuluaidd,* it was a landmark in the literature and was one of the very few early publications by the society and Lewis was one of the subscribers. That same year, Morris Prichard, father of the Morris brothers, died and was buried on 28th November in Llanfihangel Tre'r Beirdd churchyard. The Reverend Nicholas Owen of the Llangefni Pencraig family was rector and likely officiated and he too had subscribed to the above book. For those who are interested in reading it, there is a copy free to view online on the National Library of Wales website.

William Morris wrote not only of Lewis' persistence in getting Bibles for his scholars, but also of his skill as a psalm singer and skill and good company as a pennillion singer as well as his participation in "nosweithiau llawen". It was also William who proposed Lewis as a Corresponding Member of the Cymmrodorion Society. William Morris died in late December 1763 and his brother Lewis, who had taught Goronwy Owen much of his poetic craft, died on 11th April 1765 and was buried far from his native Anglesey in Llanbadarn-fawr near Aberystwyth. Goronwy Owen was living in Virginia USA when he died in July 1769 aged only 46 and was buried on his tobacco and cotton plantation. The memorial tablets for him in the parish church of Northolt, where he as curate, and the College of William and Mary in the USA, where he was Master of the Grammar school, both bear his quote: "Dyn didol dinod ydwyf, Ac i dir Môn estron wyf". Roughly translated, it reads: I am a man of no particular note who is alone, and I am exiled from the land of Anglesey. A monument erected for him in Lawrenceville bears the following inscription in relation to Anglesey "I loved my land. My dearly beloved land".

Lewis had a couple of brushes with the law; in one he was the prosecutor and in the other he was the defendant. The National Library of Wales Crime and Punishment database records a case at the Court of Great Sessions in Wales Anglesey Circuit in 1758 when Lewis took eight men to court for *"Forcible ejectment of prosecutor and Richard Prichard, Llanbedrgoch, Gentleman."* Richard was Lewis' son-in-law; the incident was at Frigan and the men in question were:

Hugh Davies, cordwainer of Llaneugrad (of Cadwgan)
Owen Edward, yeoman of Llaniestyn
Robert Griffith, labourer of Llanfihangel TB
William Griffith, labourer of Llanallgo
Hugh Jones, labourer of Llaneugrad
Hugh Jones (alias Hugh John Parry,) freehold farmer of Llanfihangel TB
Thomas Morris, labourer of Llanallgo
Owen Owens, labourer of Llaneugrad.

Lewis and Richard were business partners, and jointly had a quarter share in one messuage, five fields of pasture of about 50 acres and the appurtenances thereof known as Frigan (this was only a part of the Frigan land,) and they were granted a lease or rental agreement for one whole year. It is not clear how much of the lease was left at the time of the event as the term remaining is obscured with string. On 13th November 1758 the above-named men, together with other *"malefactors and disturbers of the peace"* whose names were not known to the jury, entered the property *"with force and arms and with strong hand unlawfully did enter and unlawfully expel and put out"* Lewis and Richard from that day, and did *"unlawfully and injuriously did keep out and still keep out to the great damage of"* Lewis and Richard. Although the men all pleaded not guilty, the jury found them *"guilty subject to the opinion of the court"*. No reason was given for the ejection or what happened after the verdict. There are other papers in the case file in NLW that may shed light on this, but I have not reviewed those.

A couple of years later in 1760, Lewis was on the defence when labourer Lewis John Oliver of Llanallgo brought a charge against him on 10th April for attempted rape of his wife Elizabeth. The initial indictment was that on 10th April, Lewis with *"force and arms"* did *"beat, wound and ill-treat"* Elizabeth *"so that her life was greatly despaired of"* and *"with an intent against her will feloniously to ravish and carnally know and other wrongs to the said Elizabeth then and there, did to the great damage of the said Elizabeth"*. This initial indictment was crossed out and re-written by the *"Jurors upon their oath"* and the piece about the intent to rape was omitted so ended up just a case of assault. In any case, the jury found that there was insufficient evidence, and the case was dismissed as "No True Bill". Lewis was also the curate of Penrhosllugwy so he must have known the family well.

One of Reverend Lewis' older brothers, Hugh, was a cabinet maker by trade and he must have moved to Llanallgo at some point because when he died in 1762, he was buried in St Gallgo's and perhaps inside the church as the Bishop's Transcripts entry states that he was *"buried in the church of Llanallgo"* and none of the other entries specify those words.

On 2nd March 1768, a major discovery happened just a few miles from Llaneugrad and Llanallgo that would forever change the tiny parish of Amlwch, and eventually result in the Reverend Edward Hughes becoming *Lord of Llaneugrad*. On that day, a miner by the name of Rowland Pugh stumbled across what would become known as "the great lode" and, as a result, serious copper mining began on Parys Mountain. Rowland was given a bottle of whisky and a rent-free cottage for the rest of his life as a reward – no small gift in those days. Reverend Edward Hughes had married into the Llysdulas family and, through that marriage, now had half of Parys Mountain. He was about to become a very rich man indeed and would end up owning around 17,000 acres of land on Anglesey and about 85,000 acres in North Wales.

Lewis' daughter Margaret and husband, Richard Prichard, lived at Plas Thelwell, Llanbedrgoch for a time and Richard paid the Land Tax payments on that property as well as on Bengul and Tyddyn Y Pric from 1756 through 1764. Lewis had paid the Land Tax on these three properties in 1755, so I believe that their partnership extended beyond the plot at Frigan. Richard and Margaret had four children who were christened in Llanbedrgoch, Lewis in 1756, twins Griffith and Edward in 1758 and Richard in 1760. Griffith, Richard, and Edward all died young and are buried in Llanbedrgoch. By 1764 Richard and Margaret had moved to Beaumaris where he became a Tidesman (a customhouse officer who goes on board a merchant ship to secure payment of the duties) and they had two more boys there, William in 1764 and Henry in 1769. Richard died in 1773 and his Last Will and Testament was proved on 28th July that year. He owned Orsedd Ucha in Llanrhuddlad which Margaret was to have for the duration of her life, and after her death it was to go to his son Lewis and his heirs.

Lewis died on 28th May 1771 aged 71 years old. His Last Will and Testament is badly damaged with bits missing, but it is possible to see that he left £2, his turn-up bedstead with green curtains, one bolster, one coverlet, three blankets, four chairs and one small square table to his wife Ann and his daughter Mary was left some money. The rest of his estate, chattels, cattle, and goods etc. were left to daughter Margaret and her husband Richard Prichard who were the co-Executors. There is a slate memorial for him in the church that is described in the Memorials in the Church chapter.

John Williams, 1771 - 1792

John was the son of John William Ezekiel of Trefdraeth and his wife Jane Lewis of the Plas Gwyn and Llwynogan families (*JEG Pedigrees* page 54). His wife was Mary Hughes, daughter of Reverend Rowland Hughes of Bryniau, Newborough and rector of Llangadwaladr and they were married on 17th March 1739 in Newborough church. They had a daughter, Elin, who married a Thomas Lewis of Red Wharf Bay.

John's appointment was very quick after Lewis died as he took over on 5th July 1771, and he also held the curacy of Penrhosllugwy. Early in John's tenure, Thomas, the son of "mad" Tom Hervey and Dame Elizabeth Hanmer became *Lord of Llaneugrad* after his father died on 16th July 1775. Thomas had been christened with his mother's married name (Hanmer,) but his father applied to the King to change his surname to Hervey and the King granted permission for the name change and from then on, he was known as Thomas Hervey. Thomas married Elizabeth March on 5th May 1774 which substantially increased his wealth. She was the only daughter and heiress of the fabulously wealthy Francis March. Amongst other estates, he owned two large sugar plantations in Jamaica, and she inherited it all, so once again Llaneugrad had a close connection with slavery. Thomas and Elizabeth had two children, Thomas Augustus born on 15th August 1775 and William born on 11th January 1777. Thomas was a young man when he died in April 1781, leaving Elizabeth a 31-year-old widow who inherited his estates that were to be passed onto his eldest son.

Each parish took care of its poor parishioners, especially those who were unable to work due to sickness or incapacity, and because of this, the movement of people between parishes was tightly controlled. Granting permission to move parish was the responsibility of the overseers of the poor, and cases were often referred to the Quarter Sessions with examination and depositions taken to verify places of legal settlement. The time of John's tenure coincides with the earliest surviving Poor records from the Quarter Sessions, and the following cases give an insight into the parishioners struggles in his time.

Bastardy cases were not uncommon, and parishes often had to take care of the unmarried unemployed mothers and their child. In 1788, Elin David, a single woman of Llanallgo, brought a case against William Jones, blacksmith of Llanallgo alleging that he was the father of her unborn child. She did not marry William, and the following year married David Owen in Llanallgo church on 3rd July 1789. It was an all-too-common story. In January 1788, Margaret Thomas, a single woman of Llaneugrad brought a bastardy case against William Ishmael, fuller of Parkia in the parish of Llanfaes, alleging that he was the father of her unborn child. He apparently refused to appear at the next Quarter Sessions, so a warrant was issued in May to apprehend him, and his refusal could well have something to do with the fact that he was already a married man.

A sad event involving their toddler happened in 1776 to Hugh Jones and his wife Catherine of Ty Cochyn in Llanallgo. Apparently after tea, unbeknownst to his family, their three-year-old son Richard followed the herdsman out into the field then fell over a rock, fractured his skull, and died instantly. Several local men served as jurors and the inquest by Hugh Owen, Coroner of Anglesey, returned the verdict of accidental death by misfortune.

John's wife Mary died in late April 1785, and she was buried in St Gallgo's on the 23rd of that month. John died on 8th May 1792 in Llanallgo without leaving a Will, and daughter Elin was one of the guarantors on the £200 Bond for administration which was granted on 12th June 1792. John was buried in St Gallgo's on 11th April 1792.

John Richards, 1784 – 1797

It was a delight to discover John as curate of our churches in the Bishops Transcripts and to confirm that he was Reverend John Richards of Llannerch-y-medd church, grandfather of Michael Richards who was the founder of the Glanrafon Hotel in Benllech. According to a descendant, he was born in Lledrod, Cardiganshire (*JEG Pedigrees* give date of birth as 26th October 1760), the son of David Richards and Elizabeth his wife, I was not able to personally confirm his parents due to the lack of surviving church records for Lledrod and Ystrad Meurig. This descendant also told me that John's brother, Edward, attended University of Oxford and graduated with a master's degree, although, curiously, this degree is not documented in Edward's Oxford record, which only records his matriculation. The entry references the Gentleman's Magazine where Edward's death is reported and that also does not show that he had a master's degree. John attended the University of Oxford at the same time as his brother Edward, as a bible clerk or servitor, but the relative does not believe that he obtained a bachelors or master's degree even though the Oxford record for him records both a bachelors and master's degrees. Some family graves claim that he had an MA and the plaque inside Llannerch-y-medd church shows him as BA. Church records document that he is a "Lit" which means that he did not have a degree, but he was considered by the bishop determined to have adequate education to become a priest. In any case, degree or not, he was a very intelligent and educated man and quite an antiquarian. The *JEG Pedigrees* state that he was of Ystrad Meurig, and I believe that he was educated at the school there which was founded by Edward Richards to whom he was in some way related, I have not been able to find out exactly. Another brother, James, also ended up living in Llannerch-y-medd and his daughter, Elizabeth, married Robert Prichard of Llwydiarth Esgob and his eldest son, John, was the bard Iocyn Ddu.

John married Ann Parry on 8th August 1796 in Llanfair ME church and she was from the Pendref, Rhodogeidio family and her parents were Michael Parry of Plas Llanfair ME (son of Richard Parry, Pendref) and Ann, daughter of William Owen of Bodwrdin. They 10 children, four boys and six girls. Their eldest son Michael married Harriet Jones, daughter of Captain Henry Jones of Llysdulas, and Michael was tenant of Parciau Farm (aka Bryn Ddiol) for several years where they had 10 children to add to the three that were born in Llanfair ME. It was their son, Michael, who together with his wife Ann Williams of Tyn Craig, Llanallgo (sister of Margaret who married William Roberts Tyn Lôn Marian-glas), who would go on to establish the Glanrafon Hotel in Benllech. The family also founded another Benllech hotel - Michael and Ann's daughter Harriet married draper Richard Edward Williams, and they founded the Garreglwyd (and later called The Nautilus).

As already mentioned, John was an antiquarian, and he was exceptionally well versed in the local ancient monuments and their history and stories. This was evident in a book published by Reverend John Skinner, who at the end of 1802, conducted a ten-day tour of Anglesey. John was rector of Llannerch-y-medd at the time and, upon reaching Llannerch-y-medd, Reverend Skinner asked the innkeeper about an ancient stone with an inscription that was nearby. Without further ado, the innkeeper promptly took him to the house of Reverend Richards, declaring that he was the local expert. This book is available free to view at the National Library of Wales in the Journals section and gives a great picture of Anglesey life at the turn of the 18th century. His status is reinforced in an 1843 publication with the wonderful name of *The Penny Cyclopaedia of the Society for the Diffusion of Useful Knowledge*, Volume 27, describes John as an antiquarian and poet. It also says that he was the founder of Sunday Schools on Anglesey.

John was taken ill at the beginning of March 1832, and he must have known that he was not going to recover because he wrote his Last Will and Testament on 22nd March; it was witnessed by his brother James, his niece's husband, solicitor Richard Prichard of Llwydiarth Esgob and surgeon J. Evans. After three weeks of illness, he died on March 26th and was buried in Llannerch-y-medd church on the 30th possibly inside the church. In his Last Will and Testament, he left a property he owned called Bryn Issa in Lledrod, Cardiganshire to the use of his son John for the duration of his life. After John's death it was to go to eldest son Michael and his heirs forever. I was not able to find out how John came to inherit this property. Although historically various Richards owned it, at the time of the 1798 Land Tax redemption record, it was owned by a Reverend Owens and occupied by a David Jenkin. Reverend John also had two properties that he leased from William Prichard Lloyd Esq. The houses which were part of the Club houses in the village of Llannerch-y-medd were left to daughter Margaret for the rest of the lease and subject to her paying rent and observing the clauses in the lease. The other was Ty Coch in Llannerch-y-medd, and the rest of the lease was left to Ann, again subject to her paying rent and complying with lease requirements.

Elizabeth, Michael, John, Catherine, and Mary each received £1. The rest of his personal estate, including debts and funeral charges, were to be shared equally amongst his children Ann, Jane, Robert, Richard, and Margaret. Ann was sole executrix.

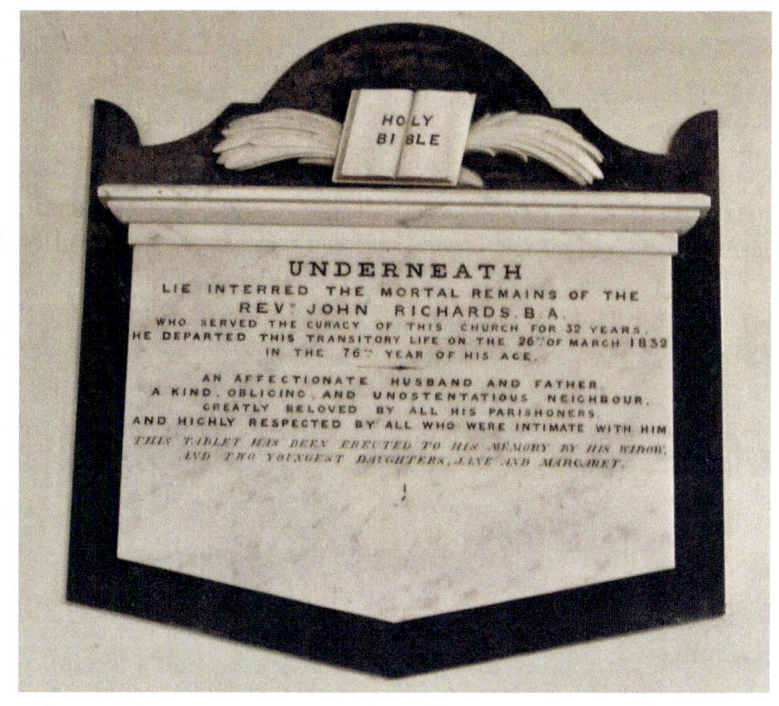

Ann then went to live with her son Richard and two youngest daughters, Margaret, and Jane, at the family farm, Plas Llanfair, in Llanfair ME. When Ann's father Michael Parry died, he had left all his property to jointly share between Ann and her two sisters, Catherine and Elizabeth and their heirs for life. I believe that this included Plas Llanfair ME. In the 1846 tithe record, the owner was listed as Richard Richards, and so I wonder if he had bought the property from the three sisters. Ann died aged 86 on 26th March 1860 and was buried in Llannerch-y-medd.

99. Memorial for John in Llannerch-y-medd Church

Pierce Owen Mealy, MA, 1792 - 1801

Pierce was born in late 1756 to John Mealy of St Georges, Middlesex and his wife Elizabeth née Parry and was christened in St George's church, Hanover Square, London on 3rd January 1757. His mother Elizabeth was a daughter of the Reverend Richard Parry, MA of Perfeddgoed, Bangor and, when her brother Owen died in 1789, she inherited the family estate which would pass to Pierce upon her death. He matriculated at the University of Oxford on 1st March 1776 aged 19, gained his BA on 11th October 1779 and MA on 6th July 1782. He was ordained at Oxford by Bishop John Butler as a deacon on 10th June 1781, and as a priest on 27th October 1782.

According to the book *Portraits of an Island,* in 1788 when he was curate at Holyhead, he responded to the questionnaire from Bishop John Warren about the Methodists and Nonconformists in the parish. He admitted to having *"a few Anabaptists and Methodists of the lowest rank, of the former there are not above fifteen, of the latter I cannot ascertain the precise number. Each of the above has a place for Divine Worship but not licenced nor is there a regular teacher belonging to either."* From the parish register we can see that in 1789 he became perpetual curate of Amlwch, a post that he held for just over 10 years before resigning on 19th December 1799. As an aside, during his time in Amlwch he officiated at the marriage of James Richards (brother of Reverend John Richards) and his wife Elizabeth Price there in 1893. He was appointed rector of our churches together with Penrhosllugwy on 5th June 1792. By way of making connections, his aunty Margaret (mother's brother's wife) was the daughter of the Reverend Hugh Jones of Brynhyrddin, Pentraeth who was rector of our churches from 1717 to 1735, and I wonder if it was this family connection and that attracted him to a post on Anglesey.

The repair of the roads continued to be a challenge, and early in Pierce's tenure, the stretch of road between Pont Sarn Gelyn and Bont Tafarn Y Wrach on the road from Brynteg to Llannerch-y-medd was a case at the 10th of October 1793 Anglesey Quarter Sessions. An order was issued to the sheriff's bailiffs to fine the inhabitants of Llaneugrad. Quite what happened in the meantime I was not able to find out, but at the 13th of January 1795 Sessions, it was recorded that the sheriff had fined the inhabitants one iron pot. Since people had little or no money back then, they usually had to give up some sort of household item and quite often it was spoons or bowls. I do not know what the process was for choosing who would relinquish their iron pot.

There were several instances of legal settlement that went to the Quarter Sessions in Pierce's time, and the following is one example. On 21st March 1795 an Examination and Deposition was presented establishing Penrhosllugwy as the legal settlement of William Thomas of Llaneugrad in the right of his grandfather Lewis John Oliver who had a freehold lease on a tenement and lands there for three lives (having a freehold in a parish meant that you were a legal "citizen" of that parish). This came up because William's single daughter, Catherine Williams, was with child and the Llaneugrad overseers to avoid the burden on the Llaneugrad poor rates. The Overseers of the Poor prepared a Removal Order requiring Catherine to move to her parish of legal settlement, Penrhosllugwy. These were usually done whilst the woman was pregnant because, although the parish could remove the woman following the birth of the child, the Overseers would not have the same ability to remove the child after it had been born in the parish. So, it was easier to remove the pregnant woman back to her place of legal settlement before the child was born.

There were three bastardy cases that were taken to the Quarter Sessions, one in Llanallgo and two in Llaneugrad, and these three examples show that there was more intermingling of people between parishes than might be imagined. Elin Rowland (aka Williams) was the wife of John Prichard, and they were living in Llanfaes when he died, leaving her a young widow. John's father, Richard Morris, had been hired by Reverend Lewis Owen of Llanallgo as a servant in husbandry, as such was a legal "citizen" of the parish and therefore John and Elin could also claim Llanallgo as their parish of settlement. Her case came up on 10th of October 1794 when Owen Morris, yeoman of Llanddona, confirmed this information. Two and a half years later, Elin was living in Llanallgo and found herself pregnant. On 3rd March 1797, she claimed that John Anwyl, an excise officer of Amlwch, was the father of her unborn child. Another case involved Elin Williams of Llaneugrad who filed a bastardy claim against Henry

Williams, a joiner of Llantrisant on 19th January 1793 and on 30th November 1798, Margaret Williams of Llaneugrad filed a claim against Hugh Williams who was a servant in husbandry at Cae Mawr in Llanfechell.

Although I am not able to prove this one way or another, I assume that the rectory was always in Llanallgo and next to the church as Llaneugrad church did not have any land other than the cemetery associated with it. I do not know how big it was or what condition it was in when Pierce arrived, but, coming from a wealthy family and growing up in London, it must not have met the standards that he was used to, or wanted, and he decided to build a new house. Under an Act that was passed in 1776 during the reign of George III, it was possible for an incumbent rector to borrow money and use the glebe (church land that supplied income) and other income such as the tithe, salary etc to secure a mortgage of a value up to three year's net income. On 19th October 1796, Pierce borrowed £200 from Reverend Peter Williams of The Friars, Bangor (headmaster of the grammar school from 1794 to1803.) The mortgage was to be repaid over 25 years and would be passed to the next incumbent if Pierce vacated the position before the 25 years were up. The monies were to be paid to Reverend Richard Williams, curate of Penrhosllugwy, (who would later become rector of Llaneugrad and Llanallgo) and Richard would be make payments for the work completed. According to the Act, if Pierce did not live in the new rectory, the repayments against the principal borrowed would be doubled and should he then go to live in the rectory, he would have to obtain a certificate of residency. The Act was also quite strict on the quality of the renovation/building work stipulating the processes to be followed for planning and the building work.

It was quite grand house, perhaps the precursor to, or even the same house, that is now called The Cloister. Eileen Clarke, who lives there now, tells me that she thinks the house may have been built in two parts – perhaps the original was a two up two down because half of the house has slanting floors, so likely that was the older part. A drawing completed by Reverend Skinner in December 1802 (Illustration 40) on his visit shows the finished house and it looks like The Cloister today, but with only two floors, so either another floor must have been added at some point, or his drawing was just a quick crude one and he didn't draw all three floors. Skinner also tells a story that was told to him by the Reverend John Richards who was incumbent during his visit. When the workers were digging the foundations of the new parsonage, they discovered a square vault formed of a solid composition resembling thick tile which was supposed to be an ancient burying place. He did not mention whether any bones were found or whether the vault was removed or left in place.

Perhaps Pierce's motivation in building the house was also in preparation for his upcoming marriage. He married his cousin Susannah Burnett in 1800 in Dublin. She was the daughter of Richard Burnett Esq. of Richmond, County Dublin. Their only child, Richard Ridgeway Parry Mealy, was born the following year in Bangor. Sadly, he would never know his father as Pierce died on 2nd April 1801, only about 44 years old, and he was buried in Bangor Cathedral on 6th April. He likely died unexpectedly as he did not make a Last Will and Testament.

Other notable events that occurred during Pierce's tenure include a medical breakthrough and an invasion in Wales. his lifetime the first vaccine, Smallpox was a nasty disease which at that time killed almost a third of people who contracted it and left those who survived with scars for life. The very first vaccine for it was administered on 14th May 1796 in England by vaccine pioneer, Edward Jenner and was the first step in the journey to eradicating smallpox.

The very last invasion of mainland Britain happened in Wales beginning on 22nd February 1797 at Fishguard. I will digress and tell the story paraphrased from the historic-uk.com website which I found quite amusing, although I am sure it was not amusing to the residents of that town. In 1797, Napoleon Bonaparte was busy conquering in central Europe, and in his absence, the newly formed French revolutionary government devised a 'cunning plan' based on the assumption that the poor country folk of Britain would rally to the support of their French liberators. The French invasion force of about 1400 troops set sail from Camaret on February 18th and the man entrusted to implement their 'cunning plan' was an Irish American septuagenarian, Colonel William Tate. Napoleon had apparently taken the cream of the Republican army with him and so Col. Tate's force was a ragtag collection of soldiers including many newly released jailbirds. Tate's orders were to land near Bristol and destroy it, then to cross over into Wales and march north onto Chester and Liverpool. From the outset all did not go as planned. Wind conditions made it impossible for the four French warships to land anywhere near Bristol, so Tate moved to 'plan B', and set a course for Cardigan Bay in southwest Wales. On Wednesday February 22nd, the warships sailed into Fishguard Bay to be greeted by cannon fire from the local fort. Unbeknown to the French, the cannon was only being fired as an alarm to the local townsfolk and so, nervously, the ships withdrew and sailed on until they reached a small sandy beach near the village of Llanwnda where the men, arms and gunpowder were unloaded by 2 am Thursday morning. The ships then returned to France and sent a special despatch to the government in Paris informing them of the successful landing. After they landed, the invasion force ran out of enthusiasm for the 'cunning plan' and, perhaps because of years of prison food, they were more interested in the rich food and wine that the locals had recently removed from a grounded Portuguese ship. After a looting spree, many of the invaders were too drunk to fight and within two days, the invasion had collapsed, and on 25th February 1797, Tate's force surrendered to a local militia force led by Lord Cawdor.

One woman became a local heroine known as Jemima Fawr. Jemima Nicholas was the 47-year-old wife of a Fishguard cobbler and, when she heard of the invasion, she marched out to Llanwnda, pitchfork in hand, and rounded up twelve Frenchmen. She 'persuaded' them to go with her back into town, where she locked them inside St Mary's Church and promptly left to look for some more! Her bravery is commemorated on her tombstone. I wonder if the news of this invasion made our parishioners nervous and fearful of a similar occurrence on Anglesey, and how many of our farmers wives kept a pitchfork handy just in case…

The Parys Mountain copper mines were the largest in the world in the 1780s and dominated the copper market. It was shipped all over the world and used for a variety of purposes. In 1797 the America warship, the USS Constitution, was launched and she was built using copper bolts forged from the Anglesey mine and it was also used to coat the warships of the Royal Navy at Trafalgar in 1805. The Anglesey copper also found its way to the Caribbean and was used in for sugar boiling pans on the sugar plantations.

The heir to the Llaneugrad lands, Thomas Augustus Hervey had not yet reached legal age to inherit when he contracted whooping cough in 1795 and went to Portugal to recover his health. On 3rd January 1796 he died from complications of the disease and his estates then passed to his younger brother, 18-year-old William, who would become the new *Lord of Llaneugrad* when he turned 21.

Pierce and Susannah's son Richard matriculated at St John's College, University of Oxford on 22nd January 1820 aged 18 and obtained his BA in 1823 and MA in 1827. He followed in his father's footsteps with a career in the church and was ordained a Deacon on 19th December 1824 in the same ceremony that a curate of our churches, Hugh Hughes Wynne, was ordained a priest. Richard had inherited the Perfeddgoed estate, so was quite a wealthy man, and thus, when he graduated with his MA, he was a "Grand Compounder" and had to pay £40 instead of £14 for his degree. This gave him the privilege of wearing a scarlet gown and the ability to walk to convocation and back with the vice-chancellor of the university!

Susannah did not re-marry and was living in Bangor High Street at the time of the 1861 census and when she died on 26th March 1864. After university, Richard returned to North Wales and lived with his mother in Bangor as well as on Victoria Terrace, Beaumaris and ultimately in Tyn Coed in Llandegfan. He was a very generous man, supporting many different charities through monetary contributions and sitting on committees. Richard also got to meet Victoria before she became Queen. Her and her mother, the Duchess of Kent, attended the Beaumaris eisteddfod in 1832. As the Duchess had made some substantial contributions to local charities, the Bishop of Bangor drew up an address of thanks and selected a small delegation to deliver it in the Bulkeley Hotel on Friday 17th August, which also happened to be the Duchess' birthday. The delegation consisted of the Bishop of Bangor, G.H.D. Pennant Esq., T.A. Smith, Capt. Walker, Reverend J.H. Cotton, Reverend J. Hamer, J.H. Cottingham Esq., Reverend H. Price P. Berthon Esq., and Reverend Richard Mealy. What an honour.

Richard Lloyd, 1801 - 1830

Richard was born in Llanfachreth, Merionethshire in 1744 to Richard and Margaret Lloyd, and was christened on 27th May in the church there. A newspaper announcing his successor in 1830 credits Richard with a BA, but I do not believe that he graduated from university. According to the alumni database, he matriculated at University of Oxford on 15th May 1766 but there is no degree listed for him. The clergy database also supports this as he is in there as "Lit." He was curate of Llangeinwen from around November 1772 until

May 1778, curate of Trefdraeth from January 1778 until the early 1800s and perpetual curate of Talyllyn from 1st June 1790 until 26th February 1803 when Owen Jones replaced him. He was appointed rector of our churches on 13th July 1801 by William Cleaver, Bishop of Bangor.

Richard married Elin Lewis, daughter of Hugh Lewis and Ann née Edwards who were both of the Quirtai family of Aberffraw, and they had six children. The first child was born in Llangeinwen in 1776 and so they must have married a couple of years before that. The other five children were born in Trefdraeth and three of them died as young babies. Two of the daughters lived with them in Llanallgo, Margaret who was born in 1778 and Grace who was born in 1785. I believe that another daughter, Ann, born in 1776 might have survived to adulthood, but I was unable to find out anything else about her in any of the records.

Richard came to Anglesey at a time when the numbers of Nonconformists was growing quickly. By 1797, there were 24 chapels on the island compared to about 70 churches. Two famous preachers had settled on the island. They were Christmas Evans, minister of Ebenezer chapel in Llangefni and John Elias, two dominant figures who were extremely influential in the growth of Nonconformity in the 1800s. Between 1784 and 1800, 11 chapels and meeting houses were registered, but in the year 1801 alone, 23 certificates were granted! It must have been very concerning for Richard and the other clergymen to see this rate of growth, and their own shrinking congregations. In the beginning, meetings were held in houses, but chapels were built at a rate to accommodate the increasing congregations. In Llanallgo, the Bishop of Bangor granted Certificates to three chapels. A chapel (now in ruins) for Independents at Gell Bach received certification in 1801, Paradwys chapel on the Llanallgo roundabout was certified in 1823 but was established well before that with the earliest christening recorded in 1805. Carmel chapel for Independents in Moelfre was certified in 1823, but here again, christenings date as far back as 1814. It is interesting to see that several of the christenings in Paradwys chapel were conducted by three of the great Calvinistic Methodist preachers of the time, John Elias, Richard Lloyd (not our rector) and Cadwaladr Williams of Pen Ceint. Nazareth chapel in Llaneugrad came much later, after Richard Lloyd's death, but several chapels were established in the neighbouring parish of Llanfair ME, all of which would only be what was considered back then a short walk for the inhabitants of Llaneugrad. They were Tanrallt for Independents, Bethesda and Tabernacl for Calvinistic Methodists, Seion for Baptists (founded as far back as 1782) and Capel Soar for Independents, built in 1814.

Another contributor to the growth of Nonconformity was the advent of Sunday Schools. A Carmarthenshire man, Thomas Charles, was the developer of the movement in Wales and, whilst he initially supported the Circulating Schools, he became convinced that if he was to achieve his ambition of teaching children to read in their native language and to instruct them in the principles of Christianity, then schools on a Sunday (like those in England) was the answer. Although he was not the originator, he was a very capable organizer, and the schools proliferated in Anglesey and other parts of Wales. In a letter to the Secretary of the Sunday School Association in London in 1798, he says: *"In Anglesey there are now 20 schools with*

1200 scholars and new ones rising every week." As the number of Sunday Schools grew, so did the number of chapels and the size of their congregations and it was because of the work of both Thomas Charles and Griffith Jones (Circulating Schools), that most people in Wales could read Welsh and were able to discuss theology, a great achievement at that time.

William Hervey had now come into his inheritance and was the *Lord of Llaneugrad*. He held the office of Sheriff of Anglesey for 1800 and must have lived somewhere on the island for that time. He married Dorothea Arabella Primrose daughter of Neil, Earl of Roseberry on 1st September 1801 in her father's house in London and the newlyweds lived in Bodvel Hall as he was Sheriff of Caernarfonshire that year. William's heart was not in Wales. He was an Englishman born and raised and his ancestors had spent little, if any, time in Wales. In 1804, he bought an estate in Broadwell (aka Bradwell) in Oxfordshire and made the decision to sell his other lands to invest in this English estate. In 1809 he sold his Anglesey lands to local copper magnate, the Reverend Edward Hughes of Llysdulas. An Indenture dated 9th/10th March 1809, shows that Edward bought lands in Llanallgo, Llaneugrad, Cerrigceinwen, Llanfihangel Tre'r Beirdd and Pentraeth for £20,996 from William Hervey. Edward was now the new *Lord of Llaneugrad*, and I am sure that he and Richard knew each other, and that Richard, together with other local clergymen, was a frequent guest at the Llysdulas house during Edward's visit there.

Richard and Elin's daughter Margaret made Croesallgo her home. On 18th August 1809, she married shopkeeper John Owen of Caernarvon in Llanallgo church. The newlyweds initially lived in Caernarfonshire, before moving to Ty'n y Pwll, Llanddaniel Fab for a couple of years but by 1819 they had settled in Creosallgo in Llanallgo, where they ran a shop.

In 1810 a dreadful thing happened in the rectory. Richard and Elin's daughter Grace struck their maid, Jane Hughes, on the head with a poker and the next day, because the maid was not waking up, Elin hit her on the head with tin pitcher. Jane later died from the wound and Grace stood trial for murder but was found not guilty. The full story is given in the chapter on Ghosts and a Goblin, as I believe that it was Jane who came to haunt the stairs in the rectory and frighten so many future servants. An article in the North Wales Gazette on 6th September 1810 reported on her acquittal. The word "manslaughter" was handwritten in pencil on the court document, but I do not believe that Grace was charged with manslaughter. In those days the jury were only allowed to return a verdict on the charges brought against her, and it was not possible for the jury to return a verdict on a lesser crime. Grace stayed in the area and had a daughter, Elizabeth Lloyd, who was christened by Richard on 17th June 1820 in Llanallgo church. Mariner, Rice Lloyd, was listed as the father, but I do not believe that he

> There was no trial of any interest at the assizes at Beaumaris, except that of Grace Lloyd, for the murder of her father's servant. The charge could not be proved, and she was acquitted.—We are further informed, that the evidence of the Coroner of the county, reflected great credit on his professional knowledge, and obtained the just tribute of a handsome compliment from the Judge, on delivering the charge to the jury.

100. *North Wales Gazette*, 6th September 1810

and Grace were married; there is no record in any parish registers. Grace later married mariner, William Jones, although I was unable to find a record of this marriage either. Their daughter Elin was born in December 1830 but died as a baby in May of 1832 and is buried with her mother in St Gallgo's. In the 1841 census, Grace used her maiden name. This was a bit unusual for that time as the patronymic system had largely fallen out of use, adding to the suspicion that she was never married. She was living with daughter Elizabeth and husband Israel Matthews (of Aelwyd Isaf). In the 1851 census she called herself Grace Jones, a widow, and was still living with her daughter and family. Grace died on 14th May 1851 and is buried in St Gallgo's, her gravestone is inscribed *"Sacred to the memory of Grace Lloyd who departed this life May 14, 1851 aged 65."* There is no mention of William, and he is not buried with her, so I suspect that he might have been lost at sea.

On New Year's Day 1801, England and Ireland were united under one government, and the United Kingdom of Great Britain and Ireland came into being. This was a red-letter day in the history of Anglesey because the island was an important connecting link to Ireland, and the port of Holyhead began to get much busier with a dramatic increase in both road and sea traffic. The waters on the approach to the harbour were treacherous and the only lighthouse at the time was on the Skerries. In August 1808 the foundation stone was laid on Ynys Lawd (South Stack) by Trinity House for a new lighthouse and a light was lit for the first time on the night of 9th February 1809.

James Henry Cotton, Dean of Bangor cathedral, was a founder of the Caernarfonshire & Anglesey hospital (C&A) in Bangor which opened its doors for the first time in May 1819. Over the years, thousands of people from Anglesey have travelled over the Menai Bridge to the C&A for medical treatment, but in those early days, there was no bridge and a sometimes-perilous journey on one of the ferries had to be made. Building a bridge had been talked about for many years and Thomas Telford, who had already begun construction of a road from Shrewsbury to Holyhead, was invited to submit a plan. An Act of Parliament was passed which became law in May 1818 and included an initial grant of twenty thousand pounds. Although the first stone was laid in August 1819, the building work took a few years, and the bridge was formally opened to wheeled vehicles on 30th January 1826. It shortened the journey time from London to Holyhead substantially, and it was much cheaper for coaches. It made for a much safer journey onto and off the island for those who could afford the prices and was the beginning of the end for the ferries. The bridge is a beautiful one and it was quite a radical development for the people of Anglesey, and I wonder if Richard or any of our parishioners were able to use it.

The never-ending task of keeping the roads in good repair was quite a financial burden on our parishioners who found themselves in trouble again during Richard's tenure. The road from Beaumaris to Amlwch was still a very busy one early in the 1800s and the Llanallgo inhabitants had failed to keep it in good order from the boundary with Llaneugrad to the boundary with Penrhosllugwy. They were fined one spoon at the very end of 1803. The Llaneugrad parishioners were not so lucky in July 1820. Their failure to repair the highway to Llannerch-y-medd from Graigfryn farm to Pont Fari on the boundary with Llanfair ME

(3,014 yards at a width of 8 yards) cost them one heifer – and that was a lot for someone to give up in those days. A decade or so before this though, in 1809, an unusual crime was heard at the Quarter Sessions. For some reason that shall probably remain forever unknown, on 1st March 1809, yeoman Robert Parry, a fine upstanding and successful businessman of Llaneugrad parish decided to dig (or have dug) pits in the *"King's Common Highway"* to Llannerch-y-medd, known at the time as Frigan road. The area he dug up was a huge 30 yards in circumference and two yards deep and the pits remained in the road until 1st June the same year. The jury decided that there was sufficient evidence for the charges to be heard in court and that Robert had *"with force and arms, unlawfully and injuriously"* dug pits which prevented people from using the highway without *"great peril and danger to their lives and to the great damage and common nuisance of the king's subjects."* I was unable to find out how this ended for Robert or the reason behind his seemingly bizarre actions.

Elin died on 28th December 1825 and was buried in Aberffraw churchyard on 3rd January 1826. When Richard died on 28th May 1830, he was not buried with his wife, but in St Eugrad's on 2nd June 1830. He did not write a Last Will and Testament. Richard was 86 years old when he died, and I suspect that perhaps his health had been failing him for three or four years before he passed away because from about the middle of 1826, he no longer conducted any christenings, marriages, or burials in either church. A few services were conducted by the curate of Llangwyllog, O.G. Williams, and then a young curate was appointed to our parishes, Hugh Hughes Wynne, and it was he who carried out the services until Richard's death in 1830.

Hugh Hughes Wynne, BA, 1826 - 1830

Hugh was born in 1800 in Bryngoleu, Llangwyllog to surgeon Hugh Wynne of the Chwaen Ddu family and Mary née Hughes, heiress of William Hughes of Bryngoleu. Hugh's paternal grandfather (also a Hugh, and surgeon and Apothecary of Beaumaris) had died the year Hugh was born and, as his only grandchild, he left Hugh a legacy of £1,000 in Trust "at interest" to be paid annually which was a plentiful sum in those days. Hugh attended Jesus College Oxford, matriculating on 28th May 1819 aged 18, was a scholar from 1822 to 1826 and he obtained his BA in 1823. On 19th December 1824, he was ordained a priest, and the son of Reverend Pierce Owen Mealy was ordained a deacon, in Llandegai church by the Bishop of Bangor. According to a newspaper report of the event, Reverend Bulkeley Williams of Beaumaris preached at the occasion and *"a more appropriate and impressive discourse we have seldom heard"*.

Hugh married Elizabeth Pierce, the daughter of William Pierce of the Taihirion family of Llangaffo, on 13th February 1826 in Llangaffo church. The couple initially lived at his paternal great-grandmothers' home, Cae Mawr, in Llaniestyn where they had two children, William Morris in 1827 and Richard Pierce in 1830. Hugh served in Llaniestyn church on occasion as officiating minister at the same time that he served in our churches. After Richard died in May 1830, Hugh became curate of his home parish of Llangwyllog, and they lived in the family home, Bryngoleu. There they had two more children, Ann Pierce in 1833 and Rowland Hughes in 1835. Hugh stayed in Llangwyllog until May 1836. He was in Warrenpoint, Northern Ireland, a small port town in county Down, Northern Ireland when he died on 17th May 1839 aged only 38. He was not buried in Anglesey so perhaps he was buried in the church at Warrenpoint.

Elizabeth was left a young widow with four children between the ages of four and twelve and she went to live in her mother's house, Taihirion in Llangaffo before moving to Liverpool with her children and she appears to have been left financially independent. Elizabeth died on 18th January 1880 at 4 Stanfield Rd., Liverpool and was brought back to Anglesey to be buried in St Caffo's church, Llangaffo. None of the children married and Richard, Ann and Rowland are all buried in St Caffo's. William is buried in Cincinnati USA where he had moved later in life.

Robert Davies, MA, 1830 - 1834

Robert was born on 29th August 1787 in Garneddwen, Ysceifiog in Flintshire to Reverend Robert Davies and his wife Mary née Edwards from Garneddwen. Reverend Robert senior was curate of that parish at the time Robert was born and he was later rector of Mallwyd and vicar of St Cadfan's, Tywyn, which is famous for housing the Cadfan stone which dates from the 9th century or earlier, and upon which is inscribed the oldest known written Welsh. Robert was the eldest son and he attended Jesus College, University of Oxford, matriculating on 18th June 1806 age 18, he obtained his BA in 1810 and MA in 1813. He was ordained a priest by the Bishop of St David's at St Peter's church, Carmarthen on Sunday 29th September 1811, and was perpetual curate of Llangristiolus and Cerrigceinwen by January 1814, where he stayed until he was promoted to rector of our churches on 5th July 1830.

On 23rd July 1830, two and a half weeks after he arrived in our parishes, the Beerhouse Act was implemented, and breweries and ale houses began springing up in great numbers all over the country. The Act enabled any ratepayer to brew and sell beer on payment of a licence costing two guineas, and one of its intentions was to get people to drink beer instead of spirits such as gin which had long been a great problem amongst the poorer classes. Gin (short for genever, a traditionally Dutch drink) became the most popular drink in the country after William III, who was Dutch, was crowned in 1689. One element of the corn laws passed during his reign gave a tax break on spirits, and distilleries sprung up everywhere, thus beginning the first "gin craze" when a pint of gin was actually cheaper than a pint of beer! (The second gin craze of course is our current time where all the lovely flavoured and small batch distillery gins are now popular.) Gin drinking was a huge problem, especially for women who ended up drinking so much that they neglected their homes and their children, resulting in gin being nicknamed "mothers ruin". The Act also reduced the price of beer to below that of gin (and other spirits) and Britain once more became a nation of beer drinkers...

On Sundays the alehouses were crowded with farm servants drinking themselves into a stupor and apparently such sights had not been seen on Anglesey before the act was passed.

Robert's next-door neighbour at Glanrafon Uchaf was maltster Edward Williams (later of Glanrafon Isaf) and his brother Joseph, also a maltster, lived with the family. It was actually a rare profession in the area, and he was the only one in the parishes of Llaneugrad, Llanallgo and Penrhosllugwy at the time of the 1841 census. Maltsters processed barley into malted barley for brewing beer, and I believe that Joseph had his malting house at Glanrafon Uchaf. Local brewers bought the malted barley and many of the establishments brewing and selling their home-made beer were run by wives and daughters rather than the man of the house. Based on reading the Wills of Glanrafon inhabitants over time, I believe that there was a tavern at Glanrafon Isaf which on the busy road to Amlwch, and there were a couple of ale houses in Moelfre village at Tanyfron and Dalar Gam at the time of the 1841 census. A record dated 1808 in Anglesey Archives, records three ale houses and their proprietors in Llanallgo – Jane Thomas at Storehouse, Elizabeth Roberts at Boldon and David Owens at Dalar Gam. From the names of the properties, there appears to be two alehouses in Llaneugrad on the road to Llannerch-y-medd -Tafarn Y Wrach at the corner of Lôn Las and Frigan Dafarn further up the road.

A letter to the *North Wales Chronicle* newspaper was published on 24th July 1832 and highlighted a big problem in Llaneugrad, Llanallgo and Penrhosllugwy – foxes! Quite how long the problem persisted in our parishes or how it was dealt with, I do not know.

> ANGLESEY.—A correspondent informs us that the parishes of Llaneugrad, Llanalltgo, and Penrhoslligwy, are very much infested with foxes, which commit great depredations amongst the poultry, thereby occasioning very heavy losses to farmers, cottagers, and the inhabitants at large. Our informant wishes this fact to be publicly known throughout the island, in the hope that something may be done amongst the landed proprietors, either by the establishment of a subscription pack of fox hounds or otherwise, to abate the nuisance. We do not pretend to say whether this plan is or is not feasible; but we can inform our correspondent of a mode pretty generally adopted in the southern parts of Scotland, with the view of preventing the over increase of the fox. When the foxes get so numerous as to occasion any thing like serious loss amongst the lambs or poultry, the resident proprietors and farmers of the district assemble with their shepherds, husbandry servants, and dogs of all sorts.
> "Terrier, hound, and puppy dog,
> "And cur of low degree,"
> and beat up the enemies' quarters, making an indiscriminate slaughter of all they can get at. This sport is repeated for two or three days at the period of the year when the shepherds and agriculturists can be best spared from their usual labours, and it generally has the effect of clearing the district of foxes for several years afterwards.

101. *North Wales Chronicle* 24th July 1832

There were several illegitimate children born in the parishes in the four years that Richard was rector, three cases came up at the Quarter Sessions and several were christened in our churches. As I was reading through the christenings, I was delighted to find that on 14th November 1830, Robert christened my great-great-grandfather, Owen Thomas who was born in Penterfyn on Bodafon Mountain and also his two sisters, Jane on 17th February 1833 and Elizabeth on 30th May 1834.

Robert died at the young age of 47 on 22nd October 1834 and it must have been an unexpected death as he did not make a Last Will and Testament. His next of kin was his eldest sister Mary who applied for, and was granted, administration. Mary was a single woman of Llanallgo parish, so I suspect that she was his live-in housekeeper, as was common in those times. She was one of the guarantors on the Bond which was for the sum of £527 and 10 shillings. Thomas Williams of Glanrafon and William Owen of Caeau Gleision were the other guarantors and the inventory taken of his goods amounted to £263.15.0. The items he left paint a picture of the life of a well-off rural parish rector:

Table, chairs, Fire Iron in the parlour	£8.0.0
Table and chairs in the other parlour	£1.10.0
Kitchen Furniture	£4.0.0
Two bedrooms	£10.0.0
Room over the kitchen	£2.0.0
Lumber in the garret	£1.0.0
Books	£10.0.0
One cow	£5.0.0
Two pigs	£1.10.0
Hay	£2.0.0
Potatoes	£0.15.0
Tithe	£153.0.0
Arrears of Richard Williams	£5.0.0
Rent	£30.0.0
Purse and Apparel	£30.0.0

The £10 worth of books is impressive, although with a master's degree, we would expect that he was a studious man who enjoyed reading, the value of his books is greater than his wealthiest parishioners owned in those times. For example, farmer Robert Parry of Frigan who died in 1833 was a wealthy man and his inventory was valued at £279 16s, with £2 10s worth of books. Wealthy maltster Edward Williams of Glanrafon Uchaf died in 1831 leaving inventory worth £1149 18s including £1 7s worth of books.

Robert died on 22nd October 1834 and was buried in Llanallgo with Hugh Hughes Wynne officiating. Mary had a lovely headstone made for him, which reads: *"Underneath are interred the remains of the Reverend Robert Davies Rector of this parish and eldest son of the late Reverend Robert Davies Rector of Mallwyd and Vicar of Towyn. Merioneth. Robert Davies to whose memory is erected this small token of sisterly affection was Born August the 29th AD 1787 and died October the 22nd AD 1834."*

John Griffith, MA, 1834 - 1852

According to the 1851 census, John was born about 1790/1 in Llanfihangel TB, and the Oxford alumni database gives his birth around the same timeframe and states that his father is William from Llandrygarn. In the parish register, there is only one possibility and that is a John Griffith christened in St Mihangel's church on 24th June 1792, son of George Griffith and his wife Jane, but it is noted that he is a "natural" child (the polite term for illegitimate), so George was not his biological father. According to page 36 of the *JEG Pedigrees,* his biological father was William Griffith of Llandrygarn from the Cymunod family of

Bodedern. I believe that John was raised by William, and perhaps his mother died because George appears to have married for a second time and lived and raised a family in Amlwch. The Land Tax records for Llandrygarn of this time period show only one William Griffith, and he paid the tax on Clegir Gwynion which was owned by a Dr Jones, but I was not able to find any information that would confirm that he was John's father. When John married in 1820, he was a widower of Cymunod in Bodedern. This property was owned by a different branch of the family from his father's branch and William Evans was a tenant in 1814 (the last tax record that survives for Bodedern), so perhaps John himself was the tenant at the time, a later letter would support this is not out of the realms of possibility.

The Cymunod family boasted many clergymen over the generations - John's grandfather was rector of Rhoscolyn and his great-grandfather was the Reverend Evan Griffith of Penmorfa. John also had a connection to our churches - he was the three times great grandson of the Reverend Richard Hughes who was rector from 1670 to 1687. His other "claim to fame" so to speak was that he was the five times great grandson of the famous diarist, William Bulkeley of Brynddu. John attended Jesus College, University of Oxford matriculating on 10th October 1807 aged 17 and obtained his BA on 18th October 1813. There is no record of him obtaining an MA at Oxford and, although JEG in the Pedigrees and his 1930 article give him this title, I suspect that this is either an error or an honorary degree listed in a document that I have been unable to find. John was curate of Llanbabo for a time before being appointed stipendiary curate of Llechylched on 12th September 1834, and on 26th November that year, he became rector of our churches.

John married Frances Dorothea "Fanny" Lewis of Llangoed in the church there on 15th September 1820. Fanny's father was the Reverend John Lewis who was rector of Llanfechell from 1816, and her brother, the Reverend William John Lewis, was the officiating minister at their wedding. John and Fanny had six children: Ellis Owen, Owen Owen, Robert Lewis, Henry Lewis, Mary Grace, and Frances Jane (who was perhaps named after both their mothers).

Something that has puzzled me for a number of years is why there are several years' worth of missing records from the parish registers and as they are all during John's tenure, I set out to find a reason for this. I initially assumed that the register books were lost or damaged, but as I reviewed them page by page, I came across a curious situation. Before I go on, I should add that the Bishops Transcripts (BTs), which are the annual reports sent to the bishop of all christenings, marriages, and burials in a parish that year, are also missing the exact same records. This is an exceptionally rare as the BTs usually escape damage because they are stored in the cathedral files under mostly better conditions. By this time period the christenings, marriages, and burials each had their own register, and they were forms specifying the information required and the individual events and pages were numbered making it easy to check whether there were missing pages, or an entry was not made. In fact, it was the case that John did not make the entries. I should imagine that he was chastised by the bishop for not sending in his BTs, but as they too are missing, any admonishment was not effective.

On 1st July 1837, civil registration of births, marriages and deaths began. It was a very big change for people and there was, as we might expect, variable compliance, perhaps due to confusion or people finding it difficult or not wanting to accept change. Up until then the parish registers (and some chapel records) of christenings, marriages and burials served as the official records of life-events and it was not up to the family to take any action as these events were all conducted in a religious establishment with ceremony. However, from 1837, a family member or representative had to take an action to register births and deaths and had to travel to a Register Office in order to do so. Marriages were still recorded by the minister who conducted the service, and they sent the information to the Register Office to issue the official marriage certificate. A new marriage parish register was introduced at the same time to record the other details needed for civil registration. The new registers were received for Llaneugrad and Llanallgo, and the Llanallgo register was duly completed, albeit with occasional missing bits of information. For marriages taking place in St Eugrad's it was an entirely different kettle of fish. The last entry made by John is on page 4 and was the marriage of Thomas Owen, shoemaker of Tyn Llidiart and Mary Williams of Penrallt on 20th October 1841. The next eight pages and 16 marriages are blank. These 16 marriages appear in the civil register, so they are not lost for all time. Giving John the benefit of the doubt, I am sure that he must have intended to go back and complete these entries, but somehow, he never got round to it.

The christening and burial records are in worse shape. The last christening properly documented by him in Llaneugrad occurred on 11th February 1838, and in Llanallgo, the last documented christening was on 20th May 1838, but it has no details whatsoever. The next entries in both the Llanallgo and Llaneugrad registers are by his successor in 1852. The last Llanallgo burial recorded by him is one after 4th September in 1837 but no date is given, and the person buried is recorded as William Owen of Caeau Gleision aged 23. In fact, according to the headstone on his grave and death records of the time, it was actually Robert Owen, William's son, and he died on 22nd September 1837. In Llaneugrad the last burial recorded by John was on April 18th, 1837, and once again the next entries in both registers are by his successor.

Throughout the registers there is some sloppiness in the entries with errors and missing information, blank entries here and there, but quite why he stopped recording events altogether from the late 1830s/early 1840s except for the Llanallgo marriages is a secret that went with him to the grave. Perhaps he hated paperwork (he certainly would not be the first) and he put his efforts elsewhere.

A newspaper article paints a picture of a kind and compassionate man who was devoted to helping his parishioners and on 21st May 1844 the North Wales Chronicle printed an article entitled *Clerical Liberality*. Perhaps he had always been generous in this way, or perhaps it was as a result of a major change in how the poor were dealt with that happened in 1834.

CLERICAL LIBERALITY.—A noble feature in the character of the Rev. J. Griffith, of Llanallgo, Anglesey, is, that whenever a burial of one of his poor parishioners takes place, that he gives the offering to the survivors of the deceased; lately when a poor man of the name of Hugh Jones, of Ynys, was buried, the Rev. Gentleman, after making enquiries respecting his circumstances, on being informed that he left an aged widow and an idiot son in a very helpless state, he called Capt. Hughes, of Lligwy, a respectable parishioner, and delivered the offering to him, desiring that Mr. Hughes would see it laid out in some articles of clothing of which they were then mostly in want. This is not a solitary instance of his liberality, but his constant practice, and when we consider that the worthy rector has but a small living, and a large family to support, these almsdues are still more praiseworthy. CHARITY is the most prominent feature of *Christianity*.

103. *North Wales Chronicle,* 21st May 1844

The amendment to the Poor Act was intended to ensure that the poor were housed in workhouses, clothed and fed. Anglesey did not have a workhouse at that time and in 1837, Commissioners decided how to split up the island's 76 parishes into Unions. Llanallgo and Llaneugrad, together with 51 other parishes, became part of what was called the "Anglesey Union". Each parish had an elected Guardian (larger parishes had more than one) and there was a chairman of the Guardians; in the early years this was Mr Charles Henry Evans of Henblas, and the secretary was Mr Samuel Dew of Llangefni. All of the incumbents were elected annually, which made any attempts at lasting change nigh on impossible.

There was a lot of discontent with the new law and rectors and curates were not happy as the vestry was no longer the sole decision maker in the care of its poor and the setting of parish rates. Ratepayers were unhappy because with centralized control and the added expenditures required by the amended Act, poor rates rose quite steeply in the early years. A petition was presented to both Houses of Parliament in an attempt to have Anglesey excused from the new law, which was (not surprisingly) unsuccessful. Apparently, the poor were also no better off than they had been, and in many cases were worse off. Reverend William Jones, curate of Llanbeulan, wrote in 1840: "*We hear nothing these days but great bemoaning on account of the law both by ratepayers and those in receipt of charity from the parish. The former say they have never paid such heavy rates while the latter say that never have they suffered such hardship as at the present time.*" He goes on to say "*how a poor woman can subsist on a shilling a week and two persons on eighteen pence is beyond my comprehension. In the depth of Winter such people are often without a fire; their sustenance is meagre at best, and sometimes they are without any. When not tramping the countryside to beg they have to stay in their beds of straw or chaff which are in any case very imperfect shelters against the cold, but they retire so as to reduce their pangs of hunger. These are no idle advertisements, but facts, the truth of which can be relied upon.*" What a heart-wrenching picture that paints, and I can now appreciate why John felt compelled to donate the offering from funerals to the poor relatives, it would have meant such a lot to them.

Two censuses were taken during John's tenure, in 1841 and 1851. In 1841 Llanallgo had a population of 384 and there were 15 paupers including seven children aged 13 and under. Of the adults, all were female other than 85-year-old Henry Williams of Aelwyd Isaf. Llaneugrad had a population of 331 and 11 paupers including eight children aged 11 and under, and all of the adults were female. The 1851 census includes parish of birth and marital status. There were 19 paupers amongst the Llanallgo population of 431, eight children under the age of 14 and seven widows. All were born in Llanallgo except a visitor from Amlwch, and Ann Jones aged 75 of Tai Newydd, who was born in Llaneilian. Of the 330 Llaneugrad inhabitants, ten were paupers and five of these were children under the age of 11. There were two widows, one unmarried female and a married couple, Lewis, and Mary Jones of Tynypwll, and he was unable to work because he was blind. There were therefore plenty of cases on whose behalf John and the Guardians of Llanallgo and Llaneugrad had to plead to obtain the right amount of funds in the biweekly meetings, and I do hope that the recipients of these monies fared much better than the desperate examples given by the Reverend William Jones of Llanbeulan. It breaks my heart to think otherwise.

On August 17th, 1836, John saw the biggest change to marriages come into effect since the Clandestine Marriages Act of 1753 which had legally required marriages to take place in a church either by licence or after calling of Banns. Marriages were now allowed to take place in nonconformist chapels and the newly introduced Registry Offices. In reviewing the number of marriages recorded in St Eugrad's and St Gallgo's in the five years before and after civil registration (and even for the following decade), they were fairly constant in number, so John did not see any major decline in church marriages locally during his tenure. In fact, the nonconformist chapels were quite slow in taking advantage of these new provisions and Capel Tabernacl Llanfair ME was the first in the area to start conducting marriages, and that was in 1849; it would not be until the 20th century that Carmel and Paradwys would follow suit.

Early on in his tenure he must have had some sort of contretemps with Thomas Williams Esq. of Glanrafon Isaf, and the case was taken to the Anglesey Assizes. On 24th July 1839 he was bound £50 to keep the peace to Thomas for a year. I have not been able to find out what this was about, and whatever the situation, it did not make it into the newspaper report of the Quarter Sessions.

It was curious to see in the 1841 census that John and Fanny were living in Llanallgo rectory, but their children were living elsewhere. Ellis (16), Owen (14), Robert (12), Henry (10), Mary Grace (8) and Fanny Jane (6) were living in Beaumaris on Steeple Lane and the head of the household was a 20-year-old female servant called Margaret Matthews. I wondered why the children would be living apart from their parents, and a letter written by John in 1839 might shed some light. It was addressed to Lord Newborough and asked if John had any prospect of becoming the tenant of the property called "Glyn". I believe this was Plas Y Glyn in Llanfwrog, previously known as Bodafon Y Glyn and which was the home of Owen ap Robert Owen of Caerfryn, a *Lord of Llaneugrad* and grandfather of Sir John Bodvel.

The letter has a begging tone. In it he points out that *"all Mr Elias's brothers are provided with farms except the one at Bangor late tenant of Porthamel. Even a young man now residing with his brother at Plas Y Glyn has a farm in the neighbourhood called Blew to retire to whenever he thinks proper."* It sounds like he is saying that the Elias brothers have no need for this tenancy of Glyn that he himself wants. The Elias' were descendants of the noted poet William Elias (1708 – 1787) who had moved to Plas Y Glyn and died there. He says that he would accede to Lord Newborough's terms and would even do more; he would pay the present tenant for all of the building he had erected at his own expense and allow the old man a cottage and the keep of a cow during his lifetime. He goes on to say that he has a very numerous young family, and the living of Llanallgo and Llaneugrad does not exceed £130 a year with only two and a half acres of land. He says that he finds it impossible to support his family as milk, bread and butter which are the principal ingredients to keep a young family cannot be had for love nor money. So, perhaps this is why the children were living in Beaumaris in 1841, it might have been easier there to find milk, bread, and butter for them. He was obviously not successful in his pleas because at the time of the 1841 census, the occupant of Plas Y Glyn was Thomas Elias (grandson of poet William) who was living there with wife Catherine and their young family, and he lived there until his death in 1859.

Like many young boys in the area, sons 15-year-old Robert and 13-year-old Henry went to sea in the merchant navy. They signed up together as apprentices on 25th August 1843, on the ship *Old England* sailing out of Liverpool. Henry was only 19 when he died on 12th January 1848 in Shanghai whilst serving this same ship. Owen later followed his brothers to sea, becoming an able seaman in 1850 and earning his 2nd mate certificate on 9th May 1856. By the time of the 1851 census Ellis, Mary Grace and Frances Jane were all living with their parents in Llanallgo rectory. They also had two domestic servants living with them, 30-year-old Ann Rowlands from Rhodogeidio and 16-year-old William Rowlands from Llandyfrydog and 22-year-old farm servant Richard Owen from Llanddyfnan. They must have been quite well-off to afford these servants.

John was also very keen on educating his parishioners and when he came to our parishes, there were no schools in the area, but before his time was up, there would be a large school in both Llaneugrad and Llanallgo. One of them would be a British School and the other a church school. John was a contemporary of the famous Reverend John Phillips (Reverend JP), a Calvinistic Methodist minister who was the first principal of Bangor Normal College, and who was appointed representative of the British and Foreign Schools Society for North Wales in November 1843. This was a nonconformist-supported Society with a mission to supply cheap basic education for the children of the labouring and manufacturing classes of the country, regardless of religious persuasion. Between them, Reverend JP and an Anglesey man, Sir Hugh Owen from Llangeinwen, did more for education in Wales than anyone else in their era.

Reverend JP married Eleanor Parry of Frigan, Llaneugrad, whose father, Robert Parry, was a farmer and millstone manufacturer, owning several millstone quarries in the area. In 1843 they came to live in Brynteg, and he was able to further the British Society mission by setting up a British school (as they were called) in Llaneugrad. Together with his father-in-law and eleven local farmers and tradesmen, the 13 Trustees began fund-raising in earnest, and they secured some land alongside *The Marian* common from the then-owner of the whole parish, Lord Dinorben. At a meeting in the vestry room of Tabernacl chapel, Llanfair ME on 5th July 1844, ten of the school Trustees signed the Plans for the school building and the attached master's house. The school was to serve children of Llaneugrad and Llanfair

ME and had an initial planned capacity of around 140 children. It was opened in 1845 with a school master who was paid from the pennies that students paid to attend, amounting to a sum of £18 a year. The Indenture formally conveying the land with its premises to the Trustees and their heirs and assigns was not signed until March 1847. It was a gift of deed and made clear that the school was for the purposes of educating *"children and adults or children of labouring, manufacturing and other poorer classes."*

The church schools were run by the rector who served as the chairman of a group of "managers" responsible for oversight of the school. Perhaps it was the plan to build the British school in Marian-glas that inspired John to follow suit and provide a church school for the Llanallgo children, or it might have been the idea of another great supporter of education at the time, the Reverend Richard Williams Mason (RWM) of the Plas Bodafon family. He was appointed perpetual curate of Penrhosllugwy in 1844, and the curacy at that time owned Pentyddyn farm (historically called Tyn Y Pwll) in Llanallgo. The School Sites Act of 1841 allowed landowners to donate up to an acre of land to charities for the provision of schooling for poor children and, under this Act, RWM donated one rood (quarter of an acre) of land belonging to Pentyddyn for a school. The land was conveyed to John and his successors by Deed in 1846 with the agreement of the Bishop of Bangor, Christopher Bethell. Three beneficed clergymen had to certify the location and size of the land, and they were Owen Gethin Williams, Perpetual Curate of Pentraeth, William Williams, Rector of Llanddyfnan and William John Lewis, Perpetual Curate of Penrhoslligwy. The Deed stipulated that the land was to be used to build a school to educate the poor people of Llanallgo, Penrhosllugwy and Llaneugrad. Whilst the rector had *"sole care order and direction of the religious instruction of the scholars"*, a committee consisting of the rector or his curate, the churchwardens, perpetual curate of Penrhosllugwy and five residents who had a life beneficial interest in real property in the three parishes and who were subscribers to the school of at least 20 shillings a year, would manage all other aspects of the school. The first five men were Michael Richards of Parciau, Isaac Williams of Glanrafon Uchaf, Farmer William Williams of Glanrafon Isaf, farmer Edward Williams of Tan y Fron and merchant David Owen of Glandon. The willingness or enthusiasm of RWM to provide this particular piece of land determined the school's unfortunate location, which as it turned out, was not the best from either the Board of Education's or the parents' viewpoints. For the Board, it was too close to the Llaneugrad British School and later on the Llanallgo parents complained that it was too far from the village of Moelfre where most of the children lived, but that is a story for a different book.

I will include a few words on RWM and his life. He was the grandson of the Reverend Richard Williams of Plas Bodafon, also curate of Penrhosllugwy at one time. RWM was the son of Richard's only child, Ann, who married William Mason an M.D. from Caernarfon, and they inherited the Plas Bodafon estate and RWM was their eldest son and heir born in Llanbeblig, Caernarfonshire. He attended Jesus College University of Oxford, matriculating on 26th February 1835 aged 17, he obtained his BA in 1839, his MA in 1841 and was ordained by the Bishop of Oxford. He was an official school examiner and, together with his friend and companion, Mr Robert Williams Howell, he spent many years training young gentlemen in preparation for attending university. When he came to the parish of his ancestral home in 1844, he was said to be one of the best scholars in the diocese. I believe that when he saw that there was no school in the area, he must have determined to do something about it, and found a willing partner in the Reverend John Griffith. Interestingly, RWM was the 5th great grandson of John Griffith Lewis who left perpetual legacies to the poor of seven Anglesey parishes, including Llaneugrad and his story is told in the chapter on the Charities.

The Llanallgo school was opened six months after the Llaneugrad British school. By 1846, John had employed a 17-year-old (untrained) school master and was paying him 3 shillings a week plus his room and board and there were 69 pupils in attendance. The 1846 inquiry into the state of education in Wales reports were published in 1847, and they give us an interesting insight into the state of the two new schools. The main point of contention appears to be that the two schools catered for more pupils than were available and, because they were so close to each other, they were each struggling to bring in enough income to be efficient/financially viable. The harsh words of the report must have been very disappointing to the Reverend JP, John and RWM who were all simply trying to do good work by providing an education for the children (and some adults) of the parishes. The report claimed that placing two schools so near to each other *"has been to impoverish and render both schools practically useless."* The commissioners mused that had the schools been better separated they might have been able to better serve the neighbouring parishes as well because as none of these parishes had schools of their own. However, the locations of the respective schools were wholly dependent on what land was available for the purposes at the time and the generosity of the donors, and the term "beggars can't be choosers" comes to mind. In any event, both schools survived for a considerable period of time despite their proximity, and it wouldn't be the last time that controversy between the British and National schools would simmer, and the rector of our churches would find himself squarely in the middle of it.

In John's time, a second bridge was built over the Menai Straits with a local casualty. On 30th June 1845 the young Queen Victoria gave her royal assent to a Parliamentary Bill covering the construction of the Britannia Bridge, and the foundation stone was laid on 10th April 1846. Four years later on 5th March 1850, its designer and builder, Robert Stephenson, fitted the last rivet and the first tube was opened to rail traffic on 18th March and the second one on 21st October. As with all such construction projects of the era, there were a number of deaths, and all of those who perished are named on a memorial outside St Mary's Church, Llanfair PG with the exception of one young man. He was 27-year-old Robert Jones of Ty Coch, Llaneugrad, and he died after falling from the scaffolding at the Anglesey end of the bridge. His death was reported in the *Caernarvonshire and Denbigh Herald* on 6th November 1847. Robert was from a farming family and born at Ty Coch and christened in St Eugrad's on 13th February 1820. His parents were Henry Jones from Llandyfrydog, and Elizabeth Roberts from

> FATAL ACCIDENT.—Last Wednesday morning, Robert Jones, son of Henry Jones, of Ty-coch, Llaneugrad, Anglesey, fell from the main scaffolding on the Anglesey side of the Britannia Bridge, survived the accident only for about twenty minutes, as his head was much bruised. He was about 23 years of age, and was a steady and good workman. An inquest was held on the remains the following night, when a verdict of "accidental death" was returned.

103. *Caernarvonshire and Denbigh Herald*, 6th Nov 1847

Llanfair ME. Elizabeth, who had died giving birth to their last child in 1835, is buried in St Mary's Llanfair ME and Robert was laid to rest next to his mother.

The Reverend John Griffith died on 27th January 1852 aged 62 and was buried in St Gallgo's on 2nd February. His headstone bears the following poignant verse:

Grieve not for him though sad the task to part,
With one so gentle, true, and kind of heart,
Since pain and grief can break his rest no more,
And heaven has gained what sorrowing friends deplore.

Fanny and her daughters moved to Liverpool, where they both married. Mary Grace married Thomas Travis in 1853 and Fanny Jane married William Johnston in 1857. Fanny died on 4th July 1854 at 20 Elizabeth St, Pembroke Place, Liverpool age 62 and is buried with John in St Gallgo's. Thomas Henry Travis who is commemorated on his grandparent's grave, was the son of Mary Grace who died in 1860 age five.

Stephen Roose Hughes, MA, 1852 - 1862

104. Stephen Roose

Without a doubt Stephen is the most famous of all of the rectors of our churches, and that fame is exclusively associated with St Gallgo's because of his devoted caring for the victims of the Royal Charter wreck and their families, the stress and intense effort of which likely helped him to an early grave.

Stephen was born in Amlwch, one of ten children of farmer William Hughes and his wife Sarah née Roose of Madyn Dysw, and he was christened in Amlwch church on 17th April 1814. By Griffith Herbert. William was quite a well-off farmer and he leased about 25 ½ acres at Madyn Dysw with a house, garden and offices and he also had other properties. He made his Last Will and Testament on 25th June 1828, some 12 years before he died. He left his wife and family very well provided for, including money for the education of his sons so that they could take up respectable trades or professions. The second eldest son, William, was to study law in London after he finished his clerkship with his uncle, and Stephen was to go to Beaumaris school before attending college and entering Holy Orders. He put all his property in Trust with his eldest son John, who was 19 at the time, and the profits from them were to be used to pay the legacies in his Will. He also specified that as long as they stayed single and *"behave themselves properly"*, the children would be entitled to *"make their homestead in their mother's house"*. William, and the youngest son, Hugh Robert, remained bachelors and must have behaved themselves properly as they continued living with their mother in

Madyn Dysw until she died, and Hugh Robert continued to live there after her death.

Stephen attended Jesus College, University of Oxford matriculating on 15th March 1832, he obtained his BA in 1835 and MA in 1838. He was ordained a Deacon in Bangor on Sunday 20th July 1837 and became curate of Bodewryd, performing his first christening there on 27th August 1837. For those who are interested/related, the baby in question was Robert Jones, son of labourer William and his wife Ellen of Tynyfelin Nant. Stephen was ordained priest in Bangor on Sunday 5th August 1838, and was licenced to the perpetual curacy of Bodewryd on 6th August at the nomination of Sir John Thomas Stanley, Baronet. William lived to see Stephen fulfil his ambitions before he passed away on 7th April 1840 at his home. His mother, Sarah, outlived her son, and so saw his extraordinary work for the Royal Charter victims and their families and she died on 11th February 1863. Sarah and William are buried together in St Eleth's, Amlwch and there is a lovely three verse "*Englyn*" (type of poem) on their grave. I include it here with apologies to my English readers that I have not tried to express it in English.

Dau fyddlon cyfion eu caid – drwy einioes
Dra anwyl, ddiniwaid;
I Dduw byw'n ufudd ddibaid
O wir anian yr enaid.

Mewn doethder: heb brinder bri – un ydoedd
E'n odiaeth ragori
Mewn dawn ac mewn daioni
Pwy fwynach haelach na hi.

Yn lan drwy'r Iorddonen li – ehedodd
Ar eu hadain gwisgi
Eu dau enaid i weini
Byth ewch y ser i'n ner ni.

A year after his father's death, Stephen travelled to Liverpool where he officiated over a double wedding of two of his siblings in St James Church, Walton on the Hill on 20th April 1841. His eldest brother John married Anna Maria Pearson, whose father David was a surgeon of Liverpool, and his sister Margaret Ellen married John Jones, a Gentleman from Amlwch. Both couples returned to the island to live, John and Anna to Tyddyn Dai, Amlwch and Margaret and John to Mona Brewery in Llanfachraeth where he was a brewer and maltster until his death in 1870; Margaret carried on the business after he died, eventually moving to Mona Stores where she passed away in 1882.

On 16th September 1841 Stephen was married to his first cousin, Jane Anne Moulsdale, in Corwen church. She was the daughter of the Reverend Thomas Gorst Moulsdale and his wife Elinor (known as Ellen) née Roose. Stephen's mother and Jane's mother were sisters. Thomas and Ellen had two other daughters, Mary Hester, and Margaret Augusta who, together with their mother, would support Jane and her husband throughout the gruelling months following the Royal Charter wreck. Stephen and Jane first lived in Glanydon, Amlwch, and in the 1851 census their nephew, three-year-old Thomas Henry Platt Moulsdale, was living with them. He was the son of Jane's brother, Stephen Thomas Moulsdale, and wife Catherine née Keeley who also lived in Amlwch. In early January that year the generosity of the family was highlighted in a newspaper article. It began with "*At this time, when the sufferings of the poor acquire an unusual degree of intensity*" and went on to relate that the Hughes family had given sustenance to the poor. John (of Tyddyn Dai) had provided all of the poor widows in the town with roast beef and plum pudding as well as soup to others. Sarah, William, and Hugh Robert gave food at Madyn Dysw as did Stephen at Glanydon. Of course, they were not the only providers, many other individuals and businesses also contributed, and the newspaper declared that "*the poor were liberally regaled.*"

Stephen served in Bodewryd church until mid-March 1852 when he was appointed Rector of Llaneugrad and Llanallgo. His appointment was reported in several newspapers and with varying values of the living; the London Globe reported £135, and the Caernarfon and Denbigh Herald reported £345. In 1846/7 the joint tithe for the parishes was £216 which probably explains the difference in how the reported values – with and without tithes. These values reported in the newspapers were a bone of contention with many clergymen and Stephen's brother, Hugh Robert, would later have an argument, via letters to a newspaper, with the rector of Llanfairfechan for making false claims about the value of his Penrhosllugwy living.

Hugh Robert was born in 1825 and attended Jesus College, University of Oxford, matriculating on 30th March 1843 aged 18. He migrated to New Inn Hall and gained his BA in 1848 and an MA in 1852. He was ordained in Bangor as a Deacon on 21st December 1851 and on 19th December 1852 as a priest. By 17th September 1852, he was curate of Llanwenllwyfo, a post he held for the rest of his life. The Buckinghamshire Herald newspaper reported on 13th February 1858 that he had been appointed to the perpetual curacy of Penrhosllugwy, which was then worth £75. The brothers worked side by side in their neighbouring parishes and Hugh Robert was instrumental in helping his older brother with the Royal Charter victims and relatives.

The main event during Stephen's tenure eclipsed every other in the decade. The wrecking of the Royal Charter on the night of 25th/early hours of the 26th of October 1859 at Moelfre is quite famous, but I will include a brief summary anyway for those who may be unfamiliar with the event or its details. The Royal Charter was a steam clipper returning from Melbourne and bound for Liverpool with around 480 people on board, the exact numbers are not known as the final passenger list was lost with her. She was carrying a fortune in gold, and some of the passengers were returning miners who had struck it rich and were carrying gold on their persons or in the stronghold. In what was the most severe storm of the 19th century, with over 100mph winds, she was driven onto the rocks and broke up sending around 450 souls to their deaths. Only 40 people survived, and it was the greatest loss of life of any shipwreck on the Welsh coast – it rocked the small community of Moelfre to its core.

The bodies that were recovered that night and in the ensuing weeks along the Moelfre coastline were brought to St Gallgo's, which essentially became a mortuary. The furniture was taken out of the church and the victims, whole and parts, were laid out on the floor. The sea and the rocks had not been kind, and the mutilations were dreadful. Stephen tried to identify each and every one of them for their families and friends, and he meticulously noted details and characteristics such as hair and eye colour, tattoos, and other markings, detailing their clothing and any possessions found in pockets or about their body.

In the following weeks and months, family members not only wrote to Stephen to find out if their loved one had been found, but they also travelled from across Britain to the church to identify the remains. Stephen and Jane, her mother Ellen and sisters Mary Hester and Margaret Augusta, who had moved in with them, cared for and comforted each and every one. Stephen personally replied to the relatives and friends and is said to have written well over a thousand letters. The sheer scale of the tragedy did not weaken his resolve or compassion and he was thanked by the relatives who appreciated such duty and devotion. He bore the cost of all this work himself spending nearly half his annual stipend.

He was critical of the authorities who he believed were far more concerned with recovery of the lost gold than the bodies of those still trapped on board or being washed up along the coast in the days and weeks after it sank. He became so agitated at one point that he was threatened with arrest if he did not stop interfering. Whilst the church was used as a mortuary, church services were moved to the Llanallgo school just down the road.

That same year, the famous author Charles Dickens brought out a new weekly literary magazine called "All the Year Round" which made its debut on Saturday 30th April 1859 and featured the first instalment of Dickens's *A Tale of Two Cities*. Dickens travelled extensively to Europe, America, and all over Britain, and wrote a variety of articles which were published in his weekly magazine under his adopted title *The Uncommercial Traveller*. These articles were eventually published in a book, and the second chapter records his visit to the scene of the Royal Charter wreck and with the Reverend Stephen Roose Hughes. The article originally appeared in the 28th of January 1860 *All the Year Round* edition, and in order to ensure that his facts were in order, Dickens had his publisher mail a proof copy to Stephen. Under separate cover, Dickens wrote a now very famous letter to Stephen asking that he return the proof by return post and hoping that if they visited London they would come to his house in Kent. The letter is famous because several facsimile copies of this letter were made in 1933 and given to those who contributed to a restoration fund for St Gallgo's. At the time of writing this there were a couple of these copies for sale from booksellers for round $2,500. A copy of the letter appears on the following two pages.

Office of All the Year Round.
A WEEKLY JOURNAL CONDUCTED BY CHARLES DICKENS.

No. 11 Wellington Street North, Strand, London WC
Tuesday Tenth January 1860

My Dear Mr Hughes.

You will receive from my printer's office by this same post, a Proof of the little article I have written on the subject of my late visit. I am under the necessity of asking you to send it back to Mr Wills here, by return of post. For, although a fortnight will elapse before it is published, the mechanical necessities of this Journal, and its simultaneous publication in England and America, render its going to press at once imperative.

I doubt whether I am quite right respecting the number of the drowned buried in your churchyard, and the greatest number that lay in the church at one time. Will you do me the favor to correct me on those points? And if you should observe any similar inaccuracy, will you do me the additional kindness to mark it?

I trust that there is nothing in the article that you, or your household, will find displeasing.

105. Page 1 of the Charles Dickens Letter

I have written it out of the honest convictions of my heart, and in the hope that it will at least soften the distress of many people from whom you have not yet heard. It says for me all that I should otherwise have attempted to say to you in this note, and merely strives to express what any visitor to you must surely feel.

My daughters have taken a great interest in all I have told them, and particularly in Mrs Hughes's idea of coming to London in the summer. They earnestly beg me to assure her and you, that they hope to know you both very well, and that it will be an uncommon gratification to them if you will come and see us, down at my Kentish house on the top of Shakespeare's Gad's Hill, which is little more than an hour's railway ride from town.

Beg to present my true regard to the ladies of your house and to your brother, and to assure you of the hearty esteem and respect with which I am

Very faithfully yours

Charles Dickens

This same post will also bring you the documents you lately lent me, returned with thanks.

The Rev. Stephen Roose Hughes

106. Page 2 of the Charles Dickens Letter

It is worth reproducing a large portion of Dickens' article as it paints a vivid picture of Stephen's character, the work that he and his family did and the general circumstances of the time:

THE SHIPWRECK

It was the kind and wholesome face I have made mention of as being then beside me, that I had purposed to myself to see, when I left home for Wales. I had heard of that clergyman, as having buried many scores of the shipwrecked people; of his having opened his house and heart to their agonised friends; of his having used a most sweet and patient diligence for weeks and weeks, in the performance of the forlornest offices that Man can render to his kind; of his having most tenderly and thoroughly devoted himself to the dead, and to those who were sorrowing for the dead. I had said to myself, 'In the Christmas season of the year, I should like to see that man!' And he had swung the gate of his little garden in coming out to meet me, not half an hour ago.

So cheerful of spirit and guiltless of affectation, as true practical Christianity ever is! I read more of the New Testament in the fresh frank face going up the village beside me, in five minutes, than I have read in anathematising discourses (albeit put to press with enormous flourishing of trumpets), in all my life. I heard more of the Sacred Book in the cordial voice that had nothing to say about its owner, than in all the would-be celestial pairs of bellows that have ever blown conceit at me.

We climbed towards the little church, at a cheery pace, among the loose stones, the deep mud, the wet coarse grass, the outlying water, and other obstructions from which frost and snow had lately thawed. It was a mistake (my friend was glad to tell me, on the way) to suppose that the peasantry had shown any superstitious avoidance of the drowned; on the whole, they had done very well, and had assisted readily. Ten shillings had been paid for the bringing of each body up to the church, but the way was steep, and a horse and cart (in which it was wrapped in a sheet) were necessary, and three or four men, and, all things considered, it was not a great price. The people were none the richer for the wreck, for it was the season of the herring-shoal—and who could cast nets for fish, and find dead men and women in the draught?

He had the church keys in his hand, and opened the churchyard gate, and opened the church door; and we went in. It is a little church of great antiquity; there is reason to believe that some church has occupied the spot, these thousand years or more. The pulpit was gone, and other things usually belonging to the church were gone, owing to its living congregation having deserted it for the neighbouring schoolroom, and yielded it up to the dead. The very Commandments had been shouldered out of their places, in the bringing in of the dead; the black wooden tables on which they were painted, were askew, and on the stone pavement below them, and on the stone pavement all over the church, were the marks and stains where the drowned had been laid down. The eye, with little or no aid from the imagination, could yet see how the bodies had been turned, and where the head had been and where the feet.

Some faded traces of the wreck of the Australian ship may be discernible on the stone pavement of this little church, hundreds of years hence, when the digging for gold in Australia shall have long and long ceased out of the land.

Forty-four shipwrecked men and women lay here at one time, awaiting burial. Here, with weeping and wailing in every room of his house, my companion worked alone for hours, solemnly surrounded by eyes that could not see him, and by lips that could not speak to him, patiently examining the tattered clothing, cutting off buttons, hair, marks from linen, anything that might lead to subsequent identification, studying faces, looking for a scar, a bent finger, a crooked toe, comparing letters sent to him with the ruin about him. 'My dearest brother had bright grey eyes and a pleasant smile,' one sister wrote. O poor sister! well for you to be far from here and keep that as your last remembrance of him!

The ladies of the clergyman's family, his wife and two sisters-in-law, came in among the bodies often. It grew to be the business of their lives to do so. Any new arrival of a bereaved woman would stimulate their pity to compare the description brought, with the dread realities. Sometimes, they would go back able to say, 'I have found him,' or, 'I think she lies there.' Perhaps, the mourner, unable to bear the sight of all that lay in the church, would be led in blindfold. Conducted to the spot with many compassionate words, and encouraged to look, she would say, with a piercing cry, 'This is my boy!' and drop insensible on the insensible figure.

He soon observed that in some cases of women, the identification of persons, though complete, was quite at variance with the marks upon the linen; this led him to notice that even the marks upon the linen were sometimes inconsistent with one another; and thus, he came to understand that they had dressed in great haste and agitation, and that their clothes had become mixed together. The identification of men by their dress, was rendered extremely difficult, in consequence of a large proportion of them being dressed alike—in clothes of one kind, that is to say, supplied by slopsellers and outfitters, and not made by single garments but by hundreds. Many of the men were bringing over parrots and had receipts upon them for the price of the birds; others had bills of exchange in their pockets, or in belts. Some of these documents, carefully unwrinkled and dried, were little less fresh in appearance that day, than the present page will be under ordinary circumstances, after having been opened three or four times.

In that lonely place, it had not been easy to obtain even such common commodities in towns, as ordinary disinfectants. Pitch had been burnt in the church, as the readiest thing at hand, and the frying-pan in which it had bubbled over a brazier of coals was still there, with its ashes. Hard by the Communion-Table, were some boots that had been taken off the drowned and preserved—a gold-digger's boot, cut down the leg for its removal—a trodden-down man's ankle-boot with a buff cloth top—and others—soaked and sandy, weedy, and salt.

From the church, we passed out into the churchyard. Here, there lay, at that time, one hundred and forty-five bodies, that had come ashore from the wreck. He had buried them, when not identified, in graves containing four each. He had numbered each body in a register describing it, and had placed a corresponding number on each coffin, and over each grave. Identified bodies he had buried singly, in private graves, in another part of the churchyard. Several bodies had been exhumed from the graves of four, as relatives had come from a distance and seen his register; and, when recognised, these have been reburied in private graves, so that the mourners might erect separate headstones over the remains. In all such cases he had performed the funeral service a second time, and the ladies of his house had attended. There had been no offence in the poor ashes when they were brought again to the light of day; the beneficent Earth had already absorbed it. The drowned were buried in their clothes. To supply the great sudden demand for coffins, he had got all the neighbouring people handy at tools, to work the livelong day, and Sunday likewise. The coffins were neatly formed; I had seen two, waiting for occupants, under the lee of the ruined walls of a stone hut on the beach, within call of the tent where the Christmas Feast was held. Similarly, one of the graves for four was lying open and ready, here, in the churchyard. So much of the scanty space was already devoted to the wrecked people, that the villagers had begun to express uneasy doubts whether they themselves could lie in their own ground, with their forefathers and descendants, by-and-by. The churchyard being but a step from the clergyman's dwelling-house, we crossed to the latter; the white surplice was hanging up near the door ready to be put on at any time, for a funeral service.

The cheerful earnestness of this good Christian minister was as consolatory, as the circumstances out of which it shone were sad. I never have seen anything more delightfully genuine than the calm dismissal by himself and his household of all they had undergone, as a simple duty that was quietly done and ended. In speaking of it, they spoke of it with great compassion for the bereaved; but laid no stress upon their own hard share in those weary weeks, except as it had attached many people to them as friends and elicited many touching expressions of gratitude. This clergyman's brother—himself the clergyman of two adjoining parishes, who had buried thirty-four of the bodies in his own churchyard, and who had done to them all that his brother had done as to the larger number—must be understood as included in the family. He was there, with his neatly arranged papers, and made no more account of his trouble than anybody else did. Down to yesterday's post outward, my clergyman alone had written one thousand and seventy-five letters to relatives and friends of the lost people. In the absence of self-assertion, it was only through my now and then delicately putting a question as the occasion arose, that I became informed of these things. It was only when I had remarked again and again, in the church, on the awful nature of the scene of death he had been required so closely to familiarise himself with for the soothing of the living, that he had casually said, without the least abatement of his cheerfulness, 'indeed, it had rendered him unable for a time to eat or drink more than a little coffee now and then, and a piece of bread.'

In this noble modesty, in this beautiful simplicity, in this serene avoidance of the least attempt to 'improve' an occasion which might be supposed to have sunk of its own weight into my heart, I seemed to have happily come, in a few steps, from the churchyard with its open grave, which was the type of Death, to the Christian dwelling side by side with it, which was the type of Resurrection. I never shall think of the former, without the latter. The two will always rest side by side in my memory. If I had lost any one dear to me in this unfortunate ship, if I had made a voyage from Australia to look at the grave in the churchyard, I should go away, thankful to God that that house was so close to it, and that its shadow by day and its domestic lights by night fell upon the earth in which its Master had so tenderly laid my dear one's head.

The references that naturally arose out of our conversation, to the descriptions sent down of shipwrecked persons, and to the gratitude of relations and friends, made me very anxious to see some of those letters. I was presently seated before a shipwreck of papers, all bordered with black, and from them I made the following few extracts.

A mother writes:
Reverend Sir. Amongst the many who perished on your shore was numbered my beloved son. I was only just recovering from a severe illness, and this fearful affliction has caused a relapse, so that I am unable at present to go to identify the remains of the loved and lost. My darling son would have been sixteen on Christmas-day next. He was a most amiable and obedient child, early taught the way of salvation. We fondly hoped that as a British seaman he might be an ornament to his profession, but 'it is well;' I feel assured my dear boy is now with the redeemed. Oh, he did not wish to go this last voyage! On the fifteenth of October, I received a letter from him from Melbourne, date August twelfth; he wrote in high spirits, and in conclusion he says: 'Pray for a fair breeze, dear mamma, and I'll not forget to whistle for it! and, God permitting, I shall see you and all my little pets again. Good-bye, dear mother—good-bye, dearest parents. Good-bye, dear brother.' Oh, it was indeed an eternal farewell. I do not apologise for thus writing you, for oh, my heart is so very sorrowful.

A husband writes:
My dear kind Sir. Will you kindly inform me whether there are any initials upon the ring and guard you have in possession, found, as the Standard says, last Tuesday? Believe me, my dear sir, when I say that I cannot express my deep gratitude in words sufficiently for your kindness to me on that fearful and appalling day. Will you tell me what I can do for you, and will you write me a consoling letter to prevent my mind from going astray?

A widow writes:
Left in such a state as I am, my friends and I thought it best that my dear husband should be buried where he lies, and, much as I should have liked to have had it otherwise, I must submit. I feel, from all I have heard of you, that you will see it done decently and in order. Little does it signify to us, when the soul has departed, where this poor body lies, but we who are left behind would do all we can to show how we loved them. This is denied me, but it is God's hand that afflicts us, and I try to submit. Someday I may be able to visit the spot, and see where he lies, and erect a simple stone to his memory. Oh! it will be long, long before I forget that dreadful night! Is there such a thing in the vicinity, or any shop in Bangor, to which I could send for a small picture of Moelfre or Llanallgo church, a spot now sacred to me?

Another widow writes:
I have received your letter this morning and do thank you most kindly for the interest you have taken about my dear husband, as well for the sentiments yours contains, evincing the spirit of a Christian who can sympathise with those who, like myself, are broken down with grief. May God bless and sustain you, and all in connection with you, in this great trial. Time may roll on and bear all its sons away, but your name as a disinterested person will stand in history, and, as successive years pass, many a widow will think of your noble conduct, and the tears of gratitude flow down many a cheek, the tribute of a thankful heart, when other things are forgotten for ever.

A father writes:
I am at a loss to find words to sufficiently express my gratitude to you for your kindness to my son Richard upon the melancholy occasion of his visit to his dear brother's body, and also for your ready attention in pronouncing our beautiful burial service over my poor unfortunate son's remains. God grant that your prayers over him may reach the Mercy Seat, and that his soul may be received (through Christ's intercession) into heaven! His dear mother begs me to convey to you her heartfelt thanks.

Those who were received at the clergyman's house, write thus, after leaving it:
Dear and never-to-be-forgotten Friends. I arrived here yesterday morning without accident and am about to proceed to my home by railway. I am overpowered when I think of you and your hospitable home. No words could speak language suited to my heart. I refrain. God reward you with the same measure you have meted with! I enumerate no names but embrace you all.

My beloved Friends. This is the first day that I have been able to leave my bedroom since I returned, which will explain the reason of my not writing sooner. If I could only have had my last melancholy hope realised in recovering the body of my beloved and lamented son, I should have returned home somewhat comforted, and I think I could then have been comparatively resigned. I fear now there is but little prospect, and I mourn as one without hope. The only consolation to my distressed mind is in having been so feelingly allowed by you to leave the matter in your hands, by whom I well know that everything will be done that can be, according to arrangements made before I left the scene of the awful catastrophe, both as to the identification of my dear son, and also his interment. I feel most anxious to hear whether anything fresh has transpired since I left you; will you add another to the many deep obligations I am under to you by writing to me? And should the body of my dear and unfortunate son be identified, let me hear from you immediately, and I will come again. Words cannot express the gratitude I feel I owe to you all for your benevolent aid, your kindness, and your sympathy.

My dearly beloved Friends. I arrived in safety at my house yesterday, and a night's rest has restored and tranquillised me. I must again repeat, that language has no words by which I can express my sense of obligation to you. You are enshrined in my heart of hearts. I have seen him! and can now realise my misfortune more than I have hitherto been able to do. Oh, the bitterness of the cup I drink! But I bow submissive. God must have done right. I do not want to feel less, but to acquiesce more simply.

There were some Jewish passengers on board the Royal Charter, and the gratitude of the Jewish people is feelingly expressed in the following letter bearing date from 'the office of the Chief Rabbi:'

Reverend Sir. I cannot refrain from expressing to you my heartfelt thanks on behalf of those of my flock whose relatives have unfortunately been among those who perished at the late wreck of the Royal Charter. You have, indeed, like Boaz, 'not left off your kindness to the living and the dead.' You have not alone acted kindly towards the living by receiving them hospitably at your house, and energetically assisting them in their mournful duty, but also towards the dead, by exerting yourself to have our co-religionists buried in our ground, and according to our rites. May our heavenly Father reward you for your acts of humanity and true philanthropy!

The 'Old Hebrew congregation of Liverpool' thus express themselves through their secretary: Reverend Sir. The wardens of this congregation have learned with great pleasure that, in addition to those indefatigable exertions, at the scene of the late disaster to the Royal Charter, which have received universal recognition, you have very benevolently employed your valuable efforts to assist such members of our faith as have sought the bodies of lost friends to give them burial in our consecrated grounds, with the observances and rites prescribed by the ordinances of our religion. The wardens desire me to take the earliest available opportunity to offer to you, on behalf of our community, the expression of their warm acknowledgments and grateful thanks, and their sincere wishes for your continued welfare and prosperity.

A Jewish gentleman writes:
Reverend and dear Sir. I take the opportunity of thanking you right earnestly for the promptness you displayed in answering my note with full particulars concerning my much-lamented brother, and I also herein beg to express my sincere regard for the willingness you displayed and for the facility you afforded for getting the remains of my poor brother exhumed. It has been to us a most sorrowful and painful event, but when we meet with such friends as yourself, it in a measure, somehow or other, abates that mental anguish, and makes the suffering so much easier to be borne. Considering the circumstances connected with my poor brother's fate, it does, indeed, appear a hard one. He had been away in all seven years; he returned four years ago to see his family. He was then engaged to a very amiable young lady. He had been very successful abroad and was now returning to fulfil his sacred vow; he brought all his property with him in gold uninsured. We heard from him

when the ship stopped at Queenstown, when he was in the highest of hope, and in a few short hours afterwards all was washed away.

Mournful in the deepest degree, but too sacred for quotation here, were the numerous references to those miniatures of women worn round the necks of rough men (and found there after death), those locks of hair, those scraps of letters, those many slight memorials of hidden tenderness. One man cast up by the sea bore about him, printed on a perforated lace card, the following singular (and unavailing) charm: A BLESSING. May the blessing of God await thee. May the sun of glory shine around thy bed; and may the gates of plenty, honour, and happiness be ever open to thee. May no sorrow distress thy days; may no grief disturb thy nights. May the pillow of peace kiss thy cheek, and the pleasures of imagination attend thy dreams; and when length of years makes thee tired of earthly joys, and the curtain of death gently closes around thy last sleep of human existence, may the Angel of God attend thy bed, and take care that the expiring lamp of life shall not receive one rude blast to hasten on its extinction.

A sailor had these devices on his right arm. 'Our Saviour on the Cross, the forehead of the Crucifix and the vesture stained red; on the lower part of the arm, a man and woman; on one side of the Cross, the appearance of a half moon, with a face; on the other side, the sun; on the top of the Cross, the letters I.H.S.; on the left arm, a man and woman dancing, with an effort to delineate the female's dress; under which, initials.' Another seaman 'had, on the lower part of the right arm, the device of a sailor and a female; the man holding the Union Jack with a streamer, the folds of which waved over her head, and the end of it was held in her hand. On the upper part of the arm, a device of Our Lord on the Cross, with stars surrounding the head of the Cross, and one large star on the side in Indian Ink. On the left arm, a flag, a true lover's knot, a face, and initials.' This tattooing was found still plain, below the discoloured outer surface of a mutilated arm, when such surface was carefully scraped away with a knife. It is not improbable that the perpetuation of this marking custom among seamen, may be referred back to their desire to be identified, if drowned and flung ashore.

It was some time before I could sever myself from the many interesting papers on the table, and then I broke bread and drank wine with the kind family before I left them. As I brought the Coastguard down, so I took the Postman back, with his leathern wallet, walking-stick, bugle, and terrier dog. Many a heart-broken letter had he brought to the Rectory House within two months many; a benignantly painstaking answer had he carried back.

As I rode along, I thought of the many people, inhabitants of this mother country, who would make pilgrimages to the little churchyard in the years to come; I thought of the many people in Australia, who would have an interest in such a shipwreck, and would find their way here when they visit the Old World; I thought of the writers of all the wreck of letters I had left upon the table; and I resolved to place this little record where it stands. Convocations, Conferences, Diocesan Epistles, and the like, will do a great deal for Religion, I dare say, and Heaven send they may! but I doubt if they will ever do their Master's

The Clergymen

service half so well, in all the time they last, as the Heavens have seen it done in this bleak spot upon the rugged coast of Wales.

Had I lost the friend of my life, in the wreck of the Royal Charter; had I lost my betrothed, the more than friend of my life; had I lost my maiden daughter, had I lost my hopeful boy, had I lost my little child; I would kiss the hands that worked so busily and gently in the church, and say, 'None better could have touched the form, though it had lain at home.' I could be sure of it, I could be thankful for it: I could be content to leave the grave near the house the good family pass in and out of every day, undisturbed, in the little churchyard where so many are so strangely brought together.

Without the name of the clergyman to whom—I hope, not without carrying comfort to some heart at some time—I have referred, my reference would be as nothing. He is the Reverend Stephen Roose Hughes, of Llanallgo, near Moelfre, Anglesey. His brother is the Reverend Hugh Robert Hughes, of Penrhosllugwy.

By the time of the 1861 census, the now 12-year-old Thomas Henry Platt Moulsdale is their adopted son, and Jane's mother Ellen and sisters Mary Hester and Margaret Augusta were still living with them. The intensity of Stephen's effort took a great toll on him and in 1860 he fell ill for three months and ended up with rheumatic fever. He was probably so run down from his efforts and lack of proper food that an infection likely led to the rheumatic fever. He never fully regained his health and strength as he likely had heart damage. According to the Luton Times 3rd May 1862 edition, on the morning of 4th February 1862, he went on his rounds visiting poor parishioners, and returned to his home happy and cheerful. After having tea, he sat in his chair next to the fire and 10 minutes later died without a sigh, and smiling, even in death. He had died of paralysis, the old term for a stroke and a John Roberts, who was present at his death and who could not write, was the informant. He was buried in his beloved St Gallgo's on 11th February, only 47 years old.

> THE FUNERAL OF THE LATE REV. STEPHEN ROOSE HUGHES, M.A.—The funeral of the above lamented gentleman, took place on Tuesday last, when his remains were consigned to their last resting place, at Llanallgo church yard. The following is the order of procession:
> Dr. Parry, Medical Attendant   Rev. H. Owen
> Rev. M. Hughes, Pentraeth   Rev. W. Williams
> O. Griffith, Esq.   E. Richards, Esq.
> Then followed the Churchwardens and eight of the Principal Parishioners.
> Mr E. Jones Coffin-maker, and Mr G. Davies, Undertaker
> Bearers   THE BODY.   Bearers
> Chief Mourners.
> Master T. H. Moulsdale   J. Hughes, Esq., Llynon
> Geo. Hughes, Esq.   Wm. Hughes, Esq.
> R. O. Moulsdale, Esq.   Rev. H. R. Hughes
> S. Moulsdale, Esq.   John Jones, Esq?

106a. *North Wales Chronicle*, 15th February 1862

Even with a subscription that was opened in February 1860 to refund him the money that he had spent on the Royal Charter victims, Stephen was left with little money, and Jane was essentially unprovided for. A fund was opened by Messrs Coutts in their Bank to which they donated £10. By the time this fund was advertised on 3rd May 1862, several others had donated to the cause including Gentlemen of the Bank £6; Angela Georgina Burdett-Coutts (the wealthy philanthropist) £10; Charles Dickens £15 15s and Elder Brethren of the Trinity House £50. Several newspapers all over the country carried the advertisement for this fund.

Jane, her mother, and sisters first moved to Summer Hill Terrace in Bangor (per the 1871 census) and later to 4 Menai Villas in Menai Bridge where Jane died on 19th January 1887, aged 68 from acute gout and congestion of the liver. Her sister, Mary Hester, who was living with her and was present when she died, was the informant. She was buried on 25th January in Llandysilio church where her two sisters and daughter-in-law Amy Caroline Moulsdale are also buried, and not with her husband in Llanallgo. Their son Thomas died in Sligo, Ireland on 19th May 1894 when he was only about 46 years old.

Alban Griffith, 1862 - 1863

Alban was born at Dolgwartheg Farm, Aberaeron on 5th August 1829 to farmer Thomas Griffith and his wife Mary, and he was the youngest of their seven children. Thomas was a yeoman, and they were in easy, but not affluent, circumstances. Alban began working life with a career on the sea and in April 1845, aged 16, he was an ordinary seaman on a 90-tonne coasting vessel sailing out of New Quay. He gained his Mates certificate in Limerick, Ireland on 5th May 1851, and on 14th January 1852, he was admitted to the Dreadnought Seamen's Hospital at Greenwich, a floating hospital for sick and injured seafarers of all nations. He was 23 years old, 5 feet 10 inches tall, had last served on the *Mary Taylor* sailing out of Liverpool, and had spent a total of seven years at sea. His condition was described as "cutaneous", and so some sort of skin ailment. He received 20 days of treatment, was cured, and discharged back to his ship.

On 31st December 1852 he married Jane Edwards, a farmer's daughter who was then living in Aberaeron, in Llanddewi Church, Aberarth. He was living at Dolgwartheg with his widowed mother (his father had died in 1845) and he described himself as a farmer, so he must have retired from the sea. Jane died in 1855 and was buried in Henfynyw church on 11th September, leaving Alban a young widower.

Alban's eldest brother was the Reverend John Griffith, rector of Neath and archdeacon of Llandaff, who was both a clergyman and an educationalist and who contributed a great deal to the Eisteddfodau, both national and local. He was much loved and respected by churchgoers and nonconformists alike and was a powerful and popular speaker. I wonder if it was brother John who influenced Alban to take up a career in the church. John had done a lot to promote and help establish secondary and further education and Alban had not attended university. He was ordained as a Literate (one who doesn't have a formal degree but who is considered by the bishop to have satisfactory knowledge) in Llandaff cathedral on 21st March 1859, and then as a priest in the same church on 4th March 1860. Like his brother, Alban was a gifted speaker and there are several newspapers reports on various events that describe him as an eloquent orator with very engaging sermons. He served for a while as missionary within the Llandaff diocese and, when the incumbent rector of Porthmadog died, he was appointed there in April of 1862. It was only a few short weeks later that he was appointed rector of our churches taking up his position on 10th August 1862. He made quite an impact on his first day, conducting a morning service and in the evening a "*most eloquent and impressive sermon was delivered to a very numerous congregation"* according to an article in the .

LLANALLGO.

The inhabitants of the parishes of Llanallgo and Llaneugrad were thrown into great grief last Saturday by the arrival of the very melancholy news of the death of their beloved Pastor, the Rev. Alban Griffiths. It is but a few months ago that his initiation into the living was noticed by a correspondent in this paper ; now the heavy duty devolves upon us of announcing his departure from this mortal life. He had been ailing for some time, and had gone to Pwllheli, intending to proceed from thence to his family in South Wales, hoping by a change of scene to be relieved. But, at Carnarvon, in returning from the former place, he found himself unable to proceed, and on the 4th inst. expired at the Uxbridge Arms Hotel in that town. His untiring labours as a minister, his unaffected piety and gentle considerate manners, had won for him the love of all who had become acquainted with him during the short time he was here ; and all such no doubt would endorse our confident belief that he has changed the mortal and sickly for the immortal and glorious—the labour for the reward—the cross for a crown. Though his stay here was but short, his name will be long venerated as a faithful minister and a sincere Christian.

107. *North Wales Chronicle*, 14th February 1863

Alban was also something of an aspiring poet. He attended the National Eisteddfod which was held in Caernarfon from 26th to 29th August 1862. On Friday 29th over 100 "cantorion" trekked to the summit of Snowdon to watch the sunrise and then returned to Caernarfon for a Gorsedd and ordination ceremony. According to the Welsh newspaper Seren Cymru, Alban was ordained an Ovate and his bardic name was "Alban Allgo".

Within a couple of weeks, he was in the newspaper again, this time the North Wales Chronicle reported that on Sunday 7th September he had conducted an open-air service at St Eugrad's with between 200 and 300 attendees. Apparently, the church was a dilapidated wreck, and he was about to launch a fund-raiser to enable the church to be renovated. The service, conducted in Welsh, was designed to appeal to the generosity of the congregation gathered. The full story is in the chapter on church buildings.

Sadly, Alban would never see the church restored to its former glory. He was an asthmatic and suffered from chronic laryngitis. In early 1863 he was taken ill and left the island for Pwllheli from where he intended to go to South Wales to his family hoping that a change of scene would aid in his recovery. However, upon arrival in Caernarfon, he decided he was not well enough to go any further, and he checked into the Uxbridge and Royal Hotel. The surgeon Watkin William Roberts of Castle Street was in attendance when he died on 5th February 1863 from chronic laryngitis and asthma of nine days duration; he was only 34 years old. He was buried on 12th February in the parish of his birth, in St. David's & Holy Trinity Church, Henfynyw. The 14th February 1863 edition of the *North Wales Chronicle* reported on his death.

SALE AT THE RECTORY, LLANALLGO.

MR. W. DEW

Has been instructed by the Representatives of the late Reverend Alban Griffith, deceased,

TO SELL BY PUBLIC AUCTION,

On TUESDAY, 14th April, 1863, (commencing punctually a 12 o'clock at noon),

THE whole of the neat HOUSEHOLD FURNITURE, and other effects, comprising Mahogany Chairs, Sofas, Easy Chairs, Cheffoneer, Bookcase, Fender and Fire Irons, Carpets, Iron Bedseads, Mattresses, Feather Beds and Bedding, Mahogany and painted Chests of Drawers, Toilet Tables, &c., (the greater portion of which are new); Kitchen Furniture and Culinery Utensils ; an assortment of Glass and China ; a Select LIBRARY of BOOKS, and a few OUT of DOOR EFFECTS, consisting of a very useful Mare, steady in Harness (in foal), a light WHITECHAPEL, and an excellent set of Silver Mounted Harness, &c.

May be Viewed on the morning of Sale.

108. *North Wales Chronicle*, 4th April 1863

A few weeks later, his worldly goods were auctioned off, and the auction was reported in the North Wales Chronicle on 4th April 1863. For such a young man and widower, he had quite a bit of furniture. He left a Last Will and Testament, with effects under £450 and probate was granted to his brother the Reverend John Griffiths. I do wonder whether amongst his books was a copy of *Wild Wales* by George Henry Borrow which was newly published in 1862 and tells the tale of his journey to Llanfair ME in search of the home of Goronwy Owen.

James Morris, 1863 - 1874

James was born in the Summer of 1825 in Pont, Llanglydwen, Carmarthenshire to blacksmith David from Llanfyrnach in Pembrokeshire and Esther née Thomas from Llanwinio, Carmarthenshire. They were a nonconformist family who worshipped in the local Hebron Independent chapel where five-week-old James was christened on 10th September 1825. His elder brothers John and Caleb followed in their father's footsteps and became blacksmiths, but James was an accomplished scholar and attended Brecon Congregational Memorial College as a student of the clergy. On the 13th and 14th July 1852, James was ordained a Minister in connection with the Presbyterian church at Ynysgau where he served for three years.

He was very active in the local community and entered the Merthyr Tydfil Temperance Eisteddfod in 1852 with a composition on mental science and phrenology, a subject about which he was apparently quite passionate and opinionated. The Reverend Thomas Thomas of Pontypool judged the category and James won the second prize of £2. On 27th November the Cardiff and Merthyr Guardian reported on a meeting of the Young Man's Society: "*Some little excitement has prevailed among the members of this society in reference to the truth or falsehood of phrenology and arising from a paper on that subject read to the members by Reverend James Morris, the new minister of Ynysgau, who denied the soundness of the popular opinion.*" James was a sceptic but several of the members were believers and disputed the position he took on the subject. There followed a most lively discussion without a clear winner in the debate. Phrenology enjoyed great popular appeal well into the 20th century, but it has now been discredited by scientific research so James was ahead of his time on this one!

The temperance movement was taking off at that time and on the evening of Monday 6th June 1853, there was a meeting in Temperance Hall, Merthyr where Reverend C.P. Millea, a Roman Catholic priest from Dowlais, delivered a lecture to a "*numerous and highly delighted assembly.*" James was chairman for the evening and gained a great deal of respect that night. The newspaper said, "*In thus associating himself with a papal priest, he displayed more manliness than most of his brethren would have done, and we tender him our commendation.*" The writer went on to say that this is a time to unite all temperance reformers in hearty co-operations as drunkenness was perceptibly increasing and it behoves temperance reformers to be "*up and doing!*" Once again James was, perhaps, ahead of his peers.

In April 1855, Ynysgau chapel was celebrating its 50th anniversary, and a newspaper reported that the closing services were marked by an incident of a sudden and unexpected character, the public resignation of resident minister, the Reverend James Morris, who had by now been minister there for three years. Apparently, James went to the pulpit and announced his resignation then and there, without advance notice. The newspaper clipping is very faded, and it is difficult to make out much of the rest of it, but he was complimentary about his congregation and said that he was abandoning the dissent and joining the Church of England. It was in a newspaper article 100 years later covering the 150th anniversary of Ynysgau chapel that I found the reason for his resignation - he had met the love of his life who was a member of the Church of England, so he left his own church for that of his future wife.

His wife was Ann Kirkhouse, born in 1828 to Mineral Agent Henry and wife Barbara at Llwyn Celyn in Merthyr Tydfil. She and James were married in the church there on 17th April 1856 and their first child, Mary Esther Barbara, was born at the end of 1857 in Neath. Three more children were born in Glamorganshire when the family were living in Oakwood: Augusta Eliza in 1859, Henry Cranmer in 1861 and Alfred Tudor in 1863.

> **LLANALLGO.**
> On Sunday last the Rev. J. Morris, late of Oakwood, near Cwmavon, Glamorganshire, commenced his duties as rector of this and the adjoining parish of Llaneugrad. The congregation was but thin in the morning, but in the evening the venerable edifice was crowded by an attentive audience. After service was read a very powerful sermon was delivered, which proved that in this respect we have had in our new rector a worthy successor to the faithful minister of Jesus Christ which preceded him here for so short a time, the Rev. A. Griffiths. We sincerely hope that many years shall be given to Mr. Morris in happiness with his partner and increasing family, and that he will be the means, under Providence, of effecting much good in our neighbourhood.

109. North Wales Chronicle, 6th June 1863

The *North Wales Chronicle* of 6th Jun 1863 reported on his first service in Llanallgo and noted that he delivered a very powerful sermon.

A few notable events during James' tenure include the first group of Welsh emigrants setting sail for Patagonia on the *Mimosa* on 28th May 1865 but I have not come across anyone from our parishes on that first uncertain venture, but I am sure that James and our parishioners would have followed news of it very closely. The following year in the National Eisteddfod, a song titled *Hen Wlad Fy Nhadau* was sung and which would later become the national anthem and on 3rd June 1867, the Anglesey Central Railway was opened to passenger traffic on the almost 18-mile route from Gaerwen to Amlwch, making crossing the island very fast and convenient.

James and his wife settled down to life in rural Anglesey and had two more children in Llanallgo, Catherine Jane Kirkhouse in December 1864 and Bedlington Herbert "Howell" Kirkhouse in April 1868. He was kept busy with his parish work and also served as Vice-chairman of the Board of Guardians of the Anglesey Poor Law Union when Edward Richards Esq. of Ynys Fawr, Llandyfrydog was Chairman (Edward was the nephew of the Reverend John Richards who was a curate of Llanallgo and Llaneugrad.) Hel also played a key role with the lifeboat. The *North Wales Chronicle* reported on 23rd May 1868 that James *"has kindly undertaken the duties of honorary secretary to the Royal National Society's Lifeboat, stationed at Moelfre"*, succeeding the late Reverend William Williams, rector of Llanddyfnan. He also picked up where Alban had left off, raising money for the restoration of the dilapidated St Eugrad's. The work was completed by 3rd October 1868 when a Harvest Thanksgiving service was held there.

109a. William Williams

1868 was the year that the Llaneugrad lands, with the exception of Bodgynda and farms bought by Edward Richards of Ynys Fawr, were auctioned off by Hugh Robert Hughes, "HRH", of the Kinmel estate. William Williams bought 1140 acres and his nephew Robert Williams bought about 800 acres. William was the son of Sir John Williams, 1st Baronet of Bodelwyddan, and Margaret née Hughes, the heiress of Ty Fry, Pentraeth. William's first wife, Arabella née Pretyman died in June 1867 after 12 years of marriage and he then married Marian Scott in Thorpe, Surrey. She was the eldest child of Major-General Sir William Henry Scott of Thorpe House, Thorpe and Harriet Alethea née Stanley who was the daughter of Sir John Thomas Stanley, 1st Baron Stanley. William brought his bride to live in what is known as Old Parciau today whilst his mansion house was being built, and it was the first time since the days of Col. John Bodvel that the *Lord of Llaneugrad* lived in the parish. It was to be life-changing for the parishioners of Llaneugrad because it would trigger the development of the village of Marian-glas. 1868 was the last year in which all the Llaneugrad lands (more or less) were owned by a single individual. In the same auction, several local men were able to buy properties such as Griffith Williams who bought Ponc Yr Efail.

109b. Parciau Mansion House

By far the largest funeral ever held at Llaneugrad (or likely any of the nearby churches) was that of the Reverend John Phillips, who had done so much for education not only in Llaneugrad and Llanfair ME but in the whole of Wales. James had the honour of officiating at the burial of this great man who died on 9th October 1867 aged only 57, leaving his wife and five children. The North Wales Chronicle covered the event:

"FUNERAL OF THE REV. JOHN PHILLIPS. The mortal remains of the Reverend John Phillips, of Bangor, whose death it was last week our painful duty to record, were consigned, on Monday last, the 14th inst., to their last resting-place, in the small churchyard of the parish church of Llaneugrad. Mr Phillips was one of the ablest and most eloquent of Welsh preachers; his earnestness, his kindness, his stainless life, the strict integrity of his conduct, the zeal and activity with which he laboured in the cause of education, had endeared him to the hearts of the people; and wherever the sad tidings of his death, so sudden, so unexpected, was told, it created in the minds of every one the most profound sorrow for the loss of so beloved a minister, and the most heartfelt sympathy for his afflicted family.

It was announced that his funeral would be a public one; and many persons came from a distance to testify their respect to the memory of the deceased. In Bangor, where he resided, the loss of Mr Phillips was most severely felt. Everything wore the most gloomy aspect. People could hardly realize the sad fact that their highly esteemed fellow-citizen, who was so lately amongst them, was numbered with the dead. Everyone who could attend his funeral, resolved to do so. Every available conveyance in the town was speedily hired and many persons found the greatest difficulty in securing seats. Early in the morning of Monday, the day fixed for the funeral, vehicles of all descriptions poured forth from the city, and it is computed that no less than seventy-three conveyances in all passed-over the Menai Bridge up to ten o'clock that morning. The Normal College was emptied of its inmates, the students, about forty in number, being conveyed in the fine large omnibus which runs between Bangor and Bethesda, and which had been hired for the occasion.

The funeral took place at Llaneugrad, a small and secluded locality, distant about four miles from the towns of Llangefni and Llannerch-y-medd respectively. The roads (were they worthy of the name) leading to this remote and almost inaccessible corner of the island of Anglesey, are of the worst description, and on this day, they were especially dirty and filthy, on account of the late heavy rains. It had been arranged that the procession should start from Brynteg as soon after noon as possible. Between eleven and twelve the crowd of sympathising spectators received constant accessions, and the number of persons present at this time must have been between two and three thousand, many of whom had wended their way hither from a great distance. Soon after twelve the procession was formed, which was nearly a mile in length. But before it started, the Reverend Owen Thomas, of Liverpool, read a chapter of the Bible, most appropriate to the occasion, and offered up a short prayer. Reverend Dr Edwards, of Bala, also delivered a brief but feeling address. Both these eminent Welsh divines were deeply affected by the death of their intimate friend and fellow labourer in the vineyard of the Lord.

The funeral cortege then began its slow and solemn march to the churchyard. It was indeed an imposing, yet melancholy, spectacle. A long train of persons on foot, followed by the hearse with its jet-black plumes, and by a long train of carriages, stretching as far as the eye could reach, wended its way to the sequestered cemetery. The order of the procession was as follows: Mr Price and Mr Thomas-the Vice-Principal and Tutor at the Normal College. The students. The Marian-glas British School. Ministers of the Gospel-about sixty in number. Deacons. The Medical attendants—Dr Lloyd, Llangefni, and Dr Humphreys, Bangor. THE HEARSE. The Family of the deceased. About fifty-two carriages and several hundreds of people on foot. But the sky was overcast; the roads were in the worst possible state; and a drizzling rain still fell. The distance from the house to the church is about a mile. A little while, however, before the churchyard gate was reached, the rain ceased. At length the procession entered the churchyard. It is a churchyard used only occasionally for ages past, and of very small extent. The church itself is of a corresponding size. For some years past it has been in a very dilapidated condition but it is now undergoing some repairs, the funds being provided through the strenuous and disinterested exertions of the worthy rector, Mr Morris.

The Reverend James Morris, the officiating clergyman, took his stand by the side of the grave, which is enclosed by iron railings. The coffin was borne thither and lowered, amidst the sobs of relations and friends, into its appointed place. After a short pause, the Reverend James Morris proceeded in the most solemn and effective manner, to read the burial service. A hymn was next sung; and the Reverend Henry Rees, Moderator of the Connexion for the present year, briefly addressed the assembled people, saying, that after the beautiful service they had just heard, it would be unnecessary to make any further remark, were he disposed to do so; concluding by uttering a fervent prayer that the sad event would be blessed to his hearers, that they would remember that they too would soon be laid in the grave, and that the reflection would turn their hearts to the consideration of heavenly things while there was yet time. Another hymn was sung, and the solemn ceremony was brought to a close. Those of Mr Phillips's relations who were there gave a last farewell look into the vault. The bystanders did the same, and then turned their steps homewards. Five of Mr Phillips's children lie buried in the same vault. Mr Phillips seemed to have a fondness for this quiet rural graveyard, he used to visit it frequently when staying at Brynteg. He paid his last visit to this secluded spot about six or seven weeks before he was carried thither and laid with his children. The deceased had only just passed the meridian of life, yet the work which he accomplished was the work of no ordinary man of a life of no ordinary length. While yet in his youth, he entered with his whole soul into the good work of elevating the minds of his fellow-creatures and in leading their souls to Christ, he turned neither to the right hand nor to the left; he directed the roused energies of his countrymen into the proper channels; and under his guidance, the good work prospered. As was stated in our last, it is chiefly to his strenuous exertions that most of the British Schools in Wales owe their existence, as well as the Bangor Normal College, which forms one of the noblest ornaments of the city, and which shows, in the most effectual manner, what perseverance and determination can effect."

Neither Bangor Lodge nor the current road down to the church existed in 1867. The track or path to the church was a short way down Lôn Las from Bangor Lodge towards Brynteg. There was a gatehouse at the entrance, and the track was across what are now fields and woods to a walled entrance on the north-western side of the churchyard, the remains of which can still be seen today. The gatehouse was centuries old and originally called Greglas before becoming Tynllidiart y Greglas in the early 1800s and then Tynllidiart by the 1861 census time. Its occupants at the time of John Phillips' funeral were 38-year-old agricultural labourer Hugh Jones who was born in Marian Bach, Llaneugrad and his 37-year-old wife Sarah née Hughes who was born at Pen Y Graig, Llanfair ME and their young family. The month before the funeral in September 1867, John had been naughty and was caught poaching conies, an offence back then. His case came up at the 2nd of September Quarter Sessions where he was fined 2 shillings and sixpence or 14 days hard labour in Beaumaris Gaol. Whether he paid up or served his time, I do not know, but hopefully he was free when the funeral procession passed his house on that rainy day in October. What a spectacular sight it must have been for his daughters, Margaret age 12, Elizabeth age 8 and Grace age 5. Baby Mary was far too young to be able to remember, but I have to believe that the sight of this vast funeral procession stayed vividly in the minds of the three older girls for the rest of their lives. By the 1871 census, the family had moved to Cae Ysgawen, Llanfair ME and Tynllidiart was empty. It then fell into ruins and today not a single stone remains visible today to mark its location.

The Elementary Education Act was passed in 1870, and the government assumed responsibility for elementary education (ages 5 through 12). Locally administered boards were set up, and they took over the British schools, including the one in Marian-glas. There was great competition between the nonconformists and established church with regards to schools. The majority of people in our parishes now belonged to one of the so-called nonconformist religions, and the church saw the schools as a means to combat their dwindling congregations by influencing young minds to prefer the church. Whether this was the motivation or not, a new National school was about to be built in Llaneugrad. By an Indenture dated 27th March 1869, HRH conveyed for free about a quarter of an acre of a field called Cae'r Chwarel which was part of Tyddyn Cadwgan farm to the church for the purpose of building a school and schoolhouse. In 1871, James and William Williams of Parciau, together with the Bangor Church Extension Society, decided to go ahead with building the new school in. From the surviving documents, it seems that there were so many Llanfair ME children attending the Marian-glas school that there was not enough room for the Llaneugrad children, although I suspect that this might have been a "cover-up" for their religious motivation. At the time it was planned, the new school was also intended to be used for church worship because St Eugrad's was in such a dilapidated state. However, since the church had been renovated in 1868, I am also quite sceptical of this claim, as I find it hard to believe that it had fallen back into disrepair so soon after its recent restoration.

The location drew complaints from parishioners as it was inconvenient to the children of the lower parish of Llaneugrad. However, I would imagine that they wanted to have the school as far away from the British school as possible since the school inspectorate had been very critical of the proximity of the Llanallgo school to the British school given how lightly populated these parishes were. At the time the school was planned it was stated that the British school had a capacity of 15 and I believe this was the number of Llaneugrad children that could be accommodated rather than the total number of all children. In the School Board documents, various notes show that they were considering recommending merging several parishes together from a school perspective as well as recommending the relocation of the British school to Llanfair ME as most of the children attending were from that parish. For those with a further interest, Emyr Roberts has written a fascinating account of the struggle to establish the Tabernacl Board School in Ty'nygongl, and it can be found in the 2019 *Anglesey Antiquarian Society & Field Club Transactions*.

Yr Ysgol nad yw mwy

110. Photo Dated 1920 of Llaneugrad School from *Yr Arwydd*

The only photo I was able to find of the Llaneugrad school was dated 1920 and it was in an article in *Yr Arwydd* local newspaper written by Mr Alun Jones entitled "The School that is no More". The new Llaneugrad school was opened in 1873 and James had earlier thoroughly refurbished its sister school in Llanallgo which was reopened on 12th July 1872. In a later letter to the Board of Education, James stated that he hoped Llanallgo would be found to be an efficient school at the next inspection. Both schools he claimed were able to accommodate upwards of 87 pupils. It seems to me that whatever the political or religious whys and wherefores of what happened with the schools, the poor children of our two parishes were the clear winners, as they ended up with ample opportunity to find a place in school regardless of where they lived in the parish. A major challenge for the new Llaneugrad school, though, was to find a certificated teacher in order to be eligible for support by the local Education Board, and that proved to be a lot more difficult than James might have imagined. He would not have the chance to personally solve this challenge as he was promoted by the bishop in early 1874 and took up a new appointment in the parish of Cwm, St Asaph. The parishioners must have been very sad to learn that James was to leave Llaneugrad and Llanallgo and he performed his last services in our churches in February of 1874.

James served his new parish for just over 10 years and died on 28th July 1884 at his home after being in feeble health for many months and was buried in Cwm on 1st August. Anne died on 11th May 1887 and was buried on 16th May in the family vault.

The Congregationalist Minister, the Reverend John Lloyd Jones, who went by the pseudonym Clwydwenfro, wrote a piece for 5th August edition of the newspaper, Y Tyst titled *My Fellow Scholars*. The original Welsh version is in photo 11 and is a wonderful memory of James and roughly translates as follows. He remembers James as the son of Dafydd Morris, blacksmith, Pont Llanglydwen and learning Latin grammar. James went to Brecon College, and was ordained a minister in Ynysgau, Merthyr Tydfil. He then became a churchman, and was a priest in North Anglesey, and elsewhere afterwards.

He said that they used to go to where the Reverend W Griffith's widow and one or two of her daughters lived. There was tap water and a china cup always ready for a drink. One time, he and several others were in a hurry to get some water before going to school in the afternoon. He rushed to the cup, and drank from it, and gave it to another. This other person happened to let it slip from his hand and the cup fell and broke and he had left by that time. Mrs Griffiths complained about the broken cup to James Morris. James came into the school and to the two boys. He asked, "who broke the cup?" They both denied they had done it. "I want to know soon", James said. He went outside and came back in with three small twigs of wood of the same length. He compared them, and gave one to each of us, and placed the third in his Latin Grammar book, and said: "The twig of the one who broke the cup will grow taller than the others in a quarter of an hour. Each of us went to his place. After a quarter of an hour, he brought us together, and asked for our twigs. He compared them with his twig in the Latin book. Clwydwenfro's twig was the same length as that from the book, but that of William Davies, was shortened because the boy had broken off a piece of it. "You broke the cup" James said to Wil; and he had to admit and bring pennies the next day to pay for it. "There are many ways to kill a dog

111. *Y Tyst*, 5th August 1914

without hanging" said James, who had kept an eye on Wil, and saw him take out his knife and cut some of the wood. What a wonderful memory of the man and his character.

John Evans, 1874 - 1883

John was born on 16th November 1821 on Water St, Carmarthen to ostler Benjamin and his wife, Dinah née Davies. I could not find any information on how he entered the ministry, or his life in between, and the next record is a notice in the 13th of June 1874 edition of the *Leamington Spa Courier* announcing his appointment to our churches. Later that year an anniversary service was held for the re-opening of the parish church and opening of the Amlwch Port church at Amlwch, and according to the *Caernarfon and Denbigh Herald* dated 10th October, John delivered a very impressive sermon, preaching "very powerfully".

John took over the role of Honorary Secretary to the Moelfre lifeboat and, at the beginning of November, he gave a report to the newspapers on the first rescue by the brand-new lifeboat, the *Lady Vivian*. There was a dense fog and the barque, *Sarah M. Dudman* of Yarmouth, Nova Scotia was grounded on Dulas rocks and, for seven hours, was attended to by the lifeboat until a tug was secured from Holyhead to tow her to safety in Beaumaris where she was repaired. The *Vivian* was named after Lady Vivian who had raised the funds to build her and, slightly larger than her predecessor, was a self-righting type of boat. The coxswain at the time was Rowland Hughes who served for 34 years before retiring in 1884 at the grand old age of 82 and was awarded the R.N.L.I. silver medal for his service by the Prince of Wales in Marlborough House.

John's first task on the school front was to find a certificated teacher for Llaneugrad national school. By now the Board of Education were hounding he and the managers to get a trained teacher in place as it was so long after the opening without progress. At the request of the school managers, he wrote a letter to the Education Department on 22nd August 1874 to inform them that they were taking steps to hire a certificated teacher. There must have been some sort of confusion in the communication back to John from the Education Department, because William Williams of Parciau stepped in and wrote a letter on 31st October informing them that John had put the current school mistress on notice and had secured the services of a certificated teacher who would start at Christmas.

In his role as "owner" of the National school and chair of the managers, John provided a treat for the Llanallgo school pupils that was recorded in the *North Wales Express* 24th September 1880.

Mrs Williams Frondeg was Mary, the sister of Margaret who married mariner William Roberts Tyn Lôn and whose family built a whole corner of Marian-glas village. Mrs Williams Glanrafon (Isaf) was Elizabeth née Jones married to farmer Edward Williams. Miss Owen of Croes Allgo was Ellen, the granddaughter of Reverend Richard Lloyd who was rector of our churches from 1801 to 1830. Miss Williams of Tanyfron was Elizabeth, eldest daughter of Captain Owen Williams and his wife Margaret née Roberts of Dalar. Finally, the schoolteacher Mrs Roberts was Annie Barrett Bloom who married Robert Roberts born in

The Clergymen

> **LLANALLGO.**
>
> LLANALLGO NATIONAL SCHOOLS. — On Thursday, the 16th inst., the children attending the above school—120 in number—were entertained to a "tea treat" through the genorsity of the Rev J. Evans, rector of the parish, who very kindly presided at the meeting. Advantage was taken of the favourable weather by taking the children out in a procession to Marian Glas and back, calling on their return at the rectory, where they sang a choice selection of glees, &c. We need not enter into details respecting the way in which all was carried out. Suffice it to mention the names of the ladies who assisted at the tables, viz., Mrs Williams, Frondeg; Mrs Williams, Glan'rafon; Miss Owen, Croes Allgo; Miss Williams, Tanyfron; and Mrs Roberts, schoolmistress. In the evening, the children assembled together in a field kindly lent for the occasion by Mr Edward Williams, when they indulged in games and sports. In addition to this, Mrs Roberts gave them an additional treat in the form of fruit, nuts, &c. Before leaving the field, the children of one accord gave a hearty round of cheers to the Rev J. Evans and their teacher, Mrs Roberts. Great praise is due to all who took active part in conducting the affair in so satisfactory a manner. It will be a day long to be remembered by the children. The school is evidently increasing in number, the children evince an aptitude for learning which certainly is encouraging to their teacher, seeing by the result of the examinations that the teaching reflects such credit upon it.

112. North Wales Express, 24th September 1880

Liverpool. Annie was born in Lancaster and was a trained teacher, obtaining her certification in Warrington.

I do not know what John's opinion was about drinking on a Sunday, but on 27th August 1881, The Sunday Closing Act came into effect. It was notable because it was the first Act of Parliament since the Act of Union in the 1500s to apply ONLY to Wales. But apparently, it was not the whole of Wales because for some strange reason Monmouthshire was exempt. The Act was as a result of pressure by the Temperance movement and the nonconformist chapels, and it would last for the next 80 years. Many private social clubs sprang up in the towns because of the "dry Sundays" as they were not covered by the Act, so were allowed to serve alcohol. It was repealed in 1961 by the Licensing Act and local authorities could then poll residents on whether to continue the ban or not. The last poll was run in 1996 when every area of Wales voted to allow Sunday drinking.

The village of Moelfre dates back to at least medieval times, when that area by the coast consisted of two townships, Moelfre and Nant Bychan. Nant Bychan became a farm of around 60 or so acres, and Moelfre grew as a village around the coast. By the time John came to our parishes, Llanallgo parish was just over 400 people in 100 dwellings, about 50 – 60 of which were houses in and around the village. There were many mariners, fishermen, farmers, and various labourers as well a number of shops and tradespeople such as tailors and dressmakers, joiners, butchers, boot and shoemakers and there was a pub at Tanyfron, a grocer and draper at Croesallgo and a wool factory down by the beach. By 1881 there was a Post Office at Minydon which must have been very handy indeed as I don't know how far the nearest Post Office must have been before that, and there was even a car proprietor living on Penrhos terrace.

Llaneugrad was an entirely different kettle of fish. It was larger than Llanallgo - in the 1846 tithe report, 2695 of its acres were subject to tithes as compared with only 659 acres in Llanallgo. The village of Marian-glas did not exist when John took up his appointment, and alongside the common land known as *The Marian*, there was only a couple of houses (Bryn Eugrad and Grandies/Penmarian), the school and its associated house and four tiny cottages (Cae Eithin and three on the land that would become Pretoria Mount, Marianfa and

Gorphwysfa).

By 1881, several more houses had been built and the drapery shop, Bryn Hafod, was open as well as the bakery next to Bryn Eugrad. I am sure the bread was just as wonderful back then as it was when I grew up in the village, and it must have been quite a novelty to be able to buy ready-made loaves. Being a bachelor, John had a housekeeper, and in 1881 it was my 23-year-old first cousin (3 times removed), Jane Thomas, whose family were living in Sea View in Marian-glas, which was built by her joiner brother, William. Jane must have baked bread for John, but I do wonder if, after the bakery opened, she would walk up to the village on occasion to buy fresh from the oven to save her making her own.

> DEATH OF THE RECTOR OF LLANALLGO AND LLANEUGRAD.—With regret we announce the death of the Rev John Evans, rector of Llanallgo and Llaneugrad, which occurred on Tuesday, the 29th ult. The rev. gentleman's health had been indifferent for some time, and his death might be said to have been anticipated. In manners he was modest and unassuming, and in disposition amiable and agreeable; in short, he possessed sterling good qualities, and his death was deeply lamented by a large circle of friends. The funeral took place on Saturday at Llanallgo Churchyard, when the services, both in church and at the grave, were impressively read by the Rev R. Richards, Pen-rhosllugwy. The following were present at the funeral:—Dr Evans, Llanerch-y-medd; Dr Williams, Llangefni; Rev M. Robert, Llanddyfnan; Rev Mr Evans, Pentraeth; Rev Mr Davies, Llanerch-y-medd; Rev Mr Davies, Llandyfrdog; Rev Mr Evans, Amlwch; Rev R. Roberts, Amlwch; Rev James Smyth, Rhos-y-bol; Mr Prichard, Pen-rhosllugwy School; Mr Ellis, Llaneugrad School, &c.

113. *North Wales Express*, 15th June 1883

> LLANALLGO.—On Saturday last the mortal remains of the Rev. John Evans, the deeply-lamented rector of the parishes of Llaneugrad and Llanallgo, were laid aside three of his predecessors, in the ever-memorable churchyard of Llanallgo. The sublime service of the Church was impressively read by the vicar of Penrhosllugwy, the Rev. R. Richards; and as the body was being borne into the church, Handel's "Dead March" in Saul was played by Mr Ellis, organist of Llaneugrad. Eight clergymen of the deanery attended, and much regretted the sacred tie death had so ruthlessly torn asunder.— *Durum ! sed levius fit patientiâ.*

114. *North Wales Chronicle*, 9th June 1883

John passed away in the Rectory on 29th May 1883, and perhaps it was Jane who found him and fetched brother William to help, because it was William who registered John's death. He was a popular man with many friends. John was laid to rest in St Gallgo's in very good company next to the Reverends Stephen Roose Hughes and Robert Davies. His funeral was reported in the *North Wales Chronicle* on 9th June 1883. The Reverend Richard Richards was born in Blaenpennal, Cardiganshire, and he was living in Glanrafon Uchaf at the time.

Although his headstone and burial record state that he was 55, John was 61, but as he was not married and had no relatives in the area, I suppose his age was assumed, or perhaps he had passed himself off as younger than he was, it was by no means unusual for those times. I was unable to find out who the third predecessor is that aside him according to the newspaper article. He died intestate leaving £323 9s 6d with £196 7s left after payment of debts and funeral expenses. Administration was granted to his sister Mary Evans of 24 Davistown near Carmarthen who was one of the next of kin and the guarantors were Edward Williams of Glanrafon and the Reverend Richard Richards of Glanrafon Uchaf.

John Williams aka Glanmor, 1883 - 1891

John was christened on 11th August 1811 in Abergele, and his parents were William King, Gentleman and his "concubine", Elizabeth Parry. John adopted the surname Williams, but I do not know if he adopted his patronymic name, or whether his mother later married a Williams thereby giving him the Williams surname. In the 1841 and 1851 census records, farmer William King was living in Bagillt Hall with wife Margaret, and I assume (since the name is very unusual in that area) that this was John's father. According to an article in the Journal *Y Geninen* in 1898, John was born on the same day that he was christened, and Elizabeth was the daughter of William Parry of Bodoryn. One of John's books notes that William Parry of Bodoryn was a churchwarden. John was an intelligent boy, he attended teachers training college and became a schoolmaster until he was about 53 years old. In 1849 he was appointed master at the National school, Llangernyw, Denbighshire and in 1852 he moved to the Blue Coat school at Denbigh where he remained until 1859. From Denbigh he went to the National school at Gwersyllt until 1863 and on 31st October that year he was elected a member of the Royal College of Preceptors, London.

By this time, he had decided to pursue a career in the church, and had enrolled in St Bees theological college, Cumberland in 1863. He was ordained as a Deacon on Sunday 17th December 1865 and assigned the curacy of Christ Church, Whitehaven. On Sunday 23rd December 1866 he was ordained as a priest, continuing in Whitehaven. After spending two years there, he returned to his native Wales and to a post in Amlwch church where he spent three years, followed by a post in Ebbw Vale for 12 years from 1871. By now his health had deteriorated somewhat and the Bishop of Bangor appointed him to our churches in 1883. This was the fulfilment of one of his dreams according to a talk he had given a few years earlier as a visiting rector, when he expressed his great desire to move to a parish in North Wales. Now here he was and, according to the newspapers, the living was worth £250 a year which was quite an increase in income and very welcome as we shall see later.

John married Elizabeth Deer in St George's church Birmingham on 18th June 1854. She was the daughter of William Deer, a parish cleric, and I wonder if his father-in-law influenced his late-in-life career change. The couple had four children, Ifan in 1856, Mary Elizabeth in 1859, Rosa in 1866 and Emily Francis in 1868 and their three daughters moved with them to the Rectory in Llanallgo in 1883. Ifan, who had become an engineer/mechanic, moved to England where he lived for the rest of his life.

John chose his Bardic title after the district of his birth, Glan Y Môr, and abbreviated it to Glanmor. He was very famous for his literary works, as an adjudicator in the National Eisteddfodau and in his contributions to Welsh history. William Jones, foreman of The Traeth Bychan Quarries and Lay Reader, wrote a eulogy for him which was printed in the July 1891 edition of *Yr Haul,* and summarized his works as follows: "*Ancient and Modern Denbigh; Records of Denbigh and its Lordships; Town and Castle of Denbigh; Gwaith Glanmor; Carolau Priffeirdd Cymru; Hanes yr Eglwys yng Nghymru o ddyddiau Elizabeth I waered; Translation of parts of Tacitus and Cesar into Welsh; English Grammar, or the Peculiarities of the Celtic Tongue explained in English; Translation of some of the works of the S.P.C.K.; Cywyddau Nineveh; Castell Dinbych; Y Gloch Osper and other bardic and poetic pieces.*" To this I would add the awdlau (poems) Y Gwanwyn, Yr Eira and Diwedd y Cynhauaf. His works on the history of Denbighshire were an important contribution to the history of Wales in the Middle Ages and are considered his greatest achievement.

One contribution of his not mentioned in any of the pieces written about him, is to the National Library of Wales. The National Eisteddfod was held in Mold in 1873 and the newspapers reported a meeting held under the presidency of Reverend T.R. Lloyd (Estyn) during which Glanmor put forward a motion (seconded by Mr Isaac Foulkes of Liverpool), "*that it is desirable on many grounds that a National Library should be formed, consisting chiefly of rare books and manuscripts in the Welsh language, and in other languages, where they relate to Wales or its people.*" The motion was passed unanimously, and a provisional committee was appointed to adopt "*such preparatory measures as they may deem fitting, with a view to carrying out the establishment of a National Library.*" John was a member of the committee, and it began to ask for materials from all sorts of sources that would eventually populate the library, and they were initially stored at the University College Wales, Aberystwyth. There was no progress towards building a physical library, though, until the Royal Charter in 1907. Aberystwyth was chosen as the location over Cardiff, primarily because of the existing collections at the University there. King George V and Queen Mary laid the foundation stone on 15th July 1911, almost 38 years after the meeting of the Bards in Mold. I think John would be absolutely thrilled to see the library today and to know that I am only able to tell his complete story because of this library – their online newspapers and Journals have been instrumental in piecing together the story of his life.

There were several meetings of the Bards at that Eisteddfod, and one in particular was attended by John where he played a prominent role in a discussion on the use of "f" and "ff" in the Welsh language, which was seen by the attendees to "*throw an unnecessary difficulty in the way of Englishmen and Welshmen reading the two languages.*" After an exhaustive debate, it was approved that there should be a return to the ancient usage of "v" for the single "f" and "f" for the present "ff" in Welsh. They concluded that "*we may, therefore, expect to see the use of the "v" instead of "f" become common, by degrees in Wales, especially among our young rising literati.*" I do not believe that this ever caught on, but if it did, I stand corrected!

Elizabeth died on 24th September 1885 aged 57 and was buried in St Gallgo's. The Rural Dean the Reverend H. Thomas and Reverend Richard Richards of Penrhosllugwy conducted the service. John was 17 years older than his wife, and his health must have continued to deteriorate during his three years in our parishes because, when he attended the National Eisteddfod in Caernarvon in 1886, a newspaper article read "*Glanmor, an aged clergyman, almost too feeble to walk, was assisted to the logan, and in tremulous and touching accents delivered some beautiful lines in which he besought the Creator to impart dignity to the ceremonies of the gorsedd: Duw ar weddi derwydd, Rhodda widedd i widdai hon*". The writer noted that "*the alliterative charm of the Welsh cannot be reproduced with fidelity in English.*"

His health cannot have been helped by what must have been a very traumatic and distressing experience earlier that same year. He had to attend Bankruptcy Court on Thursday 11th March 1886 for public examination. At the time he owed £288.1s.5d and had £90 in assets, including £60 in furniture. He said the cause of his situation was the fact that he was not earning enough as curate of Ebbw Vale to support his large family, pay for his wife's prolonged illness and death as well as the permanent incapacity of his daughter (Mary Elizabeth) who was an epileptic. His Ebbw Vale salary was only £120 without a house, or any extra fees and the accumulated debts were for *"articles of household consumption"*. His gross income from his current living was £195 and, if it were to be sequestered, there would be a surplus of about £30 available for the creditors.

Under examination, he said that *"he had been greatly deceived in the value of the living of Llaneugrad, and also in not receiving a grant from the Corporation of the Sons of the Clergy towards the education of his children."* The Registrar asked him if, after giving them this expensive education, had his children not helped him. He replied no, and that his son was a mechanic and was paid when orders come in, but work was slack at the time. Glanmor had received £68 worth of furniture on leaving Ebbw Vale and had bought a piano on the "hire system" with one last instalment of thirty guineas to make. He was asked how he had come into debt in Llanallgo and replied that he had to pay upwards of £100 out of his income to settle debts from Ebbw Vale. He had also borrowed £35 from a Birmingham money lender to whom he had to repay £50, and the Receiver noted that he had already paid back more than he borrowed and hoped this would *"be a warning to other persons against going to this class of persons for loans"*. He was then asked about his writing and said that he wrote for magazines and periodicals such as the new historical edition of *Yr Haul*. The Receiver responded, *"it is generally admitted that contributions to religious papers published in Wales are paid for at the resurrection of the just"* which was met with laughter and the questioner, a creditor, said *"then these will never be paid for"*. He had received less than £5 a year for the last three years for literary labour and he had received 200 copies of his book *The Records of Denbigh* as payment from the publisher, but he was able to sell very few of them. He also wrote *The Church in Wales,* but that book did not sell very well either. He also wrote a book on the grammar of the Welsh language, for which he was to be paid £20, but it is not published as the publisher believed it to be *"too much of a digest and not elementary enough."* The proceedings were then closed, and I do not know how it this ended for him. How sad to think that he was put through something like this and was not able to profit from his wonderful contribution to Welsh literature and historical works.

It is interesting that he says in the bankruptcy hearing that he had been "greatly deceived" in the value of the Llaneugrad living. I could not imagine that the bishop had fibbed about the prospective income, but a newspaper article in 1886 gives a clue as to how Griffith might view things that way. *Y Genedl Gymreig* published attendance numbers for the Anglesey churches for the 19th December morning service. There was a single service held and, out of a population of 534, only four people attended the service. Having such a small congregation would reduce the value of the living, so perhaps they omitted to tell him and perhaps hoped that he could attract more people back to the church.

Despite the financial hardship, he was a generous man and on the last Friday in August 1886 he hosted the children of the Llaneugrad and Llanallgo Sunday schools for their half-yearly tea party at the Rectory according to the 11th September *North Wales Chronicle*. I wonder if the children behaved remarkably well because of the presence of some of the mothers.

> LLANALLGO SUNDAY SCHOOL.—On the last Friday in August the children of the Llanallgo and Llaneugrad Sunday School were, through the hospitality of the rector, the Rev. J. Williams, Glanmor, entertained to their half-yearly tea party at the Rectory. A very pleasant afternoon was spent, although the day was too rainy for them to enjoy themselves on the beautiful grounds as usual after tea. They were addressed by the rector and superintendent, Mr E. Roberts, Nant Bychan, on the duty of attending Church regularly and the singing class, and warned against the sin of untruthfulness, the use of profane language, disobedience to parents, and neglect of morning and evening prayer at home. Several hymns and songs were sung by the children, who devoutly joined in prayer at the close. The children behaved remarkably well; some of the mothers were present, as well as the teachers, viz., the Misses R. and E. F. Williams, rectory; Miss Owen, Croesallgo; Mrs Roberts School House; and Mr E. Roberts, Nant Bychan.

115. *North Wales Chronicle*, 11th September 1886

As an educator, John would have been pleased to see the major progress in furthering higher education. On the 18th of October 1884, the University College of North Wales in Bangor opened in the former Penrhyn Arms Hotel and in 1888, it was the first British university to start an agricultural department. The Welsh Intermediate Education Act was passed on 12th August 1889, about a dozen years before similar legislation in England. The intention was simple: "*to make further provision for the intermediate and technical education of the inhabitants of Wales and the county of Monmouth.*" A pathway now existed for children to become engineers, surveyors, clerks, technicians, and other professions, via schools known as the County Schools, and the children from Llanallgo and Llaneugrad who qualified, would attend the one in Llangefni.

In the Llaneugrad parish burial register, entry number 314 has been left blank. The entry before it is dated 12th May 1890 and entry after it is dated 27th of September 1890. When I first saw this a few years ago, I assumed that it was unintentional, and that the rector had probably simply forgotten to complete the entry. I now realize that this could not have been the case. Little one month old Elizabeth Thomas of Henefail was buried on the 27th, and John deliberately left a record blank before recording her burial. As I was researching the stories of the men named on the Marian-glas and Moelfre War Memorials, I came across a likely answer – it was perhaps the burial of a woman who ended her own life. The following is her story.

Griffith Thomas of Bro Dawel in Moelfre, was killed on 3rd October 1942 on the SS Lycaon. His parents, grandparents and great grandparents lived at Tafarn y Wrach, situated on the corner of Lôn Las and the Llannerch-y-medd road next to what is Eugrad House today. It was one of the older properties in the parish and built on what was originally common land. By its name, it was some sort of Tavern at one time, but by the late 1880s it was a smallholding with just about 3 acres of land. Griffith's grandparents were Richard Jones born in Penrhosllugwy and Margaret née Parry born in Llanfairfechan and, after their marriage in Llaneugrad church in 1836, Richard and Margaret lived in Tafarn y Wrach with a Griffith

The Clergymen

Parry, who was most likely Margaret's grandfather. Richard started out life as a tailor, but by the 1851 census he was working the land and then by 1871 he was a pig butcher. They had nine children in the tiny house, and their youngest child, Margaret, was born in 1853. She married a local man, Owen Thomas, who was born in Llaneugrad in 1848, and they lived with her parents.

Owen was a labourer, and she was a seamstress, so she had her own income, which was rare for a wife at that time. The couple had three children: Ellen in 1878, Griffith Parry in 1880 (he died in WWII) and Edward Ellis in 1882. Owen became ill with tuberculosis and died on 10th October 1884, leaving Margaret with their three young children. Margaret did not re-marry and continued living with her widowed father at Tafarn y Wrach. It must have been financially very difficult for her, although I imagine that her father would have helped her out, and she likely received support from the Poor Union. She appeared to manage for a few years, but her circumstances must have changed, because on 13th August 1890, she made her way to the outhouse and hung herself. The inquest was held on 16th August, and the jury decided that it was "suicide during temporary insanity" and noted that it was as a result of money worries. She was only 37 years old, and her children were 8, 10 and 11.

After her death, her father and youngest son Edward Ellis went to live with her married sister, Jane Cox, in Bangor. The eldest two children stayed in Llaneugrad and were taken in by her sister Mary who had married farmer and grocer, John Jones, son of blacksmith Hugh Jones of Llaneugrad. John had built a house and shop next to Tafarn y Wrach which he named Eugrad House, presumably because the land was owned by the church. The Tafarn y Wrach house was left empty, and the name was no longer used, I would imagine for superstitious reasons.

The family grave in St Eugrad's has had a new headstone erected since the Memorial Inscriptions of the cemetery were recorded in 1990. The earlier headstone was in the memory of Margaret and Richard, their baby daughter Elizabeth who died in 1842 and their four sons who all drowned: Edward and Richard were both 19, Griffith was 36 and John was 29. The new headstone is also in memory of Margaret, Griffith Parry of Tafarn y Wrach and Griffith Parry of Tyn Lon, Llanddyfnan, Margaret's daughter Ellen whose son, William Owen Jones, and grandson, John Jones, were both killed in WWII serving on the Atlantic convoy.

I am fairly sure that Margaret is buried in St Eugrad's, and I hope she is with her husband. The ancient tradition of burying suicide victims at crossroads with a stake in their hearts was long gone, and an Act passed in 1823 allowed them a private burial in a churchyard, but only between 9 pm and midnight, and without a Christian service. Another Act in 1882 allowed the burial to take place during daylight hours and with the usual religious rites, but it is possible that John might not have agreed or been comfortable with this new Act and, given that suicide was illegal (Parliament did not decriminalise suicide until 1961), perhaps this is the reason he left this entry blank. Whatever the reason, he took it to his grave with him.

A week before John's death, the 1891 census was taken, and it was the first time in a census that the question was asked about which language the individual spoke. Across Wales

54.4% (1,685,614 people) were able to speak Welsh, but it was a different story in rural Anglesey. Out of 433 people in Llanallgo, there was only a single English speaker – 42-year-old Alfred Tucker who was born in Chatham, Kent was living in Pen Y Bonc. He had married Annie, daughter of mariner John Jones from Amlwch and his wife Jane who was from Llanallgo. It is interesting that although Annie could speak both Welsh and English, her parents and brother, who was living at home, could only speak Welsh. In fact, there was only 12 people in Llanallgo parish that could speak both English and Welsh, so communication for him must have been a bit of a challenge. With so few English speakers around him, I would have thought that he would make the effort to learn Welsh, but ten years later according to the 1901 census, Alfred could still only speak English.

Out of 285 people in Llaneugrad, there were ten who spoke only English, and all but two of them lived in the mansion house at Parciau. One of those was 14-year-old Margaret Elizabeth Percival, who had been born in Liverpool and then come to Anglesey to live with her maternal grandparents but was now living with her Aunt Elizabeth Jones in Tyn Lon, Godrefi. Margaret married a local Welsh man, and by 1901 was also a Welsh speaker. The other person was the manager of the Traeth Bychan Quarries, Francis Young from Cadoxton, Glamorganshire, who was there for only a short time and by 1901 had moved away. In Parciau, William Williams could speak both languages, but his wife Marian spoke only English, and they had brought up their three children, Margaret, Rosamond, and Lawrence to speak only English. Of the household staff, the butler was English as was the children's governess and two ladies' maids, and all other household staff were bilingual. Llaneugrad also had a higher proportion of bilingual residents than Llanallgo with 44 residents able to speak both languages. Bryn Hafod stores was run by sisters Catherine and Mary Ackerley who were both born in Liverpool, and who had come to Marian-glas with their mother Elizabeth née Williams who was born and raised in Figin Fawr. She had brought her daughters up to speak Welsh, which was a necessity when running a shop supporting the local community of primarily Welsh-speakers. Because Marian Williams was English and her family gave financially generous support to both churches, John must have needed to conduct church services in both English and Welsh.

He passed away on 12th April 1891 aged 80 and was buried on the 17th in St Gallgo's with his wife. The website archive.org has the book *Gwaith Glanmor* published in 1865 of his earlier works, and which is free to access, and a print book can be bought on Amazon. One particularly famous poem that I very much enjoyed is Twll Bach Y Clo, so I have included it together with an English version that I very loosely "translated" with poetic licence, because as many of you may know, Welsh poetry is impossible to translate verbatim into English:

DEATH OF GLANMOR.—The death is announced, at an advanced age, of the Rev J. Williams, rector of Llaneugrad cum Llanallgo, Anglesey, parishes well known in connection with the wreck of the Royal Charter. The deceased was ordained in 1865, and preferred to the living, which is in the gift of the Bishop of Llandaff, in 1883. He was well known in Welsh literary circles as Glanmor, and was the author of several historical works bearing upon the Principality, including "The Records of Denbigh."

116. *North Wales Express*, 1st May 1891

TWLL BACH Y CLO

'Roedd cap-nos o eira ar goryn pob bryn,
Y rhew wedi gwydro pob ffos-ddw'r a llyn,
'R oedd Gweno'n gweu 'sanau wrth oleu tân glo,
A Huwcyn yn gweled drwy dwll bach y clo.

Y gath oedd yn cysgu yn dorch ar ei mat,
A'r tad yn pesychu wrth sugno ei gat,
Y fam oedd yn ffraeo, fel dynes o'i cho',
A Huwcyn yn clywed drwy dwll bach y clo.

Yr hen wraig yn synnu fod Gweno, mewn gwangc,
Mor wirion a charu rhyw leban o langc,
A Huwcyn yn gwybod mai hwnnw oedd o,
A'i galon yn crynnu wrth dwll bach y clo.

Y tad aeth i'w wely i'r lloft oedd uwch ben,
A'r fam roes agoriad y drws dan ei phen,
Ond Gweno arosodd i huddo'r tân glo,
A disgwyl am lythyr drwy dwll bach y clo.

'R oedd cŵyn y dylluan fel bwgan mewn coed,
A'r cî bach yn cyfarth wrth glywed sŵn troed,
A Huwcyn yn diangc fel lleidyr ar ffo,
'R ol d'weyd gair yn ddistaw drwy dwll bach y clo.

Cyn pen y ddwy flynedd 'r oedd Gwen Jones yn wraig,
A Huw Jones yn hwsmon I Ffowcs, Tan-y-graig,
A chanddynt un plentyn, y clysa'n y fro,
Ac arno 'n faen-geni lun twll bach y clo.

THE LITTLE KEYHOLE

The snow on the hilltops, a night-cap did make,
The ice had glazed over every pond and lake,
Gweno knitted some socks by the fire of coal
And Huwcyn was watching this through the keyhole.

The cat fast asleep on the mat she did lay,
The father was coughing on his pipe of clay,
The mother was complaining, as was her role;
Huwcyn could hear this through the little keyhole.

Gweno, the old lady lamented in woe,
Was silly to love such an awkward young beau,
And Huwcyn well knew that this youth it was he,
His heart was pounding by the hole for the key.

The father retired to the loft overhead,
And Mother put the door key under her head,
But Gweno stayed downstairs to cover the coals,
Waiting for a note through the little keyhole.

The owl gave a hoot like a ghost in the trees,
The dog barked at footsteps he heard on the breeze,
Like a thief on the run, away Huwcyn stole,
After hushed words said through the little keyhole.

Before two years were up, Gwen Jones was a wife,
Hugh Jones was a worker on farm Tan-y-graig,
And they had one child, the prettiest of all,
And on it was a birthmark - a little keyhole!

Griffith Bees Jones, 1891 - 1899

Griffith's middle name is a most unusual one and he was not born with it but adopted it later in life. I wonder if it was from someone he admired, St Bees theological college or possibly from a hobby/side-business. We shall probably never know. He was born Griffith Jones in 1832, and in early census records gives Llannerch-y-medd as his birthplace and in later ones it is Amlwch. According to his marriage certificate, his father was William Jones and, examining the records for those facts, there is only one possibility for his parents and that is William Jones who was born in Llanfihangel TB, and Martha née Evans born in Amlwch. At the time of the 1841 census, they were living at Bryn Moel in Amlwch and by 1851 had moved to Llanfechell.

Although he grew up in a church-going family, and was christened in Amlwch church on 17th March 1832, he first became a Baptist minister. In the 1861 census, he was a visitor staying with 70-year-old Elizabeth Thomas of Llanfihangel Ysceifiog. When he married 35-year-old widow Ann "Annie" Griffith on 31st August 1868 in Llanfair-is-gaer church, he was a Scripture Reader and Annie was a Grocer. She was born in Cowbridge, Glamorgan and had a four-year-old daughter, Anne Elizabeth, when they married. He was still a Scripture reader at the time of the 1871 census, and they were living at 20 Snowdon St, Llanfair-is-gaer. He then resigned from the Baptist religion to take up a career in the church and was ordained a Deacon in Bangor by Bishop James Colquhoun Campbell on Sunday 21st

February 1875 and was assigned to the church of Llanbeblig. He was a Literate, so he did not have a degree, but was judged by the bishop to have the required knowledge. He stayed in Llanbeblig until March 1879, when he was licenced to the curacy of St David's, Mountain Ash, Glamorganshire.

Later that year he had quite a traumatic experience which was reported in the 4th October edition of the *Weekly Mail*. The cottage he and Annie moved to was known locally as Petherick Cottage, although its official name was Penrhiw Pennar. It was a very isolated house about a mile from Mountain Ash in a lonely spot beside the road that leads over the mountains to Merthyr, and it was the former home of James Petherick. He was a younger brother of the famous Welsh explorer of Africa, John Petherick, whose reputation fell into tatters after he had a huge quarrel with the Captains Speke and Grant. It was over help he was supposed to be giving them on their quest for the Holy grail of African exploration – to find the head of the Nile. James, a bit of a recluse, lived in the cottage with his wife Mary and was known locally as the "Hermit of the Mountain". He would dress in rustic garb, carry a long staff and, with his fine white beard streaming in the wind, would walk about studying the local flora and fauna. He died in 1865 and his wife then moved in with relatives.

Griffith was out in his garden one Saturday evening when a man called Michael O'Neill walked by and demanded some lettuces. When Griffith told him he had none, Michael refused to leave. Griffith then threatened to set his dog on him, and Michael turned to walk to the gate with Griffith following behind. As they reached the gate he turned around and walloped Griffith violently on the head with a pair of work boots he was carrying inflicting a nasty wound that began gushing blood. Michael then made off up the road with Griffith in hot pursuit, but he wasn't able to catch up with him. Luckily, at that very moment, Lord Aberdare appeared with some of his family on horseback and, upon hearing about the attack, they went after O'Neill, captured him, and took him to the police station. The trial was reported in the newspapers and Michael was sentenced to one month in prison with hard labour.

Griffith was ordained as a priest on Sunday 9th March 1884 in Llandaff Cathedral by the Bishop Richard Lewis, and he continued his service in Mountain Ash until May 1891 when he was appointed rector of our churches. He and Annie moved to the Rectory in Llanallgo, and it was his great desire to finish his days on Anglesey, so he was very happy about his new appointment. There was a ceremony for him in St Gallgo's on 26th May 1891 at two o'clock, and Archdeacon Pryce presided in the absence of the bishop. Among others, the attendees were J. Rice Roberts of Tan y Graig, Pentraeth, Margaret and Rosamond Williams of Parciau and the daughters of Glanmor.

Griffith seemed destined to attract trouble and had a very unusual event occur during his first Christmas night service in St Gallgo's - half-way through the service a donkey came into the church! The newspapers had a field day reporting this and one of them carried the headline "*A DONKEY IN AN ANGLESEY CHURCH. Alleged Scandalous Act of Desecration.*" Whilst many in the audience were reduced to uncontrollable laughter, poor Griffith was extremely shaken and was "*so disconcerted that he was unable to proceed with the service"* according to one newspaper. He brought charges against the suspects, a group of four youths who lived in Llaneugrad, and the case was heard at the Menai Bridge Petty Sessions on Monday 1st February 1891. I looked at the census for that year to try and fathom who these lads were, and could name 18-year-old Griffith Williams of Ponc Refail, 19-year-old Owen Thomas of Cefn Du (brother of my great-grandmother Keturah Thomas) and 13-year-old Hugh Hughes who was born in Henefail and was living and working at Tyn Lôn Godrefi. There was also an Owen Parry, but I was not able to prove who he was, but a good possibility is 13-year-old Owen of Rockhouse. Testimony was taken from different witnesses, and it turned out that the teenagers had gone to Moelfre on Christmas day and drank some beer. On the way back they came across a stray donkey in the road near the church that they decided to chase with a view to getting a ride on it. There were differing opinions as to whether the church door was closed shut or partially open, but the lads' story was that the donkey raced through the church gate towards the door and pushed its head into the church without any help from them and, when they saw the donkey enter the church, they ran away. Members of the congregation had pushed the donkey back out of the church and had heard the lads running away. The lads' side of events held up and the case was dismissed, but what actually came out of this in the end was that the police were charged with investigating why these teenagers had been served beer on Christmas day. I imagine that Griffith made sure the church door was well and truly closed for every other service he conducted there!

When he took over, St Gallgo's was in quite a dilapidated state and Glanmor had been raising funds with a view to refurbishing it, so Griffith finished the fundraising and restoration; the full story is in the chapter on the church buildings. The Llanallgo National School was also in a dilapidated state when Griffith arrived, and an attempt was made by the Llanallgo parish ratepayers to establish a School Board and move the school to Moelfre village. Mr Joseph Parry of Pant Y Gaseg was assistant Overseer for the parish, and he corresponded directly with the Board of Education (BOE). The letter dated 30th November 1891 lays out the compelling case for the move from the viewpoint of the Llanallgo ratepayers. The school files in the National Archives include copies of various correspondence over the next few years, and it appears that E.J. Watts was handling the matter for the BOE. They doubted the wisdom of moving the school to Moelfre especially in light of the fact that it also supplied a portion of Llaneugrad parish. E.J. found it to be *"phenomenal"* that the Llanallgo ratepayers wanted a Board when just about every other parish that had one would be glad to be rid of theirs and felt that there *"might be a little mystery here"*. They also recommended that they pay a visit to the parish at the time of the next school inspection and provide further advice after that. The file does not contain documentation of a resolution; however, Griffith did go ahead and refurbish the existing National School and we know that the new Llanallgo Council school built a few years later was just beyond the roundabout on the Benllech road and it would not be until the 1970s that a school would be built in Moelfre village.

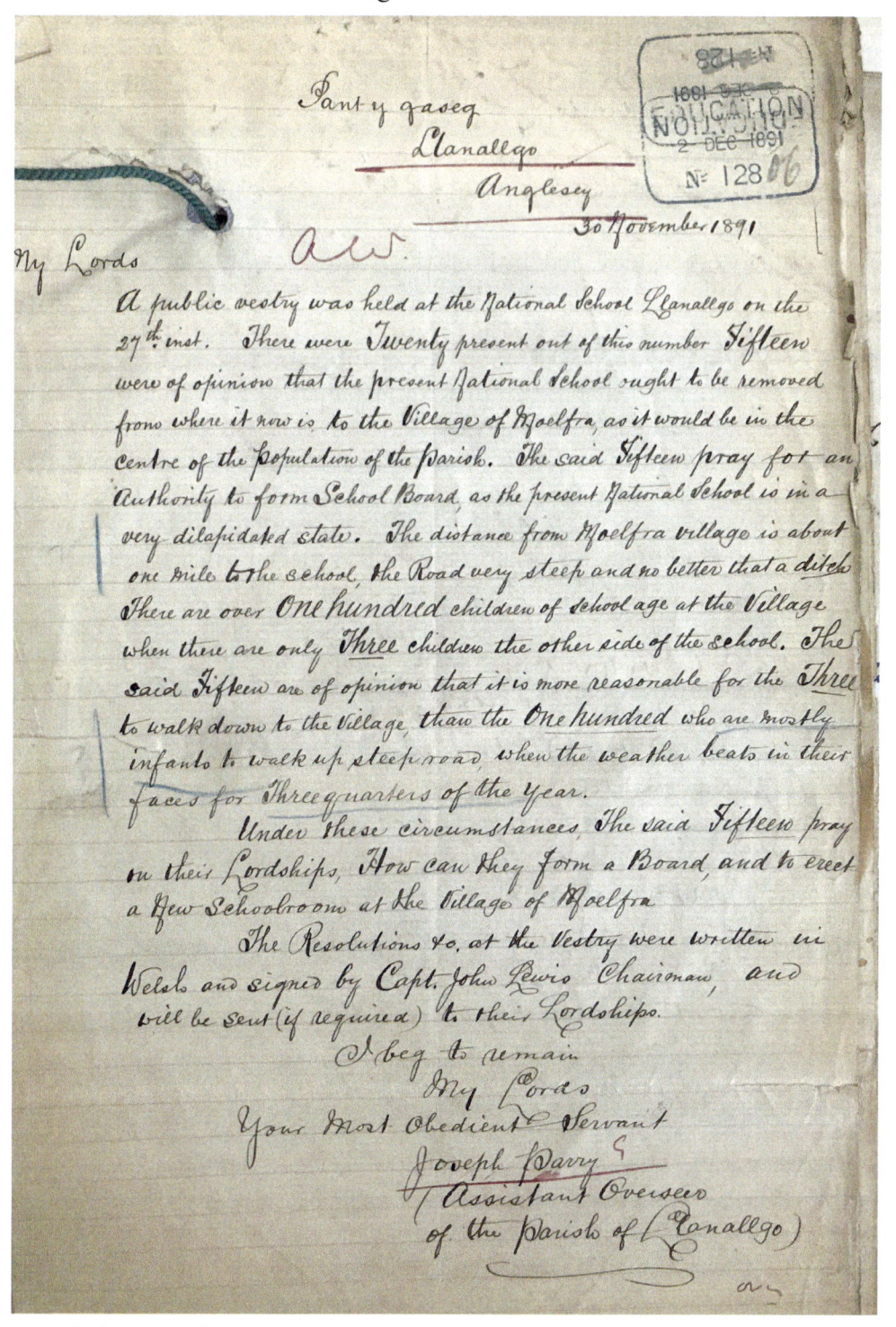

> Pant y gaseg
> Llanallgo
> Anglesey
> 30 November 1891
>
> My Lords
>
> A public vestry was held at the National School Llanallgo on the 27th inst. There were Twenty present out of this number Fifteen were of opinion that the present National School ought to be removed from where it now is to the Village of Moelfra, as it would be in the centre of the population of the parish. The said Fifteen pray for an Authority to form School Board, as the present National School is in a very dilapidated state. The distance from Moelfra village is about one mile to the school, the Road very steep and no better that a ditch. There are over One hundred children of school age at the Village when there are only Three children the other side of the school. The said Fifteen are of opinion that it is more reasonable for the Three to walk down to the village, than the One hundred who are mostly infants to walk up steep road, when the weather beats in their faces for Three quarters of the year.
>
> Under these circumstances, The said Fifteen pray on their Lordships, How can they form a Board, and to erect a New Schoolroom at the Village of Moelfra.
>
> The Resolutions &c. at the Vestry were written in Welsh and signed by Capt. John Lewis Chairman, and will be sent (if required) to their Lordships.
>
> I beg to remain
> My Lords
> Your most Obedient Servant
> Joseph Parry
> Assistant Overseer
> of the Parish of Llanallgo

117. Letter from Joseph Parry to the Board of Education, 30 November

Griffith also refurbished the Llaneugrad National School and built a "commodious" house for the Llaneugrad schoolmaster. When he submitted the initial house plans to the Education Department, the verdict was that the house could be built as long as the staircase was made "less dangerous". The house was just about complete and ready to be moved into at the time of his death. He had raised £120 but there was a shortfall of £70 which fell to his successor to raise.

I am sure that a lot of praying went on in St Gallgo's as well as all of the chapels in Moelfre and Llanallgo for the life of two little boys who were literally "blown up" (quite accidentally) by their father on New Year's Day 1892. John Matthew, the longest serving Coxswain of a lifeboat in his day, and his brother Richard Lloyd Matthew, were the boys in question. Their grandfather, Israel Matthew, was one of the 29 heroes who rescued the survivors of The Royal Charter, and perhaps it wasn't only people that Israel rescued that stormy night... Thirty-three or so years later, his son Richard (the boys' father), a butcher who had married Margaret Pritchard from Penrhosllugwy, had a catastrophic accident. Perhaps it was a classic case of "when the cats away, the mice will play" because Margaret was not at home at the time. The family lived in Bay View and Richard had reportedly inherited a barrel of gunpowder from The Royal Charter (perhaps from his father.) For whatever reason, he decided to test it out to see if it still worked. His boys were with him and Margaret's 80-year-old father, William, was in the kitchen. Richard left the cask with the rest of its contents in the house and placed a small amount of powder by the door and set it on fire. Suddenly, the flames caught the cask and there was an almighty explosion. The roof of the cottage was blown clean off, every pane of glass was blown out and shattered and all the timber of the doors were blown into matchwood. Richard was thrown about 10 yards across the street and escaped with no injuries other than badly burned hands. His sons were standing in the doorway at the time and were "much injured" with John not expected to survive. Luckily Margaret's dad was uninjured and thankfully Richard Lloyd made a full recovery, eventually becoming a Congregational minister in Caernarfonshire. I have to imagine that even with everyone surviving the ordeal, poor Richard must have been "in the doghouse" for quite some time after that. As an aside, John's sister Ellen married mariner William Evans of Penrallt, Moelfre, and their son would become another great hero of the lifeboat - Richard Matthew "Dic" Evans - who succeeded John as Coxswain, proving that bravery and heroics definitely run in that family.

Other major events that happened during Griffith's tenure include the death of 87-year-old William Williams of Parciau on 18th August 1892. He was buried in St Eugrad's on 22nd August and Griffith officiated, together with William's nephew, Archdeacon Watkin Herbert Williams of Bodelwyddan who later became Bishop of Bangor. William's son, Lawrence, was only 16 at the time, and would have to wait until he was 21 before he would inherit the estate and become the next (and last) *Lord of Llaneugrad*. Whether Griffith was a rugby union fan or not I do not know, but when Wales won the Triple Crown for the first time in 1893, I am sure that many of the parishioners were fans and very happy about this

DEATH OF THE RECTOR OF LLANALLGO.

Welsh Churchmen will learn with sincere regret of the death of the Rector of Llanallgo (the Rev. G. Bees Jones), an event which took place on Thursday at his residence in Anglesey. The deceased gentleman had been ailing for some time, and it became apparent to his friends that his constitution, which was never very robust, was breaking up. Mr. Jones was a native of Anglesey, his birthplace lying within a short distance of Llanallgo. He was ordained in 1875 to the curacy of Carnarvon, and in 1879 became Welsh curate of Mountain Ash, where he laboured with much success and to the great satisfaction of his parishioners until 1891. In that year he was promoted by the Bishop of Llandaff to Llanallgo, where he felt very happy, and did much excellent work as a parish priest and by restoring the Parish Church and two national schools, and building a commodious house for the schoolmaster. Mr. Jones was a good Welsh preacher, always in great request on popular occasions, especially at harvest-thanksgiving services and in Lent. He was a robust nationalist, though circumstances compelled him to employ English to a certain extent at Llanallgo. His parish, it may be added, was the scene of the shipwreck of the Royal Charter, and scores of the recovered bodies of men and women drowned on that memorable occasion sleep their last sleep in the well-kept little churchyard of Llanallgo.

118. Evening Express, 18th February 1899

Express on 18th February. He was laid to rest in St Gallgo's, and the funeral was held on 23rd February at 9am. Griffith must have made a great impact on the parishioners to have a crowded church with many scores unable to get in. To have 19 clergymen present was also a very high honour indeed, and it reflects the fact that he was very well respected amongst his colleagues.

Annie arranged to sell the things that she either did not want or could not take with her and the public auction was conducted by Messrs Hughes and Jones on Wednesday 29th March.

achievement. The Snowdon Mountain Railway was completed on 6th April 1896, but sadly, on its inaugural trip, the engine came off the track and a man ultimately died after jumping from the train and breaking a leg, and operations were stopped for a year to investigate and correct the problem.

Griffith's last Sunday service was on the first Sunday of Advent, 27th November 1898, and it was apparently a great sermon indeed according to *Y Clorianydd* newspaper. This was his last service of any kind as he must have fallen too ill to continue. In any case, with the small congregation, there were actually very few christenings and marriages in the two churches during this period. Of note, his last marriage ceremony in St Gallgo's was that of John Roberts of Eugrad Villa and his second wife Mary Jones on 7th May 1898. John and Mary were the parents of Annie Penmarian and nain and taid to Gwyneth Penmarian and her siblings.

Griffith passed away on 16th February 1899 at seven o'clock in the evening at his home, which was reported in the *Evening*

FUNERAL OF THE RECTOR OF LLANALLGO.

The funeral of the Rev. G. B. Jones, rector of Llanallgo and Llaneugrad, took place at Llanallgo Churchyard. At nine a.m. a celebration of Holy Communion was held, when a good number of the parishioners attended. The celebrant was the Vicar of All Saints', Cardiff, assisted by the Rev. William Jones, Ebbw Vale. The funeral service was attended by a large number of people—in fact, the church was crowded, and many scores were unable to gain admission. In all nineteen clergymen were present. The Service for the Burial of the Dead was conducted in the church by the Rev. D. Andrew Jones, rector of Llandwrog, and the Rev. J. W. Wynne Jones, vicar of Carnarvon, and at the grave the Rev. A. E. H. Hyslop officiated. The opening sentences were read by the Rev. W. Jones, Ebbw Vale.

119. Western Mail, 27th Feb 1899

THE RECTORY, LLANALLGO.

IMPORTANT TO FARMERS, PARTIES FURNISHING, BOOK VENDORS, etc.

MESSRS HUGHES and JONES have been favoured with instruction by the Relict of the late Rev. G. B. Jones, TO SELL BY PUBLIC AUCTION, on WEDNESDAY, March 29th, 1899, the Whole of the

IN AND OUT-DOOR EFFECTS,

Which comprise briefly:—A Serviceable Pony, Trap, Carriage Lamps, Harness, Saddle and Bridle, One Dairy Cow, Churn and Dairy Utensils, Three Sheep in Lamb, Quantity of Hay, Six Bee Hives, GARDEN IMPLEMENTS, a Splendid LIBRARY of THEOLOGICAL AND OTHER BOOKS, and the HOUSEHOLD FURNITURE AND EFFECTS.

Sale to Commence at ELEVEN a.m. prompt.

Further Particulars of the Auctioneers, Bodorgan and Amlwch. 17954—861

120. *Y Clorianydd*, 23rd march 1899

Y Clorianydd advertised the auction on the 23rd March. This is the first time I have seen beehives in an auction and six seems to be quite a few! Although it cannot be proved one way or the other, it does make me wonder whether this might have been the source of his unusual middle name…

Annie moved back to her native Cowbridge, and in the 1901 census she was living with her nephew William Giles (son of her sister Mary) and his wife and daughter in East Village. She died on 15th April 1908 in Cowbridge, and she does not appear to have been buried there or in St Gallgo's, so she is likely buried with her first husband in Caernarfonshire.

John Lewis Davies, 1899 - 1929

John was born in Aberystwyth in 1859 to Griffith Davies and his wife Mary née Lewis. Griffith and Mary were both born in Aberystwyth and were married in St Peter's church, Eaton Square in Pimlico London on 16th September 1858. They settled down to married life in their hometown of Aberystwyth where they had three other children: Thomas Griffith in 1860; Mary Jane in 1862 and Daniel Lewis in 1866. John grew up attending chapel as his father was nonconformist, and minister of the English Presbyterian (Calvinistic Methodist) Chapel, Aberystwyth at the time of the 1871 census.

This was no ordinary chapel - on 18th May 1871, a memorial stone was laid for a new very grand gothic style building that was to be built. Griffith was busy raising large amounts of money and by that date he already had £800! The chapel would seat 272 in the main body and 104 in a gallery and have a Sunday school which would seat 150. I was curious as to why it was called an English chapel because, coming from Anglesey, I am more used to the chapels being Welsh. An interesting address given by 43-year-old Caernarvon-born Reverend Griffith Parry of Manchester sheds some light on this and it was reported in the *Aberystwyth Observer* on 20th May as follows: *"The most palpable reasons for the erection of this building was the progress the English language had made throughout the principality.*

121. The Reverend John L Davies and Family Outside The Rectory

This was a fact to which they could not shut their eyes much longer, and for which they must

not be unprepared. If the denomination to which they belonged was to retain the position it had taken, and to exercise the influence for good in future that it hitherto had done, they must follow the times, and act according to the progress of civilization. It was a fact generally acknowledged among the wisest and most farsighted men of their denomination that the Welsh language was doomed to die. He did not venture to offer an opinion upon this disputed subject; but this he hoped and believed, that if it was to die away, Calvinistic Methodism would not die upon the same day or be buried in the same grave with it. The friends in this town had the sagacity and foresight to see the signs of the times, and had prepared themselves for the change, so that Methodism should survive the language of the country in which it flourished." So that is why it was an English chapel.

Griffith was called to the Welsh Presbyterian church on Nassau St, London as minister and moved the family to London. Mary died after a few years there and in his grief, he decided to leave the hustle and bustle of the city and took a post at the Tabernacl Chapel in Cardigan sometime before the time of the 1881 census. By now John was at University of Glasgow pursuing a Bachelor of Arts degree and was lodging with the Gould family in Partick. Although he was raised in the CM chapel, John decided to enter the Church of England instead of following in his father's footsteps. He was ordained a deacon by the Bishop of Llandaff on Sunday 23rd September 1883 and was licenced to the curacy of Pontlottyn. On 20th December 1885 he was ordained as a priest, also at Llandaff.

It was in Pontlottyn on 28th June 1886 in St Tyfaelog's church that he married Mary Snook, a schoolmistress from Cadoxton Juxta Neath. Later that year on 30th October, the *Weekly Mail* announced that John was appointed to the curacy of St Michael and All Angels in Dafen, Carmarthenshire and their first child, Irene Paschal was born there on 7th April 1887. His stay in Dafen was short, and his next appointment was in a different country – Stoke Climsland in Cornwall,

---

LLANEUGRAD CHURCH SCHOOL.

[To the Editor.]

Sir,—Will you permit me to make an appeal through the medium of your paper to those amongst your readers who are friends of Church schools.

The parish of Llaneugrad, in Anglesey, has no School Board; for many years past its educational needs have been supplied by a school in union with the National Society.

Some time ago my predecessor, the late Rev. G. B. Jones, feeling, together with his fellow-managers, the great disadvantage caused by the absence of any suitable house or lodgings for the head teacher, resolved on building a teacher's house on a portion of ground adjoining the school.

The house is now completed, and is in occupation, but there remains on it a debt of about £70. Towards the building of the house the owners of property in the neighbourhood have already done their part, and of them no more can reasonably be expected. It falls upon me and my fellow-managers to seek other means of liquidating the debt.

I venture to appeal to members of the Church of England, to all those who favour religious teaching in day schools.

It was felt by my predecessor, and rightly, that to provide a good house for the teacher would tend to the increased efficiency of the school, for it was becoming continually more difficult, without the inducement of a house, to secure the services of a well-qualified person to undertake the charge of a school so remote from a town and railway facilities.

Should any feel inclined to respond to this appeal contributions might be sent to me or to the National Provincial Bank at Llangefni.—I am, etc.,   J. LEWIS DAVIES,

Rector of Llaneugrad with Llanallgo.

122. North Wales Chronicle, 28th October 1899

where he served as curate from early 1887 until 1889 and baby Irene was christened in this church on 19th June 1887. The *South Wales Daily News* announced on 1st August 1889 that in a special service at the Palace Chapel, the Bishop of Llandaff granted him a licence to the curacy of Merthyr Tydfil. The couple's next four children were all born in Merthyr (Gwladys Tydfil in 1890, Griffith in 1891, Gwendoline Audrey in 1892 and Monica Mary in 1894) where he remained until the bishop of Llandaff offered him the benefice of Llaneugrad with Llanallgo in 1899. The *Weekly Mail* (and other newspapers) announced on 1st April that he had accepted the offer.

When John and his young family took up residence in the rectory at Llanallgo, they were moving from a predominantly English-speaking area of Wales to a predominantly Welsh-speaking area one. The 1901 census showed that the population of Wales exceeded two million for the first time and just over 15% of the population spoke only Welsh. In Llanallgo and Llaneugrad the percentage of those who only spoke Welsh had declined over the previous 10 years and was now 66% and 58% respectively. The number of bilingual speakers had increased dramatically, from 12 in 1891 to 143 in 1901 in Llanallgo and from 44 in 1891 to 111 in 1901 in Llaneugrad. Llanallgo had six English only speakers. Alfred Tucker of Pen Y Bonc had still not learned Welsh, and what was very surprising to me was the fact that all five of John's children were English only speakers, despite the fact that John and his wife were bilingual. In Llaneugrad the eight English only speakers were all either the Parciau family or the staff associated with the "big house" as it was known.

The rector continued to be Chairman of the Managers overseeing the National schools and John still had £70 to raise to cover the cost of the schoolmaster's house for the Llaneugrad school built by his predecessor. As such, he posted an advertisement in the North Wales Chronicle on 28th October 1899.

When new standards were created by the highly controversial Education Act (aka Balfour Act) in 1902, the Llaneugrad school fell significantly short. The Managers were given, and accepted, a fairly large "To Do" list by the newly named Local Education Authority (LEA) for Anglesey, a body that had been formed in 1889 under a different name. For a number of years, they did not remedy the shortcomings, and this led to a major conflict between John and the then *Lord of Llaneugrad*, Colonel Lawrence Williams of Parciau. It was a long saga,

122a. Colonel Lawrence Williams

the details of which will be included in a future publication and the following is a much-abbreviated version.

The Church still owned the National schools and did not automatically transfer them to the LEA after the 1902 Act. Financing came from the local ratepayers, and a grant was provided to the schools by the Board of Education (BOE), which also had the power to close those National schools that did not meet the required standards. Llaneugrad was a small, very poor parish, and the school suffered from a lack of funds. The Managers began negotiations to transfer the school to the LEA (other National Schools, including Bodedern were doing the same) who would then bring the school up to the required standard. As Chairman, John seems to go along with the transfer, although it dragged on for several years, and I suspect this was because John really did not want to lose the school, for whatever reason. It was late 1909 when things came to a head.

He must have realized that he had no choice but to go ahead, so he wanted it to be only for a limited time, which he tried to negotiate with LEA. They finally agreed, but it became obvious that he was pushing his own personal agenda, and not including the Managers in the decision-making. When pressed by the LEA to show evidence that the Managers concurred with the decision, he could not. Colonel Lawrence of Parciau, one of the Managers, had by now realized what was going on, and his position was clear – he wanted to avoid further burdens on the parish ratepayers and turn over the school to the LEA. If the school could not be upgraded (and there were some physical limitations that made it quite difficult), then a new school would have to be built and, if it was a National School, then the parishioners would have to foot the cost. Colonel Lawrence knew this was not going to be affordable for them and, as he owned a great part of Llaneugrad lands, he was fiercely protective of his tenants and fellow parishioners. The two men butted heads on several occasions and John apparently tried to exclude Colonel Lawrence from Managers meetings by scheduling them at the very last minute. He also refused to show him the minutes of an important meeting he was not able to attend, and in the end, John replaced a churchwarden (also a Trustee) with one he felt would take his side rather than that of the Colonel Lawrence. All of this is documented in letters that both men wrote to the BOE, Colonel Lawrence wanted to make sure that the BOE understood that John was acting on his own behalf and questioned if John's approaches were within the rights of the Chairman. The BOE replied and said that John was acting within his rights as Chairman. The following is an excerpt from The Colonel's letter dated 1st March 1910 and it sheds light on how the school was financed: *"The school has been kept going in the past mainly owing to my family, and the teachers' house was built not long ago, my mother found most of the money. When all of the church people and two of the three Trustees wish for the transfer of the school, I think it is an extraordinary thing if the clergyman should be allowed to overrule these opinions and to burden the parish with the cost of a new school."* The Trustees of the school property were the rector and the two churchwardens. The Colonel was one of the wardens and Captain William Roberts of Tyn Lôn was the other. He was the one that John replaced in the midst of this with William Davies of Nant Bychan whom John thought would be more sympathetic to his cause.

I am sure that both men were trying to do what they thought was the right thing, but John lost his battle in the end. He refused to attend a meeting of the Managers in December 1909 where an agreement was to be signed to turn over the school, despite the best efforts of the new churchwarden, William Davies. Finally, a meeting of the Managers/Trustees was called on 11th May 1910, but John also refused to attend this one. At this meeting Colonel Lawrence was appointed Chairman of the Trustees, Mr William Griffith, Angorfa, was made Secretary, and it was documented that the Reverend John Davies was no longer the authorized correspondent for the Trustees. This was all in preparation for the formal signing of the Memo of Agreement the following day that was to be sent to the LEA. The school and house were leased to the LEA for 40 years, and the Trustees had access to use the school on Sundays and two evenings each week. Given that only two of the Trustees had signed it, the LEA had to check with the BOE if it was acceptable to go ahead with the transfer. With all that had gone on (or not in the case of bringing the school up to standard) the BOE readily agreed to the transfer, and I sure that all involved were relieved to see an end to this eight-year-long saga!

I do wonder whether the deterioration in the relationship between John and Colonel Lawrence led to the publishing of an unfortunate article in the newspaper *Ye Brython Cymreig* on 26th August 1909. It was written under the pen name "Traveller" and titled "On Tour: In a fuss about a road". It complained that although there used to be several paths some years ago, today there was no public access to St Eugrad's church. There were dogs everywhere and the old pathways sign that they were only open *"to servants employed on the estate"*. The Traveller related a conversation he had with a man who had come from the church and cemetery and some quite derogatory comments were made about Colonel Lawrence, and, although his name was not specifically mentioned, it was quite obvious about whom the man was talking. On 16th September, the owners and publishers of the newspaper made a full apology. They said that they did not make the connection between the comments and Colonel Lawrence but recognize their full accountability for the pain and damage to his good reputation that this article caused. If the church was really that inaccessible, I can't help but wonder just who the man was who happened to be coming from it and would say such things about Col. Lawrence to a stranger.

In 1909, it was the 50 years since the sinking of The Royal Charter, and John wanted the St Gallgo's churchyard to look its best. He conducted a fundraising effort, placing an advertisement in the *North Wales Weekly News* on 6th August appealing for funds. With 140 of those who perished buried in the churchyard, many visitors were expected, and it was important that their final resting place be in good order.

Some of the notable events that happened during John's tenure include the very first Royal Welsh Show, held in Aberystwyth beginning on 3rd August 1904, and the birth of Marianglas' most famous son, Oscar-winning Hugh Emrys Griffiths, on 30th May 1912 in Angorfa, although no-one at that time could have guessed just how great his accomplishments would be. There must have been quite a bit of excitement on Anglesey when the first ever flight from North Wales to Ireland took place in 1912. On April 26th, Captain Vivian Hewitt of

> **Spanish Flu or Influenza.**
>
> If suffering from the above or from a bad cold, take
>
> **JONES' CHILL CURE,**
>
> which will bring immediate relief.
>
> 1/3 and 3/- or by Post 1/4½ & 3/1½; from
>
> **R. R. JONES,**
> CENTRAL PHARMACY,
> Llangefni and Amlwch.
>
> 123. *North Wales Chronicle,*

Bodfari Denbighshire, flew from Rhyl along the North Wales coast and landed in Holyhead to prepare for the main part of his flight. He then took off and managed to land in Phoenix Park in Dublin to the roar of cheering crowds before dismantling his plane and bringing it back on the ferry. I wonder if any of our parishioners travelled to Holyhead to see the historic take-off.

On 4th August 1914, war was declared on Germany. In all, more than 133 men from our parishes played their parts in the war either in the armed forces on the front lines fighting the enemy or on the sea as merchant mariners risking their lives every day to ship essential goods in waters infested with enemy submarines. Colonel Lawrence was posted overseas to the battlefront. The war was right on our Anglesey doorstep as German U-boats were patrolling the Irish Sea. At the tail end of 1917 and beginning of 1918, there was a particularly deadly set of enemy actions. Between 27th December 1917 and 14th October 1918, 199 men were killed as eight ships were sunk off the Skerries, South Stack and Point Lynas. The war memorials in Moelfre and Marian-glas name the men of our parishes who died in the Great War and my book *Lest We Forget: The Men of the Marian-glas War Memorial in WWI* (Amazon) tells their stories and that of their families. A total of 40,000 people from Wales lost their lives in this war and 28 of them were from our parishes. The men who survived would live with physical and/or mental injuries, and the horrors they saw and the terrors they endured would be with them for the rest of their lives. May all of their souls now rest in peace.

John was very active in local society arranging many activities, including a recital in the Marian-glas British School on 12th August 1915 in support of the North Wales Nursing Association which raised £4 10s. He delivered a lecture on Monks and Friars in Wales to the Bro Goronwy Literary Society in February 1917. Religious differences were set firmly aside when it came to the North Wales Heroes' Memorial, and he worked hand in glove with his chapel colleagues to raise funds for its construction.

The 11th of November 1919 was Armistice Day, and with one horror over, another came along. The Spanish flu pandemic began in December 1918 and lasted through the following year. The death toll in Wales was shocking -10,000 people which was a quarter of the number killed in the war. In reviewing the parish burial registers for that period for St Eugrad's and St Gallgo's, there does not seem to have been an excess number of deaths in either of our parishes, but perhaps in our rural environments, it was easier to take measures to prevent the spread of infection. It certainly could not have been Jones' Chill Cure, which was extensively advertised in Welsh and English newspapers, with a claim to bring immediate relief.

1918 was a big year for voting rights. The Representation of the People Act enabled virtually all men from age 21, as well as 8.5 million women over 30 who met a minimum property qualification, to vote. This was only about 2/3 of the population of women, but the age was purposely chosen so that the majority of voters would be men. Sadly, this was because so many men were killed in WWI, that if they had given the vote to women 21 and over, then women would have made up the majority of the electorate. In 1919, 71 women were registered to vote in Llaneugrad and 109 in Llanallgo, including Mary, the Reverend John's wife. It would be another decade before the Equal Franchise Act of 1928 extended the vote to all women 21 and over and, by 1929, the number of women registered to vote had increased to 100 in Llaneugrad and 171 in Llanallgo.

After centuries of Welsh churches falling under the "rule" of the Church of England, the Welsh Church Acts of 1914 and 1919 came into force resulting in the creation of the Church in Wales, and the post of Archbishop of Wales. Unlike the Archbishops of Canterbury and York, who are appointed by the Queen upon the advice of the Prime Minister, the Archbishop of Wales is one of the six diocesan bishops of Wales, elected to hold this office in addition to his or her own diocese. Alfred George Edwards, Bishop of St Asaph had the honour of becoming the first ever Archbishop of the Church in Wales in 1920.

John also saw a very important cultural aspect of Welsh life founded two years later by Sir Ifan ab Owen Edwards in 1922. His ambition was to protect the Welsh language in a world where English was now dominating every aspect of life outside the home. In an issue of the magazine *Cymru'r Plant* in 1922 Sir Ifan said, "*These days, in many villages, and in most towns in Wales, children play and read in English. They forget that they are Welsh.*" He appealed to children to join this new organization that offered opportunities through the medium of Welsh, which was called Urdd Gobaith Cymru.

John died at home in the Rectory on 27th January 1929 (Septuagesima Sunday) and his death was registered by daughter Gwendoline who was still living at home. He was still conducting services and two days before had buried Mary Jones of Bron Haul in St Eugrad's. John was buried in St Gallgo's on 31st January and Owen Evans, Archdeacon of Bangor, officiated. John's family erected a plaque in the church in his memory.

After John passed away, Mary and the children moved to Shepherd's Hill in Llanfair ME, the former home of William John and Olive Rowlands who had moved to Bryn Glas. Mary was 84 when she died on 31st January 1940 at home and was buried in St Gallgo's' on 3rd February. None of the children married and all are buried in St Gallgo's. Irene attended St Winifred's school in Bangor, and it was reported in the newspapers on 29th August 1903 that she had passed the Senior Oxford Local Examination with the title of A.A. (Associate in Arts). She attended University College of North Wales in Bangor and studied English, French and Latin and graduated with a BA. On 18th October 1918, the school governors of the Aberystwyth County school announced her appointment as classics mistress. She was still single and living in Aberystwyth at the end of September 1939 (1939 Register). She had retired to Anglesey by 1966 and lived in Shepherd's Hill. She died aged 85 on 7th June 1972 in the Druid Hospital in Llangefni and was buried in St Gallgo's on 12th June and the Reverend Rees Hughes officiated.

Gwladys was also very intelligent and won a scholarship to Howell's school in Denbigh.

She must have also had a talent for needlework as she won a prize two years running in 1905 and 1906, which was awarded on the annual Speech Day. She also became a teacher and in September 1939, according to the 1939 Register, she was living the Rickmansworth district of Hertfordshire. She had retired to Anglesey by 1969 and was living in Shepherd's Hill with her siblings, Griffith, Irene, and Monica Mary. She died aged 80 on 20th March 1971 in Valley Hospital and was buried in St Gallgo's on 24th March and the Reverend Rees Hughes officiated.

124. Griffith from his Merchant Marine Record

Griffith moved to Dowlais near Merthyr Tydfil and, in 1911, was an engineering apprentice in the ironworks there and boarding with the ironworks' lodgeman (security guard), James Jenkins at 29 White Street. In about 1919, he became a ship's engineer in the merchant navy and served through WWII. He was serving on the SS Statesman which sailed from Liverpool to New Orleans arriving on 20th February 1940 during the Battle of the Atlantic and was 2nd engineer, age 49 and 5ft 6in tall weighing 143lbs. I don't know if he was still working on the SS Statesman at the time, but the following year she was returning from New Orleans via Belfast to Liverpool, when, on 17th May, she was bombed by the enemy and sank in the waters to the west of Ireland with the loss of one soul, Geoffrey Dewar, the 2nd Officer who was 35 years old.

For his service during the war, Griffith received four medals: the 1939, Atlantic Star, Africa Star, and Italy Star. After the war, he moved to Shepherd's Hill where he spent the rest of his life. He died aged 81 in St David's Hospice on 14th January 1973 and was buried on 17th January in St Gallgo's by Reverend Rees Hughes. I have little information on Gwendoline, she was not living in Shepherd's Hill at the time of the 1939 Register and could possibly have been the Gwendoline A Davies who was a woman gardener in the London area. She was a registered voter at Shepherd's Hill that year but was not living there after that as far as I can tell from the electoral registers. She died aged 56 on 18th November 1948 in Meridale Nursing Home in Colwyn Bay and was buried in St Gallgo's on 23rd November by the Reverend Glyn Evans. Monica Mary stayed in the area, living with her mother at Shepherd's Hill and does not appear to have worked outside the home whilst her mother was alive. She died aged 89 in the Cefni Hospital, Llangefni on 14th May 1983 and was buried in St Gallgo's on 19th May by Reverend Elias Hughes from Dolgellau.

Delyth Roberts (Pwll Bachgen) tells me that Griffith's nickname at sea was "Bulldog Davies". She used to deliver the milk to them on a Sunday morning and always had some sweets or threepence or sixpence for going. They were a family that very much kept themselves to themselves as they say, so I have not been able to glean any more information.

John Henry Parry, 1929 – 1937

John was born at Plas Dulas, Penisarwaun, Llanddeiniolen on 5th August 1893 to slate quarryman Henry John Parry from Llanddeiniolen and Gwen Ellen née Jones from Llanwnda. At the time of the 1911 census, John was 17 and still in school and I was unable to find out if he attended university. He was married on 14th June 1927 in Llangeinwen church and was a clerk in holy orders living on Caroline Street, Llandudno. His bride was Ruth Williams, a hospital matron who was born in Cefn Du, Trewalchmai on 28th March 1890 to farmer John Griffith Williams from Llanidan and Sarah Ann née Jones from Llangeinwen. Ruth trained at The Royal Southern Hospital in Liverpool from 1919 to 1922 and became a registered nurse on 18th May 1923. John had taken up his appointment as rector of our churches by the middle of 1929 and the family lived in the Rectory. They had three children: Gwendoline Ruth "Gwenno", John W Lloyd and Henry "Harry" Vaughan. Harry was born in Llanallgo on 9th March 1931, so likely in the Rectory.

125. The Young John

Motor cars had been around on Anglesey since the turn of the century and Henry Paget, the 5th Marquess of Anglesey, bought his locomobile in 1902. He inherited his title and estate from his father in late 1898 and was a notoriously flamboyant spendthrift who managed to spend all of the family money and rack up debts of over half a million pounds before his early death in 1905. His young chauffeur was Camberwell-born Harold Maurice Bater, who sounds like he aspired to be a racing driver, because he was continually in the North Wales courts answering charges of "furiously driving" at speeds of 20 to 40 mph as reported in *The Motor Car Journal*. Bater incurred many fines as a result of his reckless driving, but by June 1904 was no longer in the employ of the marquess and had emigrated to Boston USA, no doubt leaving the North Wales roads a much safer place to travel on. With the growing number of cars, speeding was not the only problem, and various laws had to be updated including those relating to drunk driving. As far back as 1872, it was an offence to drive carriages, horses, cattle, and steam engines whilst under the influence of alcohol, and in 1925, this list was expanded to include any vehicle. In 1930 it became an offence to be in charge of, or drive, a motor vehicle if you were too drunk to have proper

125a John Henry Parry

control of it and in 1936 John and his family were to see a drink-driving incident first-hand. It was reported in the *Liverpool Echo* on 26th October with several eye-catching headlines. I reproduce the article here as the original newspaper print is of poor quality:

TWO GARAGE OWNERS FINED
Car Drivers and Drink
BENCH WARNING
"This Punishment Just a Commencement"
TRIBUTE TO MINISTER

LLANGEFNI, Monday: Fines of £8 each and costs were imposed at Llangefni Police Court today, on two Anglesey garage proprietors, Howel Roose Jones, of Llanfaethlu, and William Hugh Lewis Jones of Menai Bridge, for being under the influence of drink when in charge of a car on the Benllech road on the night of October 5. The defendants pleaded guilty, and the chairman of the magistrates, Colonel Lloyd, issued the warning that punishment in this case was inflicted just as a commencement. "This bench is determined, so far as it can, to put a stop to drunken people driving motor-cars" he said. "We have decided that we shall deal very severely in future with all cases that come before us of people in a drunken condition driving cars."

LICENCES SUSPENDED

The magistrates also ordered the defendants' driving licences to be suspended for twelve months. Mr E. Lloyd Jones, who prosecuted, said the case was reported by the Reverend John Parry, rector of Llanallgo, who, while driving his family home, had encountered the defendants seated in a car which was stationary in the middle of a road. With some difficulty he persuaded the driver, Howel Roose Jones, to move his vehicle, and himself averted a collision by running alongside and grasping the wheel from the defendant's hand. A telegraph pole was grazed further along the road. When a policeman overhauled them, he saw the defendant, Howel Roose Jones, give up the driving seat to his co-defendant, William Hugh Lewis Jones. Both were under the influence of drink.

FELL BACKWARDS

Howel Roose Jones fell backwards into the car while attempting to stand outside. Following a doctor's report, the defendants were taken to Llangefni police station. There, in reply to the charge, Howel Roose Jones said he had had only six glasses of beer. William Hugh Lewis Jones, who insisted that he was all right, said he had four glasses of beer and two gins. Mr Gordon Roberts, who appeared for the accused, said both men had been working without meals all that day repairing a car, "and had taken liquid refreshment without the solid." The bench complimented the Reverend John Parry upon his public-spirited action.

There were two what I call "Society" weddings in our churches during John's tenure, one each in St Eugrad's and St Gallgo's. On Friday 9th June 1933 in St Eugrad's, the Hon. Pierce Butler, youngest son of the late Earl of Carrick married Miss Eleri Llewelyn Jones, daughter of physician Dr Griffith Llewelyn Jones of Brynglas, Llangefni. One of the seven bridesmaids was seven-year-old Penelope Williams of Parciau and her little brother, three-

The Clergymen

year-old Lawrence Hugh was a page boy. John aided the Reverend J. Davies, rector of Llangefni, in the ceremony, and the wedding celebrations were held in the Parciau mansion house. The second wedding was on 6th February 1937 in St Gallgo's when Freda Violet Williams, daughter of Sir William Willoughby Williams 5th Baronet of Bodelwyddan (brother of Henrietta, The Colonel's wife,) married Sidney Hinde, eldest son of Col. Hinde of Natal, South Africa. These were very unusual sorts of wedding for our parishes and must have been wonderful spectacles for the locals and they must have turned out in some numbers to see the wedding parties; I know I would have been there!

One of John's enduring legacies is his work in organizing a memorial for the Royal Charter which is on the coast overlooking the place of the wreck. On 18th September 1935, the Western Mail newspaper reported the unveiling of the memorial.

"DISASTER THAT SHOCKED THE NATION, Memorial to Victims in Wreck of Royal Charter. A memorial in the form of an obelisk to those who lost their lives in the Royal Charter on 26th October 1859 will be unveiled at the tiny village of Llanallgo in Anglesey today". It goes on to summarize the events of the time and concludes with: *"The remains of the wreck are there to this day, and a good deal of the gold with it, in all probability. The memorial overlooks the reef which brought the Royal Charter to its doom. The movement was organized by the Reverend John Parry, rector of Llanallgo, and the memorial will be unveiled by Lord Boston this afternoon."*

125b. Royal Charter Memorial

In mid-1937 John moved to Dyffryn Ardudwy where they lived in the Rectory; the living included St. Enddwyn's church with the curacy of Llanddwywe annexed. In the war, everyone had to their bit and the 1939 Register says that John was an Air Raid Precautions (ARP) warden. The main tasks of the warden were to try and protect people during air raids, when enemy planes dropped bombs, especially on cities. They would hand out gas masks and guide people to shelters. After an air raid wardens might have to give First Aid help or help to put out fires. ARPs would also patrol and make sure that people blocked the light coming from their homes during the blackout. Although Dyffryn Ardudwy was rural, there was still a need for the blackout rules had to be strictly enforced to not give enemy bombers easy targets or navigational signposts. Although we might think that air raid shelters were in cities only, back in Marian-glas, the family living in Marianfa had built one in their back garden!

The *Western Mail* newspaper reported on 28th April 1953, that John, who was then rector of Penrhyndeudraeth, would move to Llandwrog, replacing the retiring incumbent who had spent 40 years there. John's tenure was much shorter than his predecessor's as he died on 6th April 1955 and was buried in his home parish of Llanddeiniolen with the Reverend J.M. Hughes of St Thomas' and Reverend D.M. Jones of Llanrug officiating. Ruth was living at Min Menai in Bangor when she passed away on 26th January 1981, and she is buried in Llanddeiniolen with her husband.

Robert Williams, 1937 - 1940

For the first time in almost 40 years, the rector was a local Anglesey man. Robert was born on 18th March 1902 on Church Street, Aberffraw to Robert, an agricultural labourer whose family had lived in Aberffraw for at least a few generations, and Ellen née Jones born in Holyhead, the daughter of sailor Richard and his wife Margaret née Jones. I was unable to find anything on Robert's education, but Alma Salt is a relative and she kindly provided me with the picture of him with the choir as well as some information on his life. He served as a curate at St Michael's in Valley for a time before moving to Llandinorwic as a curate.

126. Llandinorwig church choir Robert Williams center middle row

One of Robert's hobbies was entering competitions, and in 1932 he was a very big winner. The cigarette company, Kensitas, ran an advertising campaign: "*Every day, except Sunday, until further press notice, a £235 Austin Twelve-Six De Luxe Saloon will be awarded to the competitor from whom is received the best 20-word statement - best in the opinion of the judges, from the standpoint of truthfulness and advertising value - describing the quality and merits of Kensitas cigarettes.*" The car was described as "*A luxuriously modern car. Sunshine roof. Selected hide upholstery. Triplex Glass. Bumpers front and rear. Four wide doors. Four-wheel brakes. Finger-light steering. 13.9 Six-cylinder engine. Four speed twin-top gearbox. Five wire wheels. All exterior bright parts chromium plated. List price £235.*"

Each packet of 20 cigarettes had an entry form with a tear-off piece upon which you wrote just two words from your 20-word statement, numbering each word in order. To enter your entire statement, you therefore had to buy 10 packets of cigarettes – and presumably many people were lured to switch to this brand, at least for the duration of the competition. Of course, this was in the days before smoking was generally recognized as a serious health risk and, indeed, the entry ticket must have been quite reassuring to the purchaser: "*Kensitas offer the finest, choicest real Virginia tobacco plus the throat protection of that exclusive private* *process which includes the use of modern ultra-violet rays – the process that expels certain biting, harsh irritants <u>naturally present in every tobacco leaf</u>. 1,004 British doctors have stated Kensitas to be less irritating. No wonder Kensitas are always <u>kind</u> to your throat."*

126a. Kensitas Car Advertisement

The 10th of February edition of *The Dundee Courier* reported on his win. A very eloquent endorsement, and I wonder just how many people enjoyed a luxurious ride in his new car.

Robert married Nora Catherine Salt on 11th April 1934 in Llandinorwig church. His two nieces, Deryl Pritchard and Doris Williams and her two sisters, Elizabeth Alice Roberts, and Edith Myfanwy Griffith (Deputy mayoress of Caernarfon) were the bridesmaids, and his best man was the Reverend G Wright of Llangefni. Nora's uncle, the Reverend George Salt officiated together with the Reverend Walter Jones of Llandinorwig and D Jenkins of Porthmadog. The wedding tea was held in the Royal Hotel, Caernarfon. Nora was a daughter of the Reverend James Salt and Catherine Gwladys Phillips Johns. James had been rector of Llandinorwic until 1926 and afterwards became rector of Robert's home church of Aberffraw. Nora was the third of their six children, and she attended Llanberis County school, obtaining her senior certificate in English, arithmetic, mathematics, and Welsh. She then trained as a nurse in Liverpool Royal Infirmary from 1917 to 1920 and was registered as a nurse in London on 15th February 1924.

When Robert became rector of Llaneugrad and Llanallgo in 1937 they lived in the Rectory and their daughter, Rhiannon, was born in Bangor in 1938. John had a close relative as a colleague in the area. His first cousin on his father's side, Evan John Williams, also took up a career in the church and was rector of Llanwenllwyfo at the same time that Robert was rector of our churches.

The memories of WWI and the 28 lost lads were still fresh in everyone's minds when, on 1st September 1939, Hitler invaded Poland, sparking the beginning of World War II. In preparation for the wartime years, a register of all civilians in England and Wales was taken on 30th September 1939. The information was used to produce identity cards and, once rationing was introduced in January 1940, to

CURATE WINS CAR

KENSITAS STOPPED PULPIT COUGH.

A curate living in the second highest house in Wales has won the eighteenth Austin car offered daily for the best message about the merits of the Kensitas cigarette.

He is Rev. Robert Williams, of Llandinorwib Parish Church, in Deinieon, a scattered district in the heart of the hills. Mr Williams is a bachelor, 30 years of age.

"I believe in competitions of this kind," said Mr Williams in an interview yesterday. "I always have a go at them. They keep one's wits keen.

"I must have won because I wrote what I know to be true about the cigarettes, which have stopped me coughing in the pulpit. The car will enable me to visit my outlying people oftener, to take the sick to hospital, and invalids for outings."

The winning message reads—"Besides being excellent cigarettes, made of good quality tobacco, Kensitas, because of their scientific preparation, safeguard the throat against irritation."

127. *Dundee Courier*, 10th February 1932

issue ration books. At the time of this register, Nora's parents, whose home was in Cae Ddafydd in Llangefni, were living with them in the Rectory and perhaps James was ill, as he died on 5th October 1939 aged 82, in the Rectory. He was buried in Llanfair-is-gaer and his obituary in The *Liverpool Express* reads: "*DEATH OF 82-YEAR-OLD MINISTER. The death is announced at the age of 82 of the Reverend James Salt, of Llanallgo. He had been in Holy Orders for 56 years. Educated at St Aidan's College, he was ordained at Bangor Cathedral in 1883. He was curate of Llanfair-is-gaer from 1883 to 1892 when he was appointed vicar of Llandinorwic. In 1926 he became rector of Aberffraw and retired in 1935*".

I was fortunate to receive some war-time memoirs of the Oscar-winning actor, Hugh Griffith from Marian-glas, from his nephew William. I draw on these to relate the events of the early days of WWII as experienced by Hugh, who begins by addressing his experiences in WWI. "*In the far reaching past I remember a glorious August day, when we children were playing round the trees and large shrubs in the garden of Angorfa where I was born. My mother and my father were lounging on the large stone steps. I say large, they were enormous, as they still are, or were till recently. You couldn't have imagined a more perfect Summer's day. My father with his Panama and pipe and my mother so seemingly placid and watchful. Angorfa in fine weather has an uninterrupted view from Port Linus to the Great Orme's Head and even further at times to the Isle of Man and Cumberland. I must have been only two and a quarter at the time, but I can almost see now a huge explosion in the middle of the whole bay like a mini atom bomb. There was no radio then and we wondered what in the world it could be. But of course, my father knew that a war was imminent. As it turned out that was the first ship, the Tanbank, to be torpedoed on the first day of the war. This was 1914 so the submarines must have been lying in wait there for a long time to make a kill.*

The aftermath of that was panic along the bay and I very well remember that for years when I was barely growing up that a kind of dredger with divers often used to come to Moelfre seeking the copper that was bound for Liverpool. Strangely enough at the very beginning of the 1939 war a submarine called the Poseidon [later named Thetis] *on its trial run perished almost in the same spot as the Tanbank. It took a long time to raise this ultra-new submarine with all its hundred or so bodies still in it. It was brought to our local beach Traeth Bychan where I'd enjoyed so many childhood hours. You could not get near it because of the people who were morbidly drawn to this catastrophe.*" The story of this submarine is an extremely sad one, none of the men survived and it was eventually towed to Holyhead where the remaining bodies were brought out for burial.

One of the great and respected characters of Marian-glas village was Captain Thomas Jones of Ysgubor Fawr, a mariner who had survived WWI. Thomas would not live to see WWII break out, or the men of the village who had sailed with him killed, as he died on 12th January 1939 aged 83. His funeral was held on Saturday 14th and was unusual (at least to me) in two respects. Firstly, the service was held in the Marian-glas school and not Llanallgo chapel, and secondly, his burial in Llaneugrad was "*public for men only*" according to the newspaper. I have not seen such a thing before, and I wonder why it was that way. Secondly, there is no record at all of his interment in the parish register, which strikes me as odd because there are many burials recorded in the register for nonconformists – so, whether it was deliberate, or an oversight, we shall likely never know.

All 13 men killed in WWII from our parishes were sailors who risked their lives to ferry vital supplies in the mine strewn seas and under constant barrage from bombing planes. 1940 was the deadliest year, with eight casualties and four of them before Robert died. They were:

20th March 1940: 49-year-old Thomas Henry Rothwell of Tyn Pwll, Chief Office on the SS Barn Hill.
24th April 1940: 62-year-old Edward Jones of Glasfor, Chief Officer and 25-year-old Owen Edwin Owen of Penrhos Terrace, 2nd Officer on the SS Rydal Merchant when she struck a mine.
27th July 1940: 44-year-old Owen Lewis of Sychnant, 2nd Officer on the SS Durdham which struck a mine.

Robert contracted TB and died on 22nd September 1940 in the Bryn Seiont sanitorium in Caernarfon aged only 38; his daughter was only two at the time. In an article about Bryn Seiont on North Wales Live website, the author describes this time as a *'grim period when tuberculosis was a scourge in the district.'* He adds *'Bryn Seiont at that time, on its wooded site above the Seiont bridge, served as a sanatorium where an unusual feature was that the patients were housed in wooden cabins so that they would have plenty of fresh air.'* In fact, TB was one of the UK's most urgent health problems during this period, and the prognosis for those who contracted it was poor. This was before the BCG vaccination that many of us remember from our school days (that would come in the 1950s), and just a small number of years before the first effective antibiotic, streptomycin, was discovered in 1944.

Robert was buried in St Gallgo's on 26th September 1940, and the service was conducted by Henry Morgan, Archdeacon of Bangor. Sometime after his burial, Rhiannon and family members had a tablet erected in the church in his memory. Nora moved to Caernarfon and in the 1946 Nursing Register her address was listed as Erw Wen, Ael-Y-Garth. She died in 1978. The memorial inscriptions do not include a headstone for Robert, and I was unable to find where Nora is buried.

Arthur Gordon Ware, B.A, 1940 – 1943

Arthur was born on 9th November 1908 in Sunny Side, Morfa Nefyn to Jacob Ware and his wife Gwladys née Davies. Jacob was a clerk in the holy orders and Arthur was the middle of their five children. His siblings were Violet Mary, John Franklin Jones, Gwendoline Rosa, and Austin Neville. All three sons followed in their father's footsteps with careers in the church.

Arthur attended University College of North Wales in Bangor and St Michael's College in Llandaff, graduating with a bachelor's degree in Philosophy in June 1930. He was ordained a deacon by the Bishop of Bangor on 20th December 1931 and licenced to the curacy of Llanbeulan and ordained a priest the following year on 18th December. His brother

The Clergymen

Franklin obtained his BA from Oxford that same year and was also appointed to a curacy on Anglesey. The *Western Mail* thought this was quite newsworthy and on 25th July reported on their appointments in a story titled *"Brother Curates and Brother Vicars"*. Arthur reportedly served sometime after that in Gyffin, Conwy, and although I have not been able to find any details of this service, I did find that he returned to this church as a visiting priest to conduct Harvest Festival services in English and Welsh on 8th October 1941. By 1938 he was serving in Llandegfan as an assistant curate, and his sister Gwendoline was living with him as housekeeper. By the end of September 1939, he had moved to Llanbeulan and was living with Gwendoline in the Parsonage. He was curate of Llanedwen with Brynsiencyn when the Bangor Diocesan Board of Patronage offered him the living of Llanallgo and Llaneugrad in September 1940.

A very good friend of his was schoolteacher Robert Williams of Fairview, Marian-glas or "Bob Gors" as he was known. The two men were about the same age and had been in University College of North Wales in Bangor at the same time. Bob was a faithful attendee at Llanallgo church, and Arthur nominated him to be a lay reader and he was accepted and obtained his certificate on 26th May 1941. Later that year Bob volunteered to serve in the Royal Navy and in August he set off to the Naval training base at Portsmouth. On his first day there he was mortified when his name was called over the tannoy and he had to go at once to see the captain. He feared that he had already done something bad and was in terrible trouble, but in fact nothing could be further from the truth. His dear friend Arthur had written to the Chaplain asking if Bob would be able to lead some services whilst in the navy and they were simply calling him up to let him know that, yes, he could!

128. Arthur, Top left
John Franklin, Botton

Whilst in Africa at the beginning of 1943, Bob got a letter from Arthur informing him that he was to be married. Bob regretted the fact that he did not immediately reply and by the time he did, teasing Arthur and telling him that he couldn't wait for the opportunity to return and congratulate the two of them, Arthur was sadly in his grave. Arthur's wife Jean, whom Bob had never met, was the one to break the news to him. She was 28-year-old Jean Eryl Jones, and they were married on 2nd March 1943 in Bangor Cathedral. Jean was the daughter of famous author Elias Henry Jones, Registrar of the University College of North Wales in Bangor.

I have to digress and tell Elias' story because it is very interesting. In WWI Elias served in an artillery regiment in Mesopotamia and became a commissioned officer. He was captured at the surrender of Kut-el-Amara, Turkey, and was marched 700 miles to a prison camp at Yozgad. For reference that huge distance is 100 miles further than the distance between Land's End and John O'Groats as the crow flies! In the wake of his experiences, he wrote a book called *The Road to Endor* which describes how he and Lieutenant C.W. Hill (an Australian RAF officer) planned their escape. The pair used a homemade Ouija board to weave an elaborate plot, claiming to be mediums who could lead their captors to buried treasure on the Mediterranean coast, where they planned to abscond to Cyprus. Unsurprisingly the plan failed, but they persisted with the ruse of insanity for six months in an attempt to gain repatriation on medical grounds. Elias nearly killed himself in a fake suicide attempt in spring 1918, and he and Lieutenant Hill were eventually approved for a prisoner exchange, reaching Britain two months before the war ended. His book was very popular in the 1920s and sounds like a must read!

As another interesting aside, Jean's niece is the TV producer Hilary Bevan Jones who has worked on programmes such as Not the Nine O'clock News, Blackadder, and Cracker to name but a few and she started Endor Productions which was named after her grandfather's book. She was also the first female Chairman of the BAFTA from 2006 to 2008.

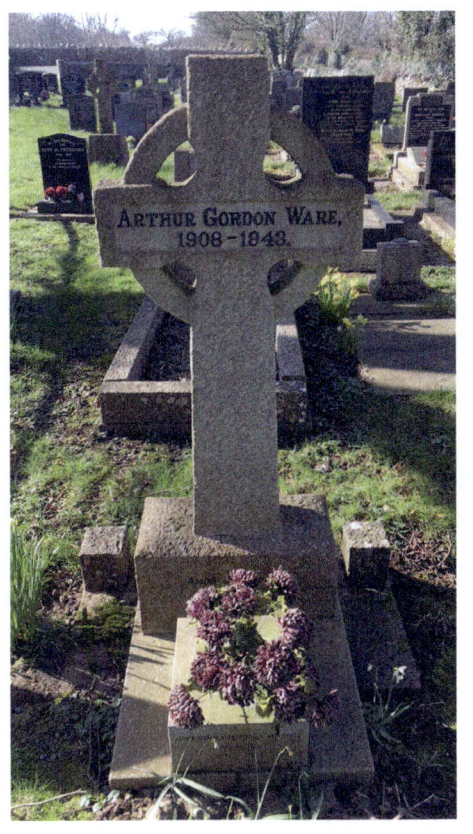

129. Arthur's Grave

In a cruel twist of fate, Arthur and Jean had only a few months together. He had an appendicitis in July 1943 and was rushed to the C&A hospital in Bangor for an appendectomy. He developed an infection from a contaminated needle and passed away on 19th July aged only 34. He was buried in St Gallgo's on the 21st of July, and his younger brother, Austin Neville, who was then curate of Drypool, Hull officiated. Bob Gors was an exceptionally talented poet, and, in honour of his dear friend, he wrote an *Englyn* (type of poem) for him:

Gwr a'i wedd yn fonheddig – llon, annwyl,
Llawn ynni brwdfrydig;
A gwr od o garedig
Hael oedd ef, heb le i ddig.

It does not translate literally, however, the general gist is that he was a man of noble character, cheerful and dear, full of enthusiasm, kind, generous and without anger.

By the time Arthur passed away, our parishes had suffered six more deaths in the war:

29th September 1940: 17-year-old Elwyn Williams of Cae Eithin and 19-year-old Robert Allan Dunsmuir of Alton Burn (this is what the family called Marianfa at the time) were neighbours and ordinary seamen when they were both killed on the SS Bassa.
18th October 1940: 48-year-old Ebenezer Williams of Ceris was master of the SS Ficus.
28th October 1940: 57-year-old John M Jones of Penrhos Terrace was chief engineer on the SS Wythburn.
7th March 1941: 29-year-old Thomas Roberts of 4 Morannedd was an able seaman on the SS Dotterel and died on upon returning to the ship to try and recover its papers.
3rd October 1942: 62-year-old Griffith Thomas of Brodawel was a Boatswain on the SS Lycaon.

Jean was pregnant when Arthur died and she gave birth to their son, Nicholas Gordon, on 6th February 1944 in Bangor County Hospital. Nicholas became a geochemist and was a contributor to the American space program. *The North Wales News* ran the following article on 9th January 1969, six months before man first landed on the moon:

Moon Dust Analyses Will be His Job

"Once on the moon", wrote a correspondent in the Times on Tuesday, "the astronauts will scoop up about 100lbs of soil and rocks. There are on earth more than 100 scientists waiting to give this material the most detailed analysis".

One of these scientists is 25 years old Mr Nicholas Gordon Ware, MSc. Son of the late Reverend Arthur Gordon Ware, who was much loved in several North Wales parishes, including Gyffin and Conway, and of Mrs E.A. Hunt (Jean Ware) now living in Surrey.

Mr Ware was flown to Canberra in the new year by the Australian National University to join the staff of Professor J.F. Lovering, the specialist in meteorology, to whose laboratory in the geochemistry department the first samples of moon dust will be sent by the Americans.

In view of his experience with electron probe machinery as research assistant to the Metallurgy Department of Imperial College of Science, Kensington, Mr Ware, as part of his work in Australia, will be responsible for the expensive machinery which will analyse the dust.

His wife, Helen, will join him in Canberra in a few months' time… He was educated at Abermad Preparatory school in Aberystwyth, St Bees School in Cumberland, and University of Durham."

Nicholas remained in Australia, and I am sure that Arthur would have been immensely proud of his son and his accomplishments. Arthur's parents had moved to Bryn Seiriol, Llanallgo and Gwladys was housekeeper for Arthur at the Rectory. Jacob passed away on 20th March 1954 and was buried in St Gallgo's and Gwladys died in Welshpool on 1st June 1963 and was brought back to Anglesey to be buried with her husband. Arthur's brothers and sisters are all also buried in St Gallgo's. Gwendoline Rosa died on 12th October 1984, Violet May on 7th August 1987 and John Franklin Jones on 9th April 1997 and they are all in the same grave as Arthur. Austin Neville died on 3rd April 2001 and is in his own grave.

Glyn Evans, BA, 1943 – 1954

Glyn was born on 23rd October 1910 at Dolgoch, Bethesda to slate quarryman Owen Evans and his wife Ellen née Owens. He was the youngest of ten children, and it was early in life that he found a calling to the priesthood. His story is taken primarily from an obituary that appeared in the *Western Telegraph* on 25th February 2009 with a few specifics added here and there as I found them in other records. I am grateful to Heather DeFer (neé Evans) for supplying the photograph. Heather is a cousin of mine that I found through DNA, and she was born and lives in Michigan but is of Welsh descent. She contacted me as I added Glyn to my Ancestry family tree for this project to let me know that he was related to her - the fourth child of her three times great-grandfather! It is indeed a small world.

Glyn graduated from the University College of North Wales in Bangor in 1933 with a degree in the classics, and went to St Stephen's House, Oxford for theological training. He was ordained a Deacon in Bangor Cathedral on 21st December 1934 by Charles Green, the newly appointed Archbishop of Wales, and it was Charles' first ordination since his enthronement only a few days before. Two days later, Glyn took up the position of curate in Dolgellau, where he met his future wife, Iola Jones whom he married in 1941 when he was curate of Llanfairfechan. Their daughter, Rhian, was born the following year. The *North Wales Weekly News* reported on 26th August 1943 that Glyn had been appointed rector of our churches, and the family moved into the Llanallgo Rectory where they had three sons, Robert Wyn, Dewi Glyn and Hugh (Huw) Glyn.

129. Glyn Evans

During Glyn's time in our parishes, three more men of our parishes were killed in the war:

28th June 1944: 20-year-old William Leonard Murley Francis of Bodawen, Moelfre, a boatswain on the SS Dalegarth Force, was struck by shrapnel and killed at sea just off Dover.

His father, Captain William Jones Francis of Bodawen, was chief officer of the ship at the time and was with his son when he died. Leonard was laid to rest in St Gallgo's by Glyn on Tuesday July 4th, 1944.

14th November 1944: 46-year-old Richard "Dick" Thomas, was another man who would be buried in his home parish with Glyn officiating; his story is a little different. From 26th May until 4th June 1940, around 198,000 British and 140,000 French and Belgian troops were evacuated from the beach at Dunkirk, with the help of both naval and civilian ships and boats. Anyone who has watched the 2017 film "Dunkirk" cannot fail to have been simultaneously horrified at the danger and impressed with the bravery, as these men risked their lives to rescue those trapped on the shores. Dick was born in 1898 in 8 Penrhos Terrace and went on the sea as a youth at the beginning of WWI. He was at Dunkirk and never fully recovered from his experience, ultimately succumbing to Hodgkin's Lymphoma with Captain Henry Roberts of Dolfor Moelfre at his bedside and registering his death.

24th February 1945: 34-year-old John Roberts was 1st mate on the SS Oriskaney when she was hit on the port side by a torpedo from a U-boat and sank about 5 miles west of Lands' End. He was the brother of the beloved cook for many years in Llanallgo school, known to us kids as "Aunty Peggy Wenvoe".

In 1953, a project that was over 50 years in the making came to fruition which benefited the older children of our parishes. Sir Thomas Jones (1870–1945) was a local doctor, and the chairman of the county council, and he had campaigned tirelessly for a secondary school at Amlwch. It was the first comprehensive school in Britain that was purpose-built, and the foundation stone was laid on 17th September 1948 by Mr D.R. Hardman, Parliamentary Secretary to the Ministry of Education. The stone was polished Moelfre limestone, and inscribed by a young Amlwch craftsman, Mr Thomas Owen Williams, with a record of the occasion and the Welsh motto "Gorau Athro Ymgais" – effort is the best teacher. It was designed for about 700 students, and the official opening took place on 19th June 1953 by the Minister of Education, although it had opened its doors to children earlier than that.

The parish mariners were also famed for their service on the Moelfre lifeboat, whose crew had saved a great number of souls from watery graves. John Matthews served as Coxswain for 37 years before retiring just after his 65th birthday and, when he began as master, he was the youngest in the country. During his record service, the lifeboat saved some 300 lives, and, upon his retirement, he was awarded a coxswain's certificate of service and received a gold watch from the National Lifeboat Association for bravery. He was the little boy who nearly died in 1892 and whose story is told in the section on Griffith Bees Jones.

On 24th December 1954 the *Western Mail* announced Glyn's appointment as vicar of St Issell's with St Mary's Kilgetty, which later included the parish of Amroth, and the family moved to Saundersfoot in 1955. Sioned Harper, whose grandfather built Cae Marl, has very fond memories of the family: "*The only vicar and family I knew really well was Glyn Evans and his wife Iona. They had 4 children around my age, and I practically lived at the Rectory always there playing with them. I remember it as very happy times and was heartbroken when they left.*"

Glyn ministered at St Issell's for 25 years until his retirement in 1980 and during that time, he had become rural Dean, then canon treasurer of St David's Cathedral. In his retirement in St Florence, he worshipped mostly at St Florence and Redberth churches and continued to take a full and active part in the local community. He was a keen gardener, especially of vegetables, and before moving to St Florence, always kept bees. He had also been an active member of Probus in Tenby.

Glyn died at home on January 28th, 2009, aged 98 and he was buried on 6th February at St Issell's church. A private service at the family home was led by Reverend Robin Webley and the officiating clergy at the church were Canon Michael Butler, Canon Richard Rees, Rt Reverend Dewi Bridges and Reverend V. F. Millgate.

Thomas "Tom" Woodings, BA, 1955 – 1958

Tom was born on 24th September 1888 at 10 Fron Square in Upper Bangor to iron moulder Thomas William Woodings and his wife Catherine née Owen(s). He was an intelligent boy and attended Friars school in Bangor. In 1906, Friars' headmaster Mr Glynn Evans announced some stellar results in the Central Welsh Board Exams. Four students achieved honours certificates, including Tom, who placed 21st in the whole of Wales! The same year he won a John Hughes scholarship for £30 and a County Exhibition for £20, so he went to the University College of North Wales in Bangor with a grant of £50 a year and graduated in July 1910 with a 1st Class Honours in Greek, one of only two students ever to achieve this. Following graduation, he attended St Michaels College in Llandaff and was ordained as a Deacon in 1911 and as a priest in December 1912.

131a. Tom in his Friar's School Uniform

His first appointment was to Pwllheli as curate, and whilst he was there, a friend and St Michaels colleague, the Reverend Eliseus Griffith Parry, committed suicide in January 1915, and Tom was one of the officiating ministers at his funeral in Rhyl. The 26-year-old Eliseus had only recently been appointed rector of St Annes and he, too, was an accomplished academic. He stepped in front of a train and died a short time afterwards in the Royal

131. Tom Woodings

Alexandria Hospital. He was very popular in his new parish and was known as a cheerful and conscientious man. It is a stark reminder that depression and despair can often hide behind the most cheerful of smiles, and it must have been heart-breaking for Tom to bury his friend.

The 22nd of December 1915 edition of the *Western Mail* announced that Tom had been appointed to Llandegfan with Beaumaris, and he spent the next eight and a half years there. In early 1924 he was appointed vicar of Llanegryn in Merionethshire where he spent ten years, becoming rural Dean during his time there. In 1934 he was appointed rector of Llanbedrog and was made honorary Chaplain at RAF Penrhos.

On the brink of the second world war, the 16th June 1939 edition of the *Liverpool Evening Express* reported on a meeting of a Welsh delegation with the air minister, and Tom was one of that group as the representative for the Church in Wales. I do not know what the ultimate outcome of the meeting was.

In February 1945 he was inducted as rector of Dolgellau and Corris church, and upon his departure from Llanbedrog, his parishioners presented him with a cheque. His unmarried sister Elizabeth lived with him as housekeeper, and she received the gift of a handbag from the members of the St Pedrog Sunday school. He spent a further ten years in Dolgellau, during which time he had quite a distressing experience. The National Eisteddfod was held in Dolgellau in the Summer of 1949, and the only flag that Tom's church owned was the Union Jack and, like many others in the town, he flew it on the flagpole atop the church tower. In the early hours of the morning on 4th August, a group of four young Nationalists especially appointed for the task, entered the church through an open door, climbed the 120 steps to the top of the tower, replaced the Union Jack with the Welsh flag and took the Union Jack with them. When it was discovered, Tom at once reported the incident to the Bishop of Bangor and, in an interview with the *Western Mail* newspaper, his sister Elizabeth said that Tom was "*most distressed*" and that "*these people got into the church during the night and took away the Union Jack. The rector feels most upset because there are many more Union Jacks flying in the town and these young fellows could have taken one of them down if they wanted to make a protest. They should not have broken into the church. It may not be sacrilege, but it is very near it. The church people here are upset indeed.*" Tom considered it a discourteous thing to have done. In response, the Nationalists said that they considered the flying of the Union Jack an insult to Wales in a thoroughly Welsh area during the national festival of the Welsh people. They suggested that the Union Jack flag would be returned undamaged at the close of the eisteddfod, and that the Welsh flag would be left there as an "*unsolicited gift*" to the church.

Tom's next appointment was to our churches, and by mid 1955, he and his sister Elizabeth had moved into the rectory. A couple of notable events that happened in Wales around this time include Cardiff being named as the official capital of Wales on 20th December 1955, and on 31st July 1957 the controversial Tryweryn Bill was signed into law, allowing the Liverpool City Council to build a reservoir thereby drowning the village of Capel Celyn.

WELSH DEPUTATION SEES AIR MINISTER

Mr. Lloyd George, accompanied by Major Owen, M.P. for Carnarvonshire, and Miss Megan Lloyd George, M.P. for Anglesey, yesterday invited Sir Kingsley Wood, Secretary of State for Air, who was accompanied by Air Vice-Marshal Portal, to meet at an informal luncheon at the House of Commons a deputation from Carnarvonshire on the subject of bombing and air-firing.

The deputation was representative of all local authorities and religious denominations in the county. Mr. William George put the case for the local authorities and the Rev. John Owen that for the religious denominations.

After a free and frank discussion, to which Sir Kingsley Wood listened sympathetically, he said he would carefully consider the representations which had been made to him on this important subject and would give his reply as soon as possible.

The full deputation was composed as follows: The Rev. John Owen, M.A., Moria Nevin, and Rev. C. Roberts-Jones, M.A., B.D., Pwllheli (representing the Welsh Presbyterian Church); the Rev. A. J. George, B.A., B.D., Four Crosses (representing the Baptist Church); the Rev. J. H. Pugh, Abersoch (representing the Congregational Church); the Rev. W. J. Jones, Pwllheli (representing the Wesleyan Church); the Rev. T Woodings, Llanbedrog (representing the Church in Wales); Dr. R. Jones-Evans, Mayor of Pwllheli, Councillor J. T. Jarrett, Nevin and Mr. S R. Jones (representing the Lleyn Rural District Council); Mr. W. Roberts (chairman Carnarvonshire County Council) and Mr. William George (representing Carnarvonshire County Council).

132. *Liverpool Evening Express*, 16th June 1939

There was fierce opposition in Wales with every Welsh MP (except one abstainer) voting against the Bill. The Minister of Welsh Affairs in Westminster at the time was Conservative politician and Englishman Henry Brooke and he caused great anger throughout Wales for his support of the Bill. As we might imagine, this was a topic of heated discussion by just about everyone at the National Eisteddfod, which took place in Llangefni a few days later. In fact, Henry Brooke was scheduled to attend the ceremony for welcoming home Welshmen from overseas, but some of the exiles made it known that they planned to walk out of the pavilion to the music of Men of Harlech if he were to be present. More controversy ensued when the leader of the Welsh Nationalists wrote to the Eisteddfod Council warning of likely trouble if Henry were to attend. In the end Henry decided not to make an appearance, and the ceremony took place without fuss. It was not only the Nationalists who were unhappy with him and his attendance, as shown by the slew of letters from individuals from a variety of political parties that appeared in the newspapers after the event, all saying how pleased they were that he did not show up. On a positive note, there was cause for much celebration locally when the actor, Hugh Griffith of Marianglas, was initiated into the Gorsedd Circle and became a bard. The eisteddfod was very well attended with Llangefni "bursting at the seams" before most of the attendees had even arrived.

On 12th December 1957, the peace and quiet of the area was shattered by, of all things, a plane crash at Ponc Refail farm. A newspaper ran the headline *"Blazing jet wreckage falls on farmhouse"* with the following account: *"A Royal Naval student pilot due to graduate in seven days' time, was killed yesterday when his Mark V Vampire jet plane disintegrated in the air over Marian-glas, Anglesey. And a farmer missed death by only a few minutes when pieces of the burning plane crashed down on a haystack where he had been standing.*

The student was Lieut. Nicholas John Lipscomb of Shard House, Hambleton near Blackpool of No. 7 Flying Training School at the R.A.F. Valley Camp, Anglesey. An R.A.F. spokesman said last night: 'Contrary to reports circulating in this area this aircraft was not engaged in the search for the missing Canberra. The pilot was on No. 64 course and was on a training flight. He has been stationed at Valley for several months and had flown solo many times before. The cause of the accident is unknown' he added.

The farmer, Mr Hugh Williams aged 35 of Ponc Refail Farm Marian-glas, who lost all his hay and farm implements including a £750 pick-up bailer, in a fire started by the wreckage said: 'I was getting ready to go to Llangefni market when I suddenly saw a plane hurtling down towards me. The next thing I knew was that wreckage was falling on my farm. I raced back to the house to see if my wife and four-month-old daughter were all right. When I found they were I saw my haystack was burning furiously so I ran to my neighbour's house 200 yards away and telephoned the fire brigade. It was a big shock to me for five minutes earlier I was standing on the very spot where a heavy piece of metal fell' he said.

Llangefni Fire Brigade commanded by Anglesey's Chief Fire Officer, Mr L.E.R. Loder, Beaumaris Fire Brigade, police officers R.A.F. personnel from Valley, ambulances and farm workers raced to the scene to help. Firemen had to run hose a quarter-of-a-mile to the nearest hydrant. The farmhouse itself suffered little damage despite the burning haystack 10 yards away. Parts of the wrecked plane, however, were found on the roof-top and a window was broken.

Mr William Jones, 43-year-old bricklayer of Rhiwlas, was working on a house at Marian-glas when the plane crashed. He said 'I heard the plane in the air and looking up I saw it coming from the direction of Benllech. The plane appeared to be losing height with her nose down. I heard an explosion which was accompanied by fire and smoke. I telephoned 999 and raced to the farm to help.'"

At the inquest it was revealed that there were three planes flying in formation on a normal training flight and they were doing a loop when the leader heard Lipscomb radio that he was bailing out. There was no ejector seat on the Vampire plane and the parachute was found burnt and torn with an empty harness; despite a thorough search, no intact body was found. The coroner said that there was no evidence as to what had happened to the plane. Nicholas was the son of engineer Robert and Phyllis née Harland and was born in 1934 in the Stockton area. He left a Last Will and Testament with probate to his father and personal effects worth £622 3s 4d. Tom Roberts was a student at Llanallgo school and remembers the day well. He told me "*I remember looking out of the windows in Miss Owen's class and seeing a huge ball of red and black flames climbing high into the sky.*" Although it is not mentioned in the newspaper, Bryn Jones says that this was the first callout for the Benllech Fire Station. Thank goodness that no-one else was hurt, and the losses were not greater.

RECORDER OF CHESTER BEREAVED

Through the death of his father, Colonel Lawrence Williams

The Recorder of Chester, Mr. Francis Williams, Q.C., was bereaved last Friday by the death of his father, Col. Lawrence Williams, aged 83, of Parciau, Marianglas, Anglesey.

Col. Williams was a magistrate from the age of 23 until he was 75, and was a member of the Anglesey County Council for 56 years.

The funeral took place in Anglesey on Monday, and a memorial service was held there on Wednesday.

133. Cheshire Observer, 14th June 1958

Tom buried three members of the Parciau Williams family in St Eugrad's within the space of less than two years. Colonel Lawrence's sister, Mona Rosamund Alice Lees, died on 18th October 1956, his daughter Rosamund died on 28th February 1957 and the 82-year-old Colonel himself died on 6th June 1958. He was what I consider the last *Lord of Llaneugrad* as by the time he died, many of the properties were now owned by other individuals and the old very large estate had dwindled in size. This was to be Tom's last burial in St Eugrad's and quite an honour to bury such an accomplished and well-respected man.

Anything that Tom had to deal with previously paled into insignificance compared to what happened in the Rectory according to an account in the book *Haunted Anglesey* by the late Bunty Austin. I will paraphrase from Bunty's book as I have not been able to contact a family member to obtain permission to reproduce the text. Tom, who had always been closely associated with Bangor Cathedral was made a Cursal Canon in 1953 and was Precentor there from 1957 until his retirement. This meant that he had to spend a month a year living in Bangor. One very windy Winter's night, he left the rectory to spend his time at the cathedral. His sister Elizabeth said goodbye on the doorstep and returned to sit and read by the warm fire in the front room. At bedtime, she secured the house as usual and turned off the downstairs lights, making her way upstairs to bed as she had done every night since they had moved to the rectory. But this night was different. Halfway up the stairs, she felt the sensation of someone's head pressing against her chest and the sound of slow breathing rang loudly in her ears. At first, she was paralyzed with fright and then turned and fled back downstairs to the front room, locking the door behind her. After waiting to see if she could hear anything except the blood pounding in her ears, she phoned her brother and begged him to come and fetch her, declaring that she could not stay in the house all night on her own. She babbled her story to him, and although he could barely understand what she was saying, he realized that she had had a very frightening experience. He told her to stay in the room and that he would come and get her. Elizabeth refused to return to the Rectory after that, and Tom ended up resigning as rector of our churches.

He attended a committee meeting which was held to decide who the next rector of our churches would be and declared that the house must not be used as a rectory in the future. He told them about Elizabeth's experience and how she had not been able to speak for three whole weeks due to shock. He had spoken to maids who had previously been in service in the rectory, and they told him that they too had the exact same experience. The committee were stunned, especially as they knew Elizabeth to be an intelligent woman who was not given to hysteria. At this time, they were also reviewing the dwindling congregations in the area and hit upon a solution that would kill two birds with one stone as the saying goes. They decided to formally combine the Llaneugrad and Llanallgo benefice with that of

Penrhosllugwy, thus making the Penrhosllugwy rectory available as a possibility for a home the next incumbent. I have a theory as to who this ghost could be, and the story is told in the chapter Ghosts and a Goblin.

Tom's tenure as rector of our churches ended in mid to late 1958, and he spent the rest of his career in Bangor Cathedral, before retiring in 1963. After his retirement, he continued to worship in Bangor Cathedral, and was particularly fond of Cathedral music. He died on 27th May 1978 aged 90 and is buried in Glanadda where his parents and other family members are buried.

William Rees Hughes, BA, 1958 – 1973

Rees was born on 3rd May 1908 on Bryn Engan farm, Capel Curig to farmer Rhys and Catherine Ann née Thomas and both his grandfather and great grandfather had farmed the 350 acres or so. Rees attended Llanrwst Grammar School followed by the University College of North Wales in Bangor, graduating in June 1930 with a BA in Welsh. He attended St Michael's College at Llandaff, and was ordained a Deacon by Dr Charles Green, Bishop of Bangor, on Saturday 18th December 1937 and licenced to Glanogwen, Bethesda where he worked for the Reverend Richard H. Hughes. He was appointed to Llanfechell in 1942 after the previous incumbent, Reverend William Morris Jones, moved to Llanbadrig.

Rector's new benefice.—The Rev. W. R. Hughes, rector of Llanfechell, Anglesey, has accepted nomination by the Bangor Diocesan Patronage Board to the benefice of Llaneugrad with Llanallgo, Anglesey.

134. *Western Mail*, 27th September 1958

On 11th August 1943 Rees married 30-year-old teacher, Daisy Williams, of 28, Bryntirion, Bethesda in Llanfechell church. On 27th September 1958, the *Western Mail* announced that Rees had accepted nomination by the Bangor Diocesan Patronage Board to the benefice of Llaneugrad and Llanallgo and by this time, Penrhosllugwy was included. I do not know if the circumstances surrounding Tom Woodings' departure were told to Rees by the Board, but I am sure that they must have been aware of Elizabeth's experience and the fact that Tom had recommended that the rectory not be used in the future. Perhaps there was some sort of exorcism performed at the rectory as Rees and Daisy did live there for a short time before moving to the Penrhosllugwy rectory. The Llanallgo rectory was later sold to Edmund and Eileen Clarke, and it was re-named The Cloister.

There were quite a number of notable events during Rees's tenure and include Shirley Bassey becoming the first Welsh singer to have a number one hit in the singles charts with "As I Love You" at the beginning of 1959, and on 29th September 1960, Ricky Valance made his own mark as the first male Welsh singer to have a number one hit with "Tell Laura I Love Her". In 1959, the current flag was made the official flag of Wales by the Queen and in 1961 the film Ben Hur, which featured Marian-glas born Hugh Griffith as Sheik Ilderim (for which he won an Oscar,) played for the whole Summer in the Savoy cinema Llandudno and proved to be a "great attraction" according to the newspapers.

CLASSICAL TRADITION

In his address Mr. Rees Hughes contrasted the sense of values represented by the school of 350 years ago in which religion and the classical tradition were prominent, with the uncertainty about values in modern industrialised society. There had been a loss of a true sense of values where people often earned a lot of money but were without joy in their hearts, he said.

Teachers, particularly in secondary schools, had a tremendous responsibility because children were in their care at the critical time of their lives when they chose careers for the future. The claims of posts which were worthwhile, although they might not offer the most money, had to be remembered.

135. *North Wales Weekly News,* 22nd December 1960

The school that Rees attended, Llanrwst Grammar School (now called Ysgol Dyffryn Conwy) is one of the five ancient Grammar schools of the country. It was founded in 1610 by Sir John Wynne of Gwydir, father-in-law of Sir John Bodvel and grandfather of Colonel John Bodvel. In the "Orders, Rules, Statutes and Ordinances" made by Sir John in 1612, he decided that it should be a Free School (Ysgol Râd), which was very progressive for the time. It was the 350th anniversary of the school in 1960, and a memorable celebration was held in December, with Rees giving one of the addresses which was reported in the *North Wales Weekly News* on 22nd December.

The Moelfre lifeboat was as busy as ever performing rescues, especially in the Summer with the influx of tourists, and sometimes they were called upon for different purposes. Major Thomas Corrigan of Parciau had taken over as Lifeboat secretary upon the retirement of his father-in-law, Col. Lawrence Williams, and when he died, the lifeboat carried his ashes in a casket draped in the Union Jack out into Moelfre Bay where they were scattered by Coxswain Dic Evans, with Rees conducting the committal service. Hundreds of villagers and visitors attended, filling the clifftops along the coast.

St Gallgo's has been host to visitors from all over the world coming to view the site of the *Royal Charter* disaster and the graves of those who perished. On 24th May 1962, Rees and others hosted

WHERE ROYAL CHARTER SANK

HISTORICAL SOCIETY VISIT LLANALLGO

A strong party from Aberconwy Historical Society on Wednesday, last week, visited the church at Llanallgo where the memory is preserved of the 434 victims of the Royal Charter disaster. On October 26, 1859, the then famous auxiliary clipper ship was driven ashore at Porth Helaeth near Moelfre, in one of the worst gales of all time.

The 66 members of the excursion were received by the vicar, Rev. W. R. Hughes, and were shown the interesting church, contemporary records of the shipwreck, and other items of interest, including the memorial column raised to the victims near their mass graves in the churchyard.

The vicar mentioned that by a coincidence in October, 1959, as a service was being held in Llanallgo Church, during which the memory of the Royal Charter was very much in mind it being the centenary of the event, the coaster Hindlea was being driven on to the rocks very near to where the Royal Charter was wrecked.

From Llanallgo the party went to Moelfre and members walked down to Porth Helaeth to see the rock on which the ship foundered. A few yards away stands a commemorative pillar.

136. *North Wales Weekly News,* 24th May 1962

sixty-six members of the Aberconwy Historical Society and *The North Wales Weekly* news covered the visit. Rees told the visitors about the wreck of the *Hindlea* almost exactly 100 years after the Royal Charter was wrecked. There was a fierce gale that turned into a hurricane with gusts of up to 104 mph recorded at RAF and coastguard stations around Anglesey. The *Hindlea* had been anchored in Dulas Bay, but when the wind direction changed, she started dragging her anchor and drifting towards the shore. There was no time to lose, and Coxswain Dic Evans and mechanic Evan Owen tried to assemble a crew. Hampered by downed telephone lines, they were only able to reach 2nd Cox Donald Murley Francis (who also served as assistant mechanic) and Bowman Hugh Owen who was also hero of the 1927 Excel rescue. The fifth and last recruit was a volunteer who was a helper on the slipway, and who had never been out on service on the lifeboat - talk about trial by fire! They launched the temporary lifeboat, the *Edmund & Mary Robinson* (the *Watkin Williams* was being refitted) in what would prove to be an extraordinarily dangerous rescue mission. Time and again, Dic brought the lifeboat alongside the listing ship, often being pounded into it by the raging sea, and on each attempt, a *Hindlea* crew member was able to jump to safety into the lifeboat. They managed to rescue all eight crew members before the *Hindlea* was pounded to pieces on the rocks. Dic was awarded the Gold Medal for Gallantry, Evan the Silver Medal and Donald and Hugh Jones the Bronze Medal and Hugh Owen was awarded a second clasp to add to his Bronze Medal earned on the prior rescue. Later that year, all five of the crew were awarded the Silver Medal for Gallantry at Sea by the Queen in Buckingham Palace.

The construction of Wylfa power station began in 1963, with employment opportunities for locals and bringing in workers from elsewhere. People also began coming to Anglesey to retire, and all of this stimulated the expansion of several villages, including Moelfre and bolstered church congregations. The *North Wales Weekly News* carried an advertisement on 24th May 1962 for the upcoming construction of the Sea View estate. It was to consist of 12 luxury bungalows priced from £2,500 to £3,500.

"SEA VIEW" ESTATE,
MOELFRE BAY, ANGLESEY.
Construction to commence soon on
12 LUXURY BUNGALOWS
PRICED FROM £2,500 TO £3,550.
Complete details from—
SOLE AGENTS: IRFONWY JONES & CO., Tel. 75178.
Builders: Case North Western (Builders) Ltd.
Developed by: Palmrose Properties Ltd.

137. *North Wales Weekly News*, 24th May 1962

My earliest memory of disastrous news that affected just about everyone was in 1966. I vividly remember coming home from school on Friday 21st October and hearing about the disaster at Aberfan. This was by far the saddest and most shocking of all colliery disasters as 116 children and 28 adults were killed as the contents of a coal spoil tip cascaded down the mountainside, burying Pantglas Junior School and a row of houses. I was only seven and it frightened me to the core that so many primary school children could go to school and never come home. We prayed very hard that Sunday morning in Llanallgo Paraduys chapel for all those little lost souls, as I am sure they did in St Eugrad's and St Gallgo's.

Charles was made Prince of Wales on 26th July 1958, and on 1st July 1969, the official investiture was held in Caernarfon Castle. Huge crowds gathered on the streets of Caernarvon, and we watched it on television. I do not know who was invited to the event, but I wonder if Rees was able to attend in person. There was a lovely tea party held to celebrate the event in the old British School in Marian-glas, and I think just about the whole village was there. It has become an annual event and the 50th anniversary tea party was held in 2019 before two years of Covid temporarily halted it.

The Britannia Bridge over the straits today looks nothing like it originally did when it was first built. During the evening of 23rd May 1970, some boys playing in the tunnel dropped a burning torch which set alight the tar-coated wooden roof of the tubes. Even with the best efforts of the Caernarfonshire and Anglesey fire brigades, the fire could not be controlled, and it spread all the way across from the mainland to the Anglesey side. The bridge was no longer useable and had to be closed to rail traffic – a huge inconvenience to those travelling from the mainland to and from Holyhead. It was decided to rebuild it as a road-and-rail bridge, and it opened to rail traffic on 30th January 1972 and to road traffic in 1980.

The following are some of my own memories of Rees and Daisy as well as a couple from others:

My mother was from Marian-glas and had moved to Nelson Lancashire to get work, where she met and married my dad and had my sister, Lynne, and I. We moved to Marian-glas in the Summer of 1965 and, as Mum's family were chapel, she had us go to Llanallgo Paraduys chapel on Sunday morning and to the Sunday school in the afternoon in the old British School. Sad to say that we did not like giving up our Sunday afternoons for more "school", and eventually pestered our mother to let us go to church (they did not have a Sunday school in St Eugrad's so that was a great attraction to us.) She eventually agreed but it was a bit daunting going to the first service, and we stepped into the old church with a bit of trepidation. We need not have worried, though, as Rees and the St Eugrad's congregation welcomed us with open arms. We were the youngest by far and, with the aging congregation, it must have been heart-warming to see children in attendance, whatever their motivation.

In the early 1970s, Lynne and I prepared for our confirmation together with children from St Gallgo's and St Michael's Penrhosllugwy. The classes were held in St Gallgo's on a weekday evening, and I remember that Daisy would provide us with a drink as well as, what were for me, "upscale" biscuits – ones with a very nice filling, possibly custard creams. Looking back, I think it was a ploy to make sure we turned up every week as I remember everyone (including myself) being very excited indeed for those biscuits. Rees was a very kind and patient teacher; we were suitably prepared and all of us did a splendid job at the confirmation ceremony. It was held in early Summer at St Michael's and the Bishop of Bangor officiated, which was extremely exciting for us. My paternal grandparents were visiting from Burnley and attended, and we had a lovely tea afterwards in the Penrhosllugwy school. We felt very grown up indeed to then be able to take holy communion with the adults in the church on the first Sunday of the month.

A couple of people have told me that Daisy continued her passion for teaching, and she had a very small nursery class that she held at the Penrhosllugwy vicarage which they both attended, this being some time before nursery schools became popular.

Eleanor Jones (née Thomas) Bronallt, remembers that Daisy played the organ in St Eugrad's before her grandmother, Margaret Wild, took over, and that Rees christened both Eleanor and her brother Tudor. He also christened the author's brother, Justin, in 1970.

Rees retired in late 1973, and he and Daisy moved to Rhianfa Estate in Benllech, and they named their house "Siabod". I suspect that it was named after the 872-meter-high mountain, Moel Siabod, the highest peak in the area around Capel Curig and the farm Bryn Engan where Rees grew up. Rees died on 21st February 1979 in Bangor and is buried in St Eugrad's with Daisy who passed away in 2001.

Hugh Hughes, BA, 1974 – 1982

Hugh was born on 6th September 1913 in his grandmother's house, Beehive, in Llannerch-y-medd to farmer Hugh Thomas Hughes and wife Lizzie née Jones, the third of their five children. Beehive was both a house and a shop, and it was Lizzies family who lived there. Her father, Elizeus, was a farmer and grocer who had grown up in Bryn Gwallen in Rhodogeidio. Hugh's father, Hugh Thomas, was born in Llandrygarn and brought up in Ynys Goed, Coedana.

Hugh Thomas and Lizzie were married in Moriah Chapel, Llangefni on 30th December and the family lived at Tyddyn Melys, Llanfihangel Tre'r Beirdd which is quite famous as the birthplace of Lewis Morris in 1701, the eldest of the Morris brothers (Morisiaid Môn). Lizzie died of TB in Beehive on 4th March 1920 when Hugh was only six years old, and the siblings were split up to be raised by relatives. Hugh was brought up by an aunty who would guide him through his education and career choices, and he once told his son David that his two best career choices were teaching or the church, and it was his aunty who decided that the church was for him, even though he excelled in mathematics!

138. A Very Young Hugh

He went to St David's College in Lampeter, graduating in July 1935 with a bachelor's degree. He then attended St Michael's College at Llandaff and was ordained Deacon by the Bishop of Llandaff in September 1936 and was licenced to the curacy of Llanfaethlu and Llanfwrog. Charles Green, the Archbishop of Wales, and Bishop of Bangor, was unwell at the time, and so the ordination took place by Letters Dimissory process (this type of letter testifies that the subject has all the qualities demanded by canon law for the reception of the order in question and requests the bishop to whom they are addressed to ordain him.) The following September, he was ordained a priest

The Clergymen

by the Archbishop of Wales and Bishop of Bangor in Bangor Cathedral. Whilst the vicar travelled around in a large Austin 16, curate Hugh had an old motorbike to get around his parishes and perform his parochial duties.

He stayed in Llanfaethlu & Llanfwrog until 1941 and during his time there, he caught the eye of a lady from Benllech, a regular visitor at her aunty and uncle's farm, Bodowen and a courtship began. Hugh was a lodger at the farm and the lady's name was Rhonwen Eirlys Jones. He was curate in Holyhead church for a short time and was living in Holyhead when he married Rhonwen on 14th July 1942 in Llanfair ME church.

She was born 25th February 1920, the daughter of Thomas Jones and Ellen Grace née Roberts of Mynachlog in Benllech. Thomas was the grandson of blacksmith Hugh Jones of Refail Newydd and later Ponciau, Llaneugrad whose story is told in the book *The People of Llaneugrad Volume 1*. Hugh stayed in Holyhead at least through 1945, but by the time Rhonwen's father passed away in 1952, he had

139. Hugh and Rhonwen on their Wedding Day

moved to Dolwyddelan, and he was still there in 1956 when a newspaper article makes mention that he was ill. Rhonwen told the story that the Llanfaethlu motorbike had been dismantled during the war and was taken in a sack to Dolwyddelan where Hugh rebuilt it. He was apparently quite the mechanic as their sons John and David remember that if they ever had problems with their early unreliable cars that their father could be relied upon to fix the problem and on more than one occasion this involved a total engine strip down. Hugh was also an excellent clock repairer and carpenter, a skill that would come in very handy in retirement!

He became rector of Llanfaelog at the beginning of 1957 and remained there until 1970, when he came to our

140. Author's Wedding St Eugrad's 1981

The Clergymen

parishes according to the parish magazine reporting on Rhonwen's passing. It was in 1974 that he was appointed rector of Llanallgo, Llaneugrad, Penrhosllugwy and Llanfihangel Tre'r Beirdd and he and Rhonwen moved into the rectory in Moelfre. Rhonwen was very active supporting all four churches in the Benefice with her boundless energy and enthusiasm, and people remember her kindness, good humour, and infectious laugh.

Hugh officiated at both mine and my sister's weddings in Llaneugrad church. I was married on 19th September 1981, and the unforgettable John Hanks played the organ for us. Hugh retired the following year and so I think that my marriage must have been either the last, or one of the last, that he conducted in Llaneugrad.

Hugh and Rhonwen retired to Craig y Don in Benllech where his first job was to install a new kitchen and then work on other renovations in their new home. Hugh continued to help with church services until his 80s and the two of them were always together, sharing the same interests and promoting the same goodwill and friendship. They had been happily married for just about 65 years when Rhonwen passed away aged 86 on 2nd February 2007.

In his later years Hugh suffered with dementia and moved to Plas Mona Residential home. In his time there, his early years in Llannerch-y-medd became very prominent for him and he would regularly recite an old Welsh poem, that he likely learned at school, to anyone who would listen:

Yn Llannerch-y-medd ym Mondo
Y claddwyd Brenin Pabo
A'r frenhines deg ei gwedd
Yn Llannerch-y-medd mae hono.

In Llannerch-y-medd Anglesey
King Pabo was buried
And the fair-faced Queen
In Llannerch-y-medd is she.

141. Hugh and Rhowen in Retirement

Hugh passed away in Plas Mona on 2nd January 2011 aged 97 and is remembered as a very cordial and easy-going personality, proud but gentle and mild-mannered, always polite and who liked to tease in a light-hearted way.

Elena Johnson says of her father "He was indeed a gentle and kind man who loved being with his family and friends. He did love to tease - particularly the grandchildren - but they loved him for it. Such happy memories of him."

Granddaughter Vicki Louise Smith tells me "Ahh you've made me cry. So lovely reading this about Taid. He was genuinely the most loveliest man, and we were so lucky to have him as our Taid. He adored Nain and did whatever he was told 😊. Such fond memories of him teasing us and wheeling us around in wheelbarrows. He was also brilliant at drawing horses!"

Grandson Chris Hughes saw my post on the Llaneugrad Facebook page telling Hugh's story and says: "Fascinating to see Taid on Facebook. Completely agree with final comments regarding his personality although a competitive spirit lurked whenever we played a game. Each summer he happily taught me a lesson or two playing croquet in the back garden in Benllech".

Philip Hughes, 1983 – 1995

142. Ordination in 1982 with Archbishop Gwilym

Everyone seems to agree that Philip was the most successful and effective modern-day rector of our parishes. Under his leadership, he did so much for the services, worship and three levels of youth groups. His wife Sandy says *"So much could not have been done without the practical and ongoing support of so many (you all know who you are) and sadly many who are no longer with us. It was a time of great generosity of spirit and action, and we praise God for blessing those years of ministry. A very special time and place and people which will never be forgotten."* She is of course right in that it takes the support and work of people in the community to make a difference, but it really all starts with an extraordinary leader who has a vision for what they want to accomplish and who can engage and inspire people to help fulfil the vision. Philip was that extraordinary leader.

He was born in Bangor in November 1947, the only child of local bus driver and RAC Patrolman Norman from Dwygyfylchi and Lily née Lewis who was the fourth of nine daughters born to quarryman Hugh Lewis, a smallholder from Llanfairfechan. Although he was baptised at St Gwynin's Church, Dwygyfylchi, he later attended Salem, Capel yr Annibynwyr (the Congregational Chapel) in Penmaenmawr and after marriage returned to the Anglican fold attending Church of our Saviour on the West Shore, Llandudno.

Philip grew up in Penmaenmawr and attended the National Primary School followed by the local Secondary Modern School for two years and then transferred to John Bright

Grammar School in Llandudno. After completing a year at Bangor Normal College, he embarked on a 12-year career with Lloyds Bank starting in Rhyl and then moving on to Y Felinheli, Llandudno and finally Oswestry.

In 1970 Philip married Sandra Cuthbertson (who had grown up on the Great Orme in Llandudno) in Holy Trinity Church in Llandudno and they had two daughters whilst living in Llandudno, Catrin and Rhian.

It was during the two years working for Lloyds Bank in Oswestry and attending St John the Baptist Church in Whittington that Philip discerned God's call to the ordained ministry and, following training at St John's College, Nottingham (founded as the London College of Divinity), he was ordained at Bangor Cathedral in June 1981. He then began a two-year curacy with Canon Elias Hughes in Dolgellau.

143. Installation as Canon at Bangor Cathedral 2010

It was in the Summer of 1983 that Philip was appointed to Llaneugrad, Llanallgo, Penrhosllugwy and Llanfihangel Tre'r Beirdd churches, and he and his family moved to the Rectory in Moelfre at the top of Nant Bychan which is now called Tŷ Ni. As a new incumbent, Philip was glad of the help and support of two Readers, John Roberts, and David Irons and, over the years, the Wardens at Llaneugrad, Captain Lawrence Williams, Bert Albiston, Tom Meakin and Elma Verrinder. The organists during his tenure were Margaret Wild, Patti Doreen Records and latterly Mair Muir. The Reverend Canon Dr Graham Loveluck, who would be the very last rector of Llaneugrad and Llanallgo, joined Philip as a NSM Associate Priest in 1987.

During the years in Moelfre, Mothers' Union was reintroduced, and an extensive child and teenager's ministry was started with Pathfinder and CYFA groups. Monthly outdoor Songs of Praise Services were held in the summer months down by the sea in Moelfre. The churches in Llaneugrad and Llanallgo were reroofed, and the 'new' churchyard in Llanallgo was consecrated and opened.

144. Sandy and Philip in 2012

In January 1995 Philip was appointed to the Parishes of Llanberis and Llanrug, returning to Anglesey to the Parishes of Llanfairpwll with Llanddaniel-Fab, Llanedwen and Penmynydd in 2003, where he remained until retirement in July 2012 when he moved to

Conwy.

Philip was made a Canon of Bangor Cathedral in 2010 and is currently a member of the Bro Celynnin Ministry Team which includes St Mary and All Saints Church, Conwy; St Benedict's Church, Gyffin; St Mary's Church, Caerhun; St Peter's Church, Llanbedr y Cennin and Yr Hen Eglwys Llangelynnin (Llangelynnin Old Church).

Graham D. Loveluck, BSc., Ph.D., F.R.S.C., 1987 – 2004

Graham was born and brought up in Kenfig Hill, a vibrant mining village in the south Wales coalfields where his father Clifford and mother Elvina, née David, ran a boot and shoe business. An accomplished scholar, Graham went to the grammar school in Bridgend followed by the university at Aberystwyth where he studied Chemistry. He graduated with Honours in 1955 and stayed on at Aber for a further three years doing a Ph.D. in Chemistry. It was during this time that he met a fellow student, Llio Rhydderch Williams from Bangor who would later become his wife.

On June 18th, 1958, the Western Mail newspaper announced that three graduates who had been carrying out research in the chemistry department of the University College of Wales at Aberystwyth had been awarded major scholarships to go to the USA. One of those lucky students was Graham, who got to spend two years at Brown University, Providence, Rhode Island, as a Research Associate to Prof. Robert Cole, the chairman of the Chemistry Department. During his time at Brown, he was licenced as a Reader in the Anglican Cathedral in Providence by the English-born diocesan Bishop of Rhode Island, John Seville Higgins.

After returning to the UK, he spent two years as Lecturer in Polymer Chemistry at the Welsh College of Advanced Technology (WCAT) in Cardiff and he and Llio were married in 1961. In 1962 he was appointed Head of Chemistry and later Head of the Science Department at the newly established Atlantic College at St Donat's Castle in Llantwit Major. This was the founding college of the United World College Movement which today has 18 global schools and colleges. St Donat's is a medieval castle that was bought in 1925 by William Randolph Hearst, the American newspaper tycoon, and transformed into what George Bernard Shaw described as *"what God would have built if he had had the money"*. Nine years after Hearst died, it was bought in 1960 by the son of the businessman and educational philanthropist Antonin Besse, who donated it to the trustees of UWC Atlantic. It must have been quite exciting and rewarding to be a part of founding such a college and what a beautiful building to work in! Although Graham was later invited to set up the Science Department at the Lester Pearson UWC in Vancouver, he declined the opportunity and in 1973 he was appointed Deputy Headmaster at Ysgol David Hughes at Menai Bridge.

On a spiritual level, he was Secretary of the Llandaff Diocesan Association of Readers from 1967 to 1972 and Secretary of the Archbishop's Commission on Boundaries and Structure of the Church in Wales from 1969 to 1977. After training at St Deiniol's Library, Hawarden, and gaining his General Ordination Certificate, he was ordained in Bangor

Cathedral as Deacon in 1978 and Priest in 1979.

He and Llio moved to Benllech in 1978 and Graham was appointed non-Stipendiary curate of the parish of Llanfair ME. They moved from Benllech to Gwenallt in Marian-glas in 1987 and he became the non-stipendiary curate to then rector of our parishes, Philip Hughes. After retiring as Deputy Headmaster in 1990, he was appointed Diocesan Director of Education in 1992 responsible for the 19 church schools in the diocese and for supervising the team of School Visitors. After Philip moved on, Graham became the Curate in charge of the parishes and continued as such until 2003 when he was made Rector.

Philip left Llaneugrad and Llanallgo churches in good repair having renewed the roof of each church and during Graham's tenure the roof of Penrhosllugwy church was renewed and the rectory house in Moelfre was sold. The Church Hall received an expensive and extensive renovation and Kay Hitchen was the moving power behind this; there is a plaque to her in the Hall. Despite being confined to a wheelchair she was a dynamic person and was the editor of the parish magazine which had a wide circulation. In Graham's monthly contribution he always detailed parish activities for posterity and when he retired, he deposited a complete run of 10 years of the magazine in the Llangefni Archives.

It wasn't just our churches that Philip left in a fine state, under his exceptional leadership the parish that Graham took over was a very cohesive and lively one. There were the weekly coffee mornings in the Church Hall at Moelfre which was too small for the Christmas concerts and Fairs, and they had to be moved to the Hall of Moelfre school. Each year on February 4th the Reverend Stephen Roose Hughes, who died on that day, was remembered with a service in the church which the senior pupils at Ysgol Moelfre attended. In Philip's time there was a flourishing Sunday School which continued after he left. The Summer Holiday Club was attended by 30 children, and teenagers were involved in the church in the Youth Alpha course. There was a weekly prayer meeting, and, during Advent and Lent, there were fortnightly Bible Studies which regularly attracted 15-20 adults. In addition to the regular Wednesday morning Eucharists, mid-week evening services were held during Lent.

Obviously, he could not carry out all these activities in the parish and carry on his work as Diocesan Director of Education - all of this could be achieved because there was a lay ministerial team. Together they worked out the fact they were the church – the people of God. Graham has a specialist ministry to administer the Sacraments, but others had specialist ministries too – organising youth work, running the bible studies, visiting, Mothers' Union, maintenance of the physical fabric and finance. They had five Readers, three of whom were licenced to administer the Sacrament. When the team went to the Cathedral to be licenced, they were 24 in number. This team also ran Parish Retreats in a retreat house in Penmaenmawr and Graham would attend the final session to celebrate the Eucharist.

Graham recalls that *"A unique event, possibly in the long history of the parish, occurred on the 25th of February 2001. A group of teenagers, who were to be confirmed, had never been christened. A decision was made to baptise them by immersion. Capel Sardis, the Baptist chapel at City Dulas, allowed us the use of their baptistry for the service."* The water in the baptistry was icy cold but the teenagers insisted on carrying on.

On September 1st, 2004. a near disaster occurred with a fire in Llanallgo church. Fortunately, it was discovered by a church member taking flowers to the church (the story is told in the Buildings chapter.) The church was redecorated and reopened on the 20th of October for Graham's final service as rector.

Graham was made Canon in 2000 and was the Canonicus Quartus. When he retired in 2004 at 70 years of age, it was the end of a very long era indeed and he had the honour of being the last Rector of our parishes and the last resident Anglican priest. At his ministerial review Bishop Barry Morgan had asked him what he aiming to do in his ministry, and he had replied 'Make myself redundant' and he achieved this. Of his time as curate and then rector, Graham says *"What a wonderful and exhilarating time those eight years were!"*

Of course, Graham's story would not be complete without a mention of his very famous and highly accomplished wife, Llio Rhydderch née Williams. She was born in Bangor to John Prydderch Williams and Margaret née Williams and is the granddaughter of William Daniel Williams who ran the Ty'nygongl Post Office for many years and who also held the tenancy of Bryn Hafod stores in Marian-glas for a period. Llio attended the girl's grammar school in Bangor followed by university in Aberystwyth studying Welsh and Music. She graduated with Honours and was a Lady Gladstone Music Scholar. She taught Welsh in Pontarddulais at secondary level, and at primary level in Cowbridge where they lived while Graham was at Atlantic College. She later taught Welsh at Ysgol David Hughes and was a peripatetic harp teacher in Anglesey.

A highly accomplished harpist, composer, and improviser, she has made several CDs (I have all of them) which are a delight to listen to. She is one of the very few harpists who play the triple harp, an instrument that originated in Italy but was adopted by Welsh harpists in London in the 17th century and came to be known as the Welsh harp. She was a student of Nansi Richards who was known as "Queen of the Harp" or by her bardic name, Telynores Maldwyn and Llio herself has concentrated on teaching the skill to as many young harpists as possible. In 2021 she was interviewed remotely, and played for, the Edinburgh Harp Festival and the following biography appears on their website: *"At Llio's touch, the Welsh triple harp is a meeting point of tradition and creativity and two Welsh harp lineages that extend back many centuries. Raised in a living tradition, music has been a constant in Llio's life, shared around the family hearth from her earliest memories. Her creative explorations and boundary-breaking artistry have taken traditional Welsh music and the triple harp to sound worlds of exquisite vision and emotional depth. Celebrated around the world through her recordings and international performances, Llio's monumental contribution to Welsh culture was finally recognized with an Honorary Fellowship from Bangor University in 2019."* In 2020, RootsWorld magazine published a very flattering review written by Andrew Cronshaw of her CD *Sir Fôn Bach*. He called Llio a "national treasure", and absolutely nobody would argue with that! The full review can be found on the internet at https://www.rootsworld.com/reviews/llio-rhydderch-20.shtml.

Usually when a rector has finished their term of office in a parish he or she will move away, but in Graham's case, his home was in the Parish and where he lived before being appointed, so he and Llio remained. Despite Graham's advanced years he continues as a faithful volunteer at the Moelfre Lifeboat Seawatch Centre, is a member of many local societies and is an asset to the community. Graham and Llio are still enjoying their retirement living in Marian-glas in Gwenallt, which used to be called Fair View and was renamed sometime in the 1970s by the former owners.

Honourable Mention: Peter and Pat Day

Peter was not a rector of our churches, but a Lay Reader and someone, who with his wife Pat née Smart, has made a tremendous impact in our churches over the years. He is well deserving of an honourable mention in this book, not only in his service to the churches, but also for his tireless work and efforts with regards to the Royal Charter Wreck – keeping the memories alive and linking descendants of the victims with their ancestors' stories and graves. Here is a bit of his story.

In early summer of 1944, Lt. Commander Frank Day, RN came to Benllech whilst on leave and bought the Wendon Cafe and all the surrounding land. Very soon after making the purchase he was urgently recalled joining the D Day operations in his role commanding a Motor Torpedo Boat. At the time, the Day family lived in Deganwy and in September Frank, Monica and their three children, Margaret, Rita, and baby Peter moved to live in a bungalow close to the Wendon Cafe at Benllech Beach. Peter had been born on 1st May that year in Colwyn Bay.

Peter's schooling began in a kindergarten run by two German ladies who luckily had left Germany in the early months of WWII, escaping almost certain death. At the age of five he moved to the Primary School at Llanallgo with class teachers Miss Parry and Henry Davies and Headmaster Mr. Trevor Owen. At age eight Peter became a weekly boarder at Hillgrove School, Bangor and then joined his old Benllech friends in attending Sir Thomas Jones School, Amlwch. He recalls that those were happy years of playing rugby and attending lessons, in that order!

When he was 13, Peter borrowed the book *Lively She Goes* from the school library. It was a story about deep water trawling in the North Sea and this very much piqued Peter's interest in becoming a trawlerman, so much so that he wrote to a number of fishing companies in Grimsby inquiring about opportunities. In the summer of 1958, aged 14, he made two twenty-four-day trips to Icelandic fishing waters working as a "deckie learner". By the end of the second trip, the Icelandic Fishing War was well under way, and this ended the opportunity for youngsters to be taken to sea. Peter then took a Board of Trade medical and failed the eyesight tests due to a weak eye and this put an end to his becoming a deep-sea fisherman with any hope of progressing to become a mate or skipper. Non-the-less, Peter continued going to sea on the Conwy trawler *Kilravoch* owned and skippered by Jack Williams, originally of Sport Y Gwynt, Benllech (now Llys Y Gwynt.) Jack was part of the

Williams family of Benllech, who in older times were herring fishermen and of course one person of distinction in the village was Nurse Williams, wife of Bob "Glandŵr".

At 15, Peter worked in school holidays for the diving company laying the seaward section of the new sewage outfall. Whilst working for this firm, he was dressed in the old-fashioned diving suit with large copper helmet. Having gone down the ladder and to the bottom of the sea, it was then time to come back to the surface, and in this type of diving equipment, it was always important to be feet down, body up. However, as he returned to the surface, the team on the boat gave a sharp tug on the safety rope and air pipe which pulled Peter into the horizontal position...then the whole suit inflated into the form of a Michelin Man with no ability to bend arm or legs. This was greatly amusing to the men working as diving tenders.

Peter, like many of his contemporaries, occasionally got up to quite some mischief. When the Rector of Benllech, the Reverend Hugh Pierce Jones heard tales of some boys "borrowing" the odd stick of gelignite, cutting it into smaller pieces with a pen knife, adding a detonator and burning fuse, the throwing it over the cliffs near the creek, just as they did in the "Westerns", he determined to "save" them and quickly brought into being tamer activities such as Boy Scouts etc to occupy the lads before someone got hurt, or arrested! Hugh's endeavours were very effective, and Peter was the proud recipient of a Gold Duke of Edinburgh Award in 1959, the first in North Wales!

After leaving school Peter started training to become a Civil Engineer/Site Engineer on projects at St. Mary's College, the University College North Wales Refectory and John Phillips Hall at Normal College, all in Bangor. After a period of training at the company head office in Cheshire he went to Aberystwyth as second engineer in the early construction of Bronglais Hospital, and later served as Site Engineer on the multi-storey "Crown Building", Plas Crug Avenue, Aberystwyth.

He returned to Anglesey with a new job at Wylfa in 1965 and married Patricia Elizabeth "Pat" Smart of Harbour House, Traeth Bychan at St. Andrew's Church, Benllech on 1st February 1969. Later that month Peter started a new job working for an international Fire Protection company with whom his father had worked for some twelve years or more. Seeing the local potential, Peter started his own company, Anglesey Fire Protection, in October 1969 and after many successful years sold all the non-marine elements of the firm in December 2005. His marine business still flourishes in countries world-wide. In addition, Peter served for over twenty years in the Royal Naval X Service during the 1960's and 70's.

Peter and Pat had two sons, Michael (b 1972) and Simon (b 1974), and as the boys grew up, Pat became involved in running the Sunday School at St. Andrew's and Peter became a Churchwarden. Their work in the church brought them into a close working contact with the Curate Graham Loveluck. In 1987 Peter, Pat and Graham left St. Andrew's and the parish of Llanfair ME to become involved in the Llaneugrad cum Llanallgo benefice, which also by then included churches at Llanfihangel TB and Penrhosllugwy. Their collective devotion and considerable contributions to the benefice has been appreciated by many over the years.

Peter is also quite famous for his other interest - diving on shipwrecks and in particular studying the story of, and diving on, the *Royal Charter* at Moelfre. Working for about three months every summer from 1972 into the mid-1990's, a vast number of artefacts were recovered together with some interesting items of gold. In 1971, the team found the wreck of the Royal Yacht *Mary*. She was the first Royal Yacht of the Royal Navy and was built in 1660 by the Dutch East India Company and bought by the City of Amsterdam to give to Charles II on the restoration of the monarchy, as part of the Dutch Gift. She struck The Skerries in thick fog on 25th March 1665 while en route from Dublin to Chester, and quickly broke up and sank with the loss of 35 lives. It is interesting to note that with all his contributions on the *Royal Charter*, Peter discovered that his two great, great uncles, Robert, and Charles Williams (who trained at Gallows Point, when the family lived in Beaumaris,) worked as Shipwrights on the building of the ill-fated ship. Peter has organized and held anniversary events of the wreck and has been instrumental in the preservation of a variety of artifacts from the ship, including most recently obtaining permission to have one of the drag anchors moved inside St Gallgo's to prevent further deterioration. He also continues to travel around giving presentations on the wreck and the dives and finds.

In the church, Peter soon became a churchwarden at St. Gallgo's, a position he kept for almost thirty years. In addition, he began assisting in services led by Lay Reader David Irons in the late 1990's and, after training, became a Licenced Lay Reader in 2001. In 2000 the Bishop of Bangor asked that specific people in parishes be identified for the work they were doing with a view to Commissioning those people for their efforts. When Bishop Saunders asked the Reverend Graham Loveluck for names, Graham suggested that all current worshippers be included as they all had an important part to play in the successful life of the church. His suggestion was accepted, and, on the 17th of May 2001, Bishop Saunders issued his Commissioning Certificate.

Chapter Five: Charity

One of the responsibilities of the Church for hundreds of years was care of the poor and sick. Before the drastic changes to the church instigated by Henry VIII (the separation from Rome and dissolution of the monasteries) the church was a very wealthy institution and helped the poor by both administering relief and by encouraging parishioners towards Christian charity. After Henry's changes, the church became considerably poorer, and charity then had to come from the community and wealthy individuals. It wasn't until the Poor Act of 1552 that the parishes were given the power to levy taxes (called poor rates) on property to provide for those who were considered to be deserving of relief. The rate was set once a year by the group of men called the vestry, named after the meeting place in the vestry and which was chaired by the rector, and an overseer of the poor was appointed by them to collect the rate. Even after this, the wealthier people tended to leave some sort of charitable donation in their Wills for the poor of the parish. Being a poor institution and with many buildings especially on Anglesey, the churches also depended on charitable donations and legacies in Wills to keep the buildings in good repair as did the Cathedral church of Bangor. Such was the case in our parishes until the early part of the 1700s. There is also evidence that the bishop was able to demand monies from the wealthy landowners to keep his Cathedral in good repair as we shall see in the Last Will and Testament of Owen of Caerfryn.

Wills and Bonds

Wills that were proved in the ecclesiastical court in Bangor between 1576 and 1858 are free to view online at the National Library of Wales, and copies of those proved in the Prerogative Court of Canterbury between 1384 and 1858 can be bought from the National Archives for a small fee. These were the two sources of Wills that I reviewed of people who lived in our two parishes. There are 28 Wills for Llaneugrad dated between 1608 to 1855 and 33 Wills for Llanallgo dated between 1638 – 1855. Our parishes were very poor and there were only a few people who left legacies to the poor or the churches, so each one is described.

Owen ap Robert Owen ap Meurig of Caerfryn, 1608

As covered in the chapter on rectors, Owen was *Lord of Llaneugrad* during the time of the Reverend David Rowlands. By the time he died in 1608, Owen had moved to his house that he had built called Bodavon on the other side of the island, but he did not forget the Llaneugrad parishioners. He left five shillings to the poor as well as five shillings each to the poor of Llanallgo, Llanfair ME and Llanfihangel TB as he also owned lands in all these parishes.

Owen's grandson, Sir John Bodvel, married Bess, the daughter of Sir John Wynn of Gwydir in Gwydir with the Bishop of Bangor, Henry Rowlands officiating. Henry was a half-brother of our Reverend David Rowlands and is a well-remembered bishop as he replaced the four bells that were taken down by his predecessor, and he also repaired the cathedral, including a new roof. These repairs must have been very costly, and no doubt Henry leaned on his brother David to help with fund-raising. He may not have been that successful, however, because according to Owen's Last Will and Testament, he was ordered to the Court of Bangor to give £40 towards the repair of the Cathedral. A court order seems a bit harsh! Owen duly delivered that sum to a Dr Mosten and perhaps none of this money had yet been used for the restoration because in his will, Owen stated that he required Dr Mosten to make a payment of £20 to be bestowed upon the Cathedral Church. He also left sixpence towards its repair. As an aside, Henry himself bequeathed £20 to the Cathedral repairs in his Last Will and Testament.

Sir John Bodvel 1631/2

He was born in 1583, I believe in Bodvel Hall based on a eulogy written for his mother who died shortly after giving birth to him. His grandfathers had made a covenant that Sir John would directly inherit their lands and, after graduating from Oxford with a degree in law in 1602, he took Caerfryn as his residence as his grandfather had moved out by then. His first wife died in 1605 and John then married Elizabeth (known as Bess), the equally formidable daughter of the very formidable Sir John Wynn of Gwydir, Llanrwst. The couple lived in Caerfryn, and this would be about the time that John built the Dovecote and began work on a new house next to it. However, after his father died, the couple made Bodvel Hall their main residence, and the new house never got further than having the foundations set as far as we know. I do not know how much time they then spent on Anglesey, but by 1631 Sir John's health was failing him he drew up his Last Will and Testament on 18th September. Perhaps he was reflecting on his life and wanting to do some extra good before his day of judgement, or perhaps he was just a very generous and caring man, but he added a Codicil shortly afterwards with some personal and added large monetary and livestock bequeathments. His first legacy was to the poor of Llaneugrad parish to whom he left 40 shillings a year forever. This was an exceptional sum of money back then and an annual payment in perpetuity was even more exceptional. The legacy has not endured, there is no later record, and it is not mentioned in the 1818 charities inquiry. I suspect that it probably vanished during the time of Sir John's son, Colonel John Bodvel, as he got into severe financial difficulties because of his royalist loyalties, Parliament sequestered his estates, and he died in debt in 1663. The next owners of the Llaneugrad (and some Llanallgo) lands until 1868 were all absentee landowners whose charitable legacies were to the parishes where they lived or were born.

Sir John left monies for the repair of various churches, 10 shillings each to Bangor Cathedral and Llanor church (the Bodvel local church) and 20 shillings each to Llaneugrad and Llanallgo, a small fortune in those days.

David ap John Thomas of Llaneugrad 1636
I have not been able to place him in any of the pedigree families, but I suspect that he lived in Caerfryn and managed the Bodvel estate. His Will was proved on 13th March 1636, and he left small legacies and worldly possessions to family, but the largest part of his Will records monies owed to him by a variety of people in Llaneugrad and Llanallgo. The list is long, and I suspect that they were either rents due from tenants, or perhaps tithes. It was during this period after Sir John Bodvel had died, and his son John was a ward of King Charles I until he reached the age of 21 when he would inherit his father's estate. In the meantime, the king took the income of the estate and likely employed his own men to run it and collect the rents. David also left sixpence to St Gallgo's, and the Will is damaged in the middle so it is not clear what this would have been for, but an educated guess would be towards repairs. Quite why the sixpence was left to St Gallgo's and not St Eugrad's is not clear from the Will, but perhaps it may be linked to the fact that it was St Gallgo's and not St Eugrad's that had the memorial of the Knight in front of the altar, supposed to be in honour of Sir John Bodvel, as perhaps that is where the family worshipped. This is pure speculation on my part and the true reason may never come to light.

William Lewys 1638
Llanallgo property owner William Lewys wrote his Last Will and Testament in January 1638 when he was quite sick, and he wished to be buried in Llanallgo church. He left money for that church as well as Bangor Cathedral, but the Last Will and Testament is too illegible to read the amounts. His mansion house and lands etc he left to his wife Elizabeth vch (daughter of) David ap John Wynne for her life and, after her death, it was to go to his grandson Lewys ap William Thomas (William had married his only daughter Ann.) Elizabeth was still alive in 1650 and the Land Tax value of her property was £2, but the property name is not specified.

William John Ivan, 1660
William lived in Llaneugrad and was a tenant of "my Lady Bodvel", Ann, the wife of Colonel John Bodvel, who appears to be directly receiving the rent monies (which were part of her joynture). In 1650 the value of his rented property for Land Tax was £1 10s, so it was one of the smaller holdings in the parish. When he died, William owed monies to several people and although the inventory taken in February 1660 is quite a long one, he died in debt to the sum of £9. However, that did not stop him from leaving sixpence towards the repair of the church.

Owen Woods, 1668
Owen was rector of our churches for a very brief time and his story is told in the chapter on the rectors. Despite his short tenure and the fact that he was the son and heir of Arnold Wood of Isallt, Holyhead (and apparently of the Rhosmor family according to the JEG Pedigrees,) he wished to be buried in Llanallgo church and left two shillings towards its repair.

John ap Evan of Bodgynda, 1684

He and his wife Sydney Hughes both died in May 1684 and were buried together in Llaneugrad church towards the repair of which he left one shilling. He wrote his Last Will and Testament on 3rd April, and she wrote hers on 20th May after she was widowed. They do not appear to have had any surviving children and their worldly goods were left to their brothers, Owen ap Evan and Richard Hughes, nephew Thomas Owen and nieces Margery Hughes and Margaret Matthew. His godson John David also received a sheep and a lamb. He was quite wealthy for his time with goods and chattels worth £72 16s including many livestock.

William Watkin, 1718

William was a Yeoman and, in his Last Will and Testament dated 18th July 1718, he left his lands, houses, outhouses, and his share of a boat with nets to his wife for her life. After her death it was all to go to their daughter Jane and her heirs. One of his daughters received a Heifer that was at Glanrafon, but I do not know if this is where he lived as his residence is not specified. He left a lump sum of 10 shillings to the poor of Llanallgo without any stipulation as to how or when it was to be administered, that was left presumably up to his wife to decide as she was the sole executrix.

Charities Commission Inquiries of 1833 and 1895

A key source of information on legacies from Wills and other sources is the report of the Endowed Charities Inquiry for the County of Anglesey which was returned to The House of Commons on 17th March 1896. This report updated the results of an earlier Inquiry commissioned by Parliament in 1818 and which took 19 years to complete. The Anglesey parishes were completed in 1833 and the report dated 10th January. There are a couple of charities for which the Inquiry was not able to identify the origins because the information was based on living people's memories and no documents could be found. Thankfully, with the online Wills at the NLW, I was able to discover the origins and details of both of these charities as well as some information contradicts that in the 1896 report. I include my findings here and its sources.

Llanallgo

The Inquiry for Llanallgo was held on Monday August 19th, 1895, at the National School in Penrhosllugwy on the same day as the Inquiry for that parish. This must have been a very big deal for the parishioners, who apparently turned out in number and the room was crowded. The Llanallgo section of the report lists those present as rector Reverend G.B. Jones and Messrs Edward Williams of Glanrafon etc. The Bishop of Bangor was present at the Penrhosllugwy Inquiry so I would assume that he stayed for the Llanallgo Inquiry.

According to the charities report, *"In the Returns made to Parliament in 1786 it is stated that William Roberts, by his Last Will and Testament dated in 1719 gave £3 for the use of the poor not receiving parochial relief, which was then vested in John Prichard. This sum was last in the hands of one Hugh Evans, a parish officer in the year 1812, who died in very indigent circumstances, and the money is consequently lost to the parish"*. The 1895 update states that the donation is irretrievably lost, and nothing was then known of it in the parish.

A review of the Wills dated 1719, found the Last Will and Testament of one William Probert Humphrey of Llanallgo. It was written on 4th April when he was very sick, and he wished to be buried in Llanallgo. He was a herring fisherman and had built some storehouses which he left to niece Elin Jones for her life and then they would go to his nephew William Rowland. He also owned part of a sloop called the Hopewell which he left to his brother Ellis Probert Humphrey.

I am very confident that this is the same William Roberts who left money to the poor. Based on the patronymic naming conventions in use at the time his last name would be his father's first name and that could explain why he was recorded as William Roberts. This man left £3 to the poor of Llanallgo and specified that 10 shillings every year for six years were to be spent by the churchwardens before Christmas. It would seem that he did not leave this as an annual charity, and I wonder why the churchwardens/overseers of the poor saw fit to pass the money down from year to year rather than fulfil the testators wishes of a six-year legacy. In any case Hugh Evans, who apparently last had the money, sounds like he was probably in great need of it if he died in very indigent circumstances.

I have not been able to find any more concrete information on the other charity discussed in the report which was a legacy of land. A terrier dated September 1821 records that there were two quillets or strips of land in Glanrafon estate (4 X 60 yds and 4 X 30 yds) and one in Tynllan estate of 4 X 40 yds, the yearly rent of which was left towards repairing the parish church. No Last Will and Testament or deed of the donor could then be found. In a search of Llanallgo Wills I was also not able to find the donor, but the quillets in Glanrafon must have come from an owner of Glanrafon, and possibly the Bishop of Bangor. Leaving a rent-charge to charity seems to be more common in the 17th century, and looking at the owners at that time, John Hughes who married Blanch Lloyd, daughter of Henry Lloyd of the Garreglwyd, Dwygyfylchi family seems to be a prime candidate. He was buried on 27th May 1689 according to the JEG Pedigrees and he died without leaving a Last Will and Testament. His wife Blanch was granted administration, and the inventory is by far the largest that I have come across in any Last Will and Testament of the time, with £602 13d 4d worth of goods and chattels! Given how rich he was, and the fact that he died intestate, it must have been a sudden death or incapacitation as the wealthy landowners usually left a Last Will and Testament if they were sick but were still in possession of their faculties. Perhaps it was his intent to leave something to the poor of the parish, and Blanch was the one to set up the charity with the rent-charge of the two quillets, which would explain why there is no documentation on the donor. If Blanch left a Last Will and Testament, it has not survived.

In the 1895 Inquiry it was stated that the Glanrafon strips were sold about 70 years prior to fund repairs to the east end and roof of the church. The sale must have happened prior to 16th September 1831 as there is no mention of them in the terrier of that date. Interestingly, the Tynllan quillet was being let to Edward Williams (tenant of that farm), not for money, but on condition that he undertook to have the rector's surplice washed twice a year. This is known in Welsh as "y llain i olchi'r wenwisg" i.e., "the quillet to have the surplice washed". The same family had lived in Tynllan for the previous 70 years and had faithfully followed the condition - what a laundry service!

Llaneugrad

The Inquiry for Llaneugrad (and Llanfair ME) was held on Thursday August 15th at the British School in Marian-glas. The attendees were John Roberts Bodgynda, chair of the parish council; Henry Williams Bron Haul, churchwarden; Thomas Parry Dinas and Captain Robert Williams Glynllifon, overseers of the poor; Ellen Roberts Tyddyn Tlodion; Thomas Griffiths Gamdda Fawr; Henry Owen Gloddfa Bach; John Jones Eugrad House; Owen Roberts and Edward Williams Ty Coch; William Roberts Tyn Lon; Henry Parry Llwyn and others; Edward Williams Glanrafon Llanallgo; J.P. Williams Ty'nygongl; Humphrey Evans Tan Y Marian and Hugh Williams of Pant Y Saer of the parish of Llanfair ME.

Llaneugrad may only be a small parish, but it had more charities than most of the Anglesey parishes. They include the John Williams Charity, John Griffith Lewis Charity, Eugrad House Tenement, and the Sites of the British and National schools.

John Williams Charity

This is notable for two reasons. Firstly, although the Last Will and Testament of the donor does not appear to have survived, the legacy is carved on a memorial slate tablet inside Llaneugrad church (where John Williams is buried) ensuring the legacy can never be forgotten, and secondly, this charity has survived for over 300 years which is quite rare for the charities of that era! John was born in Llanddona in about 1648 and married Hester Parry. He lived at Bodgynda for 33 years and died on 17th January 1721 aged 73. His inventory of his goods and chattels was valued at £86 16s and he had £202 5s in Bills and ready money. There appears to be some issue with his Last Will and Testament, perhaps he did not sign it, as witnesses had to come forward in the consistory court in Bangor to vouch for the document which, at the time, was annexed to a note to that effect. The Last Will and Testament was proved on 9th February and Hester and his nephew Roland Jones were the joint executors.

John left £50 to be laid out at interest to benefit the poor of Llanddona, Llanfair ME and Llaneugrad. According to the 1833 charities report, the £50 was lent to William Lewis Esq of Llysdulas who, *"to avoid the trouble of paying interest thereon, at an unknown time gave in lieu of the principal a farm called Tyddyn y Tlodion in Llanfair ME consisting of a cottage and six acres two roods and 20 perches of land."* On the inclosure of the Llanfair ME common land in 1815 a further acre and a half were added and the tenant in 1833, Anne Thomas, was paying £6 12s rent. The rents were split evenly between the three parishes and the 1895 update showed that the tenant was now Mrs Ellen Roberts paying the same rent which was considered fair value.

At the Inquiry, there was a bit of controversy with how the money had been used in Llaneugrad as apparently the poor of the parish had not derived any benefit from this charity for upwards of 40 years until 1895 when the overseers distributed the money between three farmers whom they believed were the poorest persons in the parish not receiving parochial relief. It was stated that the overseers had selected their favourites and had acted somewhat hurriedly when they heard that the parish council contemplated moving in the matter and the churchwardens, who were the trustees, had not been consulted. The overseers were Thomas Parry of Dinas and Capt. Robert Williams of Glynllifon and they defended their actions, saying that there were no poor in the parish who did not receive parochial relief, and these farmers were as comparatively badly off as any workmen. John Roberts of Bodgynda, who was chair of the parish council, said that for the last 24 years the vestry had decided on how to use the money. Churchwarden Henry Williams stated that the churchwardens had not taken part in administering the charity since 1886 because it was thought they were not trustees. In an 1892 vestry meeting, the overseers claimed that they could use the money for such parochial objects as they considered advisable, whilst the rector stated that it was expressly left for the benefit of the poor (as is actually written on the tablet in the church.) Further, the Commissioners had not received any accounts since 1875 and nothing has been communicated to them with regard to the future administration of the charities. No further information was given in the report.

I was very curious as to why the very wealthy William Lewis Esq. of Llysdulas would want to borrow £50 from this charity, and why (and when) would he then give a property in lieu of paying interest on the £50, which surely would have been such a trivial amount of money to him. Drawing from my book *The Lords of Llaneugrad* and reviewing the Land Tax records for Llanfair ME, I managed to find the answers.

It all began with a man by the name of Owen Hughes who was born into a poorer gentry family of Porthllongdy, Llanbedrgoch, in the early 17th century and who had a fire in his belly and ambitions way beyond his humble beginnings. He was quite famous in his day, and his success earned him the nickname "Yr Arian Mawr" or "The Big Money". He was the son of Thomas and Jane Hughes who had seven children and Thomas ended up having to sell their small estate to make ends meet and support his family. After his education, Yr Arian was bound to an attorney, second Cousin Owen Wynne, with whom he spent 16 years as apprentice and servant. According to the Biography of Wales website, this meant "wiping his shoes and boots, riding after him, scribbling Bonds and faring on a hard diet". But to be clear, compared to most, he had it good! In 1661 he married Margaret, the daughter of Ifan Wynn of Penllech and then succeeded his teacher to the post of recorder of Beaumaris. He then secured lucrative posts with the Bulkeley family and the Wynn family of Gwydir as advisor and agent and began to build wealth starting with a lease of land from the Bulkeleys in Beaumaris. In a very strategic move, he gained a monopoly over the most important of the Menai Strait's ferries at the time, later securing a 30-year lease on it from the crown that would not be contested until he had made quite a fortune for himself. He was known as a "rich attorney of Beaumaris" and gradually bought up estates in Caernarfonshire and Anglesey, including the Madryn estate and the Llysdulas estate on Anglesey. An interesting aside is that, according to the JEG Pedigrees, he bought Bodgynda in Llaneugrad from Tudur Thomas, the illegitimate son of William Thomas who had inherited the property and who died in London.

Yr Arian did not have any children and, when he died in 1708, he left a large estate that he described in his Last Will and Testament as "not very great but far beyond my deserts". Talk about the understatement of the year! Perhaps by then he had just got too big for his boots, because his accumulated wealth and estates jump-started a new dynasty whose property ownership and influence were to rival, if not exceed, that of the other great Anglesey landowners (the Llysdulas and Kinmel Estate family). Had he lived to see it, I believe Yr Arian would have been delighted about that!

He left various lump sum legacies totalling £2,700 and annual payments of around £200 for the life of the recipients and his real estate was divided into two parts. Properties in the Anglesey commotes of Talybolion, Twrcelyn and Llifon were left to the above William Lewis Esq. who was the eldest son of his niece Martha by her husband Ambrose Lewis and William took up residence at Llysdulas. The Anglesey properties in the commotes of Tindaethwy, Menai and Malltraeth, and in Beaumaris, together with his Caernarfonshire estates, were left to Peter Bodvel who was the eldest son of his niece Ann by her husband Lloyd Bodvel. All of his legacies were chargeable against these estates and his joint Executrixes were his nieces Ann Bodvel and Martha Lewis who received all of his personal estate, goods, chattels etc to share between them.

Peter Bodvel died three years later aged only 21 years old, and because Yr Arian had put an entail in the male line on the estate, the properties now passed to his brother, William Bodvel. William became Constable of Beaumaris castle, was High Sheriff of Anglesey in 1718 and MP for Caernarfonshire in 1741 and 1747. He had a long and profitable life from the estate and died childless on 30th June 1759 aged 64. Curiously, there is a memorial plaque inside Llanfair ME church engraved with the words *"This burying place belongs to William Bodvel Esq"*. Whether William wished to be buried there, or whether the rector was simply saving a spot for him inside the church we will never know, but I can confirm that he was buried in the family church of Llandwrog, according to the parish register. William was the last surviving male of the family and so the estate now fell to the rightful heirs of Yr Arian, and that was William's sister Gwen. She was a 63-year-old spinster and would not live long enough to enjoy the benefits of her inheritance as she died only six months after William on 8th January 1760, having written her own Last Will and Testament on 4th December 1759, before William's Last Will and Testament had gone through probate.

William left several cash legacies to be paid out of his estate including about £200 annually and lump sums totalling about £3,000. On top of this, Gwen left £300 annually and lump sums totalling £5,242. Gwen was now able to divide up the estate, which she did as follows. The Bodfan house, it's properties and lands, several properties in Llandwrog, Pistill, Llanor, Carnguwch, Pwllheli and Edern, two properties in Llanwnda, and some property in Newborough, Anglesey were all left to her cousin Peter's son, Hugh Hughes. Peter had been Land Agent to her brother William and he and his wife received a small legacy of £30 a year which was to be charged to this estate inherited by Hugh Hughes. The remaining properties were bequeathed to none other than her cousin William Lewis Esq. of Llysdulas adding to his already considerable estate, and also saddling him a huge financial burden.

Gwen made it very clear in her Last Will and Testament that the payment of her and brother William's legacies would fall to the estate inherited by William Lewis (with the exception of the annual £30 for Peter Hughes and his wife) and he was expressly forbidden in the Last Will and Testament from trying to get any money from Hugh Hughes. In addition, the lump sum legacies were to be paid either within three or six months of Gwen and William's death, which I believe could only be managed through selling or taking out mortgages on the Real Estate. We know from William Bodvel's Last Will and Testament that his personal estate was not expected to be enough to cover his legacies and Gwen did not have enough time to make enough from the real Estate to make up the difference. According to his Last Will and Testament, William Lewis both mortgaged properties and borrowed money to settle the legacies. To give an idea of the size of the financial burden, the £8242 lump sums legacies are the equivalent of around £1,794,000 in today's money (as of February 2022.) William may have been land rich, but he was now cash poor. Perhaps that is why he borrowed the £50 from the charity fund, or it is also possible that he had cash flow challenges before he inherited the Bodvel legacies and had borrowed it long before, no doubt supplying the churchwardens an attractive interest rate.

William Lewis Esq., married Elizabeth, daughter of William Meyrick of Bodorgan, but the couple did not have any children. He wrote his Last Will and Testament on 16th July 1759, which was about two weeks or so after William Bodvel died, and it included the properties he would inherit from Gwen Bodvel; she must have let him know what she was leaving him. He died on 20th May 1762 and left his estate to Elizabeth as tenant for life, giving her the power to obtain mortgages on his lands to pay off his debts if, and when, they were called in. He directed her (and her successors who were also tenants for life) to pay down as much principal as they could manage after paying off the interest. From this I surmise that the interest on his debts must have been quite crippling and reducing the principal that he had borrowed was surely his motivation in transferring the Tyddyn Tlodion property to the parish churchwardens. It is also in line with the statement in the charities report that he gave the property "to avoid the trouble of paying the interest".

To answer the question of when the transfer of Tyddyn y Tlodion happened, I reviewed the Land Tax records for Llanfair ME. The property was called Ty'n Rhos up until 1761 when William Prichard and Philip Thomas were both responsible for the Land Tax and the value was 11 shillings. It was in 1761 that it became known as Tyddyn y Tlodion or "Land of the Poor" and it was variously recorded by its Welsh and English name from then on. Therefore 1761 must have been the year that it was given to the churchwardens as trustees, and it was William himself who made the transfer.

John Griffith Lewis Charity

In the Returns made to Parliament in 1786 it is stated that John Griffith Lewis (JGL) gave 5 shillings a year charged on land for the use of the poor. Nothing was said of how, or the year it was left. In the Charities report of 1833, it was stated that *"there is a quillet in the middle of a farm called Trevor, in the parish of Llansadwrn, for which the Reverend William*

Thomas, rector of that parish and proprietor of the farm, now pays an acknowledgement of 5s per annum to the churchwardens and overseers of Llaneugrad, which is understood to be in respect of the above-mentioned donation, but the size and boundaries of the quillet are not accurately ascertained. This sum is regularly received by the churchwardens and is carried by them to the poor rates; but this improper mode of application will in future be rectified by giving it to the most necessitous poor." By the time of the 1872-4 General Digest of Endowed Charities, the payment was recorded as being withheld. At the 1895 Inquiry, it was noted from a letter written on 8th May 1868 by the then rector of Llaneugrad and Llanallgo, Reverend James Morris, that the 5s had not been paid *"for the last 10 years"* although an application for the money had been made later than that. John Roberts (chair of the parish council) added that payment had not been received for at least 25 years and that a vestry was held in 1872 to consider what steps should be taken to recover the money. The assistant overseer had been to Llansadwrn several times to demand the rent on behalf of the vestry but the present tenant, Captain Thomas of Plas Llansadwrn had refused to pay since the exact quillet could not be pointed out. That was all that was reported in 1895 for Llaneugrad but I found several other parishes that also benefited from the generosity of this man, and I decided to try to find out who he was.

Finding the original bequeathment turned out to be quite easy, as his Last Will and Testament has survived and is online at the NLW. Finding his origins with 100% certainty, though, has proved to be an impossible task to date despite several weeks of research. The JEG Pedigrees are an excellent piece of work, but they occasionally prove to be incorrect as shown by information I uncover in Wills or other legal documents. This is the case for JGL. The JEG Pedigrees place him in the Penhesgin, Llanfaethlu family and claim that he is the John Griffith of that family who is noted to be living in 1608. Aside from the fact that he would have been over 100 when he died, the information in both he and his brother's Last Will and Testament, as well as the Plas Bodafon Pedigree in JEG's Pedigrees, prove that he was not the John Griffith of the Penhesgin family.

JGL was of Llangwyllog and sick when he wrote his Last Will and Testament on 16th June 1708, and he wished to be buried with his wife, Jane Owen, and son John in St Cwyllog's. Jane had died in 1689 and was buried on 1st August and JGL died in 1709 and was buried on the 19th of June. His Will was proved on 9th January 1709/10 and he left annual sums to the poor of seven Anglesey parishes, all of which were to be paid out of the rent of his properties:

Parish:	Amount:	Property to be Charged:
Bodedern	10s	Cerrig y Baban, Bodedern
Llanbedrgoch	5s	Trefollwyn, Llangefni
Llaneugrad	5s	Cerrig y Baban, Bodedern
Llangefni	5s	Trefollwyn, Llangefni
Llangristiolus	10s	Ty yn y Coed, Llangristiolus
Llangwyllog	15s	Trescawen, Llangwyllog
Tregaian	2s	Cae yn Mynydd, Tregaian

He noted that Llaneugrad was the parish in which he was born. There are no records of his exact age, but the available information gives clues as to where he was born and roughly when. First, his brother Richard Griffith Lewis of Llanddyfnan died in 1668 leaving about £42 in cash legacies, his wool, and yarns, but no properties. Richard made no mention a wife or children and so I believe that he was still single or widowed. His father Griffith Lewis and stepmother, Margaret Lewis, were both still alive as he left £20 to Griffith and his wool and yarns to Margaret, whom he called his mother-in-law which appears to be a common term in the area for stepmother back in those times. He left monetary legacies to the children of his brothers, John Griffith, and Rees, who each had three children, and sister Grace who had two children. Given he left wool and yarns, I believe that he must have been a weaver and as such would be more likely to stay closer to his childhood home and I therefore imagine that his father would live nearby.

By 1708 when JGL wrote his Last Will and Testament, he had great grandchildren by his daughter Elizabeth who had married into the Plas Bodafon family and one was known to have been christened in 1706, so using about 25 years between generations, this places JGL's birth around the 1630's or before. Reviewing the Hearth Tax records for parishes around Llanddyfnan, there is a Griffith Lewis in Llanbedrgoch in 1672 who was a miller, and I believe this was the father of JGL. Millers underwent an apprenticeship and when they were qualified, they usually had to move to another parish when a vacancy arose for them to take up tenure of their own mill. This could explain why and where JGL was born in Llaneugrad. There was only one mill in Llaneugrad parish, and it was at Dinas and so an obvious candidate for where JGL was born. However, I should mention that there was also another mill situated where the entrance of Home Farm Caravan Park is today, and although it was in Llanallgo, the *Lord of Llaneugrad* owned it. Whilst it is possible that miller might have had a house in Llaneugrad parish, I doubt this was the case, and I believe it is much more probable that Griffith Lewis was the miller of Dinas mill when JGL was born.

A curious event happened in 1728. William Lewis of Trysglwyn borrowed JGL's original Last Will and Testament from the Consistory Court of Bangor and a Bond was taken out to ensure it was returned safe and intact. The Bond does not describe why he wanted the Will and perhaps he was simply buying some land or giving a mortgage to one of the grandsons of JGL and wanted proof of inheritance or proof of a charitable donation; but it is curious nevertheless and especially since this happened almost 20 years after JGL had died. This made me wonder whether JGL was from a branch of the Lewis of Trysglwyn family and also perhaps connected to the Griffiths of Llanddyfnan, but I could not find anything in the JEG Pedigrees. I also wonder how the son of a miller could have become so well off and acquired so many properties in his time, but it was in the era when land was easily leased and was still profitable, although I would imagine that he would have needed some sort of means to get started.

JGL's three children all adopted the patronymic surname Jones. His son John died before him, and I do not know if he married. His son Richard married Margaret Hughes, a daughter of Hugh Bowen Hughes of Trefollwyn, and they had two children, Hugh, and Alice. Margaret brought "messuages, lands and tenements" into the marriage, and there was a legal agreement at the time of the marriage that committed Margaret to convey this property over to her children, and to Hugh and his heirs before Alice and her heirs. In his Last Will and Testament, JGL asked that Margaret do this at the first Great Sessions court to be held after his death, and if she did so, he would give his lands that he had bought in in Llangefni to her son Hugh. If she did not do this, then he would give them to his great grandson John Williams, the son of Richard Williams of Plas Bodafon (Richard was his daughter Elizabeth's son.) The properties that JGL owned were all left to his grandchildren, and I will only address what happened with the Llaneugrad charity in this book, the other charities will be included in a more comprehensive article that I will write on the JGL charities.

Cerrig y Baban in Bodedern was the property charged with paying 5 shillings to the Llaneugrad poor and 10 shillings to the Bodedern poor out of the rent for that property. JGL also owned Cefn Caergeiliog in that parish, and both of these properties were left to granddaughter Alice Jones (daughter of his son Richard and Margaret Hughes) and her heirs forever, essentially putting them in entail so they could therefore only be inherited and not sold. At the time of the 1895 Inquiry, the Bodedern charity was still being paid by the tenant of Cerrig y Baban which was now the owned by Col. William Hugh Thomas of the Trevor family of Llansadwrn. The Reverend William Thomas who was paying the Llaneugrad charity per the 1833 report previously mentioned, was from this same family. Although the 1833 report calls him the proprietor, he did not own Trevor farm, it was his brother Hugh who had inherited the estate, including this farm, from their father, also called Hugh.

A review of the Wills of several of the Trevor family members, including that of William Thomas who died in 1670, shows that the information at the top of the JEG Pedigree tree for this family is not quite right. In his Last Will and Testament, William Thomas mentions the following children - Richard, William, Grace, and Ellen. He left his estate property to grandson Henry who was his son Richard's son. Henry was not the son of William as shown on the JEG Pedigrees. Somehow the Bodedern properties left to Alice came into this Llansadwrn family and, because the entail was still intact in 1773, either she or a child of hers must have married one of the heirs of this family. The surviving Anglesey parish records are sparse for this time period, so it is not possible to find out exactly how this came about but we can assume that they were in the family by the time of the 1833 Charities report when the Llaneugrad legacy had been transferred to Trevor farm and the Reverend William Thomas, the great great great grandson of William Thomas. Perhaps the burden of 15 shillings a year had become too great for the 57 or so acre Cerrig y Baban and that is why it was transferred to the 125-acre Trevor farm. In the parish terrier of 13th August 1817, the money was still being paid out of the Cerrig y Baban rent and so the transfer happened sometime after this.

In 1773, Reverend William Thomas' father, Hugh Thomas of Trevor (1737 – 1819), went through the legal process for breaking the entail on the Bodedern farms as well as on other properties that he had come to inherit. He was now free to either sell those properties, or to bequeath them to whomever he wanted. He appears to have kept them in the family and after he died in 1819, his son Hugh inherited them. Hugh died childless in 1852 and in his Last Will and Testament, he placed the freehold properties of Trevor Mawr and his properties in Llaneilian and Bodedern, in trust with Sir Harry Dent Goring, Baronet, of Highden in Sussex and Robert Wynn Jones, Surgeon of Beaumaris. They were to sell or mortgage these properties, in whole or part, by auction or private sale, to raise £1500 to be held in trust for his nephew William Hugh Thomas (son of his brother Reverend William Thomas). The money would be invested, and the dividends and interest were to be paid to various family members, including Ann, the widow of his brother Reverend William Thomas. Reverend William Thomas had died in 1845 and his son William Hugh was only 19 when he inherited from his uncle. He must have continued to pay the 5 shillings until 1858 when it was recorded as being stopped. This would have been a paltry sum to this young man who had also inherited several other properties on and off the island from his uncle, but it is a story that has repeated itself time and again for the legacies to the poor by older generations.

The Eugrad House Charity

Eugrad House is on the corner of Lôn Las and the Llannerch-y-medd road on what was originally common land. It was built by John Jones, a son of blacksmith Hugh Jones who had a smithy across the road from Eugrad House on what is now Frigan land and described in a 6th April 1885 mortgage document as "recently built." The property upon which it was built was originally known as Llwyn y Chwilbo and after that Tafarn y Wrach as the house there likely was a tavern serving travellers on what was a very busy Llannerch-y-medd road. The Tafarn y Wrach house and name was abandoned when John's sister-in-law, 37-year-old Margaret Thomas sadly committed suicide; her story is told in the section on rector John Williams aka Glanmor.

The story of this charity goes back to before the time of the Inclosures in around 1819/20 when there was around 148 acres of common land in Llaneugrad parish. Common land was a legacy from the feudal system of the Middle Ages when the Crown owned it and was part of the feudal grant to the Lord of the manor. Different classes of citizens living in the manor had different rights over land and those who had right in, or over, the common land jointly with others were called commoners. In Llaneugrad, it extended from the top of Lôn Las down to *The Marian*, segregated into three areas. There were 59 acres at the top on the other side of the Llannerch-y-medd road, 59 acres alongside Lôn Las and 30 acres around what is *The Marian* today. Next to the common land at the Marian-glas end of Lôn Las, there were around 20 acres of common land in Llanfair ME. The roads were also common land and accounted for an added nine or so acres in the parish.

In 1756, a licence was granted by the rector, churchwardens, and parishioners of Llaneugrad to Evan Prees, a yeoman of Llanfair ME, to build a cottage 21 feet 9 inches long by 12 feet wide and to enclose a piece of land measuring 132 feet by 107 feet, about 0.325 acres. Evan and his executors, administrators and assigns were to have this house and land for 500 years at a yearly rent of 25 pence clear of all deductions and it was to be paid for the use of the parish church of Llaneugrad. The agreement was signed by the rector, Reverend Lewis Owen, churchwarden Daniel Parry who was a blacksmith, Harry Williams of Nant Uchaf among others. The cottage was built at the top of Lôn Las on the land next to where the Eugrad House is today, and a date stone was created for it bearing the letters "E P M and 1756." On 18th April 1811 an Agreement was made between the parish vestry and then occupier of what was by now called Dafarn Wrach, Griffith Parry to enclose a further acre of land. Apparently, a road had been built through his land and this acre was to be compensation for that loss of land. It was noted that as Griffith had enclosed more than an acre, the rent was to be adjusted to a guinea (£1 1s) a year for the whole piece of land. No overall dimensions were given in that document, but on a map created in 1820 for William Lewis Hughes, the son and heir of Reverend Edward Hughes of Llysdulas, the property measured two acres, three roods and seven perches, so almost three acres.

The fate of common land in Britain was defined by the Inclosure Act of 1773, which was passed during the reign of George III. It created a law that enabled enclosure of common land, at the same time removing the right of commoners' access. As you can imagine, this created all sorts of unrest and riots and hardships for those relying on this land on which to graze their animals. The Act required the procedure to start with a petition delivered to Parliament signed by the landowner, tithe holders and a majority of people affected. The petition then went through the stages of a bill with a committee meeting to hear any objections. The petition would then go through to Royal Assent after passing through both Houses of Parliament. Commissioners would then visit the area and distribute the land accordingly. This appears to be irrelevant in Llaneugrad because it was unique amongst the Anglesey parishes in that all its lands except the Llwyn y Chwilbo property and the small plot that the church is situated on was exclusively owned at the time by only one man, William Lewis Hughes, who would become Lord Dinorben, so this made the inclosure of the common a straightforward matter. In fact, in the 1895 Inquiry, it was stated by Edward Williams of Ty Coch that his father had told him some 47 years before that all of the common land except Llwyn y Chwilbo was awarded by the Inclosures Commissioner to Lord Dinorben. Llwyn y Chwilbo was either awarded to, or simply remained, the property of the church with a guinea a year income.

The property remained in the family of Griffith Parry for many years and so I would imagine that they faithfully paid the annual guinea to the church. Griffith had married Ann Richard of Llaneugrad on 1st April 1777 in Llaneugrad church, and their six children (two daughters and four sons) were christened in the church. I believe that one of their sons had an illegitimate daughter with a Mary Hugh in Llanfairfechan in 1811, and that this daughter was brought to her grandparents in Anglesey to be brought up; her name was Margaret. In 1836, Margaret married Richard Jones, a tailor from Penrhosllugwy, and they lived in Tafarn y Wrach with Griffith and where they had nine children: four sons and five daughters. Griffith died in November 1841 and Richard became the tenant. By 1871 Richard had become a pig butcher and he was the tenant of Tafarn y Wrach through 1890 and was living with daughter Jane and her family in Bangor when he died in February 1892. In 1868, Hugh Robert Hughes (HRH) of Kinmel, who owned all the rest of the parish lands except Tafarn

Y Wrach, decided to sell up the lands and put them up for auction. Curiously, Tafarn Y Wrach was listed as one of the properties up for auction and yet it wasn't his to sell! This wasn't the only property that was included in the auction and then withdrawn before auction day, *The Marian* common was also withdrawn when it was discovered that HRH did not have the rights to sell it at that time.

In 1883, Margaret and Richard's daughter Mary married mariner John Jones, the son of blacksmith Hugh Jones and they lived in Tafarn y Wrach after their marriage and he built Eugrad House. After Mary's sister Margaret had committed suicide in August 1890, the couple took in two of Margaret's children, Ellen and Griffith Parry Thomas and raised them with their own three daughters. John was an enterprising man for his time, and he bought the freehold Gloddfa Fawr with Bron Haul on 2nd April 1885 from a Hugh Jones. Two days later he used them as security on a mortgage of £220 at £4 5s percent per annum from Mary Thomas of Gwnhinger, Llanfair ME. Interestingly, he also used whatever term was left of his lease of Tafarn y Wrach as further security. He borrowed a further £30 from Mary on 6th November 1893 at 5% interest. Mary died intestate in 1896 and tailor Owen Hughes of Holyhead was granted Letters of Administration. He and John arranged with solicitor John Rice Roberts of Llangefni and John Blackwall of Hendre, Llainisa in Denbighshire to take over the mortgage on 10th September 1896. The mortgage was later transferred to surgeon George Osbourne Hughes and Evangeline Margaret Hughes of London on 8th June 1899. By 17th 1900 March John had paid off his £220 mortgage and by 19th March he had also paid back the £30 he had originally borrowed from Mary Thomas.

In 1890 he was able to negotiate a long lease with the churchwardens and overseers of the poor on Tafarn y Wrach. On the 6$^{th\ of}$ October 1890, he was granted a lease for 865 years starting from 13th November at an annual rent of one guinea. John was to pay all the tithes and taxes and at his own expense keep the buildings in good repair, painting the outer doors and windows every three years and the external wood, iron and other work usually painted every seven years. He would also manage the lands according to the most approved system of farming in the vicinity. The Indenture (legal agreement) does not specify a sum of money to be paid for the lease, just the fixed annual rent. The churchwardens (Farmer Hugh Evans of Caerhoslligwy and Gardener John Williams of Eugrad Terrace) and overseers of the poor (Farmer William Davies of Nant Isaf and Farmer Edward Williams of Ty Coch) signed the document on behalf of the parishioners.

Once John had the long lease, he used it as security to raise money via a mortgage. On 27th November 1890 he obtained a mortgage of £100 from Mrs Ann Jones and Mr Richard Hughes, both of Tyhen Isaf in Coedana at an annual interest rate of £4 per centum per year. He had to take out £150 worth of fire insurance on the property and supply the receipt for the annual premiums to Ann and Richard. Ann Jones was a widow who, having lost her husband in 1853, lived at Tyhen Isaf for many years with her unmarried elder sister. Richard Hughes, who was born in Llangefni, was a lodger with them since at least his early 20s and until Ann died in 1896. She left effects to the value of £1078 7s 3d and Richard, who was the executor of her Last Will and Testament, took over the mortgage. By 17th March 1900,

John had paid back all the money he had borrowed, and that mortgage was closed out.

In the records in the archives in Bangor there is a memorandum dated 1st November 1893 from William Jones of Traeth Bychan quarries to J Rice Roberts of Tan y Graig, Pentraeth in which William gives a valuation and description of both Gloddfa and Eugrad House as follows: *"Gloddfa: This place contains 4 acres of land on which a house is built which contains kitchen, parlour, and pantry with two bedrooms; The house and garden is £3-10-0 per annum. Also, a handsome stable Rent £1-0-0 per annum. I should say that this place is worth about £280-0-0. Eugrad House: This is a large house; Contains as follow: kitchen, parlour, and pantry, 3 bedrooms; Also, there is a stable, cistern and barn. The walls of these are built very near to the level. I should say that the value of this place is about £270-0-0."* There is a note written in what looks like a different had saying that the rateable value [of Eugrad House] is £200. No purpose is given for this valuation, perhaps Mary Thomas was ill in 1893 and this was in preparation for John Rice Roberts to take over the mortgage from her. Whatever the purpose of this valuation, clearly the long lease that John now had was worth a lot of money and his building the Eugrad House increased the value of the property significantly.

On 17th March 1900 John paid off his £30 loan from Mary Thomas and two days later on the 19th he paid off both his £100 and £220 mortgages. On the same day he assigned the remainder of the lease on Eugrad House and conveyed the freehold of Gloddfa and Bron Haul to Marian Williams of Parciau for £450. Assuming these were his only mortgages, he made a handsome profit for the time of around £120 and he stayed as a tenant of Eugrad House and Bron Haul paying the yearly rent of £20 to Marian. As part of the legal agreement, Marian had to commit that she would continue paying the guinea rent to the church of Llaneugrad. What I found interesting, but cannot explain, is that in the Electoral register for 1897, Gloddfa was a freehold property, and a William Jones was listed as the owner.

On 2nd August 1906, the lease on Eugrad House was assigned and the freehold on Gloddfa and Bron Haul was conveyed over to the joint ownership of Marian Williams and Samuel Richard Dew at a price of £325 and once again there was a specific commitment in the legal document to continue to pay the guinea rent to Llaneugrad church. Four years later according to the 1910 Valuation Survey, Marian's son Lawrence had the lease on Eugrad House and owned one of the Bron Haul houses and John was still living in Eugrad House. Ellen Roberts owned the other Bron Haul house and Gloddfa was now owned by William John Jones who lived there with his family including his 14-year-old son Willie who would be the first casualty of WWI when he was killed on 1st November 1914 off the coast of Chile.

John died on 21st February 1919 and his widow Mary moved to Bron Haul with daughter Grace where she died on 21st January 1929. Both are buried in Llaneugrad. John's brother Thomas died a week after him on 28th February and his widow Ann moved into Eugrad House where she lived until her own death on 23rd July 1927. Their children Robert and Lizzie Jane were living there in 1929 and then Robert lived there until 1934.

The next family moved into Eugrad House in 1935. William Roberts was a farmer form

Llechylched, and he lived there with his wife Catherine Jane, known as Katie, and their six children. Their youngest son, Tecwyn Thomas, was born in Eugrad House on 17th March 1937 and he married my mother's 2nd cousin, Margaret Catherine Rowlands. They lived in Gloddfa Fawr for many years.

By 1954, a teacher in Sir Thomas Jones School Amlwch, Mr John Thomas Jones aka "Jet" and his wife Annie Myfanwy née Jones were living there. Jet was born in 1921 in Llanddeusant and was brought up at Maes y Wrach (the witch's field) in Caergeiliog and I wonder if he knew that the old name for Eugrad House was Tafarn y Wrach?

I do not know if this guinea is still paid to the church every year; I do know that it is not paid to the Llaneugrad parish council.

Sites of the British and National Schools
Many parishes on Anglesey struggled to get even one school, and yet the tiny parish of Llaneugrad, one of the lesser populated parishes on the island at the time, found itself in what might be considered the luxurious position of having two schools within the parish and a third school that was only a short walk away for many of the children in Llanallgo. The two Llaneugrad schools also served the children of Llanfair ME and the Llanallgo served children in Llaneugrad who lived nearby. Between them the schools catered for all of the children in our parishes. According to the 1851 census, there were 34 children in Llaneugrad parish, 56 in Llanallgo parish and 78 in Llanfair ME parish between the ages of 3 and 13 which was considered to be school age (per the 1891 census report) and by the time of the 1891 census the numbers had dwindled to 22, 40 and 62 children respectively.

The story of how the schools came about is told in the sections on Reverend John Griffith (1834 – 1852) and Reverend James Morris (1863 – 1874) and so I will only address here the donations of land for the two Llaneugrad schools. There is no mention of the Llanallgo school in the Charities report of 1895.

In the 1840s, all of Llaneugrad, with the exception of the three acres or so of Llwyn y Chwilbo, was owned by one man and Llaneugrad was only small part of the enormous amount of land that his father, Reverend Edward Hughes, had bought with his profits from the Parys Mountain copper mines. He was The Right Honourable William Lewis Hughes, Lord Dinorben, had inherited after his father died in 1815, and it was he who donated 2,400 square yards of what was common land to build the school and house for the schoolmaster. It was a gift of deed, and it was stated that the school was for the purposes of educating "*children and adults or children of labouring, manufacturing and other poorer classes*" and was to be run upon the principles of the British and Foreign School Society. Although the school opened in 1845, the legal document formally conveying the land is dated 1st March 1847 and it was granted and conveyed upon trust to seven men; only one of them was from Llaneugrad:

Michael Richards, Parciau, Llaneugrad, Farmer

Robert Parry, Bryn Goronwy, Llanfair ME, Farmer
Hugh Thomas, Plaselwa, Llanbedrgoch, Farmer
David Williams, Ty'nygongl, Llanfair ME, Draper, and Grocer
John Charles, Olgra, Llanfair ME, Shopkeeper
Richard Williams, Tyddyn Fadog, Llanfair ME, Farmer
John Phillips, Brynteg, Llanfair ME, Minister

The building of the National school on the road from Brynteg to Llannerch-y-medd was the project of Reverend James Morris and William Williams of Parciau, and it was opened in 1873. The school and schoolhouse were built on land that was donated by the Hughes family of Parys Mountain copper fame. This time it was Reverend Edward Hughes' grandson, Hugh Robert Hughes (affectionately called "HRH,) and he donated about a quarter of an acre of a field called Cae'r Chwarel, part of Tyddyn Cadwgan farm. The Indenture was dated 27th March 1869 and was enrolled in Chancery on 5th April. This was around the time that HRH was selling off his Anglesey lands to fund his enormous house at Kinmel, and William Williams of Parciau and his nephew had bought a large amount of Llaneugrad parish lands from him. The land was conveyed to the minister and churchwardens and their successors, and the buildings erected on it were to be used as a school It was stipulated that the land was to be used to erect a school "for the education of *children and adults or children of labouring, manufacturing and other poorer classes*" and "*as a residence for the teacher or teachers of that said school*" and for no other purpose. It was to be "*in union with and conducted according to the principles and in furtherance of the ends and designs of the Incorporate National Society for Promoting the Education of the Poor in the principles of the Established Church throughout England and Wales*". The operation of the school was vested in a committee consisting of the rector (or his licenced curate), the churchwardens and three people who had to be members of the Established Church and subscribers to the funds of the school of not less than ten shillings annually. The religious instruction given in the school together with the entire control and management of any Sunday school held in the premises was to be vested in the incumbent rector.

Chapter Six: Ghosts and a Goblin

In the section on Canon Tom Woodings (1955 – 1958), I told the tale of his sister Elizabeth's encounter with a ghost on the stairway of the rectory. It so frightened her that they left the rectory on that same night, she was unable to speak for three weeks, and he resigned from his post as she refused to go back and live there. Elizabeth was an intelligent well-balanced woman who was not prone to hysteria, and this gave much credibility to her experience on the stairs. She was housekeeper to her brother and apparently, she was not the only "hired help" to be visited on the stairway by the ghost. Bunty Austin's *Haunted Anglesey* book also relates the experiences of three sisters who in turn worked at the rectory as domestic servants as told to Bunty by Mr John Roberts of Bronfelin, Brynteg.

The eldest sister, Mair, first encountered the spirit after she had been working there for a while and one night was taking a hot water bottle upstairs to the rector's bed. Halfway up the stairs, she felt a great pressure on her chest, which she assumed was a man's head, and then she heard a "slow tortured breathing" all around her. Terrified, she ran upstairs to deposit the bottle in the bed and then slid downstairs as close to the wall as she could manage to avoid the middle of the stairs. It happened again that week and on her half day off she told her mother about it. Her mother wanted her to leave, but Mair knew how important her meagre wages were to the family and was determined to stay on even though she had the same experience many times during her tenure and was quite frightened. She had not told her sisters about the ghost and each of them in turn took up the domestic servant post and both had the same experience on the stairway, but Mair told them that they would not be harmed so they too stuck with their jobs. Although Bunty says that John was told the story by the girl's aunt Margaret, I believe that Margaret might have been a younger sister and that the three servants were Mary Elizabeth, Jane, and Kate Francis of Trosyffordd in Moelfre who all in turn served in the rectory. If anyone knows differently, please do contact me to set the record straight.

In her book, Bunty says that the identity of the ghost has never been established but speculates that it is someone in need of comfort, perhaps one of the sorrow-stricken relatives of a Royal Charter victim, or even the poor Reverend Roose Hughes who became a shadow of his former self in helping the victims and their relatives. I am doubtful that it is either of these two.

I find it curious that the ghost seemed to appear only to servants or housekeepers and not to the clergymen or their wives and children (Elizabeth Woodings was her brother's housekeeper.) So, why would the spirit be so selective? The sceptical amongst us may say that those were individuals who were not highly educated, likely had over-active imaginations (especially on dark and windy Winter nights) and might be expecting something to happen after hearing tales that had been passed down from servant to servant over time. However, Elizabeth Woodings was a different matter, she was a highly educated woman who had no reason to imagine her terrifying experience. I suspect that the ghost was real, that it was a woman and not a man, and that she either needed comfort, or more likely, was exacting her revenge by trying to frighten away the servants. I believe that the ghost was Jane Hughes of Cegin Filwr, Llanfechell, servant to Reverend Richard Lloyd (1801 to 1830) and his wife Elin née Lewis, and who was the victim of a very cruel act on the morning of Friday 30th March 1810 in the rectory.

The surviving records do not reveal exactly what led up to the events of that morning, but according to the jury verdict, Reverend Lloyd's daughter, Grace, *"not having the fear of God before her eyes but being moved and seduced under the instigation of the devil"* and *"with malice aforethought"*, struck Jane on the head with an iron poker with such force as to cause a mortal wound three inches in diameter and one inch in depth. According to depositions taken in the murder charge brought against Grace, Jane told friends that she was *"not ruined"* on the Friday but that on the next day, Saturday, her mistress, Elin, had to wake her and struck her on the wound with a tin pitcher which made blood run down on her skirt, handkerchief, and spencer. She told Elin *"Don't beat me for you have already ruined me"*. Jane also said that she had to crawl to the well on her hands and knees to fetch water and carry the water back by carrying the pitcher on her head on the Saturday morning. If the well she talks about was the one at the back of Glanrafon Uchaf, then that was a very long way for someone with such an awful head wound.

When Jane went home to her father-in-law's house, Cegin Filwr, on Sunday 1st April, she was already quite ill. At 8 o'clock that morning she visited Ann Lewis at Tynllidiart, and Ann said that she had a slovenlier appearance than usual which she questioned. Jane showed her the wound on her head declaring that they *"have ruined me"* and *"driven me out of my senses"* and told her of the assaults. Ann said in her deposition that Jane showed sign of mental derangement and her demeanour was altogether different for what it used to be. Elizabeth Williams of Tynrodyn went to see Jane on Monday 2nd April at Cegin Filwr and found Jane sitting by the fire and looking *"quite wild"*. The doctor was called, and he testified that he found Jane quite delirious and after that she gradually worsened day by day until she passed away at Penllidiart (the home of Elizabeth Lewis and Hugh Hughes) on 8th May 1810.

It was her father-in-law, Owen Jones of Cegin Filwr who brought a charge of murder against Grace Lloyd, and she was tried by jury in the Grand Sessions later that year. After all the evidence and several depositions were considered, the jury decided that Grace was not guilty of murder. This was probably on the technicality that there was no premeditation. A note on one of the court documents states that it was a "true case" of manslaughter, but the records do not document anything else about the manslaughter charge.

Jane's story must have been well known in the community and passed down from generation to generation so that subsequent servants were aware of her fate. Whether the ghost on the stair stemmed from someone with an overactive imagination or whether Jane truly could not rest in peace and determined to seek solace on the chests of future generations of servants or frighten them out of their wits so that they would flee their post – who knows?

One thing is for sure – when Eileen and Edmund Clarke bought the rectory, the ghost was long gone as none of the Clarke family have ever had any sort of experience on the now modest staircase… This leaves me wondering if Bangor HQ had the rectory exorcised before putting it up for sale and whether the old grand 18th century staircase was replaced by a more modest one and as a result Jane decided that it was time to move on to the eternal rest that the poor girl well and truly deserved…

Another ghostly tale of the rectory was passed down from Annie Owens, the wife of the lifeboat mechanic Evan Owens and her granddaughter Sioned, the daughter of Annie's son David Arbonne, has confirmed the story and given more details. Annie worked for a period as domestic help at the rectory during the time of Reverend John Parry (1929 – 1937) when the rector was accustomed to going out in the evenings to visit with his parishioners. One evening she went out into the front garden to call the cat and saw the figure of a man dressed in black with red hair and a red beard and carrying a lantern walk up the back path alongside the churchyard wall and go in the back door. As she was expected to deliver supper to the rector as soon as he arrived home, she hurried directly to the dining room to lay the table. The rector's wife came in just as she finished and expressed surprise since he was not due to come home for another hour. Annie insisted that she had just seen him arrive home, but when the two of them searched the house from top to bottom, there was not another soul to be found. Sioned told me that Annie also heard many strange noises in the house and the combination of her seeing the man and these noises led her to give up her post as they caused her great distress.

Other tales have been told about a spectre seen in the Llanallgo graveyard by passing motorists and others visiting family graves. Given the churchyards host to many of the victims of the Royal Charter, many unidentified this does not surprise me, and I am sure that they are prime candidates…

It would be remiss of me to not include one of the most famous hauntings of the parishes, especially as Llanallgo church at one time had a relief of this individual on a wall that was later plastered over and Llaneugrad church still has a wooden panel with his son's initials carved on it from a renovation that his son had carried out in 1644. Therefore, I will reproduce here the chapter from my book *The Lords of Llaneugrad* on that most famous ghost, Sir John Bodvel. I have heard that the most recent sighting of the ghost was in August 2017 around the time of the Moelfre lifeboat day, but there have been many other sightings over the years.

As I began my research into the Bodvels and their ownership of the Llaneugrad and some Llanallgo lands, the big question for me was, is it the ghost of Sir John or his son Colonel John? Well, if the ballad of Sir John Bodvel (also reproduced in this book) is to be believed, and I have no reason to doubt it, then I am sure that it must be Sir John's ghost. I am also convinced that it was the actions of Colonel John and his men during the time of the civil wars in the 1640s that perhaps started the myth and legend of the ghost in the first place. There are various stories told of him hiding horses in Llaneugrad church and the dovecote which was likely when Cromwell's men were out looking for royalist sympathizers on the island and horses and men moving around in the dead of night, might well have fed the imagination of the locals. And there might have been some dealings and goings on that made it convenient to have the locals think there may be ghosts or goblins around the area so that they would stay away at night…

In the book *Haunted Wales: A Guide to Welsh Ghostlore* by Richard Holland, he was told a story by 84-year-old Mrs Griffiths who was told by her grandmother, passed on by her mother, who heard it from her grandmother… Her great-great-great-grandmother had apparently seen the ghost herself as a little girl in Marian-glas. She was standing in the doorway of their house with her mother and a visitor, who was just about to leave, when her mother said to the visitor "I wouldn't go just yet". Just then, *The Marian* lit up and a white horse and rider appeared, and the rider had cloven hoofs! Mrs Griffiths also told of another sighting. A midwife was walking along a country lane, having attended a mother-to-be, when she heard a clatter of hoofs coming beside her. It stopped and the rider asked if she wanted a lift. She saw his cloven hoofs and declined his kind offer.

From an undated copy of "Interesting Stories about Moelfre" by the Merched Y Wawr that I found in the Anglesey Archives, there is another story about Sir John. According to this article, he married "several" times and killed one of his wives and buried her on Lligwy beach. For this sin he is condemned for all eternity to count all the grains of sand on Lligwy beach. He had also apparently acquired some land illegally, and he can now be seen riding his white horse across the Moelfre fields shouting, "Woe to him that changes the boundaries of his neighbour's land"! Sir John was involved in all sorts of litigation including one against several tenants for Crown Lands of Nantmawr which he won and added those lands to his Llaneugrad estate. There were also many lawsuits in Caernarfonshire and one for Tyddyn Agnes on Anglesey, so there is some basis in truth for the legend of him "stealing" his neighbour's land. The same article also tells of another of his dastardly deeds as a wrecker. He was helped by Gaynor, who lived near Swnt, and they would light bonfires on the rocks to lure ships to their doom and then steal the valuables from them.

Another story told in the book "*Haunted Anglesey*" by Bunty Austin, is one about four schoolboys who, on a very cold January day, after hearing about the ghost on horseback condemned to count the grains of sand on the beach, decided to venture down to the beach in search of this ghost. Egged on by their school pals, and desperately wanting to impress the girls, off they went down the lane. Although they began to doubt themselves halfway there, they carried on and crossed the little bridge over the stream to the beach. Two of them were in front and suddenly, the pair of them saw a man standing next to a horse. The peculiar thing was that the horse did not appear to have any legs! They decided to move closer to the strange sight, and as they neared, the horse and man vanished in front of them. Strangely enough, the other two boys saw nothing at all but happily joined in the retreat as the two who saw the sight began to scream and run hell for leather back up the lane and away from the beach…

A few years ago, a family friend, who had a caravan on the Parciau Caravan Park was staying there for the Summer with her children. She knew nothing of the local history of the area, nor about any ghostly sightings. One night she had a very vivid dream of a man on a white horse riding across the caravan park and past her own caravan. The next day she told my dad about her very disturbing dream and asked if there were any stories of horses riding around. Dad told her the story of Sir John Bodvel's ghost who appears to have been visiting her in her dreams! And this tale gets stranger still. Unbeknownst to her at the time, her young daughter was having the exact same dream, a man on a horse pausing by the kitchen window of the caravan before going on his merry way! It wasn't until many years later that she told her mother of this dream, and they learned of the eerie coincidence. She also told me that she always had difficulty sleeping when the caravan was on that particular pitch, but when the caravan was moved to a private farm up the road, the dreams stopped... If you take a map of the area, and draw a line from Traeth Bychan to the Dovecote, it goes right past the pitch where their caravan was...

Another lady, who grew up in Marian-glas, told me a story from her childhood. The village children would all play together and would roam all over the village and surrounding area. On one particular day, the woods by Parciau were the chosen spot for their playground. This was somewhere around the early 1940s and so neither the pub nor the caravan site had been built. There was a stone wall to the left of where the pub is today, and to the left of the wall was a wooded area. They had just started to walk along the wall when the children in front started screaming, and they all saw a ghostly white figure wandering about in the woods. They turned and ran for their lives...

Another tale came from someone who worked on the Parciau estate, and who swore that he had seen the ghost as a headless rider on a horse on the estate lands.

There is also a story of a goblin which is quite interesting, but this one I believe has a more down to earth explanation. A Welsh paper written in the 1880s was translated by Margaret Williams of Parciau, daughter of William and Marian Williams. The author must have grown up in the parish because he says that as children, they would take care to withdraw from Parciau grounds before dark lest the goblin might catch them. Apparently, the goblin had a monster stile, or "great" as it was called, quite near the old Parciau house and tradition had it that the goblin, from the top of his stile, announced his curses "*Woe, woe unto him that moveth the boundary of his neighbour*", and wailed and moaned terrifying noises. Even the fishermen of Moelfre used to hear it whilst drawing their nets, so that peasant and peer equally dreaded being out of doors late. The goblin would also issue his proclamation from his chair which was situated about two miles from the stile on the Llannerch-y-medd road by Frigan and is known today as Cadair Bwgan. After the goblin had finished wandering between stile and chair at night, it retired to the Dovecote near the church which it used as its resting place during the day.

Apparently, the goblin disappeared in the early 1870s after William and Marian bought the Parciau estate and built their mansion house. They also renovated the old Parciau farmhouse and, according to this same author, they "*removed all the odds and ends of things that might have been the cause of the disquiet complained of, put down to the goblin's love of mischief, every relic and vestige of the goblin near the house was annihilated, so that the building of the magnificent palace and the repair of the old farmhouse scared away the goblin with his screeches and curses, and the vicinity ever since enjoys the tranquil neigh of peace.*" Margaret says that William made the mansion accessible by building roads from every direction and built several cottages about his residence so that the goblin perceived his home to be here no more. She also notes that nothing was pulled down at all around the old farmhouse as that is where they lived for two years whilst the mansion was being built.

Now here is my take on this goblin. Although, I believe that Sir John's ghost is real and probably continues to haunt the neighbourhood, I believe that the goblin was a fabricated creature that served a very specific and convenient purpose. I can imagine that the big stile and the chair would make great lookouts as well as places from which to make unearthly noises to keep prying eyes away from the lands of Llaneugrad Parke at night. Likewise, these noises heard in Moelfre by the fisherman would ensure they were all safe and sound in their houses after dark and not seeing potential happenings on the local seas around Moelfre and Traeth Bychan. Also, the Dovecote would be an ideal hiding place for all sorts of things, and what better way to keep people away from seeing what that might be in there than declaring it to be the goblins resting place in the day?

This might have started as a cover to move around the spoils of the legendary forced shipwrecks, and it also might have been convenient for smuggling goods into the country from very faraway places. Anglesey and Traeth Bychan were well out of the way of the usual ports and the customs officials, yet close enough to the North Wales coast to move on smuggled goods… Samuel Hanson, *Lord of Llaneugrad*, was a Barbados sugar plantation owner cum pirate and smuggler and I suggest that he took advantage of the remote location and local folklore to bring goods to Traeth Bychan or Moelfre. He also owned Bardsey Island, a well-known pirates haven, as part of his Bodvel estate and his full story is also told in my book *The Lords of Llaneugrad*. When the Williams came to Parciau around 1869, whatever, if anything, was still ongoing there would probably have had to stop and the goblin, no longer needed, would have simply vanished never to return…

Given the recent report of the sighting of his ghost, Sir John is apparently still "alive and well" galloping about, and probably still very busy counting the grains of sand on Lligwy beach. I would love to meet him someday, as I have so many questions that I need answers to, the very first of which is where did he bury his legendary golden treasure? I have to admit though, should he offer me a ride, I would definitely politely decline!

In order to give context to the stories of his ghost, I include here the full ballad of Sir John Bodvel – a truly epic and entertaining piece of poetry by the talented Reverend John Vaughan Lloyd, MA (1805 – 1859) who wrote Eisteddfod-winning poems and occasionally went by the name "Maelog". He was rector of Llanbeulan and Llanfaelog for a time until 1838, and I would imagine that it was during his tenure there that he heard the tales of Sir John Bodvel, perhaps from the rector of Llanallgo and Llaneugrad at the time, John Griffith (1834 – 1852). In any case, the poem was composed by a man with great credibility, and I am sure that the old adage "no smoke without fire" is applicable. In verse 57 he mentions "Allgof's Holy Priest" who I believe might be the Rev John Griffith as it seems to me exactly the sort of thing that John would be likely to say. I could not find a surviving intact version, so this epic 61 verse poem was pieced together from three fragments, part in a handwritten notebook of Margaret Williams (1874 – 1922) of Parciau, part from Llio Rhydderch handwritten by her grandfather, William Daniel Williams (1873 – 1957) and part from the National Library of Wales possibly in the handwriting of J.E. Griffith.

The Ballad of Sir John Bodvel

1 Bright shines the moon's departing light
O'er Lligwy's gentle stream
And bright is ocean's dimpled face
Beneath her silvery beam.

2 Bodafon's dark and craggy hill
With vest of heather grey
Is steeped in soft and tranquil light
By the first fading ray.

3 Oh! what a calm and holy hour
To think on ages fled
To muse on deeds enacted here
By those long gone and dead.

4 Soon, soon the placid moon will pale
And her pure radiance hide
Behind yon mountain's dusky height
Then sink 'neath ocean's side.

5 When midnight comes and darkness lowers
O'er all this lovely scene
The spirits of the past will rise
To mourn o'er what has been.

6 For oft is heard at deep midnight
When moonlight's sway is past
A dismal voice of woe afloat
Upon the cold wild blast.

7 Twas deemed when'er was heard that voice
And sad unearthly wail
Some tortured spirit rode the breeze
To tell some warning tale.

8 Twas no vain dream - it was a thought
Wise aged men proved right
It was a voice of soul condemned
Which wandered through the night.

9 The tale of John of Bodvel's crimes
Could it be duly told
Would fright the stoutest heart of man
And make sweet woman's cold.

10 Sir John of Bodvel's wealth was great
By bards his deeds were sung
And knightly fame and courtly grace
Their radiance round him flung.

11 In youth's gay morn his heart was full
Of feelings proud and high
In camp and court, he was esteemed
The flower of chivalry.

12 Enriched and honoured by his Queen
He basked in fortune's smile
And was endowed with manors fair
In Mona's ancient isle.

13 Afar from court now dwells the knight
In Bodvel's stately Halls
Which oft resounded with the voice
Of joyous festivals.

14 The dance, the feast, and revelry
Were graced by rich and fair
Who loved to hie to Bodvel's home
The mirthful scene to share.

15 Where Bodgunda's turrets rise
The sea lost barque to guide
Dwelt Lilian loveliest of her sex
Of maidenhood the pride.

16 Full oft had she in Bodvel's halls
With bright and gladsome eye
Marked the sad air of Bodvel's Lord
And heard his deep drawn sigh.

17 She deemed he loved her, so he did
But not with passion pure
His was a loveless passion, base,
That short space would endure.

18 How changed alas was now the chief
Of Bodvel's broad domains
Some demon lure possesses him
And o'er his reason reigns.

19 He feigns true love, the maiden yields
Her heart and hand to him
And seemed to her the cup of joy
Filled up unto the brim.

20 And now in Eugrad's holy fane
The plighted couple stands
Each vows eternal truth to each
Each grasps the other's hand.

21 The plain gold ring her finger binds
A holy prayer is said
A solemn blessing is implored
From heaven upon their head.

22 Around, the torch and taper shone
And shed abroad their glare
But paled their fires when lightening flashed
Athwart the darkened air.

23 Heaven looked in wrath upon the scene
Of profanation foul
It was no priest who read the rites
Despite his ropes and cowl.

24 His passion sated, hate succeeds
Which Lilian sees too well
Her smitten heart in secret bleeds
To none her grief she'll tell.

25 A few short months saw Lilian pine
Away in Bodvel's halls
Her heart was sick, she could not share
The boisterous festivals.

26 One night when from his orgies risen
He calls her faithless and untrue
He calls her faithless and untrue
And swears he loves no more.

27 In vain her love and truth she pleads
And harmless babe unborn
With accents frantic he replies
And treats her vows with scorn.

28 In vain she strives to gain his ear
By speech devoid of art
The ruthless monster plunges deep
A dagger in her heart.

29 And now a vile and ruffian crew
That form as cold as clay
Bear off in moody drunkenness
To Dulas distant bay.

30 A skiff unmoored; the oarsmen plied
Five miles from land they be
And down that beauteous corpse is plunged
Into the deep, deep sea.

31 Strange 'tis, but true, at morning dawn
Some wanderers on the strand

32 With secrecy they buried her
In Eugrad's fair churchyard

Her pale and mangled corpse discerned
High up upon the sand.

33 Sir John still heads the revel rout

And still his halls are gay
But peace has left proud Bodvel's Lord
For age has fled away.

35 One crime another will beget,
And in a hellish race
Sir John his compeers all surpassed
And won the highest place.

37 There many a costly ship was wrecked
And many a sailor brave
By his fell art were hurried on
To an untimely grave.

39 In vain the harp sends forth sweet sounds
In vain the wine cup's foam
For in his heart on earth again
Shall peace ne'er make her home.

41 His conscience now awakes at night
As strength and life decay
Now fain would he make peace with God
Insulted many a day.

43 He knows himself the guilt - he feels
How changed a man is he
By night by day his prayers arise
To God in agony.

45 The solemn priest his sins confessed
Hath absolution given
Yet still deep horror chains his heart
For he despairs of heaven.

47 In human view it nothing can
But all in heaven's it may
The priceless worth of Jesus blood
Can wash all sins away.

Not lovelier form has 'ere reposed
Beneath its emerald sward.

34 His diminished wealth and mortgaged lands
Now scarce his wants supply
And soon to crimes of blackest hue
We see him reckless fly.

36 False beacon lights would he make blaze
When storms the ocean tore
To lure the helpless sea lost barque
To Moelfre's rugged shore.

38 But time rolled on and with old age
Came racking soul deep fears
The thought of Lilian, all his crimes
Rose up from vanished years.

40 Now sickness and wild pangs come on
With fierce and rapid stride
And he must fearfully sail down
Dread times unsleeping tide.

42 Cold anguish now his bosom fills
And penetrates his soul
Can naught dispense the gloomy clouds
Which round him darkly roll!

44 That stubborn heart at length is bow'd
In dread unhoping fear
But gladly does our gracious God
Guilt's cries for mercy hear.

46 Can penitence alas! restore
Life robbed from fellow man
Can it the virgins pride bring back?
Oh! answer if it can?

48 He dies at length in terrors dread
The livid lightening's flash
And echoing with a voice of wrath
God's living thunders crash.

49 And may this godless - graceless man
Find slumber in the tomb
Oh! no! the righteous wrath of heaven
Gives him a fearsome doom.

50 When darkness broods o'er nature's face
And silence reigns with her
And ye might hear a snowflake fall
And nothing seems to stir

51 Then at the awful midnight hour
Is he compelled to stray
In air a viewless, shapeless ghost
Till dawns the blessed day.

52 Each night to hover o'er the scenes
Where his foul crimes were wrought
Till the great day of reckoning comes
When earth and time are nought.

53 His cold heart-freezing voice is heard
To wail upon the breeze
Where soft o'er Lilian's bed of rest
It sighs amid the trees.

54 And over Moelfre's storm vexed coast
The self-same wail is heard
It chills the breast - such voice ne'er came
From man, from beast, from bird.

55 His punishment is thus to roam
Until the judgement day
When, may we hope, his fearful guilt
May all be purged away.

56 For Allgof's holy Priest hath said
Some visions have been his
Which shewed him that his penance o'er
He yet should taste heavens bliss.

57 Forsooth! the blessed son of God
Who died upon the tree
Can make our crimson crimes all white
And set guilt's bondsmen free.

58 Full oft the fated traveller hears
When on his lonely way
What seems Sir John of Bodvel's voice
And shudders in dismay.

59 And sure, this voice may well be deemed
A sermon deep to preach
That we should use but righteous means
Our ends and aims to reach.

60 For here or in a future world
The wrath of heaven will make,
A dread example of such men
As dare his laws to break.

61 And from it too, this truth we learn
That penitence and prayer
If sent to heaven in Jesus' name
Will find acceptance there.

References and Sources

Photographs, Illustrations & Newspaper Articles

1 Wikimedia Commons, Filename: Treouergat_-_Fontaine_St_Ergat.jpeg User yfig.
2 Website: https://www.patrimoine-iroise.fr/culturel/civil/Ergat.php?lang=en
3 *The Lives of British Saints* colourized and enhanced by the author
4 Guy Singleton
5 The Author
6 The Author
7 Gwen Meredith Williams
8 Dawn Hughes
9 Dawn Hughes
10 Cassini Folded Sheet Map, 1841 Anglesey
11 *Archaeologica Cambrensis*, April 1859 with colour added by The Author
12a National Library Wales Online Newspapers
12b National Library Wales Online Newspapers
13 National Library Wales Online Newspapers
14 National Library Wales Online Newspapers
15 The Author
16 The Author
17 The Author
18 Gwen Meredith Williams
19 Dawn Hughes
20 Dawn Hughes
21 Peter Day
22 Dawn Hughes
23 Dawn Hughes
24 Gwen Meredith Williams
25 The Author
26 Dawn Hughes
27 Dawn Hughes
28 Dawn Hughes
29 Peter Day
30 The Author
31 The Author
32 The Author
33 The Author
34 The Author
35 Graham Loveluck

36 Graham Loveluck
37 Graham Loveluck
38 Graham Loveluck
39 Dawn Hughes
40 Website https://archive.org/details/tendaystourthrou00skin
41 *Archaeologica Cambrensis*, April 1859
42 FindMyPast Newspapers Online
43 Graham and Llio Loveluck
44 National Library Wales Online Newspapers
45 National Library Wales Online Newspapers
45a Graham Loveluck
45b Dawn Hughes
46 National Library Wales Online Newspapers
47 Anglesey Archives Ref. WPE/55/41. Edited and Colourized by The Author
48 National Library Wales Online Newspapers
49 National Library Wales Online Newspapers
50 Dawn Hughes
51 Dawn Hughes
52 Dawn Hughes
53 Dawn Hughes
54 Dawn Hughes
55 Dawn Hughes
56 Dawn Hughes
57 Dawn Hughes
58 Dawn Hughes
59 Dawn Hughes
60 Dawn Hughes
61 Dawn Hughes
62 The Author
63 Dawn Hughes
64 The Author
65 The Author
66 Peter Day
67 Dawn Hughes
68 The Author
69 The Author
70 The Author
71 Peter Day
72 Dawn Hughes
72a The Author
73 The Author
74 The Author
75 Peter Day

76 Eleanor Jones
77 Dawn Hughes
78 The Author
79 Dawn Hughes
80 Dawn Hughes
81 Dawn Hughes
82 Dawn Hughes
83 Dawn Hughes
84 Dawn Hughes
85 Dawn Hughes
86 Dawn Hughes
87 Dawn Hughes
88 Dawn Hughes
89 Dawn Hughes
90 Graham Loveluck
91 Dawn Hughes
92 Dawn Hughes
93 Dawn Hughes
94 FindMyPast Newspapers Online
95 Dawn Hughes
96 Valmai Jones
96a The Author
97 National Archives
98 National Archives
99 Arwyn Owen
100 National Library Wales Online Newspapers
101 National Library Wales Online Newspapers
102 National Library Wales Online Newspapers
103 National Library Wales Online Newspapers
104 Website Casgliad Y Werin, Colourized by The Author
105 Alma Salt
106 Alma Salt
106a National Library Wales Online Newspapers
107 National Library Wales Online Newspapers
108 National Library Wales Online Newspapers
109 National Library Wales Online Newspapers
110 Yr Arwydd
111 National Library Wales Online Newspapers
111a National Library Wales Online Newspapers
112 National Library Wales Online Newspapers
113 National Library Wales Online Newspapers
114 National Library Wales Online Newspapers
115 National Library Wales Online Newspapers

116 National Library Wales Online Newspapers
117 National Archives ED 2/558/4
118 National Library Wales Online Newspapers
119 National Library Wales Online Newspapers
120 National Library Wales Online Newspapers
121 Eileen Clarke, Colourized by The Author
122 National Library Wales Online Newspapers
122a The Author
123 National Library Wales Online Newspapers
124 FindMyPast Merchant Marine Records
125 & 125a Philippa Parry
125b https://commons.wikimedia.org/wiki/File:Royal_Charter_disaster_memorial,_Moelfre_%28geograph_2696583%29.jpg Author: Meirion
126 Alma Salt
126a Website https://www.oldclassiccar.co.uk/austintwelvesix.htm
127 National Library Wales Online Newspapers
128 Patrick Hussey
129 Patrick Hussey
130 Heather DeFer
131 Colin Haywood, Colourized by Author
131a Colin Haywood
132 FindMyPast Newspapers Online
133 FindMyPast Newspapers Online
134 FindMyPast Newspapers Online
135 FindMyPast Newspapers Online
136 FindMyPast Newspapers Online
137 FindMyPast Newspapers Online
138 David Hughes
139 David Hughes
140 The Author
141 David Hughes
142 Philip Hughes
143 Philip Hughes
144 Philip Hughes
Cover Photos St Eugrad's – The Author
Cover Photos St Gallgo's – Dawn Hughes

Journal Articles

Prof. A.H. Dodd "The Tragedy of Colonel John Bodvel", *Transactions of the Anglesey Antiquarian Society* (1945)
W. Gilbert Williams 'Y Cyrnol John Bodvel', *Cymru*, Vol 45 (1913)

HLJ, 'Mona Mediaeva Hundred of Twrcelyn', *Archaeologica Cambrensis,* (April 1859), pp 121 – 124
Richard Fenton, Edited by John Fisher, 'Tours in Wales (1804 – 1813)', *Cambrian Archaeological Association,* 1917 Supplemental Volume

A.D. Carr, 'Extent of Anglesey 1352', *Transactions of the Anglesey Antiquarian Society*, 1971
Irene George, 'Syr Dafydd Trefor, an Anglesey Bard', *Transactions of the Anglesey Antiquarian Society,* 1934
'Poems by Richard Llwyd', *Cambrian Register* Vol III 1818
J.E. Griffith, 'A List of the Clergy of Anglesey', *Transactions of the Anglesey Antiquarian Society,* 1930
Arthur Ivor Pryce, 'Sidelights on the Rise of Nonconformity in the Diocese of Bangor', *Transactions of the Anglesey Antiquarian Society,* (1922) Pg 47, (1924) Pg 52
George Eyre Evans, 'The Non-Parochial Registers of Anglesey', *Transactions of the Anglesey Antiquarian Society,* (1923) Pg 59
Foljambe Hall, 'Dr Michael Roberts: The Corrector for the Press of the Welsh Bible of 1630', *Journal of the Welsh Bibliographical Society, Vol. 2, No. 8,* (1923)
Rev. H.M. Pennant Lewis, 'A Thomas Coke Letter', *Bathafarn* (1963) pp 18 – 21

Books, Essays, Articles

S. Baring-Gould and John Fisher, *The Lives of the British Saints Vol II*, 1908
Monk of Rhuys, *Life of Gildas*, 9th Century
Angharad Llwyd, *A History of the Island of Mona*, 1832
Samuel Lewis, *A Topographical Dictionary of Wales Vol. II,* , 1833
Anthony D. Carr, *Medieval Anglesey,* 2011
Rev. John Skinner *Ten Days Tour Through The Isle of Anglesea*, December 1802
J.E. Griffith, *Pedigrees of Anglesey and Caernarvonshire Families*, 1914
Henry Rowlands, *Mona Antiqua Restaurata*, 1766
William Edward Lunt Editor), *The Valuation of Norwich*, 1926
Charles Dickens, *All the Year Round,* 28th January 1860
Gillian Kellett Hodkinson and Iwan T. Kellett ,*The Lords of Llaneugrad,* 2020
Arthur Ivor Pryce, *The Diocese of Bangor in the Sixteenth Century,* 1867-1940
Edward Alfred Jones, *The Church Plate of the Diocese of Bangor,* 1906
Donald C. Richter, *Lionel Sotheby's Great War, Diaries and letters from the Western Front,* 1997
Rhiannon Ifans (Editor), *Gwaith Syr Dafydd Trefor,* 2005
Richard Holland, *Haunted Wales: A Guide to Welsh Ghostlore,* 2011
Geraint Wyn Hughes, *Secret Anglesey*, 2019
Helen Ramage, *Portraits of an Island: Eighteenth Century Anglesey,* 2001
Griffith Jones, *Welch piety: or, a farther account of the circulating Welch charity schools, from Michaelmas 1751 to Michaelmas 1752.,* June 10, 2010

Harri Parri, *Elen Roger Portread*, 2000
John Williams, *Gwaith Glanmor*, 1865
Gillian Kellett Hodkinson, *Lest We Forget: The Men of the Marian-glas War Memorial in WWI*, 2020
Bunty Austin, *Haunted Anglesey*, 2005
Glanmor Williams, *The Welsh Church From Conquest to Reformation*, 1976
W. M. Jacob, *The Clerical Profession in the Long Eighteenth Century 1680 - 1840*, 2007
E. A Williams, *The day before yesterday: Anglesey in the nineteenth century*, 1988
Y Parch Dafydd Wyn William, *Y Canu Mawl I Teulr'r Caerfryn*,

Crown, Legal, Church and Misc. Other Documents

Calendar of Patent Rolls, multiple references
Calendar of Papal Register, multiple references
Calendar of Inquisitions Postmortem, multiple references
National Archives ED 21/21410, Llaneugrad National and Council School
National Archives ED 2/558/4, Llanallgo National and Council School
The Calendar of Wynn Papers
Dictionary of Welsh Biography
National Archives E 179/351/1/110, E 179/351/1/103, Hearth Tax Llanallgo and Llaneugrad
National Library Wales: Crime and Punishment Database 4/252/3 Doc 24 and 115, 4/258/1 Doc 26 Cases of Lewis Owen and Grace Lloyd
Bangor Archives Online Database, The Diaries of William Bulkeley of Brynddu, 1734 – 1743 and 1747 – 1760
Samuel Hanson, *The Case of Samuel Hanson Merchant and Planter in Barbadoes, Humbly Offer'd and Submitted to the Kings Most Excellent Majesty's Consideration, and Royal Determination in Council*, Undated
Commissioners for Inquiring Concerning Charities, *Further report of the commissioners for inquiring concerning charities. 32-Part II*, 1938
Commissioners for Inquiring Concerning Charities, *Report of the Endowed Charities Inquiry for the County of Anglesey*, (1896)
B. Jones (Editor), *Fasti Ecclesiae Anglicanae* 1300-1541: Volume 11, the Welsh Dioceses (Bangor, Llandaff, St Asaph, St David's), 1965
Joseph Foster, *Index Ecclesiasticus*, 1890
The Royal Commission on Ancient and Historical Monuments in Wales & Monmouthshire *An Inventory of the Ancient Monuments in Anglesey*, 1960
Browne Willis, *Survey of the Cathedral Church of Bangor and the Edifices Belonging to it*, 1721
Anglesey Archives WQ/S/1776/M/4, Certificate of Inquisition Richard Hughes Ty Cochyn
National Library of Wales, B/DL/264, Mortgage of the livings of Llaneugrad and Llanallgo to secure £200 and interest raised for the rebuilding of the parsonage
Anglesey Archives WQ/S/1809/T/5, Presentment: Robert Parry late of parish Llaneugrad, yeoman, for digging pits two yards deep in the highway, Anglesey Quarter Sessions,

Anglesey Archives WQA/LIC/49/3, Ale Houses of Llanallgo,
Anglesey Archives XD2/18783, Letter Rev. John Griffith to Lord Newborough,
Indenture Conveying Land for British School Marian-glas by Lord Dinorben 1st March 1847, (Llio Rhydderch)
Bangor Archives CV/188, Draft Conveyance of Lot of Land in Llanallgo for a School by the Rev. Richard Williams Mason, Perpetual Curate of Penrhosllugwy, 1845
Indenture Conveying Land in Llaneugrad for National School by Hugh Robert Hughes of Kinmel, 27th March 1869
Bangor Archives, BMSS/28620, Legal Release, Hugh Thomas of Trevor, 1773
Bangor Archives, PARC/1/1, 2, 3, 4, 7, 8, 9, 10, 11, Eugrad House Charity
The Old Dominicans' Association Friars School Newsletter, 450th Anniversary Edition, Summer 2007
National Library of Wales MS 19068C, Ballad of Sir John Bodvel
Parish Registers and Bishops Transcripts: Christenings, Marriages and Burials

Wills

Owen of Caerfryn 1607	Sir Jon Bodvel 1631
David ap John Thomas 1636	William Lewys 1638
William John Ivan 1660	Owen Wood 1668
William Thomas Trevor 1670	Michael Roberts 1678
Hugh Humphreys 1680	Edward Wynne 1680/1
John ap Evan 1684	Sydney wife of John ap Evan 1684
Samuel Hanson 1687	Samuel Hanson Jr 1692
Richard Hughes 1693/4	Francis Prichard 1704
John Griffith Lewis 1708	Owen Hughes Yr Arian 1708
William Wynne 1709	William Watkin 1718
William Probert Humphrey 1719	Maurice Jones 1725
Richard Jones 1730	Silence Folkes 1735/6
Elizabeth [Folkes] Hanmer 1739	Hugh Jones 1754
Rowland Jones 1758	William Bodvel 1759
Gwen Bodvel 1759	William Lewis 1759
Leonard Jones 1769	Lewis Owen 1761
William Thomas 1772	Richard Prichard 1773
Rev Edward Hughes 1815	William Hughes 1828
John Richards 1832	Hugh Thomas 1852
Alban Griffith 1863	Ann Jones 1896
Lionel Sotheby 1915	

Websites

Names of Clergymen, theclergydatabase.org.uk
Story of The Last Invasion of Britain,
https://www.historic-uk.com/HistoryUK/HistoryofWales/The-Last-Invasion-of-Britain/

Bryn Seiont Sanitorium Article: https://www.dailypost.co.uk/news/local-news/memories-of-bryn-seiont-hospital-2827214
John Griffiths Biography, cynonculture.co.uk/wordpress/Welsh-preachers/john-griffiths/
CADW, https://cadw.gov.wales/

Subscription and Free Online Databases -Various Records

Ancestry (e.g. Census, Parish Records, Oxford Alumni, Calenda of Wynn Papers, Welsh Wills, 1939 Register, Military, Electoral Registers, FindaGrave, Military etc)
FindMyPast - various
MyHeritage - various
BritishHistoryOnline.ac.uk – various Crown and Parliamentary Records
National Library of Wales: Wills, Newspapers, Journals online
UK General Records office – Various Birth, marriage & death Certificates
CDs via Dave Wilson of Stone Science and Anglesey Archives: Birth, Christening, Marriage, Death, Burial Registrations and Parish Records/Bishops Transcripts for Anglesey
Wikipedia (judicious use of) with cross-referencing other sources such as Encyclopaedia Britannica

Personal Contribution/Memoirs

Alma Salt
Bryn Jones
Chris Hughes
David Hughes (on his father Hugh Hughes)
Delyth Roberts
Eileen Clarke
Eleanor Jones
Elena Johnson
Emyr Roberts
Graham D. Loveluck (autobiography)
Hugh Griffith Memoirs of Marian-glas, from nephew William Roger Jones
Lynne Kellett
Patrick Hussey (nephew of Arthur Gordon Ware)
Peter Day
Philip Hughes (autobiography)
Philippa Parry
Sioned Boardmen
Sioned Harper
Sue Watkinson
Tom Roberts
Valmai Jones
Vicki Louise Smith

Printed in Great Britain
by Amazon